KU-570-903

Skagen

Frederikshavn

Northwestern Zealand
Pages 120–155

Southern Zealand and the Islands
Pages 156–175

Copenhagen
Pages 50–115

Grenå

Aarhus

Helsingør

Frederiksværk

Hillerød

Hørsholm

Frederikssund

Holbæk

COPENHAGEN

Kalundborg

Roskilde

NORTHWESTERN
ZEALAND

Bornholm
Pages 220–231

Sorø

Køge

Ringsted

Odense

Slagelse

FUNEN

Nyborg

Næstved

Faaborg

Svendborg

SOUTHERN
ZEALAND AND
THE ISLANDS

Stege

Rudkøbing

borg

BORNHOLM

Nakskov

Nykøbing F.

Denmark

BORNHOLM

Gedser

Denmark

4000000131578 9

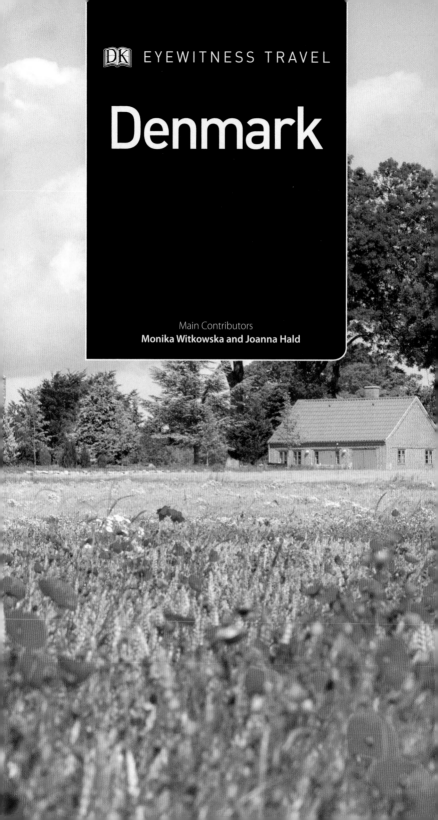

DK EYEWITNESS TRAVEL

Denmark

Main Contributors
Monika Witkowska and Joanna Hald

Produced by Wydawnictwo
Wiedza i Życie, Warsaw

Senior Graphic Designer Paweł Pasternak
Editors Maria Betlejewska,
Joanna Egert-Romanowska
Authors Joanna Hald, Marek Pernal,
Jakub Sito, Barbara Sudnik-Wójcikowska,
Monika Witkowska

Cartographers Magdalena Polak,
Olaf Rodowald, Jarosław Talacha
Photographers Dorota and
Mariusz Jarymowiczowie
Illustrators Michał Burkiewicz,
Paweł Marcza
Graphic Design Paweł Pasternak
DTP Elżbieta Dudzińska

For Dorling Kindersley
Translator Magda Hannay
Editor Matthew Tanner
Senior Dtp Designer Jason Little
Production Controller Rita Sinha

Printed in China

First published in the UK in 2005
by Dorling Kindersley Limited, 80 Strand,
London WC2R 0RL, UK

17 18 19 20 10 9 8 7 6 5 4 3 2 1

**Reprinted with revisions 2008,
2010, 2013, 2015, 2018**

Copyright © 2005, 2018 Dorling Kindersley,
London
A Penguin Random House Company

A CIP catalogue record is available from
the British Library.

ISBN: 978-0-24130-597-3

Floors are referred to throughout in
accordance with european usage; i.e. the
"first floor" is the floor above ground level.

MIX
Paper from
responsible sources
FSC
www.fsc.org   FSC™ C018179

Introducing Denmark

Copenhagen Area by Area

Colourful buildings along Nyhavn, Copenhagen

◀ **Title page** Glim Kirke, a church near Roskilde. **Front cover main image** Traditional architecture in the town of of Upernavik,
Greenland. **Back cover image** Boats lining Nyhavn waterfront, Copenhagen.

Contents

Lighthouse on the cliffs of Mykines, the Faroe Islands

Frederiksborg Slot, Hillerød

HOW TO USE THIS GUIDE

This guide will help you get the most out of a visit to Denmark. The first section, *Introducing Denmark*, provides information about the country's geographic location, its history and culture. The sections devoted to the capital and other large cities, as well as to individual regions, describe the major sights and visitor attractions. Information on accommodation and restaurants can be found in the *Travellers' Needs* section. The *Survival Guide* provides practical tips on everything a visitor may need to know, from money and language to getting around and seeking medical care.

Copenhagen

This section has been divided into three parts, each devoted to a separate part of the city. Sights outside the capital's centre are described in the *Further Afield* section. All sights are numbered and plotted on the area map. Detailed information for each sight is given in numerical order.

Sights at a Glance lists the sights in an area by category: churches, museums and art galleries; streets and squares; parks and gardens.

A suggested route for sightseeing is indicated by a dotted red line.

2 Street-by-Street Map
Provides a bird's-eye view of the town centre described in the section.

Pages referring to Copenhagen are marked in red.

A locator map shows where visitors are in relation to other areas of the city.

1 Area Map
For easy reference the sights are numbered and plotted on the area map, as well as on the main map of Copenhagen (*see pp112–15*).

Star Sights indicate parts of buildings, historic sights, exhibits and monuments that no visitor should miss.

3 Detailed Information
All the major sights of Copenhagen are described individually. Practical information includes addresses, telephone numbers, the most convenient buses and trains, and opening hours.

SOUTHERN ZEALAND AND THE ISLANDS

The lowlands of southern Zealand are characterized by cultivated fields and beautiful lakes. Many visitors see only Vordingborg and Køge, two towns that have played a significant part in Denmark's history, but the islands of Lolland, Falster and Møn to the south are attractive holiday destinations and offer miles of sandy beaches, woodland and awe-inspiring views of coastal cliffs.

1 Introduction
This section deals with the landscape, history and character of each region, revealing how it has changed over time, and describing its current attractions.

Denmark Region by Region

In this guide Denmark is divided into seven regions, each of which has a separate section devoted to it. The most interesting cities, towns, villages and sights worth visiting are marked on each regional map.

2 Regional Map
The regional map shows the main road network and the overall topography of the region. All sights are numbered, and there is also information on public transport and getting around.

Boxes highlight interesting aspects or people associated with a sight.

Each region of Denmark can be found by using the colour code. The colours are explained on the inside front cover.

3 Detailed Information
Towns, villages and major tourist attractions are listed in numerical order, corresponding with the area map. Each entry contains information on important sights.

The Visitors' Checklist provides practical information to help plan your visit.

4 Major Sights
At least two pages are devoted to each major sight. Historic buildings are dissected to reveal their interiors. Major towns and town centres have street maps with the principal sights marked on them.

INTRODUCING DENMARK

DISCOVERING DENMARK

The following itineraries have been designed to take in as many of Denmark's sights as possible, without exhausting the visitor. First is a two-day tour of Copenhagen, Denmark's capital, with ideas to extend the stay with trips to Roskilde or Helsingør. There is a three-day tour of Bornholm, the "sunshine island" with its own distinct character and history in the Baltic Sea. For those able to extend their visit to Copenhagen and travel further afield,

there are suggestions for a week-long gourmet tasting tour of Zealand and its regional specialities; and ideas for making the most of three days in Jutland enjoying the region's rich artistic heritage. Finally, a one-week itinerary is designed to best explore the unique northerly landscapes of the Faroe Islands and Greenland. Choose one or two to follow, or simply take inspiration.

Holiday home on the beach
A holiday cottage perches on a small cliff at Gammel Skagen, near the Skaw in Denmark.

Gourmet Tour of Zealand, Lolland and Møn

- Sample the culinary treats of Copenhagen's gourmet marketplace, TorvehallerneKBH.
- Enjoy dining in the idyllic setting of Søllerød Kro, one of Denmark's top restaurants.
- Take a guided tour of ice cream maker Hansens Is near Jægerspris.
- Try modern-day Viking food at Restaurant

Snekken, next door to the Vikingeskibsmuseet.
- Sample freshly smoked fish from the Arne Jacobsen-designed smokehouse in Havnebyen on the Odsherred peninsula.
- Taste regional specialities *bidesild* (pickled herrings) and wheat cakes on the island of Møn.

Art Tour of Jutland

- See Arne Jacobsen's groundbreaking Kubeflex summerhouse outside Trapholt museum, Kolding.
- Stimulate your senses on the skywalk "Your Rainbow Panorama" at ARoS Kunstmuseum in Aarhus.
- Visit the Museum Jorn in Silkeborg to see works by Denmark's *enfant terrible*, Asger Jorn.
- Get inside the fantastic imaginations of CoBrA artists at HEART Herning Museum of Contemporary Art.
- Appreciate the unique quality of light in Skagen.

◀ A street scene as depicted by an oil painter from the Danish School

Locator Map

Cruise boat, Greenland
A boat trip is an essential part of a trip to Greenland. Trips can include wildlife-watching, including puffin colonies and whales, and also take in Greenland's monumental icebergs.

Key

━━━ Art tour of Jutland

━━━ Gourmet tour of Zealand, Lolland and Møn

━━━ A Week in Greenland and the Faroes

━━━ Three Days on Bornholm

A Week in Greenland and the Faroes

- Sample puffin, musk ox and other regional specialities in one of Tørshavn's innovative gourmet restaurants.

- Enjoy the breathtaking views from atop Slættaratindur peak on Eysturoy, the highest point on the Faroes.

- Take a sailing trip to Mykines island to watch the puffins.

- Visit the Norse church ruins on Hvalsey Fjord, south Greenland.

- Cross the Arctic Circle and witness climate changes first-hand on the edge of the Greenland Ice Cap.

- Experience huge whales and monumental icebergs in Disko Bay.

Three Days on Bornholm

- Enjoy a herring lunch fresh from the smokehouse in Hasle.

- Explore the ruins of Hammerhus Slot.

- Visit the picturesque villages of Gudhjem and Svaneke, on Bornholm's east coast.

- Visit Bornholm's biggest round church in Østerlars – and its smallest, in Nyker.

- Enjoy a pub lunch (or dinner) on the main square in Bornholm's award-winning brewery, Svaneke Bryghus.

Herring smokehouse at a museum in Hasle, Bornholm
Diners enjoying produce from the Silderøgerierne Museum smokehouse with its distinctive white chimneys.

Two Days in Copenhagen

Denmark's capital combines old-fashioned charm with modern design and efficient transport networks.

- **Arriving** Kastrup Airport is 8 km (5 miles) southeast of the city on the island of Amager. Both the Metro and regional trains travel to the city centre in 15 minutes.

Day 1

Morning Follow in the footsteps of Peter the Great by racing up the unique spiral walkway of the **Rundetårn** (*p75*) and be rewarded with great views over the city. Then take a leisurely stroll through the Latin Quarter to the **Nationalmuseet** (*pp88–9*); with limited time, focus perhaps on the prehistoric finds. Afterwards, cross Frederiksholms Kanal onto Slotsholmen, an island that's packed with museums, to check out **Christiansborg Slot** (*pp90–91*) current seat of Parliament with the remains of four other castles beneath. Highlights include the Great Hall and the Throne Room.

Afternoon If visiting between April and early September or in the month preceding Christmas, spend an afternoon enjoying the cafés and entertainment of **Tivoli Gardens** (*pp80–81*); if your trip is out of season, then **Ny Carlsberg Glyptotek** (*pp82–3*) makes a worthy alternative.

The Royal Room of Christian IV's Rosenborg Slot, Copenhagen

The atmospheric ruins of Hammershus Slot, Bornholm

Day 2

Morning Begin day two by visiting **Rosenborg Slot** (*pp64–5*), a magnificent Renaissance palace that guards the country's crown jewels in its basement. Stroll through the palace's green grounds, Kongens Have, into the elegant Frederiksstaden district, passing the Baroque dome of the **Marmorkirken** (*p62*) before reaching the grand **Amalienborg Slot** complex (*pp60–61*); the museum is located in Christian VIII's palace. Also worth a visit is the **Designmuseum** (*p59*), situated between Amalienborg Slot and Kastellet. If time allows, walk up Amaliegade to Kastellet; the town's citadel is a pleasant park, with plenty of great cafés.

Afternoon After recharging over lunch, hit the shops on Europe's longest pedestrian street, Strøget, which opens out into Kongens Nytorv, a busy square with the pleasant canalside street, **Nyhavn** (*p72*) at the opposite side. Take a boat tour of the city's canals, including the chance to see the famous **Little Mermaid** statue (*p58*). End your trip with a meal overlooking the canal in either Nyhavn or **Christianshavn** (*p92*).

> ### To extend your trip...
> Spend a day in **Helsingør** (*pp128–9*), the best location for **Kronborg Slot** (*pp130–31*) and **M/S Museet for Søfart** (the Danish Maritime Museum) or **Roskilde** (*pp144–7*), with its Domkirke and Vikingeskibsmuseet.

Three Days on Bornholm

The island of Bornholm, out in the Baltic, has long been a popular holiday destination for Danes. Known for its round churches and traditional smokehouses, the northern coast has a rocky coastline while the southern end offers sandy beaches. Bornholm is great for touring by car, bus or bike.

- **Arriving** Take the train to Ystad in Sweden from Copenhagen's Central Train Station, then ferry to Rønne (travel time about 3 hours).
- **Transport** Bornholm has a good bus network, though a car is more practical. The more active could cycle.
- **Booking Ahead** Not necessary, though DSB sell combined tickets.

Day 1: Rønne to Allinge

Start the tour in **Rønne**, Bornholm's biggest town (*p226*): Allow 1–2 hours to stroll around its squares and streets, including a visit to Bornholm Museum to brush up on local history before moving on to **Nyker** (*p226*), and Bornholm's smallest round church. Enjoy a *sild* lunch in the old smokehouse in **Hasle** (*p226*), a town centred around herring. Spend the afternoon in the north of the island exploring **Hammershus Slot** (*p224*), 13th-century castle ruins perched precariously on a cliff.

Spend the evening in **Allinge** and **Sandvig** *(p224)*, two pleasant seaside towns that merge into one. If time allows, check out Madsebakke Helleristninger, the bronze age rock paintings on the outskirts of Allinge; they are thought to be 4,000 years old.

Day 2: Gudhjem to Svaneke

Leave Allinge along the coastal road towards **Gudhjem** *(p230)*, stopping along the way to visit **Bornholms Kunstmuseum** *(p226)*, showcasing local art in a modern building. Take an hour or two to explore the picturesque fishing village of Gudhjem, including the **Oluf Høst Museet** *(p230)*, eating lunch in one of the town's numerous cafés. Then, head a few miles inland to view Bornholm's largest round church, **Østerlars Kirke** *(p230)*, and the medieval exhibits and demonstrations at recreated medieval village **Middelaldercenter** *(p230)*. Round off the day in **Svaneke** *(p227)*, 14 km (9 miles) down the coast. This picturesque town offers many dining options, including Røgeriet *(p275)*, a casual smokehouse eatery.

Day 3: Nexø and Aakirkeby

On the final day of the tour explore the island's southern end, with the morning spent exploring Nexø, a busy working town where you can visit the town museum. After lunch, head west to **Aakirkeby** *(p227)*, and spend at least two hours at **NaturBornholm**, a state-of-the-art natural history museum on Aakirkeby's southern outskirts.

Anna Ancher Returning From Flower Picking (1902) by Michael Peter Ancher

Art Tour of Jutland

Jutland's artistic heritage is as rich and varied as its landscape. In the late 1800s, an artists' colony was formed around a fishing village at Denmark's northernmost tip; while in the 20th century, the artist Asger Jorn pushed artistic limits from his base in Silkeborg.

- **Duration** Three day tour;
  · allow an extra day at the end to return home from Skagen.
- **Airports** Billund Airport is centrally located in the middle of Jutland.
- **Transport** This itinerary can be made by train, with direct rail connections to all destinations, or with a hire car.

Day 1: Modern Art and Design

Start in **Kolding** *(p201)*, checking out **Trapholt** *(p201)*, an excellent modern art and design museum that includes a large collection of Richard Mortensen works, a sculpture park and Arne Jacobsen's innovative Kubeflex summerhouse. From here, it's 98 km (60 miles) to **Aarhus** *(pp192–3)* north along Jutland's east coast. (The train takes 75 minutes). A 10-minute walk from the train station, the city's modern art museum, **ARoS** *(p192)*, is one of Europe's largest.

Day 2: The CoBrA Movement

After an early breakfast, make the one-hour journey to **Silkeborg** *(p191)* to learn more about the avant-garde CoBrA movement. South of the town centre, **Museum Jorn** *(p191)* houses Asger Jorn's collection, acquired from 1953–73.

Herning *(p191)*, some 37 km (22 miles) west of Silkeborg, is about 45 minutes away. On the eastern outskirts of town is Birk Centerpark, location of fascinating **HEART Herning Museum of Contemporary Art** *(p191)* with work by artists of the CoBrA movement.

Day 3: The Skagen Painters

Start the day in Aalborg with a whistle-stop tour of **Kusten Museum of Modern Art Aalborg** *(p213)* before travelling the two-hour journey to the northernmost point of Denmark, Skagen to fully appreciate the "unique quality of light" that transformed this small fishing village into a major artists' colony in the late 1800s. At **Skagens Museum** *(p209)*, you can visit the studios of Michael Ancher and P.S. Krøyer and view many important works from the period.

Olafur Eliasson's *Your Rainbow Panorama* at ARoS Kunstmuseum, Aarhus

Gourmet Tour of Zealand, Lolland and Møn

Denmark has a global reputation for its organic, seasonal and healthy kitchen, and this tour kicks off in the markets and delis of Copenhagen before heading out to the region's farms and fishing villages.

- **Duration** One week.
- **Airports** Copenhagen Airport.
- **Booking ahead** Some of the restaurants, such as Søllerød Kro, definitely require reserving in advance, as do any guided tours.

Day 1: Copenhagen

Begin the tour in **TorvehallerneKBH** *(p104)*, a gourmet marketplace built as a replacement for the original green market that once stood on Israels Plads. If nothing takes your fancy, grab lunch on the go from the Økologiske Pølsemand – an organic hot dog stand next to Rundetaarn, then breathe in the exciting atmosphere in Kødbyen, the city's old meat-packing district that buzzes with trendy eateries. Round off the day in Nørrebro, with dinner in the restaurant of micro-brewery Nørrebro Bryghus or in one of the eateries on Jægersborggade.

Day 2: Humlebæk and Holte

Travel up the coast from Copenhagen to Krogerup Avlsgaard farm in **Humlebæk** *(pp123)*, where you can visit the farm shop of Aarstiderne, a supplier of organic fruit and vegetables to many Copenhagen residents. Browse, buy or simply enjoy the peaceful natural surroundings (open daily, 10am onwards). The farm shop is located 200 m (650 ft) north of **Louisiana Museum** *(pp126–7)*, at Krogerupvej 3. Break for lunch in the art museum café. Afterwards, return southwards to Holte, for evening dining in one of Denmark's best restaurants, Søllerød Kro (advance booking is essential).

Day 3: Helsinge and Jægerspris

If you've timed it right, visit Fuglebjerggaard near Helsinge, an organic farm that opens on Saturdays. If you have time – or the farm is closed – visit the harbour at **Gilleleje** *(p132)*, an excellent place to sample fresh fish. Next, travel westwards to **Jægerspris** *(p139)* to visit Hornsherred Mejeri, home of Hansens Flødeis, an ice cream manufacturer that still uses traditional methods. The dairy arranges guided tours in summer; pre-booking is necessary.

Day 4: Roskilde and Lejre

Visit the harbour at **Roskilde** *(p144–5)*, home to the **Vikingeskibsmuseet** *(p145)* and the adjacent Restaurant Snekken, where the exhibits are brought to life with a modern interpretation of Viking food. After a hearty lunch, travel to the villages of Herslev and Kirke Hyllinge, home to the Herslev and Hornbeer micro-breweries respectively. Part of **Roskilde Museum** *(p144)*, the old water mill Tadre Mølle near Kirke Hvalsø produces flour using traditional methods.

Day 5: Odsherred

Head to Sjællands Odde on the **Odsherred** peninsula *(p155)* to see the smokehouse in Havnebyen, designed by Arne Jacobsen. The shop is open in the summer holidays. If you have already booked table, enjoy a veritable banquet in the stately surroundings of **Dragsholm Slot** *(p154)*.

Smørrebrød – a hearty Danish open sandwich on rye bread

Day 6: The Smålandshavet Archipelago

The two islands of **Fejø** and **Femø** *(p158)* are the largest islands in the Smålandshavet Archipelago; reached by ferry from Kragenæs on Lolland, just north of Bandholm. The boat takes 50 minutes to Femø, but stops at Fejø first. Both islands are famed for their fruit trees.

Day 7: Møn and Lolland

Stege *(p173)*, the largest town on the island of Møn is a great place for trying regional specialities such as *bidesild* (herring bites) and wheat cakes coated in cheese. A good lunch spot to find these delicacies is Kaj Kok in Landsled (on Klintevej between Stege and Elmelunde). Finally, head south through **Falster** *(pp170–71)*, and into **Lolland** *(pp163–70)*, to Vester Ulslev Vingaard, one of Denmark's few commercial vineyards, 14 km (8 miles) east of Rødby. The shop is open when the owner is home so call ahead to be sure.

TorvehallerneKBH, the modern covered market at Israels Plads, Copenhagen

A Week in Greenland and the Faroes

Denmark's two northern territories have remote, harsh scenery in common, but the rocky, green terrain of the Faroes is very different in character from the unique frozen landscapes of Greenland. Combine both in a week-long tour of adventure and discovery.

- **Arriving** Several airlines make regular flights from Copenhagen to Vágur Airport on the Faroes; or take the 38-hour ferry from Hirtshals in North Jutland to Tørshavn, which runs twice weekly. Between the Faroes and Greenland, the most direct route is with a stopover in Reykjavik, Iceland: flights go to several airports in the territory.

- **Transport** A car is essential for touring the Faroes; you can take a car on the boat to Tørshavn or obtain a hire car from Vágur Airport. Travel around Greenland is more difficult, as the road network is inadequate; internal flights, public helicopters and ferries can all be used.

- **Booking ahead** Any internal flights, tours or world-renowned restaurants will need pre-booking.

Day 1: Streymoy island, Faroes

Start the tour in **Tørshavn** (*p240*), exploring the Faroese capital, with modern areas as well as an old town. On the same island, head north to **Saksun** (*p240*), a small settlement where the turf-roofed **Dúvugarðar Museum** (*p240*) puts island life in a historical perspective. Head back to Tørshavn for an evening meal in one of the town's innovative restaurants.

Day 2: Eysturoy Island, Faroes

Cross the bridge at Nesvik on Streymoy to tour the north-eastern section of **Eysturoy** (*p241*), the second-largest of

Russell Glacier, on the edge of the Greenland Ice Cap

the Faroe Isles. Take in the views at the top of Slættaratindur peak, the highest point in the Faroes. Visit the Vermakelda natural springs south of Fuglafjørður, which are said to have healing properties; finally, be fascinated by the constant rocking motion of the two Rinkusteinar boulders, near Oyndarfjørður, which move as the sea ebbs around them.

Day 3: Vágar and Mykines Islands, Faroes

Reach **Vágar** island (*p240*) via the sub-sea tunnel. On your way to Sørvágur, look out for the tall, pointy rock nicknamed "Trollkonufingur'" ("Troll Woman's Finger"). Leave the car behind in Sørvágur to sail to tiny **Mykines** (*p241*) to view the puffins. Overnight close to Vágar Airport for an early morning flight to Greenland.

Landed fishing boats in the harbour at Eysturoy, the Faroe Islands

Day 4: Qaqortoq, Greenland

Start your exploration of Greenland in the south of the territory in **Qaqortoq** (*p236*), formerly Julianehåb, by choosing between visits to the Norse church ruins on Hvalsey Fjord, Uunartoq hot springs and the Upernaviarsuk agricultural research centre.

Day 5: Nuuk, Greenland

Spend a less exhausting day exploring Greenland's lively capital, **Nuuk** (*p236*). Post a letter to Father Christmas at Nuuk Post Office, and learn more about Greenland's history in the **National Museum** on Hans Egedesvej (*p236*).

Day 6: Kangerlussuaq, Greenland

Hit **Kangerlussuaq** (*p236*) and you've crossed over the Arctic Circle and into an icy, polar landscape. Take an excursion to Russell Glacier, on the edge of the Greenland Ice Cap, and/or Sugar Loaf Mountain (pre-book this via a private tour company).

Day 7: Ilulissat, Greenland

End the week in Greenland's frozen north, exploring Disko Bay, with views of immense icebergs and the UNESCO World Heritage site, Ilulissat Ice Fiord, where climate change becomes a tangible concept. If weather permits, take a whale-watching tour out into the bay. Check out too the house of polar explorer, Knud Rasmussen, the Museum of Hunting and Fishing or the Cold museum (*p237*).

Putting Denmark on the Map

Denmark is situated between the North Sea to the west and the Baltic Sea to the southeast. Most of Denmark consists of Jutland, a peninsula that covers 29,766 sq km (11,493 sq miles). The rest of the country consists of over 400 islands, of which the largest are Bornholm, Funen and Zealand. Far to the north, Greenland and the Faroe Islands are self-governing overseas regions of Denmark.

Key

═══ Motorway
▪▪▪ Motorway under construction
─── Major road
····· Other road
─── National border

Faroe Islands *(see p238)*

Streymoy
Bordoy
Eysturoy
Vágar
Tórshavn
Sandoy
Suðuroy

Hirtshals

0 km 15
0 miles 15

Greenland *(see p234)*

Qaanaaq (Thule)
Ilulissat (Jakobshavn)
Tasilaq (Ammassalik)
Nuuk (Godthåb)
Qaqortoq (Julianehåb)

0 km 400
0 miles 400

Kristiansand, Stavanger, Bergen, Tórshavn

Larvik, Langesund

Hirtshals
Hjørring
Brønderslev
Aabybro
Hantsholm
Fjerritslev
Aalborg
Limfjorden
Thisted
Nykøbing Mors
Hobro
Nissum Bredning
Lemvig
Skive
Struer
Viborg
Randers
Holstebro
Storå
Skive Å
Gudenå
Nissum Fjord
Ulfborg
Silkeborg
Julsø
Herning
Ringkøbing
Videbaek
Jutland
Mossø
Skande borg
Ringkøbing Fjord
Tarm
Ommeå
Horser
Grindsted
Billund
Vejle
Varde
Fredericia
Esbjerg
Kolding
Middelfart
Broup
Fanø
Harwich
Ribe
Fladså
Assens
Fanø Bugt
Haderslev
Helnæs
Rømø
Bojde
Åbenrå
Als
Fynshav
Tønder
Sylt
Sønderborg
Niebüll
Flensburg
Nebel
GERMANY
Schleswig
Husum
Eckernförde

Skagen

Oslo,
Gothenburg

Europe

Greenland

40

Frederikshavn

35

Læsø

E45

Greenland
Sea

Barents
Sea

ICELAND

Arctic Circle

Norwegian
Sea

Faroe Islands

NORWAY

FINLAND

*Aalborg
Bugt*

Atlantic
Ocean

SWEDEN

RUSSIA

DENMARK

Bornholm

U.K.

POLAND

BELARUS

GERMANY

UKRAINE

FRANCE

Varberg

Oslo

Grenå

16

E6

24

Örkelljunga

Ängelholm

Ronde

15

Kattegat

E4

21

21

Ebeltoft

Astorp

Aarhus

Helsingborg

Aarhus Bugt

Odden
Færgehavn

Frederiksværk *Arresø*

Helsingør

SWEDEN

Hou

Samsø

Sejerø

Hillerød

Landskrona

Saelvig

16

Hørsholm

Kolby Kås

Frederikssund

Birkerød

23

Sejerø Bugt

6

Øresund

Røsnæs

Holbæk

6

E20

E22

Kalundborg

Roskilde

Tåstrup

**COPENHAGEN
(KØBENHAVN)**

Lund

23

21

Tissø

57

Zealand

E47

Malmö

Funen

14

Amager

E20

E65

Odense

Sorø

E20

Ringsted

Køge

Køge Bugt

Slagelse

Nyborg

Korsør

Trelleborg

9

9

E20

E55

Ringe

42

8

22

54

*Baltic
Sea*

Rønne

8

Agersø

Næstved

Faaborg

Svendborg

Smålandsfarvandet

*Fakse
Bugt*

Rostock,
Sassnitz,
Travemünde

Tåsinge

Langeland

Spodsbjerg

22

Bornholm *(see p220)*

Rudkøbing

Taars

Vordingborg

59

Stege

Allinge

Ærø

Ærøskøbing

9

Nakskov

159

158

Bagenkop

E47

9

Falster

Nykøbing F.

Rønne

38

Neksø

Lolland

E55

Rødbyhavn

Gedser

Køge, Ystad,
Sassnitz

0 km   50

0 km   10

0 miles   50

Fehmarn

Rostock

0 miles   10

A PORTRAIT OF DENMARK

From the notorious Vikings to fairy tale writer Hans Christian Andersen, irresistible cuisine to contemporary interior design, Denmark has much to offer visitors. The Danish landscape is rich with breathtaking countryside, miles of sandy coastline and fascinating historic buildings. Copenhagen, the country's capital, has a rich cultural life and world-class museums, making it a perfect city-break destination.

Denmark, the southernmost and most continental of the Scandinavian countries, occupies over 480 islands, of which about 100 are inhabited. It acts as a bridge between mainland Europe and Scandinavia and is linked with the European continent by a narrow stretch of land, in the southern part of the Jutland peninsula, at the border with Germany.

Although not part of the Scandinavian peninsula, the Danes are linked with their northern neighbours by ties of common history and culture. There are also linguistic similarities and Danes can easily converse with natives of Sweden or Norway.

The country has strong links with two autonomous regions: the Faroe Islands and Greenland, both of which are represented in the Danish parliament.

Denmark exercises control over their banking, foreign policy and defence.

Denmark is a low-lying country with wide stretches of cornfields, moors and forests, and several national parks, along with vast sand dunes, fjords and long stretches of beach. The country's immaculate towns and villages are charming, with colourful flower-adorned houses that include many examples of half-timbered design. Majestic castles, palaces and historic churches pepper this landscape, plus many Viking ruins and even older remains, including ancient dolmens dating from the Stone Age.

Denmark is acknowledged to be a peaceful and liberal country, with a well-organised transport system and a comprehensive system of social welfare.

Picturesque houses along the bank of Nyhavn, Copenhagen

◀ Inscription and a Viking boat on a rune stone, Ringkøbing Fjord

Changing of the guards at Amalienborg Slot, Copenhagen

Denmark has enviably low levels of crime and corruption. In rural areas it is not unusual to see stalls by the roadside on which local farmers have left their unattended produce on sale.

Traditions and Politics

The national flag – the Dannebrog – is the world's oldest and the Danes demonstrate their patriotism by unfurling it during state and family celebrations. According to legend, the flag takes its origin from a banner bearing a white cross on a red background, which was dropped from

Statue of the Little Mermaid – a symbol of Copenhagen

heaven to rally the Danish knights during a battle fought in present-day Estonia, in the early 13th century. The Danes are proud of their heritage, and historic villages – dating from the 1800s right back to Viking times and the Stone Age – are popular excursion destinations. Most Danes regard the fact that their monarchy is the oldest in Europe with pride. The present queen, Margrethe II, has been on the throne since 1972 and is the first female monarch in Denmark since the 14th century. In addition to performing all ceremonial functions, this popular queen is credited with transforming the monarchy into a modern institution.

In political matters, the monarchy's influence is limited by the Danish constitution. The direction of national policy is determined in the Folketinget, the chamber in Christiansborg Slot, Copenhagen, where the country's 179 members of parliament sit. About a dozen parties are represented in parliament. Elections take place every four years and over 85 per cent of those eligible to vote turn out at election time. Most important national issues are decided by popular vote, however. Decisions made in referenda have included the Danes' approval of a constitutional amendment allowing a woman to inherit the throne in 1953 and, in 2000, the rejection of the Euro.

Charming half-timbered house in Rønne, on the island of Bornholm

Society and Everyday Life

Denmark is largely inhabited by ethnic Danes who are descendants of the Teutonic tribes that once populated all of Scandinavia.

Harald I (Bluetooth), Denmark's second king, was baptised as a Catholic in 960 and Denmark remained a Catholic country until well into the 16th century, when the ideas of the German Protestant reformer Martin Luther won widespread support. Lutheranism became the official religion of Denmark with the

View of Gammel Estrup, Jutland, surrounded on all sides by water

accession of Christian III in 1534. Today, about 90 per cent of the population are Protestant, and although the churches remain fairly empty, many Danes subscribe to a tax that supports the Church and observe traditions such as christenings and confirmations.

Although Denmark is largely an ethnically homogenous country, relaxed immigration policies introduced in the 1960s helped to establish communities of foreign nationals from outside Europe. Copenhagen is home to significant numbers of Turks and Palestinians as well as arrivals from Iran, Iraq and Afghanistan.

When it comes to bringing up children, many parents continue with their careers after taking parental leave. The progressive welfare system enables most women to return to work, at least part time.

Denmark's famous liberalism is perhaps best illustrated by "Christiania", a hippy commune that sprang up in the borough of Christianshavn in central Copenhagen in 1971. Allowed to remain as a social experiment, it is inhabited by about 900 people seeking an alternative lifestyle.

The Danes are similarly relaxed when it comes to issues like marriage. The country's divorce rate is one of the highest in Europe and nearly 20 per cent of couples co-habit without ever getting married. Abortion has been available "on demand" since 1973.

Harbour and sailing boat jetty, Maribo (Lolland)

A wind turbine farm on the west coast of Denmark, where conditions are ideal for generating clean energy

Economy and Ecology

The Danish economy is fairly robust and the country has among the highest per-capita Gross National Product in the EU and a high standard of living.

Denmark was for centuries a land of farmers and fishermen. Today less than 5 per cent of the country's population are employed in agriculture. Fishing, however, is still an important sector of the economy. The country is a major exporter of fish and is also popular for its pork and dairy products. Other exports include pharmaceuticals, beer, furniture and home electronics.

The Danes attach great importance to environmental issues. The country has an extensive network of alternative energy sources and the state-subsidized power-generating windmills are a common feature of the landscape. These supply over 40 per cent of the country's electricity. Major investments are also made in the use of solar power and the island of Ærø, south of Funen, has one of the world's largest solar power stations. All new building projects are scrutinized to minimize the impact on the environment. Danes take great care of their coastline, and many resorts have been awarded the blue flag, denoting clean beaches. Recycling domestic waste is normal practice in Denmark, as is the use of environmentally friendly packaging – a large amount of the country's paper production comes from recycled sources.

Culture, Art and Design

As a world leader in happiness and quality of life surveys, Denmark has captured the world's attention when it comes to the art of living well. Cycling is a major pastime across the country, with about 12,000 km (7,400 miles) of marked cycle routes peppered throughout. Various popular English-language books celebrate the Danish culture, focusing on *hygge*

Seaside scenery in Allinge, Bornholm

The beautiful interior of art museum Ny Carlsberg Glyptotek, Copenhagen

(pronounced 'hue-gah'), the Danish term for the pleasure of a relaxed, often cosy setting. The affiliated values of this homely environment, with comforting food, warm fabrics and ambient surroundings permeate daily life – its impact is visible in the country's design, art, media and events.

Among the country's best-known furniture designers are Hans Wegner and Arne Jacobsen, both driving forces behind Danish Modernism, and both known for their iconic Y and egg chairs respectively. The Designmuseum Danmark *(see p59)* in Copenhagen devotes exhibit space to the impact of Danish design. For more information about Danish design, see pp28–9.

Danish museums are noteworthy not only for their collections but also for prioritising architecture, restaurants and retail spaces that add pleasure to the visitor experience. Copenhagen has a wide variety of wonderful museums, including the Ny Carlsberg Glyptotek *(see pp82–3)*, with representatives of Denmark's "Golden Age" of painting, and the Nationalmuseet *(see pp88–9)*, as well as the modern art museums of Arken and Louisiana. Other museums throughout the country celebrate the work of respected Danish individuals and history.

Another major Danish cultural export is Nordic Noir TV drama. Famous examples include *The Killing*, *Borgen* and *The Bridge*, which have led to a number of English-language spin offs. Nordic Noir film is characterized by crime-based narratives, unhurried plots and brooding cinematography.

Denmark's cultural events range from major music festivals to local parades and concerts. One of the largest events is the July rock festival in Roskilde, which attracts over 130,000 visitors to see a mix of international acts and local Scandinavian headliners. For more information about entertainment in Denmark, see pp280–81.

Wares on display at the Designmuseum Danmark, Copenhagen

Danish Landscape and Flora

More than three quarters of Denmark is less than 100 m (330 ft) above sea level. Most of its landforms are of glacial origin, which adds variety to the lowland scenery. Forests, whose wholesale destruction was halted in the 19th century, occupy only a small percentage of the landscape and include commercial forests planted with spruce and fir, and natural forests dominated by beech and oak. Pastures and meadows are also distinctive features of the landscape and most of these are given over to crop cultivation and the rearing of livestock. A large portion of Denmark's highly diversified coastline consists of dunes, marshland and tidal flats.

Danish Fauna

Many mammals, including bears, have disappeared in Denmark. What forests remain provide a habitat for deer, marten, wild boar and hare. Excellent nesting grounds are a haven for many birds including geese, storks, swans and sandpipers. The largest wild animal to be found in Denmark is the red deer, while polar bears can still be found in Greenland.

Zealand
The island covers an area of 7,000 sq km (2,702 sq miles), and has a diverse landscape. In its northern section, on the outskirts of Copenhagen, there are fragments of natural forests – all that remains of a vast former wilderness. Elsewhere, the island has lakes, beaches and pasture land.

Bornholm
This island, largely composed of volcanic rock, has a mild climate. Its rugged granite cliffs, with stone rubble at their base, rise to over 80 m (262 ft) in height. At its northeastern end the well-preserved deciduous forests grow to the edge of the cliffs. The southern coast has long stretches of white-sand beaches.

Seaside Centaury
(Centaurium littorale) is a species associated with salt flats, but can also sometimes be found growing on seaside sands.

Bird's Eye Primrose
(Primula farinosa) is a rare peat bog species, which in Denmark is found only in isolated clusters.

Common Wintergreen
(Pyrola minor) has a distinctive rosette of slightly leathery leaves; it grows in forests and deciduous woodlands, on acid soil.

White Helleborine
(Cephalanthera damasonium) is an orchid with creamy-white flowers, and is often found in forests.

Helleborine *(Epipactis)* is found in several different varieties in Denmark. This orchid can be recognized by its labium, which is divided into two parts.

Wild Strawberry *(Fragaria vesca)* grows on woodland glades and banks. Its small red berries are sweet and fragrant.

Five species of seal can be found on the coast of Greenland. The largest of these is the hooded seal, the male of which can weigh up to 400 kg (884 lbs). The Inuit still rely on seals for clothing and food.

The greylag goose is one of Denmark's largest wild geese. Pairs mate for life; some 10,000 pairs are thought to be breeding in Denmark.

The mute swan is Denmark's national bird and can be found in many parks and ponds throughout the country.

White storks, which winter in Africa, can be seen in summer in Denmark's marshes, meadows and pastures.

Funen

The island that separates Jutland from Zealand is famous for its scenery and is known as the "garden of Denmark" because it produces much of the country's fruit and vegetables. The terrain in the north of the island eventually levels out into marshland, while in the south it is more hilly.

Jutland

Lakes, which occupy about one per cent of Denmark's total area, are clustered mainly in central Jutland. Yding Skovhøj and Møllehøj, Denmark's highest peaks, can also be found here – rising a little over 170 m (560 ft) above sea level. Himmelbjerget is 147 m (482 ft) above sea level and is a famous viewpoint.

Mountain Arnica *(Arnica montana)*, contrary to its name, is also found growing on lowlands, meadows, pastures and by roads. It is a valuable medicinal plant.

Field Fleawort *(Senecio integrifolius)* is a rare species, found in meadows, grasslands, pastures and woodlands.

Sea Rocket *(Cakile maritima)* is a delicate plant associated solely with Funen's sandy coast.

Field Gentian *(Gentiana campestris)* is in danger of extinction and is legally protected in Denmark and many other European countries.

Sea Holly *(Eryngium maritimum)* is a typical plant of the seaside dunes and comes in white and grey varieties.

Cinquefoil *(Potentilla)* belongs to the rose family. There are several varieties growing in Denmark with yellow flowers.

Danish Architecture

Denmark's architecture includes many of the styles found elsewhere in Europe. The country's vernacular architecture includes 17th-century fortress churches and half-timbered houses. The influence of Baroque and Dutch Renaissance dominated the style of palaces built in the 17th and 18th centuries. Denmark's native character re-established itself with Neo-Classicism at the end of the 19th century and this trend has continued with contemporary landmark designs.

Dutch Renaissance Frederiksborg Slot, built mainly in the 17th century

Romanesque Architecture

The first Danish churches were built of wood, but they were quickly replaced by Norman structures that were usually constructed of granite. The 10th to 12th centuries marked the arrival of brick and stone Romanesque architecture, exemplified by the churches in Viborg and Ribe. Village churches, such as the one in Hover, Jutland, were usually built as single-aisle structures, with an apse or presbytery. The historic round churches found on Bornholm represent a very distinctive style. These medieval fortress-like buildings were built in the 12th century and were used not only for religious purposes but as places of refuge. Three-storeys high, the top two storeys were used as storage rooms and also provided shelter for the local population in times of danger.

Portal finial in the form of a pediment, with ornamental carvings

The portal tympanum has been decorated with a granite relief depicting the Deposition from the Cross, reminiscent of the reliefs found in the churches of northern Spain.

Ribe Domkirke is a prime example of a Romanesque cathedral. Built on the site of a wooden structure, this stone building was begun in 1150. One of its most notable features is the "Cat's Head" door on the south side.

Sankt Bendts Kirke, Ringsted, was built during the reign of Valdemar I (1152–82) as a tomb for his father, Canute III. Later, more royals were buried here including Valdemar I. Its rich architecture encompasses an imposing edifice with a front tower, a presbytery enclosed with an apse and a mighty transept.

Round churches were used as shelters during enemy raids.

Nylars' round church on Bornholm, built around 1160

Gothic Architecture

One of the earliest Gothic buildings in Denmark is Roskilde's Domkirke (Cathedral), founded by Bishop Absalon in 1170. The most prominent example of the mature Gothic is the cathedral church in Odense. The introduction of red brick is an important element of the Danish Gothic style. Other typical features of Gothic architecture are its severe forms, ornate decorations and a façade that features stepped peaks. Many Gothic buildings have whitewashed or polychromatic interiors.

Sankt Knuds Domkirke in Odense is a magnificent example of pure Gothic church brickwork. Most of the cathedral is 13th- century but the finely detailed gilded altar dates from the early 16th century and is the work of Claus Berg, a master craftsman from Lübeck.

Renaissance Architecture

Danish Renaissance architecture grew out of the church's practice of importing architects for major projects in the late 16th century. Dutch architects and craftsmen were employed by Frederik II, and later by Christian IV in the 17th century, to build grand palaces such as Frederiksborg Slot in Hillerød and Kronberg Slot in Helsingør.

Triton figure from the Neptune fountain at Frederiksborg, by Adrian de Vries (c.1615)

Gables with richly carved ornaments

Kronborg Slot, a stately castle built in 1585 by Frederik II, and later rebuilt by Christian IV

Jens Bangs Stenhus, Aalborg, is, along with the Børsen (Stock Exchange), Copenhagen, and the quaint streets and crooked houses of Christianshavn, a fine example of town architecture from this period.

Baroque Architecture

From the mid-17th to mid-18th centuries Baroque in Denmark left its mark mainly on residential architecture. The best examples are Copenhagen's palaces – Charlottenborg and Christiansborg – along with the grand residence in Ledreborg. The main force behind Baroque in Denmark was the architect Nicolai Eigtved. His greatest achievement was the Frederiksstaden district in Copenhagen, which was built in a French style and intended as a royal quarter.

Audience Room in Frederiksborg Slot with moulded decorations

Fredensborg Slot is a sumptuous early-18th-century castle and was built by Frederik IV to a design by Johann Cornelius Krieger in an Italian Baroque style.

Altar from Vor Frelsers Kirke (Our Saviour's Church), Copenhagen

20th-century Architecture

In the early part of the 20th century Danish architecture began to reflect a desire for better design in housing and everyday objects, resulting in Modernism and, subsequently, Functionalism. A major result of this trend was the creation of the Design Council at the Association of Architects, in 1907. Characteristics of modern Danish architectural practice are an honest use of materials, clean lines and an abundance of natural light.

Water emphasises the visual link with a ship

The "Black Diamond", an extension of Det Kongelige Bibliotek (The Royal Library), Copenhagen, represents a Neo-Modernist trend that has gained favour in Denmark.

Arken Museet for Moderne Kunst (Museum of Modern Art) was designed by the then 25-year-old architect Søren Robert Lund, in metal and white concrete, and is a splendid example of Danish Deconstructivism.

Danish Design

LEGO® bricks, Arne Jacobsen's egg chair, audio-visual equipment by Bang & Olufsen – all are recognized throughout the world as examples of a Danish aesthetic. Design has a high profile in Denmark and constitutes an important source of revenue for the country, as well as being a major element of the national identity, supported by many institutions. Two good places to learn more about the traditions and history of Danish design are the Designmuseum Danmark and the Danish Design Centre, both of which are in Copenhagen.

Kähler Ceramics began building their reputation at the 1889 World Exhibition in Paris. Since then, the company has collaborated with several designers.

Bang & Olufsen high-fidelity products have been manufactured by Bang & Olufsen since 1925. The beauty of these products resides in the discreet use of the latest technology to promise first-rate sound and performance.

Large windows blur the boundary between a room's interior and the outside.

Furniture designer Kaare Klint was fascinated by the possibility of combining ergonomics with traditional furniture design. His designs draw on many sources including pieces from 18th-century England.

The Bodum company was founded at the end of World War II by Peter Bodum. His smart and simple kitchen appliances, designed in the 1950s, are produced to this day and still enjoy great popularity.

LEGO® is the name of the toy company founded in 1932 by Ole Kirk Christiansen. Christiansen started by producing wooden toys and, in 1958, introduced the now familiar plastic building bricks. The well-known brand name is a contraction of the Danish phrase *leg godt* ("play well").

The Mikado Table, by Cecilie Manz (b. 1972), has a refined, three-legged construction which is assembled without using screws or hinges.

The Y Chair is the most recognizable design created by Hans Wegner (1914–2007), a pioneer of Danish Modernism. He created over 500 wooden chairs, which combine minimalism with organic softness.

Light, open space

Functional, simple furniture

This Lamp by Poul Henningsen, from a series of lamps produced for Louis Poulsen & Co, is the result of a persistent endeavour by the designer to create lamps that give maximum natural light, while eliminating all shadows. He achieved the desired result by employing sets of curved lampshades to produce a soft, dispersed light.

Innovative use of material

Danish porcelain is epitomized in Royal Copenhagen's very first porcelain dinner service, the Blue Fluted Full Lace pattern, which debuted in 1775. Its intricate and exclusive design is both historic and timeless.

Design For Living

The Danish prioritize simple pleasures in daily life, a value that permeates Danish design. Many Danish products are geared toward creating hygge, a Danish concept of enjoying homely, social intimacy. Its impact is especially visible in interior design, with examples ranging from functional furniture made with quality materials to ambient lighting.

Arne Jacobsen

Born in 1902, Arne Jacobsen is the unquestionable "star" of Danish design. In his youth, Jacobsen was fascinated by the work of the Swiss-born architect Le Corbusier, especially his focus on functionality. As

Jacobsen's famed egg chair design

a designer Jacobsen created many well-known pieces including the Ant (1951). This plywood chair could be stacked and was the forerunner of chairs found in schools and cafés all over the world today. The majority of Jacobsen's chair designs, including the Egg and the Swan, are still being produced. He died in 1971.

Danish Art

Both painting and sculpture have an important place in Danish art and its history. Sculpture flourished during the Late Gothic and Mannerist periods. Even more so, the so-called "Golden Age," in the early 19th century, saw a flowering of Danish expression, thanks to the genius of figures like sculptor Bertel Thorvaldsen. Painting also flourished during this period and the formal portraiture of earlier painters such as Jens Juel began to be replaced with lively depictions of everyday life by artists such as Christoffer Wilhelm Eckersberg and his student Christen Købke.

View from the Loft of the Grain Store at the Bakery in the Citadel (1831), Christen Købke

Wounded Philoctetes (1774–75), Nicolai Abildgaard (Statens Museum for Kunst)

Old Masters

There are many well-preserved medieval works of art in Denmark, including Romanesque paintings and, in the churches of Zealand, the cycles of frescoes dating mainly from the 12th century.

The subsequent centuries were dominated by formal portraiture. Among the most outstanding, and the largest in size, are the oil paintings on display in Rosenborg Slot in Copenhagen, produced after 1615 by artists such as Reinhold Timm and Rembrandt. The artists working for Christian IV, in Kronborg, included the Dutch painter Gerrit van Honthorst, who painted for the court of Denmark between 1635 and 1641. During the reign of Frederik IV the influences of French painting became more pronounced. During the Rococo period a French influence was also present and can be seen in the works of Scandinavians such as

Johan Salomon Wahl and Carl Gustaf Pilo. The turning point in the development of Danish painting came with the founding of the Royal Academy of Fine Arts in 1754. Its alumni included many prominent painters from the period such as Jens Juel and Nicolai Abildgaard, who studied in Rome, from 1772 to 1776.

The "Golden Age"

The period between 1800 and 1850 saw a great surge in creativity. One of the prime movers of the "Golden Age" *(see pp46–7)* was Christoffer Wilhelm Eckersberg, who drew much of his inspiration from the native Danish landscape, as well as from scenes of everyday life. He had studied in Paris where he was taught

by Jacques Louis David to see nature for what it was. Eckersberg returned to Denmark, fired with the belief that truth is beauty. He brought back the precision of Neo-Classicism and made it a dominant trait in Danish painting. Portraiture during the "Golden Age" was also of a very high standard. Among the other outstanding artists of the period are Christian Albrecht Jensen and Christen Købke.

Modern Art

After 1880 Realism and Naturalism ruled supreme in Danish painting. Their most famous exponent was the Skagen School, which placed an emphasis on natural light and its effects. Among the leading members of this school were Peder S. Krøyer and Anna and Michael Ancher. Around 1900, Danish painting came to be dominated by Symbolism. The situation

Dead Drunk Danes (1960), Asger Jorn

changed just before World War I, when new trends, such as the experiments with form by the Expressionists and Cubists, began to challenge existing traditions in art. The ranks of Danish Cubists included Jais Nielsen and Vilhelm Lundstrom. One of the most important phenomena of the 1950s was CoBrA (Copenhagen–Brussels–Amsterdam), a movement that tried to give free expression to the unconscious. One of the movement's founders was the Danish artist Asger Jorn, whose vivid abstract paintings have received international acclaim.

High altar of Roskilde Domkirke, 16th century

Sacred Art

Before turning to Protestantism Danish churches were richly decorated. In the 16th century, after the Reformation, many frescoes were painted over, as they were considered to be examples of Catholic flamboyance. Surviving to this day are a few gilded altars dating from the Romanesque period (12th–13th centuries); two of them are still found in their original locations, in Sahl and Stadil churches. Some outstanding altarpieces were created in the Late Gothic period (late 15th and early 16th centuries) by woodcarvers from Lübeck, notably Claus Berg. The work of Berg, which includes the main altar in the cathedral in Odense, is

particularly striking. Filled with emotional charge and high in drama, his carving maintains a realism of detail that is typical of work found in southern Germany.

The Renaissance high altar in Roskilde Domkirke was made in Antwerp in 1560. It was originally intended for Gdansk, until it was requisitioned by Danish customs authorities.

The 17th century saw a culmination of the Reformation. At that time large sums of money were spent on building churches and chapels, notably Holmens Kirke in Copenhagen, for which Frederik III ordered a sumptuously decorated altarpiece sculpted from raw oak wood.

Sepulchral Sculpture

With the passing of the medieval era, funereal or sepulchral sculpture began to enjoy success in Denmark. Characteristic of this period are the works of the sculptor and architect Cornelis Floris of Antwerp, who designed the tomb of Christian III (d.1559) in Roskilde Domkirke (Cathedral), west of Copenhagen. It is made of multi-coloured marble and extraordinarily richly ornamented, with an open-plan colonnade that contains two statues of the monarch. This is one of Europe's largest royal tombs from this period.

Renaissance tombs and epitaphs of the aristocracy, found in great numbers throughout Denmark, were more modest, and usually limited to a single slab of stone bearing the image of the deceased in a prostrate position, with an inscription. A new type of tombstone appeared in the

Tomb of Christian III in Roskilde Domkirke, by Cornelis Floris

17th century. Its main creator was Thomas Quellinus of Antwerp. His marble tombs realistically depicted the deceased, and were accompanied by personified images of his or her virtues.

Modern Sculpture

Prior to the 19th century sculpture was treated in Denmark solely as a means of portraying the monarchy. This art form began to be taken more seriously with the establishment of the Royal Academy, however, and among its early exponents were Johanes Wiedeweilt (d.1802) and Nicolai Dajon (d.1823). Sculpture was only elevated to a high form of art, however, by Bertel Thorvaldsen (d.1844), who created an austere variety of Classicism based on his in-depth studies of classical antiquity while in Rome. After working in southern Europe for many years, Thorvaldsen returned home to a hero's welcome in 1838. He bequeathed many of his finest works to the city of Copenhagen on condition that a museum was established in which to house them (Thorvaldsens Museum, *see p89*).

Self-portrait, by Bertel Thorvaldsen

DENMARK THROUGH THE YEAR

Denmark is roughly on the same latitude as Moscow and southern Alaska but has a fairly mild climate in comparison. The coldest months are January and February, with most events and festivals are scheduled for spring and summer. The Danes like to enjoy themselves, and during the summer holiday season the whole country comes alive, with almost every town having its own festival. Denmark is not a large country yet it hosts many world-class events, including one of the oldest rock-music festivals, in Roskilde, which is attended by many major international acts. The world-famous Copenhagen jazz festival also attracts top performers. As elsewhere in Europe, religious festivals such as Christmas are widely observed and provide an opportunity for people to spend time with their families.

Royal family at the official celebrations of the Queen's 64th birthday (2004)

Spring

Spring arrives slowly in Denmark, but its advent is welcomed with great celebration around the country. The biggest of the festivals is Copenhagen's Whitsun Carnival, when the streets fill with Danes dressed in colourful costumes to mark the end of the long winter.

March

CPH:DOX *(late Mar)*, Copenhagen. This is the largest documentary-film festival in northern Europe.

April

H C Andersen's Birthday *(2 Apr)*, Odense. Free entry to the H C Andersen museums with special tours for children and theatrical presentations of his works.

Tivoli Gardens Concert Series *(mid-Apr)*, Copenhagen. The Tivoli amusement park and gardens open for the summer season. On Fridays the entrance fee includes access to the very popular late-night concerts.

Birthday of Queen Margrethe II *(16 Apr)*, Copenhagen. The Danish queen is very popular, and on this day large crowds of loyal Danes congregate outside Amalienborg Slot to sing "Happy Birthday", which is accompanied by the ceremonial changing of the Livgarden (royal guards).

Store Bededag *(4th Friday after Easter)*. Common Prayer Day or Great Prayer Day is a movable Easter feast. Following the introduction of Protestantism to Denmark in the 16th century, the church calendar was revised and several feasts were combined into one – the Store Bededag. On this day many Danes eat wheat buns – *varme hveder*.

May

Arbejdernes Kampdag *(1 May)*. Rallies are held to mark International Workers' Day.

Pinsedag. Whitsunday.

Viking Market *(1st weekend in May)*, Ribe. Held at the Viking Museum, this annual event recreates a Viking marketplace complete with displays of Viking crafts.

Aalborg Carnival *(Whitsun weekend)*, Aalborg. A week of celebrations leading up to Whitsunday, including a fireworks display and Northern Europe's biggest parade.

Ølfestival *(mid-May)*, Copenhagen. This lively three-day beer festival includes stalls, music and, more than 800 different beers from around 70 exhibitors, which include both Danish and foreign breweries.

Vild Med ORD - Aarhus Litteraturfestival *(mid-May)*, Aarhus. Founded in 2009, this literature festival celebrates the written word with author interviews, lectures and quizzes.

Classic Race Aarhus *(mid- to late May)*, Aarhus. Experience an historic drive through the decades in Aarhus when around 300 historical vehicles from Denmark and abroad gather for this classic race.

Copenhagen Marathon *(late May)*, Copenhagen. This race attracts around 10,000 amateur and elite runners from many European countries.

Whitsun Carnival *(Whitsun weekend)*, Copenhagen. This three-day event includes a parade, dancing and special activities for children.

Viking Market, Ribe

Average Daily Hours of Sunshine

Hours

| 10 | 8 | 6 | 4 | 2 | 0 |

Jan Feb Mar Apr May Jun Jul Aug Sep Oct Nov Dec

Hours

10 — 8 — 6 — 4 — 2 — 0

Hours of Sunshine
Most sunny days occur in late spring and early summer but visitors can also expect some fine weather through until September. November, December and January are generally the cloudiest months.

Roskilde Festival – one of Denmark's most popular events

Summer

Summer festivities begin with Sankt Hans Aften (23 June) when bonfires are lit on many beaches. Numerous attractions are scheduled for the summer holidays – from local one-day events to major festivals.

June
International Sand Sculpture Festival *(from early Jun)*, various towns. Competition to build the best sand sculptures.
International Kite Festival *(mid-Jun)*, Fanø. This four-day festival attracts over 5,000 kite-flyers.
River Boat Jazz Festival *(end Jun)*, Silkeborg. Jazz bands perform all around Silkeborg, some on boats.
Sankt Hans Eve *(23 Jun)*. Midsummer Night is celebrated around camp fires.

July
Roskilde Festival *(24 Jun–1 Jul)*, Roskilde. This rock festival has been attracting some of the biggest names in music since 1971. Past performers include Bob Dylan, Bob Marley and David Bowie.

Ringridning *(Jul)*, several towns in Sønderjylland. At this colourful festival, horse riders use a lance or spear to target a series of metal rings suspended in mid-air.
Copenhagen Jazz Festival *(early Jul)*, Copenhagen. For two weeks jazz, blues and fusion blast out of almost every public space in the city.
Aarhus International Jazz Festival *(mid-Jul)*, Aarhus. A second opportunity in this month to hear some top-class jazz.
Hans Christian Andersen Plays *(end Jul–early Aug)*, Odense. Each year, one of Andersen's fairy tales is performed outside in Den Fynske Landsby (Funen Village).

August
Cultural Harvest. Festivals celebrated in castles and stately homes, including exhibitions and theatre.
Aalborg Opera Festival Aalborg. In mid-August opera lovers congregate to hear some of the world's best performers.
Kulturhavn *(mid- to late Aug)*, Copenhagen. Festivalgoers can

enjoy the range of free cultural experiences on offer at this harbour-based festival. These include dance, music, children's activities, watersports, theatre and Secret Harbour Tours exploring little-known areas of the city's waterways.
Copenhagen International Fashion Fair *(early Aug)*, Copenhagen. Top Scandinavian and European fashion designers present their latest collections.
Hamlet Summer *(early to mid-Aug)*, Helsingør. Performances of Shakespeare's *Hamlet* and other works are staged in Kronborg Slot.
International Film Festival *(28 Aug–3 Sep)*, Odense.
Schubertiade *(mid-Aug–early Sep)*, Roskilde. Top musicians perform a selection of the works of Franz Schubert.
Copenhagen Cooking and Food Festival *(end of Aug)*, Copenhagen. Ten days of cooking events, from tastings and street kitchens to special menus.
European Medieval Festival *(end of Aug)*, Horsens. For two days the city is transformed into a 15th-century market town.

Copenhagen Cooking brings street kitchens and outdoor cooking events to the city

Average Monthly Rainfall

Rainfall
July is one of the
warmest, but also
one of the wettest,
months in Denmark.
The best time to
visit the country is
in late spring, when
it is warm and there
is very little rain.

Autumn

Early autumn provides the
final opportunity to stage
outdoor performances of jazz
and theatre. The beginning of
September marks a transition
between the carefree holiday
season and the beginning
of the new school year with
months of hard work and study
ahead. Theatres stage their first-
night performances, and cold
autumn evenings bring music-
lovers into the clubs.

Father Christmas Parade during Christmas celebrations in Tønder

September
Golden Days *(2 weeks in Sep)*,
Copenhagen. This annual event
celebrates Copenhagen's rich
cultural heritage and city life
through a series of exhibitions,
lectures, concerts, debates and
themed walks.
Around Limfjorden Race *(early
or mid-Sep)*, Løgstør, Thisted,
Struer, Nykøbing Mors, Fur and
Skive. The biggest annual sailing
event in Scandinavia is an
exciting five-day race in
traditional boats around the
Limfjord Bay.

Tour De Gudenå *(mid-Sep)*,
Skanderborg. Kayak and canoe
contest attracting many
participants and spectators.

October
Culture Night *(2nd Fri in Oct)*,
Copenhagen. A night when it is
possible to visit many exhibitions,
museums, castles, theatres
and churches, including some
buildings that are usually closed
to visitors.
Mix Copenhagen *(1st half of
Oct)*, Copenhagen. International
gay, lesbian, bi-sexual and
transgender film festival.

Tivoli Halloween *(2nd half of
Oct)*, Copenhagen. Witches,
lanterns and pumpkins.
CPH PIX *(late Oct–early Nov)*,
Copenhagen. This is the biggest
international film festival in
Denmark. Film entries include
Scandinavian ones, as well as
those from world-famous directors.

November
Tivoli Christmas *(Nov–Dec)*,
Copenhagen. Events for the
young and young at heart in
Tivoli as Christmas draws closer.
Among the attractions are a
Christmas market, ice-skating
on a frozen artificial lake and
the chance of spotting a
Christmas pixie.
Copenhagen Irish Festival *(1st
half of Nov)*, Copenhagen. Four
days of celebrations and plenty
of Irish music.
Feast of St Morten *(10 Nov)*.
St Morten's Evening is often
marked by roasting a goose.
Tønder – The Christmas Town
(mid-Nov), Tønder. A colourful
parade featuring a multitude
of Father Christmases,
accompanied by marching
bands, passes along the main
street of the town.

Fantastic Halloween decorations at Tivoli

Average Monthly Temperature

Temperature
This chart shows the average maximum and minimum temperatures for each month. Summer temperatures reach about 20° C (68° F), although temperatures can top 25° C (77° F). Winters can be cold with the temperature often dropping below zero, though severe frosts are rare.

Winter

Winter is the quietest time of the year. Little happens and the weather is not conducive to outdoor entertainment. The Christmas period abounds in concerts, however. These are often staged in churches and feature choral ensembles singing psalms and carols. Denmark's streets are beautifully decorated and illuminated at this time and Christmas fairs are held throughout the country, with plenty to eat and drink, and the occasional parade.

December

Jul *(24–26 Dec)*. The Danes celebrate Christmas in family circles. As in most of Europe, children play a central role. Danes tend to celebrate on Christmas Eve, decorating the tree the night before Christmas and often hanging it with real candles. The traditional Christmas dinner is also eaten on the

24th and usually consists of roast pork, goose or duck with red cabbage and potatoes. Rice pudding with cherry sauce is eaten for dessert; whoever finds the hidden almond receives a prize.

January

Nytårsdag *(1 Jan)*. New Year's Day witnesses a boisterous welcome to the New Year in Denmark. Many towns stage firework displays, while classical concerts are performed in most major cities.

February

Wondercool *(throughout Feb)*, Copenhagen. A fusion event, mixing music, art, food, design and architecture. On Saturdays guests can join gastronomic cruises on boats that drop them off at six different restaurants. Alternatively, visitors can enjoy an after-hours dining experience in a museum.
Fastelavn *(last Sun before Lent)*. Shrovetide is a time for fun and

Symphony orchestra performing for Aalborg's New Year concert

games. The Danish tradition of "knocking a cat out of the barrel" is still practised by children in fancy-dress. Originally the barrel, hanging from a string, contained a real cat, which was held to be a symbol of evil. Today, the barrel is reminiscent of a piñata, containing sweets, toys and fruit, which eventually fall to the ground.

Public Holidays

New Year Nytår (1 Jan)

Maundy Thursday

Good Friday

Easter Day Påske

International Workers' Day Arbejdernes Kampdag (1 May)

Common Prayer Day Store Bededag (Apr/May)

Ascension Day Kristi Himmelfartsdag (May/Jun)

Whitsunday, Whitmonday Pinse (May/Jun)

Constitution Day Grundslovsdag (5 Jun)

Christmas Day (25 Dec)

Boxing Day (26 Dec)

New Year fireworks in Tivoli, Copenhagen

THE HISTORY OF DENMARK

Denmark's history has long been associated with the sea. Viking raids on England and elsewhere between the 9th and 11th centuries marked the beginnings of Danish influence and by the late Middle Ages Denmark had a tight grip on trade in the Baltic. The country later lost its position as a world power, but continues to play an important role in the international arena.

The earliest evidence of human existence to be found in Denmark dates from about 12,000 BC after the first warm phase at the end of the last ice age. From 7000–3900 BC, the sea level rose so much that the northern parts of Denmark were divided into islands and deep fjords. Between 3900 and 1700 BC the first agricultural settlements began to emerge. The period is marked by the clearing of forests, the rise of small communities, and the mining of flint. Denmark's Bronze Age dates from around 1800 BC and jewellery and cult objects have been unearthed from this period. By about 500 BC iron had largely replaced bronze.

Unification

During the late Iron Age (5th and 6th centuries AD) a Nordic tribe known as Danes began to take control of the Jutland peninsula, forming a social order based around tribal structures.

As a result of the threat from the south presented by the Frankish empire under Charlemagne, these clans began to co-operate as a defensive measure. The Danish strategic position was strengthened in about AD 737 by the building of the Danevirke, a rampart that cut across the Jutland peninsula. This wall, and the forces of Godfred, king of Jutland, forced Charlemagne to recognize the local Eider River as the Franco-Danish border in AD 811.

After Godfred's death, rivalry between different clans again brought chaos. The first ruler to restore unity was Gorm the Old, the son of a Norwegian chieftain who had conquered the Jutland peninsula in the late 9th century. Gorm's son, Harald I (Bluetooth) took the throne in AD 950 and extended his power base across the rest of Denmark. Harald I's conquest enabled the widespread adoption of Christianity, which not only unified the country but also appeased Denmark's Frankish neighbours.

Increased security gave new impetus to a series of Viking (see pp38–9) raids on the British Isles and Ireland. These raids made it possible for Danish kings to win control of England and, for a period, an Anglo-Danish kingdom was formed under Canute I (The Great), who ruled as monarch of Denmark, England and Norway until his death in 1035. After his death, England broke away from Danish control and Denmark fell into disarray for some time.

12,000 BC Earliest evidence of humans in Denmark
Cover of a stone urn from the Bronze Age
9th century Danish Viking raids on British Isles and France
811 Army of Charlemagne stopped by Danevirke wall
1018–1035 Reign of Canute I. Unification of Denmark, England and Norway

12,000 BC | 4000 BC | AD 500 | 750 | 1000 | 1100

3900–1700 BC Earliest agricultural settlements
5th–6th century Danes occupy the Jutland peninsula
737 Building of the Danevirke rampart
Clay pot, 1700–500 BC
1013 Sweyn I conquers England
c.985 Harald I (Bluetooth) unites Jutland, the islands and southern Sweden

◀ Painting featuring the Danish flag descending from heaven during Valdemar II's campaign in present-day Estonia in 1219

The Vikings

The term Viking is generally used to refer to the Scandinavian peoples who journeyed overseas in wooden ships, between AD 800 and 1100. The Vikings raided and traded throughout the North and Irish seas and along the rivers of eastern and western Europe. Early Viking raiders targeted monasteries for their wealth and the ferocity of these lightning raids spread terror throughout Christian Europe, giving rise to the image of Vikings as plunderers and rapists. In fact these pagan people were expert farmers and sailors and ventured as far as North America, where they traded in such items as tusks and pelts.

Ornament
This silver ornament, found in Lindholm Høje in 1952, represents a typical piece of Viking jewellery.

Strong ropes holding the mast

Silver Coin
The Vikings established trade routes to the East and the West. From the 9th century, silver coins, such as this one from the market place of Hedeby, were used as currency.

Sails were made from sheep's wool or flax and were often worth more than the rest of the boat.

Viking Chieftain
In the 19th century a view of Vikings began to take hold, which saw them as barbarians. This portrait by Carl Haag is typical of the common image. Actually they were skilled farmers, craftsmen, traders, and hunters.

The bow and stern of a Viking ship had the same shape, enabling it to make a rapid change in direction.

Figurehead
The stems of ships were decorated with figureheads, in the form of a snake or a dragonhead. The loss of a figurehead was believed to be a bad omen.

Keel produced from a trunk of hard oak

Viking Ship
Viking warships were usually about 28 m (92 ft) in length. The longest one ever found measured nearly 70 m (230 ft). Along with a 60-strong crew of oarsmen, they could carry as many as 400 people.

Key

— Viking expeditions

Woman Statuette
The self-reliant Viking women were either shieldmaiden warriors, or stayed behind to run their homes and farms for many months when their men went out to sea.

The ship's planking was made of overlapping planks of oak and joined together with nails. Any gaps between the planks were sealed with tarred wool or fur.

Viking sailing ships had a very shallow draught and could sail in waters less than 1 m (3.3 ft) deep.

Viking Raids
Early raids were carried out only during spring and summer. From about 845, Vikings began wintering at the mouths of foreign rivers, making raids possible throughout the year.

Viking Architecture

Few Viking buildings, which were built of earth, wood and stone, have survived. The best preserved are the round fortresses erected during the reign of Harald I (Bluetooth), in the late 10th century, at strategic points around Fyrkat (eastern Jutland), Aggersborg (northern Jutland), Trelleborg (Zealand) and Nonnebakken (Funen). These fortified settlements were surrounded by circular embankments 120 m (394 ft) in diameter, 12 m (39.4 ft) wide and rising to a height of 4 m (13 ft).

The Frykat fortress included 16 huge buildings containing domestic quarters, and was probably inhabited by between 800 and 1,000 people. Close to where the fortress stood, there is now a replica Viking farmstead including houses, outbuildings and traditionally clothed volunteers.

This replica longhouse, near Fyrkat, was built using authentic tools and materials, with knowledge gained from archaeological research.

Viking house doors, such as these in Frederikssund, were heavily built as a defence against intruders as well as the forces of nature.

Valdemar I removing a pagan statute on the coast of Rugia

of its power. Successive monarchs were forced into enacting laws which for the time were quite progressive, including the end of imprisonment without just cause in 1282.

The Middle Ages

King Canute's son Hardicanute died in 1042 and the Anglo-Danish kingdom disintegrated as the successors of Denmark's eighth monarch, Sweyn II (1047–74), began fighting each other for the throne. As royal supremacy weakened, the power of wealthy landowners and church leaders grew and this early medieval period of Denmark's history is scarred by internal strife and corruption.

This period of unrest came to an end with the succession of Valdemar I (The Great) in 1157. He reunited the country and enacted Denmark's first written laws (the Jutland Code). With help of the powerful Bishop Absalon, he made a series of successful raids against the Wends in eastern Germany. By the time of Valdemar II's succession, Denmark had won control of Meklenburg, Holstein, Lübeck and Estonia, making it one of the greatest powers in northern Europe.

Denmark's pre-eminence ended in 1227 when the country was defeated by its German vassals at the Battle of Bornhøved. Denmark was forced to give up much of its recently acquired territory and, following the death of Valdemar II in 1241, the Danish monarchy lost much

The Kalmar Union

One of the greatest achievements of King Valdemar IV (1340–75) was to arrange the marriage of his daughter Margrete to Norway's King Haakon. Margrete succeeded in forming the Kalmar Union, an alliance uniting Denmark, Norway and Sweden under a common sovereign. The main aim of the union was to counter the dominance of the Hanseatic League, which under the influence of Germany dominated trade in the region.

Queen Margrete, regent of Denmark and the initiator of the Kalmar Union

1167 Founding of Copenhagen

Bronze amulet

1227 Denmark defeated at the Battle of Bornhøved

1397 Creation of the Kalmar Union

1361 Conquest of Gotland

1100	1175	1250	1325	14

1157 Reunification of Denmark by Valdemar I (The Great)

1241 Death of Valdemar II

1282 Erik V signs an agreement to create an annual assembly *(hof)* of feudal lords

1286 Assassination of Erik V

c.1350 Arrival of the bubonic plague in Denmark

Gustav Vasa persuading Lübeck authorities to join in the attack on Christian II

16th and 17th centuries. In addition to these battles, the Thirty Years War took place (1616–48). Denmark was involved from 1625 to 1629 and suffered a disastrous defeat, while Sweden, joining in 1630, gained power and wealth. Renewed warring between the two countries ended in 1658 with Denmark losing all of its territories on the Swedish mainland. Two more wars occurred, 1675–79 and 1709–20.

While each country remained free to follow their own policies, they were obliged to fight any wars together and elect a common monarch. In 1397, Margrete's grand-nephew Erik of Pomerania was crowned king of Denmark, Norway and Sweden.

Initially, a long line of military successes, the introduction of customs duties in the Øresund (Sound) and a growing demand for Danish produce strengthened the country's position. Soon, however, Denmark's domination in the Baltic was challenged by the growing power of Sweden. In 1520 the Danish king, Christian II, ruthlessly suppressed an insurrection by what is known as the Stockholm Bloodbath. Three years later, however, Sweden elected its own king, Gustav Vasa, effectively putting an end to the union.

Wars With Sweden

Denmark's and Sweden's aims to gain control of Øresund lead to a long series of wars between the two countries during the

Wooden altar by Abel Schrøder, 1661, in Holmens Kirke, Copenhagen

Towards Absolute Monarchy

The strength of the monarchy had been increased by the introduction of Lutheranism in 1536, which placed the wealth of the Catholic church in the hands of the Crown. The king, however, was still elected by the nobility. Although political power was divided between the Crown and Council, the nobles often had the last say. After the defeats of 1658, state coffers were empty and King Fredrik III needed to take control. This led to the instatement of absolute monarchy (see pp42–3).

Christian IV, King of Denmark, welcomed in Berlin by the Brandenburg Elector, 1595

Christian II, King of Denmark (1513–23)

1520 Stockholm Bloodbath

1660 Establishment of hereditary monarchy; rise of an absolute monarchy

1658 Treaty of Roskilde. Denmark loses its territories on the Swedish mainland

1665 Denmark begins to establish colonies in the Virgin Islands

1475	1550	1625	1700

1479 Founding of Copenhagen University

1536 Introduction of Lutheranism in Denmark

1523 Termination of the Kalmar Union

Two-crown coin dating from 1618

The Era of Absolute Monarchy

Frederik III introduced hereditary monarchy in 1660 in an effort to curtail the power of the nobles of the Council *(see p41)*. In 1665, he took the matter further and passed the Royal Act, which declared the sovereign to be beyond the law and inferior only to God. Five years later Christian V became the first monarch to be crowned under the new system. The people seemed to prefer an almighty king to the old nobility, and kings continued to rule as absolute monarchs until 1848.

Frederik III
Crowned King of Denmark and Norway in 1648, Frederik III ruled until his death in Copenhagen castle in 1670. To this day, his grave can be found in Roskilde cathedral.

Academy of Knights
Denmark's elite schools were established by Frederik III. These academies became popular in the 17th century.

Frederiksborg Chapel
The Slotskirken (Palace Chapel) is where Danish kings were crowned from 1670 to 1840.

Holmens Kirke, built in 1619 to serve the Royal Navy

Holmens Canal

The Holmens Drawbridge enabled ships to enter the canal.

The Introduction of Absolutism in Denmark

The decision by Frederik III to introduce absolute monarchy in Denmark in 1665 was met with general approval. The ceremonial meeting between the king and the parliament has been immortalized in minute detail in many paintings including examples found in Rosenborg and Frederiksborg.

Copenhagen (c.1700)
Following the introduction of absolute monarchy the Danish capital's defences were strengthened.

Corfitz Ulfeldt

Corfitz Ulfeldt, son-in-law of Christian IV, was a typical example of the powerful nobility. After a disagreement with Frederik III, he switched sides and negotiated the Roskilde Treaty on Sweden's behalf in 1658.

Colourful burgher homes were built in the form of narrow-fronted terraced houses.

Børsen (the Stock Exchange)

Numerous inhabitants of the capital attended the celebrations marking the introduction of absolute monarchy.

Boats moored along the canal

The king's troops

Frederik VII

In 1848 Frederik VII renounced absolute power and, with a new constitution, turned Denmark into a democratic country, with guaranteed freedom of speech.

Architecture

The period of absolute monarchy brought with it many magnificent buildings. The most opulent examples of the residential architecture of this period include Charlottenborg in Kongens Nytorv, Copenhagen, which was completed in 1683 as a palace for the royal family *(see pp72–3)*. Other outstanding buildings from this period are Ledreborg, a stately home designed by the architect Lauritz de Thurah *(see p143)*, Copenhagen's Børsen (Stock Exchange) and Amalienborg Slot *(see pp60–61)*, which was designed by Nicolai Eigtved, the architect also responsible for Copenhagen's Frederikstad district.

Vor Frelsers Kirke was built in 1696 by Lambert van Haven in Dutch Renaissance style. The spire was added by Lauritz de Thurah in 1752 *(see pp92–3)*.

Christian VII's Palace at Amalienborg has typically opulent Rococo interiors, designed by Nicolai Eigtved and the sculptor Le Clerk.

Painting by C.A. Lorentzen of the British attack on the Danish fleet, 1801

The Age of Reform

A peace treaty with Sweden signed in 1720 marked the beginning of the longest war-free period in Denmark's history. The absence of external threats encouraged economic growth and this in turn brought about a period of social change, which became more urgent as the French Revolution gathered pace. Under Frederik VI (1808–39) feudal obligations such as compulsory labour were abolished and large tracts of land were broken up and redistributed to peasants. At the same time landowners were given a role in government and compulsory education was introduced for all children under the age of 14.

The Napoleonic Wars

The outbreak of the Napoleonic Wars in 1796 eventually brought this period of peace and reform to a halt. Denmark, which derived major benefits from trade, tried to remain neutral in the face of the conflict in Europe but, in 1801, Britain accused Denmark of breaking the British trade embargo and attacked and destroyed the Danish fleet in Øresund. In 1807 the British, fearing the strengthening of

a Franco- Danish alliance, struck again and bombarded Copenhagen for four days. By the end of the attack much of the city was ablaze and the naval yard was destroyed. The British then sailed away with what remained of the Danish fleet, which included 170 gunboats. In the aftermath of this assault, Denmark joined the continental alliance against Britain and Britain in turn blockaded Danish waters.

The war ended with the signing of the Kiel Peace Treaty in 1814 under which Denmark lost some 385,252 sq km (148,746 sq miles) of territory, including Norway. The new boundaries left Denmark with a mere

Peasants give thanks to Christian VII for abolishing serfdom, painting by C.W. Eckersberg

1720 End of war with Sweden

1721 Denmark regains Schleswig

1750 Increase in foreign trade; end of economic crisis

1807 Bombardment of Copenhagen by Wellington's army

| 1720 | 1740 | 1760 | 1780 | 18● |

Armchair from the Chinese Room in Amalienborg Slot, Copenhagen

First Danish banknote, dating from 1713 during the reign of Frederik IV

1788 Abolishment of serfdom

1801 British attack Danish fleet

Painting by C.W. Eckersberg depicting bombardment of Copenhagen in 1807

58,000 sq km (22,388 sq miles), which included the Duchy of Schleswig, with its Danish-German population, and the Holstein and Lauenburg dukedoms.

The Napoleonic Wars had a catastrophic effect on Denmark. The British blockade led to famine and starvation while territorial losses and wartime destruction resulted in a bankrupt state treasury. Culturally, however, this was the beginning of Denmark's Golden Age (see pp46–7).

Denmark's national emblem, 1774–1820

Schleswig Conflict

Events in Europe, including the 1830 July Revolution in France, contributed to the weakening of absolute monarchy. With increasing force, demands were made for the creation of a representative government. Eventually, in 1848, pressure from liberal circles resulted in the enactment of a new constitution, ending absolute monarchy.

The new constitution included the incorporation of the duchies of Schleswig and Holstein as permanent regions of

Denmark. With the support of Prussia, the armies of Schleswig and Holstein rose up against the Danish authority. War ensued and ended in 1851 with the defeat of the duchies, but failed to solve the conflict. Trouble erupted again in 1863, when the Danish parliament agreed a new joint constitution for the Kingdom of Denmark and the Duchy of Schleswig. A year later, on the pretext of defending the German populations within the duchies, Prussia and Austria declared war on Denmark. Within months Denmark was defeated and the contested duchies were lost to Prussia and Austria.

The shock of defeat led Denmark to declare its neutrality and concentrate on rebuilding the economy. Danish agriculture entered a period of rapid growth, assisted by a high demand for grain in Britain, and the railway system was extended to cover much of the country. By the end of the 19th century Denmark had a well-developed economic base that included mature shipbuilding and brewing industries.

Return of Danish soldiers to Copenhagen in 1864 depicted in a painting by Otto Bache

1813 State Treasury declared bankrupt

1814 Kiel Peace Treaty; loss of Norway

1848–51 Civil war over the duchies of Schleswig and Holstein

Christian VIII, King of Denmark (1839–48)

1873 Banning of child labour

1820 1840 1860 1880

1835 First edition of Hans Christian Andersen's *Fairy Tales*

1848 End of absolute monarchy

1884 First Social Democrats elected to parliament

1843 First philosophical works by Søren Kierkegaard published

1864 War with Prussia and Austria

Denmark's Golden Age

The period of political and economic turmoil that occurred during the Napoleonic wars, and the years immediately following them, witnessed an unprecedented flourishing of culture. The leading figures of Denmark's "Golden Age", which lasted throughout the first half of the 19th century, achieved recognition far beyond the borders of Denmark. Among the most prominent are the sculptor Bertel Thorvaldsen, the painter Christoffer Wilhelm Eckersberg and the romantic poet Adam Oehlenschläger. More famous than these, however, are the writer Hans Christian Andersen and the philosopher Søren Kierkegaard.

Bella and Hanna Nathansson
This portrait was painted by the "father of Danish painting" Christoffer Wilhelm Eckersberg.

Interior of a House
The drawing room of a Copenhagen merchant, portrayed in this painting by Wilhelm Marstrand, represents a typical interior of a middle-class home during the 1830s.

Gottlieb Bindesbøll

Martinus Rørbye

Constantin Hansen

Bertel Thorvaldsen
This sculpture (1817) of a shepherd boy is one of many Neo-Classical statues by Bertel Thorvaldsen.

Parade
Festivals, parades and fairs coloured the lives of Copenhagen's citizens.

H C Andersen Telling his Stories
An illustration from one of the earliest editions of Hans Christian Andersen's tales, which are some of the most famous works of children's literature.

Wilhelm Marstrand, Albert Küchler and Ditlev Blunck on the balcony

Jørgen Sonne

H C Andersen
Born in humble circumstances in 1805, the popular writer later socialized with the bourgeoisie and at court.

Andersen's Inkpot
As well as writing nearly 200 fairy tales, Andersen also wrote novels, librettos and other works.

Artists of the Golden Age
This painting, entitled A Group of Danish Artists Visiting Rome *was painted in 1837 by Constantin Hansen. Like many painters of this period, Hansen learnt his craft abroad and returned to Denmark with a fresh perspective.*

Søren Kierkegaard
One of the forerunners of Existentialism, Kierkegaard (1813–55) described human life in terms of ethics, aesthetics and religion.

The Golden Age in Copenhagen

Following the ravages that befell Copenhagen at the turn of the 18th and 19th centuries, including the 1807 British bombardment *(see p44)*, the city was rebuilt in a new form. Classicism became the dominant architectural style. Christian Frederik Hansen and other Danish architects often drew their inspiration from antiquity. Office buildings, as well as the new bourgeois residences, were adorned with columns, porticoes and tympanums. The most interesting buildings include Thorvaldsens Museum, the Domhuset (Court House) in Nytorv, and the Harsdorff Hus in Kongens Nytorv.

Thorvaldsens Museum was built in 1848 and approved personally by the sculptor who had bequeathed his work to the city. This building is decorated with friezes by Jørgen Sonne *(see p89)*.

Vor Frue Kirke was designed by Christian Frederik Hansen, who took his inspiration from Classical buildings. It had an imposing façade, but no tower until Frederik VI declared that a tower was essential *(see p76)*.

Stockholm, Copenhagen and Oslo portrayed in a satirical magazine, in 1906

World War I

Before World War I Denmark had maintained good relations with both Britain and Germany and with the outbreak of war the Danish government declared its neutrality. This brought considerable benefits to the country's economy, although a third of Denmark's merchant fleet was sunk during the conflict. Also, the war drew attention to the commercial and strategic importance of Denmark's colonies in the West Indies, and the USA bought the Virgin Islands from Denmark in 1917.

Germany's defeat in 1918 revived the old Schleswig-Holstein problem. Under the Treaty of Versailles, the area was divided into two zones and, after a referendum in 1920, the northern part of the former duchy was returned to Denmark. The southern zone remained with Germany.

World War II

In September 1939, during Hitler's invasion of Poland, Denmark again confirmed its neutral status. This failed to stop the Third Reich from invading Denmark on 9 April 1940, and after a brief period of resistance by the royal guards at Amalienborg Slot Germany began a "peaceful occupation". Hoping to minimize casualties, the government in Copenhagen decided on a policy of limited co-operation. Opposition among ordinary Danes to this occupation was widespread, however, and in 1943 an increasingly strong resistance movement brought an end to the policy of collaboration. Following a wave of strikes and anti-German demonstrations, the government resigned and was replaced by a German administration.

The Nazis disarmed the Danish army and fleet and began to round up Danish Jews. Fortunately, most were spirited away at night in fishing boats by the Danish Resistance to neutral Sweden.

The final 18 months of the war saw the Danish Freedom Council, an underground movement that organized the Resistance, become increasingly active. The Danish

US State Secretary hands the Danish minister a cheque in payment for the Virgin Islands

1914–18 World War I. Denmark remains neutral

Frederik VIII with his wife, Louise

1940 Denmark occupied by the Third Reich

1944 Iceland becomes a republic

1900	1915	1930	1945	196

1901 Adoption of democratic parliamentary government

1917 Sale of the Virgin Islands to the United States

1933 Implementation of first social reform programmes

1920 Schleswig-Holstein referendum

1949 Denmark becomes a co-founder of NATO

1960 Denmark joins EFTA

Christian X (1912–47)

Germans on the streets of Copenhagen during World War II

Resistance, which by 1945 had some 50,000 operatives ready to assist the Allies, did all it could to hamper the German war effort, including blowing up railway lines and sabotaging German-run factories. With the German surrender in 1945, a new government composed of Resistance leaders and pre-war politicians was formed in Denmark.

Postwar Denmark

Thanks to the activities of the Resistance, Denmark was recognized as a member of the Allied Forces and joined the United Nations in 1945. In 1949 it joined the ranks of NATO. This move marked a departure from a policy of neutrality, which the country had followed since 1864. Denmark's participation in the Marshall Plan enabled the country to thoroughly modernize its industry and agriculture and laid the foundations for postwar prosperity. A new constitution, enacted in 1953, introduced a single-chamber parliament and changed the rules governing female succession to the throne. These new rules were applied in 1972 when Queen Margrethe II ascended the throne following the death of her father, Frederik IX.

Modern Denmark

Denmark did not participate in the talks of 1957, which resulted in the formation of the European Union, but in 1973, after a referendum, it became the first Scandinavian country to join. Denmark's EU membership has remained a controversial subject with many Danes, with 87 per cent initially voting against the adoption of the euro, while the 2000 referendum saw 53.2 per cent vote against it.

Throughout the 1960s and 1970s a series of reforms, including a generous system of social welfare and a virtual lack of censorship, bolstered the country's reputation as a liberal country. In the 1970s and 1980s Denmark entered a conservative phase with calls for curbs on immigration and tax cuts. However, it is still generally acknowledged as a tolerant society, with a high standard of living, a strong sense of social conscience and many positive policies towards protecting the environment. In 2009, Anders Fogh Rasmussen, the country's former prime minister, was appointed secretary general of NATO, and Copenhagen hosted the UN Climate Change Summit in the same year. Denmark was again ranked the world's happiest country by the UN World Happiness Report (WHR), in March 2016 – the third time since 2012.

Anders Fogh Rasmussen, secretary general of NATO

COPENHAGEN AREA BY AREA

Copenhagen at a Glance

Frequently ranked as one of the world's most liveable cities, Copenhagen is loved by locals and visitors alike. Situated on the Øresund, Copenhagen's location is unsurpassed – it is possible to swim along the beaches in summer, tour the city by boat and walk to most major sights. Cycling is a hugely popular form of transport here, with around 50 per cent of inhabitants cycling to work, and the city's up-to-date infrastructure supports this activity. Together, pedestrians and cyclists crisscross the city, stopping to take in the world-class museums and ever-evolving restaurant and retail culture.

0 metres	250
0 yards	250

Marmorkirken
The Marble Church, with its vast dome, is also known as Frederikskirken, after Frederik V who had it built. Visitors are permitted to climb the dome with a tour guide *(see p62)*.

Gefionspringvandet
The biggest fountain in Copenhagen is inspired by a popular Scandinavian myth about the creation of Zealand *(see p59)*.

◀ Pretty coloured buildings lining Nyhavn canal

Cycling
Copenhagen is synonymous with cycling – half of locals commute by bike, and the city has some 350 km (210 miles) of cycle paths that are easy for all to use.

Statens Museum for Kunst
The National Gallery has a great treasure of European art dating from the 13th to 19th centuries (see pp66–7).

Rådhuspladsen
The city's main square is a good starting point from which to explore Strøget; it is also the location of the city hall (see p79).

NORTH COPENHAGEN

Separated from Central Copenhagen's bustling pedestrian streets by garden oases, North Copenhagen is rich with cultural heritage. The focal point of this elegant neighbourhood is Amalienborg Slot, the Danish royalty's official residence, which is surrounded by the decadent 18th century Rococo mansions of the Frederiksstaden district. A short walk along Frederiksstaden's main artery, Frederiksgade, leads to the mighty Marmorkirken, crowned with one of the largest church domes in Europe. A few minutes further on foot is the Rosenborg Castle and its bucolic garden of Kongens Have – the city's oldest park. To the west and north of Rosenborg, the sizeable botanic gardens and Kastellet grounds provide more options for scenic strolls. Visitors will rediscover the crowds at the Little Mermaid statue, the icon of Copenhagen, which sits on the tip of the Kastellet grounds.

Sights at a Glance

Churches
③ Sankt Albans Kirke
⑧ Marmorkirken

Historic Buildings and Monuments
① The Little Mermaid
② Kastellet
④ Gefionspringvandet
⑦ Amalienborg Slot pp60–61
⑫ Rosenborg Slot pp64–5

Museums and Galleries
⑤ Medical Museion
⑥ Designmuseum Danmark
⑨ Davids Samling
⑪ Livgardens Historiske Samling
⑭ Geologisk Museum
⑮ Hirschsprungske Samling
⑯ Statens Museum for Kunst pp66–7

Parks and Gardens
⑩ Kongens Have
⑬ Botanisk Have

See also Street Finder
Maps 1 & 2

◀ The changing of Den Kongelige Livgarde (royal guards)   **For keys to symbols** see back flap

Street-by-Street: Around Amalienborg Slot

The main reason to come to this part of Copenhagen is to visit Amalienborg Slot, the official residence of Queen Margrethe II, which is guarded by soldiers in traditional uniforms. The best time to visit is at noon, when the daily ceremony for the changing of the guard takes place. Frederik V made Amalienborg Slot the focal point of a new, smart district, which he built to mark the 300th anniversary of the Oldenburg dynasty, celebrated in 1748. In honour of the king the district was named Frederiksstaden.

❺ Medical Museion, a medical museum, is housed in the former Danish Academy of Surgery and has on display some gruesome human remains as well as an old operating theatre.

Alexander Nevsky Kirke is a Russian Orthodox church and was completed in 1883. It was a gift from Tsar Alexander III to mark his marriage to a Danish princess.

❽ ★ Marmorkirken
Also known as Frederiks-kirken, this church is just west of Amalienborg. Its huge dome rests on 12 pillars and is one of the biggest of its kind in Europe, measuring 31 m (102 ft) across.

❼ ★ Amalienborg Slot
Consisting of four almost identical buildings, the palace has been the main residence of the Danish royal family since 1794.

| 0 metres | | 50 |
| 0 yards | | 50 |

Key

- - Suggested route

❻ ★ Designmuseum Danmark
Before this building provided an exhibition space to showcase Danish design, it served as the city hospital in the 18th century.

Locator Map
See Street Finder Map 2

Sankt Ansgars Kirke is on the site of a Roman Catholic chapel and was once used by Copenhagen's foreign population. The present building was completed in 1842 and consecrated 23 years later.

Kongelige Afstøbningssamling, or Royal Cast Collection, has over 2,000 sculpture casts, including a copy of the *Venus de Milo* and copies of statues from the Acropolis.

Amaliehaven is a modern park, donated to the city by the A.P. Møller shipping company in 1983. The gardens are next to Nyhavn and are a popular place for a walk.

❶ The Little Mermaid

Langelinie. **Map** 2 F3. Ⓢ Østerport. 🚌 26. 🆆 **mermaidsculpture.dk**

The tiny figure of the Little Mermaid *(Den Lille Havfrue)*, sitting on a rock and gazing wistfully at the passing ships, is Denmark's best-known monument. The sculpture, commissioned by Carl Jacobsen, head of the Carlsberg brewery, was inspired by the ballet version of *The Little Mermaid*, which in turn was based on Hans Christian Andersen's tale about a mermaid who falls in love with a prince.

The sculptor, Edvard Eriksen (1876–1959), wanted to use as his model Ellen Price, a prima ballerina who had played the part of the mermaid. However, when the dancer learned where the statue was to be located she refused to continue posing and allowed only her face to be used. As a result, the body was modelled on that of the sculptor's wife.

The final bronze cast was placed at the end of the harbour promenade in 1913. Since then, the sculpture has fallen victim to vandals and pranksters on a number of occasions. In 1961 she had her hair painted red. In 1964 her head was cut off; some time later she lost both arms and in 1998 she lost her head once again. Now, moved a little further towards the sea, she enjoys more peace.

One of the buildings inside the Kastellet

❷ Kastellet

Map 2 E3. **Tel** 33 11 22 33 (for tours of the grounds). Ⓢ Østerport. 🚌 1A, 15, 20E, 26. **Open** fortress grounds only. 🚶 🆆 **kastellet.info**

A fortress was first built on this site in 1626 but a Swedish attack in 1658 revealed its numerous weak points and the defences were rebuilt on the orders of Frederik III. The works were completed in 1663. The final structure, known as the Kastellet (Citadel), consisted of a fort in the shape of a five-pointed star surrounded by high embankments and a deep moat. In the 19th century the fortress was partially demolished and rebuilt once more. During World War II it was taken over by the occupying German forces who used it as their headquarters. It is now used by the Danish military, although the grounds and ramparts are open to visitors.

In the 19th century Kastellet served as a prison. The prisoner's cells were built against the church so that the convicts, unseen by the public, could participate in the mass by peering through small viewing holes cut into the walls.

❸ Sankt Albans Kirke

Churchillparken. **Map** 2 E3. **Tel** 33 11 85 18. 🚌 1A, 15. **Open** summer: 10am–4pm Mon–Fri. 🆆 **st-albans.dk**

This church was built in 1887 to serve the city's Anglican community and is named after Saint Alban, a 4th-century Roman soldier who converted to Christianity and suffered a

Churchillparken, just south of Kastellet

The Story of the Little Mermaid

The heroine of Andersen's tale is a young mermaid who lives beneath the waves with her five sisters. The little mermaid rescues a prince from a sinking ship and falls in love with him. Desperate to be with the prince, she is seduced by a wicked sea witch into giving up her beautiful voice in return for legs so that she can go ashore. The price is high, and the witch warns the mermaid that should the prince marry another she will die. For a long time the prince adores his new, mute lover but in the end he is forced into marrying a princess from another kingdom. Before the wedding is to take place on board a ship, the mermaid's sisters swim to the ship and offer the mermaid a magic knife. All she need do is stab the prince and she will be free to return to the water. The mermaid cannot bring herself to murder the prince and, as dawn breaks, she dies.

Andersen surrounded by fairytale characters

The Little Mermaid, Copenhagen's most famous landmark

martyr's death. Situated not far from the Gefion fountain, along Langelinie promenade in Churchillparken, the elegant Gothic church was a gift from Edward, Prince of Wales, who at the time was vying for the hand of Princess Alexandra, the daughter of Christian IX. They married in 1863, and the prince ascended to the throne as Edward VII in 1901. The church's interior has attractive stained-glass windows and a miniature copy of Bertel Thorvaldsen's sculpture – *St John the Baptist Praying in the Desert*. Religious services are still held here in English and the congregation often includes visitors to the city.

Visitors engaging with installations at the Medical Museion

❹ Gefionspring-vandet

Map 2 F3. 🚌 1A, 15.

Built in 1908, the Gefion fountain is an impressive work by Anders Bundgaard and one of Copenhagen's largest monuments. Its main feature is a statue of the goddess Gefion – a mythical Scandinavian figure. According to legend, the king of Sweden promised to give the goddess as much land as she could plough in one night. Gefion, who took him at his word, turned her four sons into oxen and harnessed them to a plough. By the time the cock crowed she had managed to plough a sizeable chunk of Sweden. She then picked it up and threw it into the sea, and so formed the island of Zealand. The hole left behind became Lake Vänern (whose shape closely resembles that of Zealand).

❺ Medical Museion

Bredgade 62. **Map** 2 E4. **Tel** 35 32 39 00. Ⓢ Østerport. 🚌 1A, 15, 19. **Open** 10am–4pm Tue–Fri, noon–4pm Sat & Sun. ♿ 📷 🌐 **museion.ku.dk**

A combined museum and research unit at the University of Copenhagen, the Medical Museion was founded on a private initiative in 1907. It marked the 50th anniversary of the Danish Medical Association with a public exhibition of historical medical artefacts. The museum remained public until 1918, when it was taken over by the university.

The museum's main exhibition and event site is situated on Bredgade in the former Royal Academy of Surgeons building, which dates from 1787, and the adjacent buildings in Frederiksstaden. This central Copenhagen neighbourhood is a candidate for inclusion in UNESCO's World Heritage List. Medical Museion has one of the biggest and richest historical collections of medical artefacts in Europe. The collections contain up to 250,000 artefacts. There is also a large image

The goddess Gefion and her oxen, from the Gefion Springvandet

collection, a document archive, and a historical book collection. A satellite exhibition is located in the main building of the Faculty of Health and Medical Sciences on Blegdamsvej.

❻ Designmuseum Danmark

Bredgade 68. **Map** 2 E4. **Tel** 33 18 56 56. Ⓢ Østerport. Ⓜ Kongens Nytorv. 🚌 1A, 15. **Open** 11am–5pm Tue–Sun (to 9pm Wed). ♿ 🌐 **designmuseum.dk**

Designed by the Danish architects Nicolai Eigtved and Lauritz de Thurah, and erected in the mid-18th century, the buildings that now house the Design-museum Danmark were originally the city hospital; it was here that the philosopher Søren Kierkegaard died in 1855. The hospital was closed in 1919 and renovated to suit the purposes of a museum.

Today the museum is Denmark's largest museum for Danish and international design, and a central exhibition forum for industrial design and applied arts in Scandinavia. An exhibition entitled "The Danish Chair" aims to tell the story of the inheritance of the chair – one of the strongest representatives of the development of design and a reason why furniture design has made Denmark famous worldwide. The museum shop is an excellent source of industrial design, ceramics, glass and textiles.

Nearby, on the same side of the street, is **Sankt Ansgars Kirke**, a Roman Catholic church that has a small exhibition devoted to the history of Danish Catholicism.

❼ Amalienborg Slot

The Amalienborg Palace complex consists of four buildings around an octagonal square. They were meant as residences for four wealthy families but, when Christiansborg Slot burned down in 1794, Christian VII bought one of the four palaces and turned it into his residence. Designed by Nicolai Eigtved, Christian VII's Palace is renowned for its Great Hall, which has splendid Rococo woodcarvings and stucco decoration. Since 1885, the palace has been used mostly for royal guests and ceremonial purposes.

Balustrade Statues
All the palace statues were renovated in the late 1970s by sculptor Eric Erlandsen with the help of experts from the Statens Museum for Kunst (Danish National Gallery).

Gallery
The palace gallery has a beautiful ceiling and is the work of C L Fossati. The French architect Nicolas-Henri Jardin designed the furniture.

Velvet Chamber
The tiled stove in this room comes from a factory in Lübeck. The silk velvet wall hangings were presents from Ludwig XV to an important high court official named Count Moltke.

★ Entrance Hall
The entrance hall has been renovated to appear as it would have done when the palace was first built. Its decorations have been recreated according to period designs. The statue of Andromeda is a cast of the original marble sculpture.

For hotels and restaurants in this area see pp248–50 and pp262–66

★ **Great Hall**
This elegant room is an example of the artistry of Nicolai Eigtved and is the most beautiful Rococo chamber in Denmark.

VISITORS' CHECKLIST

Practical Information
Amalienborg Slot, Christian VII's Palace, Amalienborg Slotsplads. **Tel** 33 12 21 86. **Open** May–Oct: 10am–4pm daily, Nov–Apr: 11am–4pm Tue–Sun. 🏛
📷 compulsory: 11:30am (Danish); 1pm & 2:30pm (English).
🌐 **amalienborg.dk**

Transport
Ⓜ Kongens Nytorv. Ⓢ Nørreport.
🚌 1A, 19, 26, 29, 650S.

The royal guards, sporting bearskin hats, stand watch, day and night, in front of the palace.

Clock
This grandfather clock is one of many objects on display in the palace.

Royal Residence

Key

⬜ Christian IX's Palace
⬜ Christian VII's Palace
⬜ Christian VIII's Palace
⬜ Frederik VIII's Palace

The name Amalienborg actually refers to an earlier palace, built in 1669 by Frederik III for his young bride Sophie Amalie. The present complex consists of four palaces grouped around a square, collectively known as Amalienborg, which is in the heart of Frederiksstaden. The equestrian statue of Frederick V in the middle of the complex is the work of French sculptor Jacques Saly who spent 30 years working on it. The statue reputedly cost as much as the entire complex.

Changing of the Guard
Every day at noon, the Den Kongelige Livegarde (royal guards) walk from Amalienborg Palace to Rosenborg Castle for the Changing of the Guard.

❽ Marmorkirken

Frederiksgade 4. **Map** 2 D4. **Tel** 33 15 01 44. 🚌 1A, 15, 19, 26. Church: **Open** 10am–5pm Mon–Thu & Sat (to 6:30pm Wed), noon–5pm Fri & Sun. Dome: **Open** 1pm, 3pm Sat & Sun. 📷 📶 **marmorkirken.dk**

The vast dome of the Baroque Frederikskirken, also known as Marmorkirken or the Marble Church, leads many visitors to suspect that its architect, Nikolai Eigtved, based his design on St Peter's Basilica in Rome. The church was named after Frederik V who wanted to celebrate the fact that his family had ruled Denmark for 300 years by building a new district in Copenhagen – Frederiksstaden – with the church as its focal point. When work began, in 1749, it was assumed that the church would be constructed of marble imported from Norway (hence its alternative name). However, it quickly became apparent that the cost of such a venture would exceed the financial resources of the treasury and in 1770 work was abandoned.

A century later the building was completed using local Danish marble. The most obvious feature of the church is its dome – one of the largest in Europe. Visitors can climb the 260 steps to enjoy wonderful city views from the top of the bell tower. Inside the church are frescoes by Danish artists. On the outside, the building has statues of Danish saints.

❾ Davids Samling

Kronprinsessegade 30. **Map** 2 D5. **Tel** 33 73 49 49. Ⓢ Ⓜ Nørreport. 🚌 1A, 15, 19, 26, 42, 43, 350S. **Open** 1–5pm Tue–Sun (to 9pm Wed). 📶 **davidmus.dk**

The museum's founder, Christian Ludvig David (1878–1960), was a lawyer who in 1945 established the C L David Foundation and Collection, which still owns and administers the museum and holdings. David's great-grandfather owned the building in Kronprinsessegade 30 from 1811 until his death in 1830. David acquired the building in 1917 – a century after his family had lived there – and made it his home until his death in 1960. To expand the museum, the foundation bought the neighboring building, at Kronprinsessegade 32, in 1986.

17th-century bronze vessel from India, Davids Samling

The museum is best known for its extensive collection of Islamic art, which includes items from Spain, Persia, India and elsewhere. Among the many treasures, some of which date as far back as the 6th century, are ceramics, silks, jewellery and ancient daggers inlaid with jewels. The museum also houses a small collection of European art, as well as examples of 18th-century English, French and German furniture. There is also a collection of Danish silver dating from the 17th and 18th centuries. Visitors can borrow an info-tablet free of charge from the reception to learn more about the exhibits.

❿ Kongens Have

Map 1 C5. **Open** 7am–dusk daily.

The King's Garden was established by Christian IV in 1606 and is Copenhagen's oldest park, retaining most of its original layout. In the 17th century the gardens supplied the royal court with fresh fruit, vegetables and roses to adorn the royal apartments.

Today, the shady gardens, criss-crossed by paths and with numerous benches, are one of the favourite places for Copenhagen's citizens to walk and relax. Here, visitors can also find one of the capital's most famous monuments. Unveiled in 1877, it is a statue of Hans Christian Andersen enchanting a group of children with some of his fairy tales.

Leafy Kongens Have surrounding Rosenborg Slot

⓫ Livgardens Historiske Samling

Gothersgade 100. **Map** 1 B5. **Tel** 45 99 40 00. Ⓢ Ⓜ Nørreport. 🚌 5A, 6A, 14, 42, 43, 150S, 173E, 184, 185, 350S. **Open** 11:30am–3pm Sat & Sun. 📶 **forsvaret.dk/lg**

The Kongelige Livgarde or royal guards, dressed in colourful uniforms and sporting furry busbies, are one of the symbols of Copenhagen. Many people come to watch them during the daily ceremony for the changing of the guard in front of Amalienborg Slot, but even their daily marches between Rosenborg and Amalienborg palaces are a popular sight. The museum is housed in a cluster of over 200-year-old barracks and contains background

Circular grand nave of Marmorkirken, decorated with wall paintings

Vast palm house, built in 1874, in Copenhagen's Botanisk Have

information on the guards' history. Examples of their uniforms are on display along with weapons, paintings, historical documents, and musical instruments played by the guardsmen.

⓬ Rosenborg Slot

See pp64–5.

⓭ Botanisk Have

Gothersgade 128. **Map** 1 B4. **Tel** 35 32 22 22. 🚌 5A, 6A, 14, 40, 42, 43, 150S, 173E, 184, 185, 350S. Ⓢ Ⓜ Nørreport. **Open** May–Sep: 8:30am–6pm daily; Oct–Apr: 8:30am–4pm daily. 💻 🕸 **botanik.snm.ku.dk**

The 20,000 species of plants gathered in the Botanical Gardens include native Danish plants, as well as some highly exotic ones collected from around the world. The garden was established in 1872, on the grounds of old town fortifications. Bulwarks have been turned into rockeries, and the moat that once surrounded the fortified walls is now a lake filled with water and marsh plants.

The gardens themselves have much to offer. There is a small forest, waterfalls and greenhouses, one of which contains more than 1,000 varieties of cactus. Elsewhere, it is possible to see coffee and pineapples growing. A special attraction is the roof-top walk in the steamy palmhouse. The open-air

café in front of the palmhouse offers magnificent views of the garden.

⓮ Geologisk Museum

Øster Voldgade 5–7. **Map** 1 C4. **Tel** 35 32 22 22. Ⓢ Ⓜ Nørreport. 🚌 6A, 26, 42, 43, 184, 185. **Open** 10am–4pm Tue–Sun. 🕸 **geologi.snm.ku.dk**

Standing close to the eastern end of Botanisk Have, the Geological Museum opened in 1893 and occupies an Italian Renaissance-style building. Its carved stone decorations include rosettes, columns and arches.

The earliest museum exhibits are the meteorites on display in the courtyard. The biggest of these was found in Greenland in 1963 and, at 20 tonnes (17.86 tons), is the sixth largest in the world. On the ground and first floors are glass cabinets filled with minerals and fossils including the imprint of a jellyfish made over 150 million years ago. Elsewhere, there is an exhibition devoted to volcanoes, displays relating to the history of man and collections of dinosaur bones.

A separate section is devoted to oil and gas exploration and the geology of Denmark. Colourful stones and rock crystals are on sale in the museum shop.

⓯ Hirschsprungske Samling

Stockholmsgade 20. **Map** 1 C3. **Tel** 35 42 03 36. Ⓢ Østerport. 🚌 6A, 14, 26, 40, 42, 43, 150S, 184, 185. **Open** 11am–4pm Tue–Sun. 🕸 **hirschsprung.dk**

This gallery, one of Copenhagen's best, owes its existence to the art patronage of Heinrich Hirschsprung (1836–1908), a Danish tobacco baron who supported many Danish artists. The Hirschsprung collection has been on public display since 1911 and is housed in a Neo-Classical building on the outskirts of Østre Anlæg park.

The collection includes works by prominent Danish artists from the 19th and 20th centuries such as Eckersberg, Købke, Bendz, Marstrand, Anna and Michael Ancher, P.S. Krøyer and Vilhelm Hammershøi. A free tour at 2pm on Sundays highlights the works of a different artist each week and lasts around 45 minutes.

One of the exhibition rooms inside the Hirschsprungske Samling

⑫ Rosenborg Slot

This royal palace is one of Copenhagen's most visited attractions and contains thousands of royal objects including paintings, trinkets, furniture and a small armoury. Most impressive of all is the underground treasury containing the crown jewels and other royal regalia. The exquisite Dutch-Renaissance brick palace was erected in 1606, on the orders of Christian IV, to serve as a summer residence. It was used by successive monarchs until the early 18th century when Frederik IV built a more spacious palace at Fredensborg. In the early 19th century Rosenborg was opened to the public as a museum.

★ **Long Hall**
17th-century tapestries decorate the walls of the hall, which also contains a collection of 18th-century silver furniture including three silver lions that once guarded the king's throne.

KEY

① **The spire-topped tower** was converted from a bay

② **The Main Tower** was originally shorter and was raised in the 1620s.

③ **The third floor** was completed in 1624 and was designed to provide space for the magnificent, long banqueting hall.

④ **The Tower Stairway** showcases equestrian paintings, portraits, and a series of 17th-century floral watercolours by Maria Merian.

★ **Treasury**
The underground treasury rooms house the royal jewels, including the Crown of Christian IV which weighs 2.89 kg (6.4 lbs).

Christian IV's Winter Room
The most important of King Christian IV's private chambers has a fine collection of Dutch paintings and a speaking tube connected to the wine cellar below.

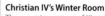

Glass Cabinet

This second-floor room, designed in 1714 and commissioned by King Frederik IV, contains his elaborately displayed collection of Venetian glass. It is the only known cabinet of its kind.

VISITORS' CHECKLIST

Practical Information

Øster Voldgade 4A. **Map** 1 C4. **Tel** 33 15 32 86. **Open** May, Sep & Oct: 10am–4pm daily; Jun–Aug: 9am–5pm daily; Nov–Apr: 10am–2pm Tue–Sun. **Closed** 1 Jan, 22–26 & 31 Dec. **W** kongernessamling.dk/en/rosenborg

Transport

Nørreport. 5A, 6A, 26, 150S, 173E, 184, 185.

Marble Hall

The hall's Baroque décor was commissioned by Frederik III. The Italian decorator Francesco Bruno gave the ceilings new stuccowork and clad the walls with imitation marble.

Chinese Drawing Room

This room was used by Sophie Hedevig, sister of Frederik IV. Some of its most distinctive items are the Chinese-style chairs, a guitar encrusted with ivory and tortoiseshell and bearing the princess's monogram, a 17th-century Japanese porcelain jug and an ebony table.

Royal Chamber of Frederik IV

The table standing at the centre of the room was given to Frederik IV in 1709 by the Grand Duke of Tuscany. The magnificent rock crystal chandelier was probably made in Vienna.

⓰ Statens Museum for Kunst

The Danish National Gallery houses a fascinating collection of European art. Among the Danish painters represented here are artists from the "Golden Age", such as Christoffer Wilhelm Eckersberg and Constantin Hansen, and members of the Skagen School, including Peder Severin Krøyer, and Anna and Michael Ancher. There are also works by Old Masters like Bruegel, Rubens and Rembrandt, as well as masterpieces by 20th-century giants such as Picasso, and contemporary installation art. Weekend workshops inspire children to make their own art.

1st floor

The Last Supper (1909)
Emil Nolde, a well-known representative of German Expressionism, has often pursued religious themes in his art.

A Mountain Climber (1912)
This Expressionist painting explores the relationship between humans and nature. It is one of a number of works by the Danish artist J.F. Willumsen.

Ground floor

★ **Portrait of Madame Matisse** (1905)
This portrait by Henri Matisse combines some of the most typical elements of Fauvism including simple lines and sharply contrasting colours.

Main entrance

Bookshop

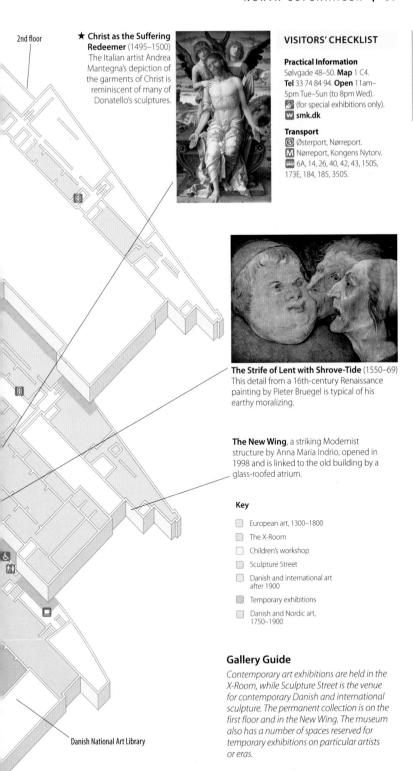

2nd floor

★ **Christ as the Suffering Redeemer** (1495–1500)
The Italian artist Andrea Mantegna's depiction of the garments of Christ is reminiscent of many of Donatello's sculptures.

VISITORS' CHECKLIST

Practical Information
Sølvgade 48–50. **Map** 1 C4.
Tel 33 74 84 94. **Open** 11am–5pm Tue–Sun (to 8pm Wed).
🎨 (for special exhibitions only).
ⓦ smk.dk

Transport
Ⓢ Østerport, Nørreport.
Ⓜ Nørreport, Kongens Nytorv.
🚍 6A, 14, 26, 40, 42, 43, 150S, 173E, 184, 185, 350S.

The Strife of Lent with Shrove-Tide (1550–69)
This detail from a 16th-century Renaissance painting by Pieter Bruegel is typical of his earthy moralizing.

The New Wing, a striking Modernist structure by Anna Maria Indrio, opened in 1998 and is linked to the old building by a glass-roofed atrium.

Key

- European art, 1300–1800
- The X-Room
- Children's workshop
- Sculpture Street
- Danish and international art after 1900
- Temporary exhibitions
- Danish and Nordic art, 1750–1900

Gallery Guide

Contemporary art exhibitions are held in the X-Room, while Sculpture Street is the venue for contemporary Danish and international sculpture. The permanent collection is on the first floor and in the New Wing. The museum also has a number of spaces reserved for temporary exhibitions on particular artists or eras.

Danish National Art Library

CENTRAL COPENHAGEN

The Strøget, a chain of five pedestrianized streets, links the city's two main squares, Kongens Nytorv and Rådhuspladsen. Shops and restaurants line the promenade, which bustles with activity well into the night. Lined with café terraces and restored 18th-century houses, Nyhavn is a quayside street that is particularly lively in the summer months. Central Copenhagen's many museums include the Ny Carlsberg Glyptotek, housing one of the world's best collections of painting and sculpture, and the Guinness World Records Museum. On a fine day Tivoli amusement park and gardens make for an entertaining morning or afternoon. The Latin Quarter, located around the old university, has some pleasant traffic-free streets, such as Fiolstræde, which is lined with second-hand bookshops. A climb up the spiral walkway of the 17th-century Rundetårn (Round Tower) is rewarded by magnificent views over the city.

Sights at a Glance

Churches
⑨ Helligåndskirken
⑮ Sankt Petri Kirke
⑯ Vor Frue Kirke

Museums and Galleries
⑤ Guinness World Records Museum
⑥ Post & Tele Museum
⑦ Nikolaj Kunsthal
⑫ Kunstforeningen GL STRAND
⑱ Ripley's Believe It Or Not!
㉒ Ny Carlsberg Glyptotek pp82–3

Streets and Squares
① Nyhavn
③ Kongens Nytorv
⑧ Højbro Plads
⑬ Gråbrødretorv
⑰ Nytorv
⑳ Rådhuspladsen

Historic Buildings
② Charlottenborg Slot and Kunsthal Charlottenborg
⑪ Rundetårn
⑭ Universitet
⑲ Rådhus pp78–9

Gardens
㉑ Tivoli pp80–81

Theatres
④ Det Kongelige Teater
⑩ Skuespilhuset

See also Street Finder Maps 3 & 4

Street-by-Street: Around Kongens Nytorv

During the late 17th century, Kongens Nytorv (King's New Square) was laid out to link the medieval parts of the city with its newer districts. Today, it is Copenhagen's biggest square and makes an excellent starting point for exploring the city. To the southeast it joins the picturesque Nyhavn district where the historic ship *Anna Møller*, part of the Nationalmuseet's collection, can be admired from a canalside café. It also marks the beginning of Strøget, which has plenty of restaurants and bars as well as specialist shops and boutiques to tempt visitors.

Hotel d'Angleterre is one of the oldest and most exclusive hotels in Scandinavia (see p72) and has entertained many celebrities on their visits to Denmark.

❺ Guinness World Records Museum
The museum collection includes numerous curios, including a figure of the world's tallest man (2.72m/ 8 ft 11 inches).

Key

▬▬ Suggested route

0 metres 50
0 yards 50

❼ Nikolaj Kunsthal
This 13th-century former church has had a number of other purposes since the early 1800s. It was used for "happenings" in the 1960s and now houses the Copenhagen Contemporary Art Center.

Magasin du Nord is more than 100 years old and is one of the biggest and most exclusive department stores in Scandinavia.

❸ ★ Kongens Nytorv
Built in 1680 by Christian V, whose huge equestrian statue is at its centre, Kongens Nytorv is one of Copenhagen's most elegant squares and contains some of the city's finest buildings. Construction of the metro will affect access to this area until 2019.

Locator Map
See Street Finder Map 4

❷ Charlottenborg Slot & Kunsthal Charlottenborg
This is the oldest building in Kongens Nytorv, and is used by Det Kongelige Kunstakademi (The Royal Academy of Fine Arts) and has exhibition space for contemporary art.

KONGENS NYTORV

An anchor from a 19th-century sailing vessel has been transformed into a monument to the victims of World War II.

❶ ★ Nyhavn
The northern side of the canal is lined with colourful houses, many of which were once brothels frequented by sailors after months at sea.

NYHAVN

HEIBERGSGADE

HERLUF TROLLES GADE

TORDENSKJOLDSGADE

Pleasure boat rides
along the 17th-century canal are one of the main visitor attractions. It has became a tradition that each year old sailing ships arriving in Copenhagen moor alongside Nyhavn.

❹ ★ Det Kongelige Teater
This 19th-century building houses a prominent theatre, staging both drama and ballet.

Nyhavn, lined with brightly-coloured buildings

❶ Nyhavn

Map 4 E1.

Lined on both sides with colourful houses, this 300-m (328-yard) long canal, known as the New Harbour, was dug by soldiers between 1671 and 1673. It was intended to enable ships loaded with merchandise to sail into the centre of Copenhagen but today is an icon of the city, with stylish yachts and old wooden boats moored along many of the quays.

When Hans Christian Andersen lived here, the area north of the canal was a notorious red-light district with a seedy reputation thanks to the cheap bars, rough-and-ready hotels, tattoo parlours and numerous brothels. Since then Nyhavn has smartened up a great deal (though a few tattoo parlours still remain) and

is one of the city's best-known districts. The boozy joints packed with sailors are long gone and have been replaced with bars, cafés and restaurants targeting a more prosperous clientele. The place is especially popular on warm summer evenings, and many of the restaurants and bars can get extremely busy – particularly on the north side of the harbour. The long awaited Inderhavnsbro (inner harbour bridge) opened here in 2016 connecting pedestrians and cyclists to the neighbourhoods of Christians-havn, Holmen and Papirøen, with the new Copenhagen Street Food Market.

❷ Charlottenborg Slot & Kunsthal Charlottenborg

Kongens Nytorv 1. **Map** 4 D1. **Tel** 33 36 90 50. Ⓜ Kongens Nytorv. 🚌 1A, 15, 19, 26, 350S. **Open** 11am–5pm Tue–Sun (to 8pm Wed). ♿
Ⓦ **kunsthalcharlottenborg.dk**

This Baroque palace was built between 1672 and 1683 for Queen Charlotte Amalie (wife of Christian V), and was named after her. In the mid-18th century King Frederik V handed over the palace to the newly created Royal Academy of Fine Arts, and it is now filled with faculty and students. An adjacent exhibition building holds both Kunsthal Charlottenborg and the Danish Art Library.

One of Charlottenborg's portals

❸ Kongens Nytorv

Map 4 D1.

King's New Square was created more than 300 years ago. This is one of Copenhagen's central points and the site of Det Kongelige Teater (The Royal Theatre) and Charlottenborg Slot. As well as marking the end of Nyhavn, it is also a good starting point for exploring Strøget, Copenhagen's famous walkway, which is lined with shops and restaurants.

At the centre of this oval square is an equestrian statue of Christian V, on whose orders the square was built. The original sculpture was made in 1688 by a French artist. Unfortunately, with time, the heavy lead monument, which depicts Christian V as a sombre Roman general, began to sink, distorting the proportions of the figure. In 1946 the monument was recast in bronze.

Each June graduates gather in the square to dance around the statue as part of a traditional matriculation ceremony.

Kongens Nytorv was once filled with elm trees, planted in the 19th century. Sadly, these fell prey to disease in 1998 and the square has since been

Hotel d'Angleterre's Romantic Origins

In the mid-18th century Jean Marchal, a young hairdresser and make-up artist travelling with a troupe of actors, arrived in Copenhagen. Jean decided to settle in town and took the job of valet to Count Conrad Danneskiold-Laurvig. At a reception, to which he accompanied the count, he met Maria Coppy, daughter of the court chef. They married in 1755 and, exploiting the culinary talents of Maria, opened a restaurant with a handful of bedrooms for passing travellers. Unfortunately neither lived long enough to fully enjoy the fruits of their enterprise. Their small hotel has survived and thrived, having undergone a great many changes including the addition of around 100 or so rooms. It receives some of the world's most distinguished figures.

Hotel d'Angleterre

Equestrian statue of Christian V in Kongens Nytorv

replanted. Construction of the city circle metro (*Cityringen*) will affect access to the square until 2019, especially near Strøget, the Danish Royal Theatre and Nyhavn.

❹ Det Kongelige Teater

August Bournonvilles Passage, Kongens Nytorv. **Map** 4 D1. **Tel** 33 69 69 33. **w** kglteater.dk

Anyone visiting the area around Kongens Nytorv is usually struck by the sight of the Royal Theatre, a vast Neo-Renaissance building that has been the main arts venue in Denmark since it was founded in 1748. The present building, which occupies the original site, dates from 1894. For many years, this theatre set itself apart by putting on ballet, opera and theatre in the same space. The complex includes two theatres – Gamle Scene (Old Stage) and Nye Scene (New Stage), the latter popularly known as Stærekassen and built in 1931. Since the opening of Operaen, the striking opera house across the harbour from Amalienborg Slot, in 2005 (*see p93*), the Old Stage primarily hosts ballet, while drama is largely staged at the Skuespilhuset (*see p75*).

The statues at the front of the theatre celebrate two distinguished Danes who made contributions to the development of theatre and the arts. One is the playwright Ludvig Holberg, often hailed as the father of Danish theatre, the other is the poet Adam Oehlenschlager.

❺ Guinness World Records Museum

Østergade 16. **Map** 4 D1. **Tel** 33 32 31 31. Ⓜ Kongens Nytorv. 🚌 1A, 15, 19, 26, 350A. **Open** Jan–mid-Jun, Sep–Dec: 10am–6pm daily (to 8pm Fri & Sat); mid-Jun–Aug: 10am–10pm daily. **Closed** 1 Jan, 24–25 Dec, 31 Dec. 🅿 **w** ripleys.com/copenhagen

Visitors to the Guinness World Records Museum are welcomed at the entrance by a replica of the world's tallest man. Inside is a collection of the biggest, smallest, fastest, heaviest, longest and shortest, as well as a number of rooms in which visitors can try to beat a world record or experience how it feels to drive a car at 500 km/h (311 mph). A film showing how people from all over the world have trained for their record-breaking attempts can also be seen. In the sports gallery, visitors can test themselves as a professional racing cyclist.

❻ Post & Tele Museum

Købmagergade 37. **Map** 3 C1. **Tel** 33 41 09 00. Ⓢ Nørreport. Ⓜ Kongens Nytorv. 🚌 1A, 15, 19, 26, 350S. **Open** 10am–4pm daily. **Closed** 1 Jan, 24, 25 & 31 Dec. 🅰 🖥 🖼 **w** ptt-museum.dk

This museum dedicated to postal and telecommunication services grew from a core collection gathered by Jens Wilken Mørch, who started his career in the Danish Post in 1856 and eventually became head postmaster. The museum opened to the public in 1913; the exhibits relating to telecommunications were incorporated in 1931, when the museum absorbed the collection of an engineer named Hans Haller.

The permanent collection consists of three sections that give an overview of the many developments in the world of postal and telecommunication services. The highlight of The King's Post Office (1624–1848) is a full-size replica of a spherical mail coach; there are also uniforms and portraits of eminent figures within the mail service. The Age of Invention (1849–1920) focuses on maritime postal history and the early years of telegraphy and telephony. The final section looks at postal and telecommunication services after the 1920s, all the way through to the Internet age. There are also temporary exhibitions and a children's playground located inside a giant 3D stamp.

Entrance to the Guinness World Records Museum

Nikolaj, Copenhagen Contemporary Centre in the former Sankt Nikolaj Kirke

❼ Nikolaj Kunsthal

Nikolaj Plads 10. **Map** 3 C1. **Tel** 33 18 17 80. Ⓢ Nørreport. Ⓜ Kongens Nytorv. 🚌 1A, 2A, 15, 19, 26, 350S. **Open** noon–6pm Tue–Thu, 11am–4pm Fri–Sun. 🎫 (free on Wed). 🌐 nikolajkunsthal.dk

This unique exhibition space, housed in the rebuilt Sankt Nikolaj Kirke, focuses on Danish and international contemporary art.

Nikolaj presents art that has not been shown before and that inspires public debate. Nikolaj Kunsthal focuses on experimental and innovative art, while also allowing a dialogue between Danish and international art, historical perspectives and the most recent trends.

Nikolaj Kunsthal presents five or six exhibitions annually. Among these, one is aimed specifically at children and young people. Another, the

Fokus Video Art Festival, takes place in February and premieres works by both Danish and international artists alongside artist talks and events.

The historical cultural heritage of the building is used in the institution's graphic identity and the exhibitions, with the large arched spaces often being included in the works on show.

❽ Højbro Plads

Map 3 C1.

This cobbled square is one of the most enchanting places in Copenhagen. Although at first glance it looks like a single large unit, it is in fact divided into Højbro Plads and Amagertorv.

Højbro Plads contains a vast monument to Bishop Absalon, who from his horse points out towards Christiansborg Slot on the other side of the canal. If you look in the opposite direction away from the canal and down the wide promenade, you will see Amagertorv. The former city market has a striking fountain called Storkespringvandet, which was added in the 19th century. Despite the misleading name, the birds here are actually herons.

The northern section of Amagertorv has an interesting twin-gabled house, built in

1616, in the style of the Dutch Renaissance. It is one of the city's oldest buildings and houses the Royal Copenhagen Porcelain Shop. Adjacent to it is the showroom of Georg Jensen, which specializes in upmarket silverware. A small museum is devoted to the work of Jensen and contains some of his early pieces.

Portal of Helligåndskirken – one of Copenhagen's oldest churches

❾ Helligåndskirken

Niels Hemmingsensgade 5. **Map** 3 C1. **Tel** 33 15 41 44. **Open** noon–4pm Mon–Fri; also 7–11:30pm Fri. 🌐 helligaandskirken.dk

Dating originally from the early 15th century when it was an Augustinian monastery, the "Church of the Holy Spirit was built on an even earlier religious site, founded in 1238. The church, which is one of the oldest in Copenhagen, acquired its towers in the late 16th century and its sandstone portal, originally intended for the Børsen (Stock Exchange), early in the 17th century. The building was ravaged by one of the city's great fires in 1728, and has been largely rebuilt, although some original 14th-century walls in the right-hand wing can still be seen. Now surrounded by a park, the church still holds religious services. It is also used for art shows and exhibitions, which provide an occasion to admire its magnificent vaults.

In the churchyard is a memorial to Danish victims of the Nazi concentration camps.

Strøget

The word "Strøget" ("pedestrian street") cannot be found on any of the plates bearing street names; nevertheless, all those who know the city are familiar with it. Copenhagen's main walkway runs east to west. It is made up of five interconnected streets: Østergade, Amagertorv, Vimmelskaftet, Nygade and Frederiks-berggade. Pedestrianized in 1962, it has since become one of the town's favourite strolling grounds. Shops range from exclusive boutiques to souvenir and toy shops, along with numerous cafés and restaurants. There are also some pretty churches and squares and a handful of museums. Every day (when the Queen is in residence), at about 11:45am, the Kongelige Livgarde march along Østergade, heading for Amalienborg Slot for the changing of the guards.

Tourist train running along Strøget

⑩ Skuespilhuset

Sankt Annæ Plads 36. **Map** 4 E1.
Tel 33 69 69 33. ♿ ✏ 🖥
🌐 **kglteater.dk**

Throughout the 1900s, a number of venues across the city were used to house the Royal Danish Theatre's Drama Department – with varying degrees of success. Although the need for a suitable playhouse was recognized as early as the 1880s, it was not until 2001 that the government unveiled plans to build a dedicated theatre.

Skuespilhuset, the Royal Danish Playhouse, was inaugurated in 2008. The strikingly modern building offers a range of performance spaces, including the main auditorium (Main Stage) seating 650, two small stages (Portscenen) seating 200 and the Studio Stage, which has seats for 100 people. There are also several open-air spaces, such as the waterfront foyer and the footbridge terrace, which are used for children's activities and other events. In addition to its seasonal repertoire of plays, the theatre hosts ballets, public lectures, concerts and Q&As with playwrights, directors and actors. Note that all drama performed here is in Danish.

Designed by Danish architects Boje Lundgaard and Lene Tranberg, the theatre incorporates a variety of materials: the dark cladding on the external walls was created with ceramic tiles; the outside of the stage tower is covered with copper; and the footbridge linking the foyer to the harbourfront promenade is made from oak.

Rundetårn's cobbled spiral ramp winding to the top of the tower

⑪ Rundetårn

Købmagergade 52A. **Map** 3 C1.
Tel 33 73 03 73. **Open** May–Sep: 10am–8pm daily; Oct–Apr: 10am–6pm daily (until 9pm Tue & Wed). 📷
🌐 **rundetaarn.dk**

The round tower, 35 m (115 ft) tall and 15 m (49 ft) in diameter, provides an excellent vantage point from which to view Copenhagen. Access to the top is via a cobbled spiral ramp, 209 m (686 ft) long, which winds seven and a half times round to the top. The Rundetårn was damaged by the Great Fire of 1728, and again by a fire in 1795, resulting in part of the observatory being rebuilt in the 18th century.

Rundetårn was erected on the orders of Christian IV, and is still used by the university for which it was originally intended, making it the oldest working observatory of its kind in Europe.

In 1642, during the tower's opening ceremony, Christian IV is said to have ridden his horse up the spiralling pathway to the top. In 1716, the Tsar of Russia, Peter the Great, allegedly repeated this stunt during a visit to Copenhagen and was followed by his wife Tsarina Catherine I who, as legend has it, climbed to the top in a coach drawn by six horses.

The modern-day equivalent of such antics is an annual bicycle race: the winner is the person who cycles to the top and back again in the fastest time, without dismounting or falling off.

⑫ Kunstforeningen GL STRAND

Gammel Strand 48. **Map** 3 C1. **Tel** 33 36 02 60. Ⓜ Kongens Nytorv. 🚌 1A, 2A, 6A, 15, 26, 29. **Open** 11am–5pm Tue–Sun (to 8pm Wed). 🎨 ♿ ✏
🖥 📷 🌐 **glstrand.dk**

GL STRAND was founded in 1825 by the artist and professor C.W. Eckersberg as a way to bridge the gap between the elitist art establishment and the viewing public, thereby making art more accessible. Its mission today is to focus on and support young, emerging artists. The gallery has occupied its current premises, a building on Gammel Strand designed by the 18th-century architect Philip de Lange, since 1952. GL STRAND doesn't have a permanent collection, relying instead on temporary shows spotlighting individual artists. During the course of its history, GL STRAND has hosted many fascinating exhibitions by the likes of Edvard Munch (1908), Asger Jorn (1953), the American film director and visual artist David Lynch (2010) and Louise Bourgeois (2011).

Skuespilhuset, on the Copenhagen waterfront

Outdoor restaurant tables in Gråbrødretorv

⑬ Gråbrødretorv

Map 3 C1. 🚌 6A.

This charming, cobblestone square is filled with music from buskers in summer when the restaurant tables spill out into the street. It is an excellent place to stop for a lunch. The square dates back to 1238, and its name refers to the so-called Grey Brothers, Franciscan monks who built the city's first monastery here. A great fire in 1728 destroyed the surrounding buildings; the present buildings date mainly from the early 18th century.

⑭ Universitet

Vor Frue Plads. **Map** 3 B1. Ⓢ
Ⓜ Nørreport. 🚌 5A, 6A, 14, 42, 43, 150S, 173E, 184, 185, 350S.
🌐 ku.dk/english

The cobbled Vor Frue Plads and its surrounding university buildings are the heart of the so-called Latin Quarter (Latin was once spoken here). Despite the fact that the university was founded by Christian I in 1479, the buildings that now stand in Vor Frue Plads date from the 19th century. They house only a handful of faculties including law; the remaining departments and staff have moved to the main campus, on the island of Amager, east of Copenhagen.

The vast, Neo-Classical university building stands opposite Vor Frue Kirke. It has an impressive entrance hall

decorated with frescoes depicting scenes from Greek mythology, which are the work of Constantin Hansen. Adjacent to the university building is the 19th-century university library. On the library's main staircase is a glass cabinet containing fragments from a cannon ball that was fired during the British bombardment in 1807. The ball struck the library and ironically hit a book entitled *The Defender of Peace*. A number of second-hand bookshops are located along Fiolstræde, which runs up to the Universitet.

⑮ Sankt Petri Kirke

Larslejstræde 11. **Map** 3 B1. **Tel** 33 13 38 33. Ⓢ Ⓜ Nørreport. 🚌 5A, 6A, 14, 42, 43, 173E, 150S, 350S. **Open** Apr–Sep: 11am–3pm daily. 🔲 🔲 burial chapel only. 🌐 sankt-petri.dk

Saint Peter's church has been the main church for Copenhagen's German community since 1586. It dates from 1450 but suffered serious damage in the course of a series of fires and the British bombardment of 1807. However, many of the bricks used in the building work are from the original structure. Particularly noteworthy is the "burial" chapel containing numerous tombs and epitaphs, mainly from the 19th century. There are also some interesting tablets

Statue of Christ from the high altar in Vor Frue Kirke

commemorating the dead which can be seen on the church's outside wall.

⑯ Vor Frue Kirke

Nørregade 8. **Map** 3 B1. **Tel** 33 37 65 40. Ⓢ Ⓜ Nørreport. 🚌 5A, 6A, 14, 42, 43, 150S, 173E, 184, 185, 350S. **Open** 8:30am–5pm Mon–Sat, noon–4pm Sun.
🌐 koebenhavnsdomkirke.dk

Copenhagen's cathedral, Vor Frue Kirke (Church of Our Lady), has a somewhat sombre look and is the third consecutive church to be built on this site. The first, a small 12th-century Gothic church, was consumed by fire in 1728, while the next one was destroyed by British bombs in 1807 (the tower presented an excellent target for the artillery). The present structure dates from 1820 and was designed by Christian Frederik Hansen. Its interior is a veritable art gallery, full of sculptures by the prominent Danish sculptor Bertel Thorvaldsen *(see p89)*. Standing on both sides are marble statues of the 12 apostles; the central section of the altar has a kneeling angel and a vast figure of Christ – one of the artist's most famous masterpieces. Thorvaldsen is also the creator of the relief depicting St John the Baptist, seen at the entrance to the cathedral. During Sunday

The imposing Neo-Classical façade of the Universitet

Interior of Vor Frue Kirke, with statues by Bertel Thordvaldsen

mass it is sometimes possible to see Queen Margrethe II among the congregation. In the past she used to occupy a special royal box. But attitudes have changed and today, not wishing to distance herself from her subjects, the Danish monarch is to be found sitting in the pews.

⓱ Nytorv

Map 3 B1.

Although Nytorv looks like one big square, it is in fact made up of two separate areas – Gammeltorv (Old Square) and Nytorv (New Square) which are separated by the Nygade section of the Strøget walkway. To the northwest of Strøget, Gammeltorv was a busy market place in the 14th century and therefore has the longest trading tradition in Copenhagen. Today, the square is dominated by a small fruit and vegetable market along with stalls selling jewellery and all kinds of handicrafts.

Standing at the centre of the square is Caritasspringvandet (The Charity Fountain), which dates from 1609. This Renaissance treasure is the work of Statius Otto, and depicts a pregnant woman carrying one child in her arms and leading another by the hand – a symbol of charity and mercy. Water flows from the woman's breasts and also from the urinating boy at her feet (the holes were blocked with lead for reasons of decency in the 19th century). The fountain was commissioned by Christian IV to draw the public's attention to his charitable virtues. At one time it supplied the city's inhabitants with water brought along wooden pipes from a lake 5 km (3 miles) north of Copenhagen.

Nytorv was established in 1606 and for a long time was used by the authorities as a place of execution. The squares were joined together and given their present form soon after the city hall was destroyed by fire in 1795. The outline of the city hall can still be seen in Nytorv's pavement.

The striking Neo-Classical Domhuset, or Court House, with its six large columns, on the south side of Nytorv was completed in 1815 to a design by Christian Frederik Hansen, the Danish architect who worked on rebuilding the town after a fire in 1795. The materials used in the rebuilding work included those taken from the ruined Christiansborg Slot, and the resulting building is redolent of an ancient temple. The building was first used as the city hall, becoming the fifth seat of the town's authorities. In the early 20th century the city hall was moved to the Rådhus. The inscription seen on the front of the Domhuset refers to its more recent function as a court house and quotes the opening words of the Jutland Code of 1241: "With law the land shall be built".

⓲ Ripley's Believe It Or Not!

Rådhuspladsen 57. **Map** 3 B2.
Tel 33 32 31 31. 🚌 2A, 5A, 6A, 10, 12, 14, 26, 29, 33, 67, 68, 69, 173E, 250S.
Open Sep–mid-Jun: 10am–6pm Sun–Thu, 10am–8pm Fri–Sat; mid-Jun–Aug: 10am–10pm daily. **Closed** 1 Jan, 24, 25 & 31 Dec. 🚻
🅦 ripleys.com/copenhagen

This museum is part of an American chain that is based on an idea of Robert L. Ripley, a radio presenter, comic book writer and adventurer, who dreamt up a freakshow in the early 20th century to stun and amaze his American audience.

The museum may well prove popular with children. Many strange exhibits are on display, some of which were collected by Ripley himself. Here, visitors can marvel at a man who eats bicycles or a doll covered in 7,000 buttons, wince at a collection of medieval torture instruments and shrunken voodoo heads, and be astounded at various freaks of nature including a fish covered in fur and a two-headed cow.

Nytorv, a colourful and bustling square

⑲ Rådhus

The red-brick Rådhus (City Hall), which opened in 1905, was designed by the Danish architect Martin Nyrop (1849–1921), who was inspired by Italian buildings but also employed some elements of Danish medieval architecture. Its large main hall, sometimes used for exhibitions and official events, is decorated with statues of Nyrop as well as three other prominent Danes – Bertel Thorvaldsen, H C Andersen and Niels Bohr. Though it is an official building, the Rådhus is open to visitors. Be sure to climb the 298 stairs to the top of the 105-m (344-ft) tower to reach the city's highest viewpoint.

Ceilings
The Rådhus rooms and chambers are full of details and architectural flourishes such as intricate brickwork, mosaics and decorated ceilings.

Copenhagen's Emblem
This has changed little since the 13th century. It consists of three castle towers, symbolically drawn waves of the Øresund and images of the sun and moon.

National flag of Denmark

★ Main Hall
This vast, rectangular hall on the first floor is flanked by cloisters and topped with a glazed roof. It has Italianate wall decorations and a number of sculptures.

Absalon's Statue
Standing above the main entrance is a gilded statue of Bishop Absalon, the 12th-century founder of Copenhagen.

Main entrance

★ World Clock
Jens Olsen spent 27 years building this clock. Its extraordinary mechanism was set in motion in 1955. One of its many functions is to provide a calendar for the next 570,000 years.

Clock Tower
The peals from the tower's bells are heard throughout the streets of Copenhagen and are also transmitted by radio across the whole of Denmark.

VISITORS' CHECKLIST

Practical Information
Rådhuspladsen 1. **Map** 3 B2.
Tel 33 66 33 66. **Open** 9am–4pm Mon–Fri, 9:30am–1pm Sat. 📷 (in English) 3pm Mon–Fri, 10am Sat. 🏛 Tower: **Open** 11am & 2pm Mon–Fri, noon Sat. 🏛 World Clock: **Open** 8:30am–4:30pm Mon–Fri, 10am–1pm Sat. 📷 🌐 **kk.dk**

Transport
Ⓢ Central Station.
🚌 6A, 11, 26, 29, 33.

Staircase
The stately rooms on the top floors are reached by graceful stairs with marble balustrades.

⑳ Rådhuspladsen

Map 3 A2 & B2.
Ⓢ Central Station. 🚌 6A, 11, 26, 29, 33.

This open space is the second biggest square in the Danish capital (after Kongens Nytorv). City Hall Square was established in the second half of the 19th century, following the dismantling of the western gate that stood on this site, and the levelling of the defensive embankments. Soon afterwards it was decided to build the present city hall, providing further impetus to the development of the surrounding area. The square has been pedestrianized since 1994 and is popular with shoppers and sightseers. It is also a gathering point for revellers on New Year's Eve.

A number of monuments in Rådhuspladsen are worthy of note. Standing immediately by the entrance to the city hall is the Dragon's Leap Fountain, erected in 1923. A little to one side, by Rådhus's tower, is a tall column, unveiled in 1914, featuring two bronze figures of Vikings blowing bronze horns. Close by, in Hans Christian Andersens Boulevard, is a sitting figure of Andersen, facing Tivoli gardens. Another curiosity is an unusual barometer hanging on a building that is covered with advertisements, located at the corner of Vesterbrogade and H C Andersens Boulevard. It includes a figure of a girl, who in fine weather rides a bicycle. When it rains she opens her umbrella. A nearby thermometer gives a reading of the daily temperature.

The Rådhus with its red brick elevations

㉑ Tivoli

When Tivoli first opened in 1843 it had only two attractions: a carousel pulled by horses and a roller coaster. Today Tivoli is an altogether grander affair. Part amusement park, part cultural venue, part wonderland, it is one of the most famous places in Denmark and much loved by the Danes themselves, who regard it as one of their national treasures. Situated in the heart of the city, this large garden is planted with almost one thousand trees and blooms with 400,000 flowers during the summer. At night, when it is lit by myriad coloured bulbs, it is a truly breathtaking sight.

Færgekroen
Located next to the jetty, this brewpub is a replica of a fisherman's house in southern Jutland and is one of 30 restaurants in Tivoli.

Frigate
The frigate *St George III*, which houses a pirate-themed family restaurant called Pirateriet, is moored on Tivoli's picturesque lake – the remains of a former moat.

Pantomime Theatre
Pantomime in Denmark dates back to the early 19th century. The Chinese-style pavilion hosts regular performances and is the oldest building in Tivoli gardens.

Main Entrance
The main gate, in Vesterbrogade, was built in 1890.

★ Pagoda
The pagoda was built in 1900 by the architect Knud Arne Petersen, when he became the director of Tivoli. The tower is an illumination tower– its primary purpose was to light up Tivoli in the evening.

Concert Hall
Tivoli's pastel-coloured concert hall was built in 1956 and updated in 2005. Concerts range from rock to symphonies, and in the basement is Europe's longest seawater aquarium.

Amusements
Rides and other amusements, including vintage cars for smaller children, are scattered throughout the park.

Tivoli Youth Guard

A group of boys and girls dressed in smart uniforms and marching to the beat of drums is a frequent sight when strolling along the park's avenues on weekends. According to promoters of the gardens, "the Queen has her own guards and the Tivoli has its own". Made up of about 100 boys and girls, aged between 8 and 16, the Tivoli Youth Guard is smartly dressed in red jackets and busbies and covers some 300 km (186 miles) a year. The marching band was founded in 1844 and is one of Tivoli's four orchestras, the other three being the Symphony Orchestra, the Tivoli Big Band and the Tivoli Promenade Orchestra.

Youth Guard marching through Tivoli

★ Nimb Building
This palatial Moorish-style building houses two restaurants, a bar and a café, as well as an upmarket boutique hotel.

㉒ Ny Carlsberg Glyptotek

This world-class art museum boasts over 10,000 treasures including Ancient Egyptian art, Greek and Roman sculptures and a huge collection of Etruscan artifacts. It also exhibits a wealth of Danish paintings and sculptures from the era known as the Golden Age *(see pp46–7)* and exquisite works by French Impressionist masters such as Degas and Renoir. It has grown from the fine collection of sculptures *(glyptotek)* donated by Carl Jacobsen, founder of the New Carlsberg Brewery, and the museum consists of three architecturally different buildings, the first one built in 1897 and the latest added in 1996.

★ Ancient Egyptian Art
The outstanding collection of Egyptian art ranges from delicate vases to monumental statues, such as this granite figure of Ramses II from the 2nd millennium BC.

Danish Sculpture
Sculptures representing the great artistic flourishing of Denmark's Golden Age include works such as Jens Adolph Jerichau's *Penelope* (1840s), as well as many pieces by H.W. Bissen.

★ The Kiss
This famous pair of lovers is one of 35 works by Auguste Rodin, which constitutes the largest collection of the artist's works anywhere outside France.

Alabaster Relief
This 9th-century BC relief depicting the Assyrian King Ashurnasirpal II is part of the multifaceted collection representing the Middle East.

Winter garden

VISITORS' CHECKLIST

Practical Information
Dantes Plads 7. **Map** 3 B3. **Tel** 33 41
81 41. **Open** 11am–6pm Tue–Sun
(until 10pm Thu). **Closed** 1 Jan,
5 Jun, 24 & 25 Dec. 🏛 (free Tue and
to under-18s). 🌐 **glyptoteket.com**

Transport
🚌 5A, 12, 33.

Landscape from Saint-Rémy
Along with this picture painted by Vincent
van Gogh during his stay in a psychiatric
hospital in 1889, the museum has numerous
works by many of the Impressionists and
Post-Impressionists, including Gauguin,
Toulouse-Lautrec, Monet and Degas.

2nd floor

The Little Dancer
The statue of a 14-year-old
dancer dates from 1880 and is
one of the most famous
sculptures to be produced by
Edgar Degas.

★ Head of Satyr
This beautiful painted terracotta *Head of Satyr* is
part of the Etruscan collection, which includes
vases, bronze sculptures and stone sarcophagi
dating from the 8th to the 2nd century BC.

1st floor

Gallery Guide
*The horseshoe-shaped Dahlerup Building
(1897) contains mainly Danish and French
sculpture. Ancient artefacts from the
Mediterranean and Egypt are found via
the Winter Garden in the Kampmann
Building (1906). The Larsen Building
(1996), rising within one of the
courtyards of the Kampmann
Building, houses French painting.*

Key
- ▢ Ancient Mediterranean
- ▢ French painting and sculpture
- ▢ Danish painting and sculpture
- ▢ Egyptian, Greek and Roman sculpture
- ▢ Temporary exhibitions
- ▢ Non-exhibition space

Ground floor

Café Glyptoteket in the Winter Garden

The Winter Garden in the centre of the
museum is the setting for Café Glyptoteket,
which serves a wide range of light, delicious
lunch dishes and cakes. It has always provided
a pleasant place in which to stroll during
a visit. Many
visitors are drawn
to the *Water
Mother* sculpture
by Kai Nielsen.
Unveiled in 1920,
it depicts a naked
woman reclining
in a small pool,
surrounded by
a group of babies.
The Winter Garden
is also used as a
concert venue.

SOUTH COPENHAGEN

Criss-crossed by canals and waterways, this part of Copenhagen contains two areas that both complement and contrast. The islet of Slotsholmen is dominated by Christianborg Slot, standing on the site of a fort built by Bishop Absalon in the 12th century, when there was nothing here but a tiny fishing village. The area flourished and, in 1443, København, or "merchant's port", was made the Danish capital. Many historical sights are situated here.

Across the water is Christianshavn where the "free state of Christiania", an alternative community, has been in existence since the 1970s. Both Christianshavn and nearby Holmen are part of an ongoing metamorphosis. The early 2000s saw the construction of Fisketorvet (a fish market turned shopping mall), Opera House and Copenhagen Street Food, a former warehouse full of food stalls, changing the waterfront's scene. Two new pedestrian and cyclist bridges have also opened here.

Waterbus tours provide an enjoyable way of getting to know the area. Alternatively, a bicycle can be useful for exploring the many nooks and crannies of Christianshavn.

Sights at a Glance

Churches
9 Vor Frelsers Kirke

Museums
1 Nationalmuseet pp88–9
2 Thorvaldsens Museum
6 Tøjhusmuseet
10 Orlogsmuseet

Historic Buildings
3 Folketinget
4 Christiansborg Slot pp90–91
5 Børsen
7 Det Kongelige Bibliotek

Places of Interest
8 Christianshavn
11 Christiania
12 Operaen

0 metres 300
0 yards 300

See also Street Finder Maps 3 & 4

◀ Den Sorte Diamant (the Black Diamond), an extension to the Royal Library

For keys to symbols *see back flap*

Street-by-Street: Around Christiansborg Slot

Christiansborg Slot, with its adjoining palace buildings including the palace church, former royal coach house and royal stables, as well as Tøjhusmuseet, Det Kongelige Bibliotek and Børsen, are all situated on the islet of Slotsholmen. The island derives its name from a castle that was built on this site in 1167 by Bishop Absalon. Opposite the palace, on the other side to the canal, is the Nationalmuseet, which has many exhibits relating to the history of Copenhagen and the rest of Denmark.

❷ Thordvaldsens Museum
The collection confirms the genius of the Danish sculptor, whose tomb can be found in the museum courtyard.

❶ ★ Nationalmuseet
This museum was founded in 1807, though its origins date back to 1650 when Frederik I established his own private collection.

0 metre 50
0 yards 50

❻ Tøjhusmuseet
Visitors interested in militaria will enjoy the huge array of arms and armour in this museum.

④ ★ Christiansborg Slot
Although this has not been the home of the royal family for more than 200 years, the palace rooms are still used for grand occasions, such as state banquets attended by Queen Margrethe II.

Locator Map
See Street Finder Maps 3 & 4

Key
— Suggested route

CENTRAL COPENHAGEN

SOUTH COPENHAGEN

BØRSGADE

SLOTSHOLMSGADE

BØRSGADE

CHRISTIANS BRYGGE

③ Folketinget
The Danish parliament building is open to visitors during the summer, when its members are on vacation.

⑤ Børsen
The former Stock Exchange, with its spire sculpted in the form of entwined dragon tails, represents an outstanding example of 17th-century public architecture.

⑦ Det Kongelige Bibliotek
The library's "Black Diamond" extension, utilizing black glass and granite imported from Zimbabwe, is one of the capital's most innovative buildings.

❶ Nationalmuseet

Exhibits in this prestigious museum include many items relating to Denmark's history as well as artifacts from all over the world. It is worth allocating several hours for a visit. Among the vast array on display are Inuit costumes and tools, rune stones, priceless Egyptian jewellery and medieval church interiors. There is a good children's section, where kids will enjoy trying on armour or "camping out" in a Bedouin tent. All exhibits are labelled in English.

Antiquities
Greek pottery, Etruscan jewellery and Egyptian mummies are on display in the Egyptian and Classical section.

★ Inuit Culture
Included in the ethnographic section are rooms devoted to the Inuit containing many costumes, including a suit made of bird feathers, as well as traditional kayaks and harpoons.

3rd floor

Ethnography
Items from around the world include exhibits from Africa, India and Japan. One room is devoted to world music.

1st floor

Key

- Pre-history (1300 BC–AD 1050)
- Middle Ages & Renaissance (1050–1660)
- Tales of Denmark (1660–2000)
- Ethnography
- History of the Museum
- Royal Collection of Coins
- Ethnographic Treasures
- Near East & Antiquities

Children's Museum

Helmet
This Bronze-Age helmet, in the museum's pre-history department, dates from the 9th century BC and was found at Viksø on Zealand.

Main entrance

VISITORS' CHECKLIST

Practical Information
Ny Vestergade 10. **Map** 3 B2.
Tel 33 13 44 11. **Open** 10am–
5pm Tue–Sun. **W** natmus.dk

Transport
🚌 1A, 2A, 6A, 12, 15, 26, 29, 33,
650S.

Gallery Guide

*The collection is spread over
four floors with pre-history,
Viking treasures and the
Children's Museum on the ground
floor. The Middle Ages shares
the first floor with Ethnography,
which continues on the second
floor with exhibits of toys and the
history of Danes. You can meet
Egyptian mummies on
the third floor.*

2nd floor

★ **Guldhorn**
The pre-history
section contains,
among other
exhibits,
fragments of
golden horns forged
around 400 BC.

Ground
floor

❼ Thorvaldsens Museum

Bertel Thorvaldsens Plads 2.
Map 3 C2. **Tel** 33 32 15 32.
Ⓢ Central. Ⓜ Nørreport, Kongens
Nytorv. 🚌 1A, 2A, 15, 26, 29.
Open 10am–5pm Tue–Sun. 🚻
W thorvaldsensmuseum.dk

Located behind the palace
church (Christiansborg Slots-
kirke), Thorvaldsens Museum
was the first art museum in
Denmark and opened in 1848.
The Danish sculptor Bertel
Thorvaldsen (1770–1844) lived
and worked in Rome for more
than 40 years, but towards the
end of his life he bequeathed
all his works and his collection
of paintings to his native
Copenhagen. The collection is
placed in Christianborg's old
Coach House. The building is
worth a visit in its own right,
with a frieze on the outside
by Jørgen Sonne and mosaic
floors within.

Despite the fact that he
worked on some of his pieces
for 25 years, Thorvaldsen's
output is staggering and
includes sculptures based on
classical mythology, busts of
well-known contemporaries
such as the English poet, Lord
Byron, monumental studies of
Christ and a number of self-
portraits. The museum also
displays Thorvaldsen's drawings
and sketches and includes
items from his private collection
of paintings and Egyptian and
Roman artefacts.

Vaulted ceiling and decorative floor in
Thorvaldsens Museum

❸ Folketinget

Christiansborg. **Map** 3 C2. 📅 Jun–
Sep: daily.

The Folketinget is the Danish
parliamentary chamber.
Seating for the 179 members
is arranged in a semi-circle
with "left wing" MPs positioned
on the left and "right wing"
MPs on the right. The civil
servants' offices occupy the
largest section of the palace.
Separate offices are used by
Queen Margrethe II, whose
duties include chairing weekly
meetings of the State Council
and presiding over the annual
state opening of parliament
in early October.

❹ Christiansborg Slot

See pp90–91.

❺ Børsen

Slotsholmsgade. **Map** 4 D2.
Closed to visitors.
W borsbygningen.dk

Copenhagen's former
Stock Exchange was built
between 1590 and 1640
on the orders of Christian
IV, to a design by
Lorentz and Hans van
Steenwinckel. Today,
the building houses
the city's Chamber
of Commerce and
is not open to
the public, but its
stunning Renaissance
façade, copper
roofs, numerous
gables and   Dragon tails
unusual spire have   forming
made it one of   Børsen's tower
Copenhagen's best-
known sights. Its
sleek 54-m (177-ft) spire, carved
to resemble the entwined tails of
four dragons, is a city landmark.
Topping the spire are three
crowns representing Denmark,
Sweden and Norway. Trade in
goods continued at Børsen until
1857, when it was purchased by
a private association of whole-
salers who pledged to maintain
the historic building.

❹ Christiansborg Slot

On the Copenhagen Castle Island visitors can experience the magnificent Royal Reception Rooms, which are richly decorated with art, chandeliers, gold and marble. The royal family lived here until the palace burned down in 1794. The grand rooms of the present palace (completed in 1928) are used by the Queen for state dinners, banquets and receptions. In the Great Hall stunning tapestries portray the history of Denmark. There are also underground ruins of medieval castles and a tower which offers splendid views of Copenhagen.

★ Throne Room
As in every royal palace, the Throne Room is one of the grandest rooms in Christiansborg. However, Queen Margrethe II is famous for her "common touch" and has apparently never sat on this magnificent royal seat.

Velvet Room
Completed in 1924, this room is noteworthy for its grand marble portals, reliefs and luxurious velvet wall linings.

Decorative Vase
This vase can be found in the Frederick VI Room, one of the many state rooms in the palace. It was a gift to Queen Juliane Marie of Brunswick, second wife of King Frederik V.

The Dining Hall is decorated with portraits of Danish kings and contains two crystal chandeliers.

★ Great Hall
The 17 tapestries on display here were commissioned in 1990 for Queen Margrethe II's 50th birthday and completed in 2000. Made by Bjørn Nørgaarde, they depict key events in Danish history.

Tower Room
Copenhagen's tallest tower is 106 m (348 ft) high and topped with a 5-m (16-ft) crown. The tower's interior has a series of tapestries created by Joakim Skovgaard depicting scenes from Danish folk tales.

VISITORS' CHECKLIST

Practical Information
Christiansborg Slotsplads. **Map** 3 C2. **Tel** 33 92 64 92. Reception Rooms: **Open** 10am–5pm Tue–Sun (May–Sep: 10am–5pm daily). **Closed** 4, 12 & 18 Jun, 9 Jul. 🖼 11am (Danish), 3pm (English). Ruins: **Open** 10am–5pm Tue–Sun (May–Sep: 10am–5pm daily). 🖼
W **christiansborg.dk**

Transport
🚌 1A, 2A, 11A, 14, 26, 40, 66.

★ **Castle Ruins**
Under the palace are the ruins of the previous castles, including parts of Bishop Absalon's castle and the Copenhagen Castle.

Library
A small portion of the vast royal collection is housed here. The remaining volumes are kept at Amalienborg Slot *(see pp60–61)*.

Alexander Room
Bertel Thorvaldsen's frieze depicting Alexander the Great entering Babylon is displayed in this room.

❻ Tøjhusmuseet

Tøjhusgade 3. **Map** 3 C2. **Tel** 33 11 60 37. 1A, 2A, 15, 26, 29. **Open** 10am–5pm Tue–Sun. **W** thm.dk

The Royal Danish Arsenal was built between 1598 and 1604 and was one of the earliest of Christian IV's building projects. When completed, the 163-m (535-ft) long complex was one of the largest buildings in Europe and was capable of equipping an entire army. In 1611 the building was extended to include a harbour pool, which was situated next door in what are today the Library Gardens. The building now serves as a museum. Its collection covers the history of artillery from the invention of gunpowder up to the present day (exhibits include artillery guns as well as firearms). Suits of armour and military uniforms are also on display.

❼ Det Kongelige Bibliotek

Christians Brygge, entrance from Søren Kierkegaards Plads 1. **Map** 4 D2. **Tel** 33 47 47 47. 9A. 991, 992. **Open** 10am–9pm Mon–Sat. **W** kb.dk

The Royal Library is a stunning example of how to merge two very different architectural forms. The original library building is 19th century.

Gate leading to the old section of Det Kongelige Bibliotek

The Neo-Classical building's courtyard has been transformed into a garden and contains a statue of the Danish philosopher and theologian Søren Kierkegaard. Next to the old building is the ultra-modern library, linked by a special passage to its historic predecessor. The black façade of the new building mirrors the sea, while the central atrium provides a wonderful view of the sea. It was built as part of the effort to reconnect Danes with their harbour in the post-industrial age. The collection includes Danish folklore as well as manuscripts from the Middle Ages and the Søren Kierkegaard Archive.

Cannon from the Tøjhusmuseet collection

❽ Christianshavn

Map 4 D & 4 E.

This district is sometimes referred to as "Little Amsterdam" because of its many canals. Built in the first half of the 17th century by Christian IV, Christianshavn was originally intended both as a fortified city and a naval base. The area was the site of the first boatyards established in Copenhagen, as well as the warehouses belonging to major shipping lines. It is also where most sailors and boatyard workers lived. Up until the 1980s, Christianshavn was known only as the site of the "free state of Christiania" and was considered to be unattractive, poor and neglected. Since the 1990s, however, Christianshavn, together with nearby Holmen, has blossomed thanks to a sustained programme of urban redevelopment. With the recent addition of a bridge for pedestrians and cyclists, linking Nyhavn to Christianshavn, the disctrict has experienced an increase in traffic. Run-down warehouses have been transformed into trendy restaurants, cafés, company offices and smart apartments.

❾ Vor Frelsers Kirke

Sankt Annæ Gade 29. **Map** 4 E2. **Tel** 32 54 68 83. Christianshavn. 2A, 19, 47, 66, 350S. **Open** 11am–3:30pm daily. Tower: **Open** 10am–4pm Mon–Sat, 10:30am–3:30pm Sun & hols (late Jun–mid-Sep: open until 7:30pm daily). **Closed** in heavy rain or strong winds. **W** vorfrelserskirke.dk

Our Saviour's Church is most famous for its extraordinary spire, completed in 1752, and accessible via a spiral staircase that runs around the exterior. Be warned – it takes considerable stamina

Yachting marina and houses built out over the water, in Christianshavn

to climb all 400 steps, not to mention a good head for heights. The spire is Copenhagen's second-highest panoramic viewpoint and once you have caught your breath at the top you will be rewarded with a fabulous view of the city from 90 m (295 ft) up.

The spire's creator was the architect Lauritz de Thurah, who struck upon the idea of a spiral staircase while visiting the church of Sant'Ivo alla Sapienza in Rome. Legend has it that Thurah was so obsessed by his work that when it was alleged that his encircling staircase wound up the wrong way he committed suicide by leaping from the top of the tower. The truth is more prosaic, however, as the architect died in his own bed, poor and destitute, seven years after completing the tower. The tale was nevertheless made into a movie by the Danish director Nils Vest in 1997.

The church itself is also worth visiting. It was built in 1696, to a design by Lambert von Haven. Inside, a Baroque altar by the Swede Nicodemus Tessin is adorned with cherubs. The huge three-storey organ dates from 1698. It has more than 4,000 pipes and is supported by two giant elephants.

Spiral stairs of Vor Frelsers Kirke's tower

⓾ Orlogsmuseet

Overgaden oven Vandet 58. **Map** 4 E2. **Tel** 33 11 60 37. Ⓜ Christianshavn. 2A, 19, 47, 66, 350S. **Open** noon–4pm Tue–Sun. 🅿 🆆 **orlogsmuseet.dk**

The Royal Danish Naval Museum's building dates from 1780 and was once a sailors' hospital. Among its exhibits are navigation instruments, ships' lights, figureheads that were once fixed to the bows of windjammers, and uniforms. A collection of over 300 model ships includes one that dates to 1687.

Entrance to Christiania – a successful example of alternative living

⓫ Christiania

Map 4 D3 & E3. Ⓜ Christianhavn. 2A, 19, 47, 66, 350S.

The "free state of Christiania" has been in existence since 13 November 1971, when a group of squatters took over some deserted military barracks to the east of Christianshavn and established a commune. The local authorities initially tried to force the squatters to leave, but as the community's numbers swelled, the government decided to treat Christiania as a "social experiment". Today the community has about 900 residents.

The community has its own kindergarten, infrastructure and system of government, which are financed in part by the proceeds of its cafés and restaurants and the sale of locally made handicrafts. Christiania was initially linked with hippy drug culture, with sales dropping following a shooting in August 2016, when two policemen and a bystander were hit during the arrest of a dealer on Pusher Street. Trade was outlawed in 2004, with Pusher Street being dismantled a few months after the incident.

⓬ Operaen

Ekvipagemestervej 10. **Map** 2 F5. **Tel** 33 69 69 69. 66. 901, 902. **Open** foyer: 3 hours before a performance. 🎫 Jul–late Aug: 2pm and 4pm daily (in English). 🆆 **kglteater.dk**

The stunning Copenhagen Opera House opened in January 2005 on the island of Holmen in Copenhagen Harbour. For over a century the Danish Royal Opera shared a space with the ballet and theatre companies at Det Kongelige Teater. The auditorium was designed by the prominent Danish architect Henning Larsen, whose works include the Ny Carlsberg Glyptotek extension and the Danish Design Centre. The modern building is clad in German limestone and covers 41,000 sq m (441,300 sq ft). It includes a 1,500-seat auditorium with a gold leaf-gilded ceiling, as well as a second, smaller stage.

Striking façade of Copenhagen's opera house

FURTHER AFIELD

There is plenty to see outside the city centre. Vibrant neighbourhoods such as Vesterbro and Nørrebro are accessible from central Copenhagen on foot or by bicycle. Once you get a taste for their laid-back village vibe and mix of restaurants and cultural sights, such as the Carlsberg Brewery and Assistens Kirkegård, you might not want to leave. Sights even further afield are served by a network of suburban trains. A visit to one or more of these places provides an alternative to the bustle of inner-city Copenhagen. Charlottenlund, in an affluent coastal suburb, has a patch of surrounding woodland that is perfect for gentle walks, as is the parkarea around Frederiksberg Slot. And, thanks to the bridge and tunnel that spans the Øresund (Sound), the sandy beach and many attractions of Malmö in Sweden are only half an hour away. The bridge is a marvel of modern engineering and can be admired from the harbour of the charming fishing village of Dragør.

Sights at a Glance

Historic Buildings
4 Frederiksberg Slot and Have

Places of Interest
1 Tycho Brahe Planetarium
2 Vesterbro
5 Cisternerne
6 Nørrebro
8 Experimentarium
10 Den Blå Planet
11 Øresund Bridge
12 Amager and Ørestad

13 Dragør

Parks and Gardens
3 Zoologisk Have
9 Charlottenlund

Museums
14 Arken Museum For Moderne Kunst

Churches
7 Grundtvigs Kirke

Key
- City centre
- Motorway
- Major road
- Other road
- Railway

0 kilometres 4
0 miles 2

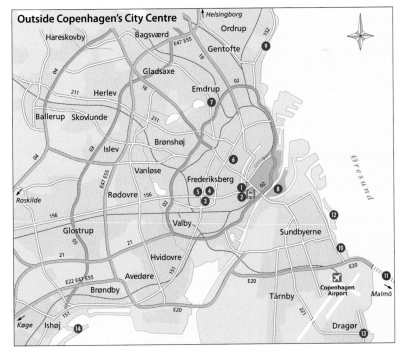

Outside Copenhagen's City Centre

◀ Charlottenlund Slot, the grand former summer residence of Princess Charlotte Amalie   For keys to symbols *see back flap*

Tycho Brahe Planetarium in the shape of a sliced-through cylinder

❶ Tycho Brahe Planetarium

Gl. Kongevej 10. **Tel** 33 12 12 24.
Ⓢ Vesterport. 🚌 14, 15, 29.
Open daily; check website for times.
🅿️ 🆆 **planetariet.dk**

Copenhagen's planetarium is the largest of its kind in western Europe and is named after Tycho Brahe (1546–1601), the renowned Danish astronomer. Brahe is credited with the discovery of a new star in the constellation of Cassiopeia, in 1572, and with making important advances in our knowledge of planetary motion. These impressive advances were made before the invention of the telescope.

The planetarium opened in 1989 in a cylindrical building designed by Knud Munk. Built from sand-coloured brick, it appears at its most attractive when viewed from across the small lake, which is one of a series that continues right up to Østerbro and that was created in the late 18th century by damming the local river. The planetarium is located on the Old Royal Route (Gammel Kongevej), which was once travelled by royal processions heading for Frederiksberg Slot.

The planetarium is Denmark's most advanced centre for popularizing astronomy and space research as well as promoting knowledge on natural science. A huge IMAX® cinema screens films daily, including one on the wonders of space travel.

❷ Vesterbro

Carlsberg Visitors Centre & Jacobsen Brewhouse: Gamle Carlsberg Vej 11.
Tel 33 27 12 82. Ⓢ Enghave, Valby.
🚌 18, 26. **Open** May–Oct:
10am–5pm daily; Nov–Apr:
10am–5pm Tue–Sun. 🅿️
🆆 **visitcarlsberg.com**

Vesterbro underwent gentrification in the early 2000s, and today is a distinctly hipster area. Visitors flock here for the high concentration of ultra-trendy restaurants and bars in the former meat-packing district of Kødbyen, and the independent boutiques and cafés that line the streets, such as Istedgade and Værnedamsvej, considered Copenhagen's little Paris.

In the southwest corner, Carlsberg Brewery is the main draw of the neighbourhood. It was founded in 1847 by Jacob Christian, whose father had worked at the king's brewery in Copenhagen. Jacob Christian

chose this site on Valby Hill for the quality of the water, and named his company Carlsberg after his son. The brewery has an exhibition centre where visitors can learn about the history of beer and manufacturing process during a 90-minute self-guided tour. This concludes with a beer tasting in a bar overlooking the huge copper kettles used in the brewing process. In 2005, the Jacobsen Brewhouse opened in part of the old brewery, with the aim of developing speciality beers. This brand is now the only one still produced at this site.

The brewery itself features examples of industrial architecture,and is recognised for the intriguing Elephant Gate (1901), which consists of four 5-m (16-ft) high granite elephants shipped from Bornholm. The streets surrounding the Carlsberg visitor centre are currently undergoing improvements.

❸ Zoologisk Have

Roskildevej 32. **Tel** 72 20 02 00.
Ⓢ Valby. Ⓜ Frederiksberg. 🚌 4A,
6A, 18, 26. **Open** Jan–Mar, Nov & Dec:
10am–4pm daily (Mar: to 5pm Sat & Sun); Apr, May & Sep: 10am–5pm daily (to 6pm Sat & Sun); Jun & mid-Aug–late Aug: 10am–6pm daily; Jul–mid-Aug: 10am–8pm daily; Oct:
10am–5pm daily. 🅿️ 🆆 **zoo.dk**

Copenhagen's zoological garden was established close to Frederiksberg Slot in 1859, making it one of Europe's oldest zoos. In the 1940s it

Elephant Gate at the entrance to Carlsberg Brewery

Frederiksberg Slot, headquarters of the Danish Military Academy

was expanded to include part of Søndermarken, with the two areas connected by a tunnel under Roskildevej. Although not large by international standards, the zoo has a wide selection of animals including giraffes, polar bears, hippos, elephants, lions, along with endangered species of some animals. The Norman Foster-designed Elephant House is especially noteworthy for its large glass domes and groundbreaking architecture. An enclosure for seals, elks and polar bears, The Arctic Ring, opened in 2012.

A tropical section houses butterflies and birds, as well as some crocodiles. Smaller children will enjoy the petting zoo, which offers close-up contact with domestic animals, pony rides and the chance to let off steam in a large play area laid out like a child-size rabbit warren. The 42-m (138-ft) high wooden observation tower, built in 1905, affords views as far as the coast of Sweden.

❹ Frederiksberg Slot and Have

Roskildevej 28. **Tel** 36 13 26 00. Ⓜ Frederiksberg. 🚌 4A, 6A, 18, 26. Palace: **Open** for tours only at 11am & 1pm on last Sat of month (except Jul & Dec). Garden: **Open** daily.

Built between 1700 and 1735 this palace was the summer residence of Frederik IV who used it to entertain visitors including, in 1716, the Tsar of Russia, Peter the Great. The king is said to have enjoyed sailing along the park canals, while Copenhagen's inhabitants lined the banks and cheered.

The palace was designed in the Italian style by the architect Ernst Brandenburger following

the king's visit to Italy. During the reign of Christian IV the building was enlarged with two additional wings, giving it its present horseshoe shape.

Since 1869 Frederiksberg Slot has been used by the Danish Military Academy. Having its origins in the Cadets' Corp established by Frederik IV in 1713, the school's emblem still bears the king's monogram. The school is not open to the public except for guided tours, though visitors are free to explore the grounds. The palace gardens, known as Frederiksberg Have, were laid out in a French style in the early 18th century. Later on they were transformed into a romantic rambling English park, criss-crossed with a network of canals and tree-lined paths, and dotted with statues and benches.

Frederiksberg Slot stands on top of a hill and, for the people of Copenhagen, marks a notional boundary of the city. In the 18th century, when it was built, the palace stood outside the city limits.

❺ Cisternerne

Søndermarken. **Tel** 30 73 80 32. Ⓢ Enghave, Valby. 🚌 4A, 6A, 18, 26, 171E. **Open** 1am–5pm Thu– Sun. **Closed** Jan, Feb & Dec. Ⓦ **cisternerne.dk**

Praised by *Forbes* magazine as one of the most unique museums in Europe, the cisterns is a long forgotten subterranean reservoir that once contained the supply of drinking water for the Danish capital. Today, the cisterns acts as a venue for art exhibitions and other events. The cisterns is located under Frederiksberg Hill in the heart of Søndermarken Park; at ground level, the presence of the museum is given away only by two modern glass pyramids. Guided tours lasting an hour take in the current exhibition at Cisternerne, as well as the geology and architecture of the cisterns.

Underground art gallery and performance space, Cisternerne

Flora Danica

This dinner service, decorated with floral designs copied from the *Flora Danica* encyclopedia of plants, was ordered in 1790 by Christian VII. The set was intended as a present for Catherine II of Russia. However, during the 12 years when the first *Flora Danica* was in production the Tsarina died, and the king decided to keep the set for himself. It was used for the first time in 1803 during a reception to celebrate the king's 37th birthday. Over 1,500 of the original 1,802 pieces have survived and are now in the possession of Queen Margrethe II. Copies of individual items are made to order and the methods of production hardly differ from those employed over 200 years ago. The pieces are hand-painted by artists who train for over 10 years to master the exquisite flower paintings. This kind of quality is expensive – a plate costs upwards of 5,000 Dkr.

An example of *Flora Danica* tableware

Assistens Kirkegård, both a park and a cemetery

❻ Nørrebro

Kapelvej 2. **Tel** 35 37 19 17. Ⓢ
Ⓜ Nørreport. 🚌 3A, 5A, 12, 18, 66,
250S 350S. **Open** Oct–Mar: 7am–7pm
daily; Apr–Sep: 7am–10pm daily.
Ⓦ **assistens.dk**

Nørrebro is connected to central Copenhagen by Dronning Louises Bro, a bridge built in the 1600s and widened in 1897 to accommodate the many cyclists and pedestrians who cross it daily. The district has come a long way since the riots in early 2000, rapidly transitioning from rundown to polished in the last 15 years.

It feels like an intimate village within Copenhagen. Young families zip around with children in carts or bikes while the sophisticated flock to destination establishments such as Jægersborggade, Elmegade and Ravnsborggade.

The star sight is Assistens Kirkegård. Conceived in 1760 as a cemetery for poor plague victims, it later became fashionable and is the final resting place for Søren Kierkegaard and Hans Christian Andersen. The cemetery is also a popular park. Visitors are as likely to see joggers, cyclists and sunbathers as well as people tending the graves.

❼ Grundtvigs Kirke

På Bjerget 14B. **Tel** 35 81 54 42.
Ⓢ Emdrup. 🚌 6A, 42, 43, 66, 69.
Open 9am–4pm Mon–Sat (to 6pm
Thu), noon–4pm Sun (to 1pm in
winter). Ⓦ **grundtvigskirke.dk**

This unusual yellow brick church, remarkable not only for its size but also its highly original shape, was designed in 1913 by P.V. Jensen Klint. Standing almost 49 m (161 ft) high, it ranks as one of Denmark's largest churches and is designed in a Danish Modernist style. It was built between 1921 and 1940 on Bisperbjerg, the highest hill in Copenhagen, and paid for by public donations to honour the memory of Nicolai Frederik Severin Grundtvig (1783–1872) – a prominent clergyman, theologian and philosopher.
In addition to his social work, this versatile man found time to write books and treatises, and composed some 1,500 hymns, many of which are sung to this day in Danish churches. For more than 10 years Grundtvig was a member of the Danish Parliament, and in 1861 he became an honorary bishop of the Danish Church.

The charismatic clergyman became famous in his country as the founder of the Danish Folkehøjskole (People's High School), a system that enabled those from the lower ranks of society to gain access to education. The shape of the church building symbolizes this sphere of his activities, being reminiscent of a typical Danish village church. In addition, the top of the tower is designed to resemble a church organ and alludes to the many religious hymns written by Grundtvig.

A climbing wall, one of the many popular attractions at Experimentarium

❽ Experimentarium

Tuborg Havnevej 7, 2900 Hellerup.
Tel 21 54 87 98. Ⓢ Hellerup or
Svanemøllen. 🚌 9A. 🚌 993. **Open**
10am–5pm Mon–Wed & Fri (until 8pm
Thu), 10am–5pm Sat & Sun. **Closed** 1
Jan, 24, 25 & 31 Dec. 🚗 🖥 📷
Ⓦ **experimentarium.dk**

This innovative science centre located in the Hellerup district has been redeveloped. The main idea behind the centre is to bring science to life through hands-on exploration. Almost all the exhibits are of the interactive kind and the experiments can be independently performed by anyone.

The place is hugely popular with children who run about trying out all the exhibits. Adults, too, will find much of interest, whether it be testing the latest in virtual technology, programming robots or playing ball with blow pipes.

At Experimentarium science is for everybody and visitors

Front elevation of Grundtvigs Kirke, inspired by small village churches

Some of the many aquatic creatures to be found at Den Blå Planet

can learn about the wonderful world that surrounds them through play and exciting experiences. There are enough activities to fill several hours of exploration. At every point, children are confronted with exhibits and puzzles to fire their curiosity, and tested with different kinds of challenges such as drawing the outline of a figure while looking in the mirror, and seeing if they can make all the muscles in their lower body work together to keep their balance on a special board. Kids can try their hand at guiding a cargo vessel into harbour, test their emotions, check their hearing from the lowest to the highest frequencies, and see which kind of ball runs the fastest in the zigzag track.

The Kids' Pavillion is a section where younger visitors between 3 and 6 years old can experiment with magnetism, build a house using a crane, hear what their voice sounds like backwards and much more.

The large outdoor area, right beside the harbour, is in use all year around with different activities depending on the season. There are also activities during which entertaining chemistry and physics experiments are carried out, and demonstrations and dissections where audience participation is encouraged. All the exhibits are labelled in Danish and English, and there are numerous lectures and special exhibitions such as navigating a light labyrinth or blowing human sized bubbles.

❾ Charlottenlund

Jægersborg Allé. 🚌 14. Ⓢ
Charlottenlund St. Palace: **Closed** to the public. Gardens: **Open** to the public.

A royal residence has stood on this site since 1690, but the present palace was built between 1731 and 1733 on the orders of Princess Charlotte Amalie. The princess, who remained single all her life, liked the place so much that it was soon named after her. She used it as her summer residence until her death in 1782.

The building was remodelled in the 19th century, when its Baroque character gave way to a Renaissance style. A number of other Danish royals have enjoyed staying here including Frederik VIII and his wife, Princess Louise, who remained here until her death in 1926. The couple are commemorated by an obelisk located at the rear of the building.

The palace is now used by the Danish Institute for Fisheries, but it is still possible to stroll in its surrounding gardens. The appearance of the park, with its pruned conifers and pleasant avenues, dates from the 1990s, though marked pathways and ponds remain from the 17th century. The vegetable garden dates from 1826 and once grew herbs and produce to be used in the palace kitchen. There are a number of ancient trees in the grounds, notably two larches that stand at the rear of the palace and are considered to be the oldest of their kind in Denmark.

❿ Den Blå Planet

Jacob Fortlingsvej 1. **Tel** 39 62 32 83. 🚌 5A, 14. Ⓜ Kastrup. **Open** 10am–9pm Mon, 10am–5pm Tue–Sun. **Closed** 1 Jan, 24, 25 & 31 Dec. 🅿 Ⓦ **denblaaplanet.dk**

Copenhagen's aquarium, Den Blå Planet (The Blue Planet), opened in spring 2013 in a modern building in Kastrup harbour, on the island of Amager. Although not as large as Nordsøen Oceanarium in Hirtshals *(see p208)*, it offers the chance to admire a wide variety of marine life; it also plays a major role in conservation, research and education.

The aquarium contains more than 90 glass tanks, the largest holding 85,000 litres (18,700 gallons) of water. The five main sections are the Amazon, the African Great Lakes, the Warm Ocean, Cold Water, and Evolution and Adaptation. The tanks are populated by over 300 species of fish from all over the world including sharks and sharp-teethed piranha. Among the other aquatic wildlife are a giant octopus, crocodiles and an electric eel (capable of producing up to 2,000 volts), as well as turtles and many hundreds of brightly coloured tropical fish.

Feeding times (displayed on the aquarium website and at the entrance) are especially animated. In the basement, kids can come close to small marine life in the touch pools.

Charlottenlund Slot, surrounded by parkland

⓫ Øresund Bridge

Tel 70 23 90 60. Toll charge: 188–800 Dkr, depending on vehicle size; no bicycles allowed; toll and passport control points are located on the Swedish side. 🖼
ⓦ **oresundsbron.com**

In 2000, when Queen Margrethe II and King Carl XVI of Sweden jointly opened the Øresund Bridge, it was the first time that the Scandinavian peninsula had been connected to mainland Europe since the Ice Age. Now, thanks to the bridge, the delights of Malmö, the largest city in southern Sweden, are only 35 minutes away from Copenhagen.

The bridge is the second longest fixed-link bridge in the world. The entire crossing is 16 km (10 miles) long and con-sists of (from the Danish side): a 430-m (1,411-ft) long artificial peninsula, a tunnel measuring more than 3.5 km (2.2 miles) and running 10 m (33 ft) below the water, a 4-km (2-mile) long artificial island and a 7,845-m (25,738-ft) long cable-stayed bridge. From either side of the sound, the sight of the structure, with its huge 204-m (670-ft) high pylons, is truly impressive.

The bridge is a marvel of modern engineering. It has a two-level structure; the top is for motor traffic, the bottom for rail. At its highest point the bridge is suspended 57 m (187 ft) above the water. At the tunnel entrance, on both sides, are light filters designed to allow drivers to adjust to the

The front of the modern looking DR Koncerthuset

dimmer conditions. About one thousand sensors are installed along the route as part of a fire alarm system.

The bridge has proved to be popular and over 32,000 rail passengers and 42,900 cars make the crossing every day. It also forms part of an annual marathon run, the first of which took place in June 2000, before the official opening.

⓬ Amager and Ørestad

3 km (2 miles) southeast of Copenhagen city centre.

For a great number of visitors arriving by plane, the island of Amager, southeast of Copenhagen's city centre, is the starting point of their explor-ation of Denmark, since it is the site of Copenhagen's inter-national airport.

Since the opening of the Øresund Bridge in 2000, Amager has gone from being a relatively undeveloped area to one characterized by

groundbreaking architecture and housing developments. The urban conglomeration of Amager, with its residential blocks, shops and restaurants, blends into the almost futuristic Ørestad. Landmark buildings here include the 23-floor skyscraper Bella Sky Comwell Hotel, whose two towers lean away from each other with insulating, alternating glass panels, and the DR Koncerthuset *(see p106)*. This world-class performance venue and studio space was designed in the shape of a giant blue cube by acclaimed French architect Jean Nouvel. Its glass façade, opaque by day, acts like blue-screen technology at night, projecting images of the activity within. Most of the University of Copenhagen *(see p76)* is now based on Amager, and Scandinavia's largest shopping centre, Fields *(see p105)*, can be found right next to Ørestad metro station. Convenient metro connections to Copenhagen have further helped rejuvenate the district. Those looking for outdoor

Øresund Bridge linking Denmark and Sweden

For hotels and restaurants in this area see pp248–50 and pp262–6

attractions can still find them here, however: Naturcenter Vestamager is an oasis for families, with play areas, pony rides and a lake, while the recreated Amager Strandpark, which replaced the former 1930s bathing huts, is a landscaped area of man-made beaches, including a lagoon and an island.

⓭ Dragør

12 km (7 miles) southeast of Copenhagen. Museum: Havnepladsen 2. **Tel** 32 53 93 07. **Open** Jun–Sep: noon–4pm Wed, Thu, Sat & Sun. 🅿 🆆 museumamager.dk

This picturesque town to the southeast of Amager used to be the place to catch a ferry for Limhamn, on the Swedish side of the Øresund (Sound), which ran from 1934 until 1999. The opening of a bridge brought about the closing of this route, and Dragør has since become a destination for those wishing to escape the hustle of central Copenhagen.

As far back as the Middle Ages, Dragør was a major centre for the Baltic herring trade. Later on, its inhabitants profited by piloting the boats that sailed

An exhibit from Dragør's museum

across the Øresund. Many houses in Dragør still have distinctive observation towers, known as "Kikkenborg". The biggest of these (now a museum) stands by Lodshuset, a building that houses the local pilot service headquarters, which was established in 1684. Surprisingly, for a long time Dragør had no proper harbour and the boats were simply dragged ashore. The word "dragør" means a sandy or pebbly strip of land up which the boats were hauled. It was not until 1520 that Dutch settlers, inhabiting nearby Store Magleby, built a proper harbour. Once built, it developed fast and by the 19th century it was the third-largest port in Denmark (after Copenhagen

Cutters moored in Dragør's harbour

and Helsingør), receiving large sailing ships. Today these maritime traditions are kept alive by a pleasant marina overlooking nearby Sweden and the stunning bridge.

The town is a pleasant place for a stroll with cobbled streets and pretty 18th-century yellow-walled houses decorated with flowers. The local museum, housed in the old town hall building and a 17th-century harbour warehouse, has a collection of items devoted to Dragør's rich maritime past. A combined ticket allows admission to four museums in the area: the Dragør Museum, the Amagermuseet in Store Magleby, the Lodshuset building and the Mølsted Museum, which is dedicated to the Danish seascape painter Christian Mølsted.

⓮ Arken Museum For Moderne Kunst

20 km (12 miles) south of Copenhagen city centre. Ishøj, Skovvej 100. **Tel** 43 54 02 22. 🆂 to and from Ishøj. 🚌 128. **Open** 10am–5pm Tue–Sun (to 9pm Wed). 🅿
🆆 arken.dk

Located a stone's throw from the beach, Arken Museum For Moderne Kunst (Arken Museum of Modern Art) is housed in a building intended to resemble a marooned ship.

The museum's permanent collection is comprised of contemporary Danish, Nordic and international art, with an emphasis on installations, sculpture and graphic art. Many of the works on display are by Danish artists such as Asger Jorn, Jeppe Hein and Per Kirkeby. One of the most fascinating installations in the gallery is Ai Weiwei's *Circle of Animals/Zodiac Heads*, which represents 12 animals of the Chinese zodiac. There are also nine huge, abstract paintings by German artist Anselm Reye, whose neon colours reference Pop Art, Minimalism and Expressionism, and ten works by Damien Hirst, which are exhibited separately in the Damien Hirst Room. In addition, the museum presents at least two major temporary exhibitions a year, ranging from international retrospectives to large group shows.

Opened in 1996, the building has proved to be as controversial as much of the work inside. Designed by Søren Robert Lund when he was 25 years old and still a student, it follows few conventional rules. Extensions built in different materials have softened the original raw finish and provide a more welcoming exterior.

Bold outline of Arken Museum For Moderne Kunst

SHOPPING IN COPENHAGEN

Copenhagen has long been the commercial centre not only of Denmark, but also of an entire region that includes Zealand and, on the Swedish side, Skåne (Skania). Shopping here is a pleasurable experience, with many of the stores concentrated in just a few areas, often in buildings as interesting as their merchandise. Strøget and the adjacent pedestrian streets offer everything from designer labels and casual fashion, to porcelain, crystal and antiques.

Copenhagen is synonymous with the best in interior style and the decorative arts, while young Danish talent has turned the city into a fashion capital, too. An array of boutiques and quirky shops have helped to revitalise previously run-down areas of the city and they deserve to be explored. Along the way, picturesque squares and cafés offer welcome respite for tired feet. For more information about shopping across the country, see pp278–9.

Magasin du Nord, one of Copenhagen's best-known department stores

Where to Shop

Most of the major international brands can be found along the city's two longest pedestrian streets, Strøget (see p74) and Købmagergade. Shops range from cheerful and inexpensive to designer and upmarket department stores (towards Kongens Nytorv). If you take detours into the side streets there is plenty of more alternative shopping on offer. On parallel Læderstræde and Kompagnistræde you will discover a variety of small independent shops; the latter is especially good for antiques. Those on tighter budgets should head west of Strøget, to Larsbjørnsstræde and Studiestræde for street fashion, secondhand shops and music stores.

On the outskirts of the old town, the Nansensgade area mixes traditional and trendy boutiques with attractive bars and cafés. There is everything here from sushi restaurants and chocolate shops to vintage clothes and accessories.

To the west of the central station, the former red light district of Vesterbro has undergone a complete transformation and is now one of Copenhagen's most vibrant areas. At its centre, Halmtorvet is a trendy café-filled square. Head to Istedgade for art and speciality shops.

Those in search of a quirky bargain should try the multicultural Nørrebro district, north of the city. Elmegade and Fælledvej are lined with secondhand stores, new Danish design and recycled goods. For secondhand jewellery try Jægersborggade and Ravnsborggade.

Opening Hours

It is not worth trying to shop in Denmark for anything other than foodstuffs before 10am. Early in the week most shops close at around 6pm, although many stores remain open on Fridays until 7 or 8pm. On Saturdays some shops close at 2pm, but the majority now stay open until 4 or 5pm.

Department stores tend to have the longest opening hours. While smaller shops in Denmark stay closed on Sundays, larger stores and shopping centres now open Sundays though hours may vary.

Department Stores and Shopping Centres

Magasin du Nord was Scandinavia's first department store and is still a huge favourite. As well as clothes, cosmetics and luxury household goods it sells books, jewellery, delicious chocolate and foodstuffs. Also popular is the light and airy **Illum** on Strøget, which has several elegant floors selling high-quality goods under a glass dome, and the added advantage of a rooftop café.

Copenhagen has several shopping centres, with shops, cafés, restaurants, and cinemas under one roof. Vesterbro's **Fisketorvet**, situated on the site of an old fish market facing the Sound, is arguably one of the best. It is also worth taking a trip out to **Fields**, one of the biggest shopping centres in Scandinavia with a total of 150 shops under one roof. Although a little way out of the city, it is conveniently situated at the Ørestad metro station.

Design and Interior Decoration

Denmark is justly famous for combining attractive design with functionality and quality materials. Most of its best-known brands have their own shops in the city centre. The **Bang & Olufsen** showroom has listening rooms where customers can appreciate the quality of its audio products. For a good selection of interior design under one roof, head for **Illums Bolighus**, which keeps an eye on tradition while displaying the latest trends in furnishing and lighting.

Winner of numerous awards for innovative design, **Normann Copenhagen** has converted an old cinema in Østerbro into a stunning showroom. As well as its own collection of kitchen accessories, here you can find a variety of contemporary lifestyle products and high-profile fashion brands from around the world – all in a truly unforgettable setting.

The **Louis Poulsen** showroom offers various designer lighting solutions set against a minimalist background, and young furniture designers display their talent for creating classics with a contemporary twist at **Hay Cph**, which has two branches in the city centre. Another sleek furniture store is **Paustian** in the dock area. Designed by architect Jørn Utzon, of Sydney Opera House fame, there is also a stylish restaurant.

Back in town, the interior design centre **Casa Shop** is well worth a look, as is the **Danish Design Centre (DDC)**, which hosts changing exhibitions showcasing Danish innovation. **Designer Zoo**, in Vesterbro, is a working design store for eight

Minimalist interior of leading fashion store Munthe plus Simonsen

Danish designers who create furniture, jewellery, knitwear and artistic glass. **Bolia** is a nationwide interior design store that celebrates Scandinavian traditions.

Clothes and Accessories

From high fashion to second-hand chic, Copenhagen has it all. Top international designers congregate at the Kongens Nytorv end of Strøget, while less expensive labels stretch down the street towards the town hall. Købmagergade is good for mid-price clothes while Kronprinsensgade, which runs off it, is known as "Copenhagen's Catwalk" for the cutting-edge clothes shops located here. **Bruuns Bazaar** is a favourite, selling men's and women's modern designs.

The narrow streets of the Grønnegade quarter are lined with half-timbered buildings housing Danish streetwear and classic labels. **Munthe plus Simonsen**, renowned for classy yet casual ladieswear, is found here. Nearby, on Pilestræde, **Designers Remix** have opened a large flagship store of their sexy, edgy womenswear. **Day Birger et Mikkelsen**, has also gathered all of their seven lines under one roof here: women's, men's and children's wear, lingerie, jewellery, accessories and home. **Holly Golightly** sells elegant Danish womenswear and accessories.

Secondhand chic lies in the "Pisserenden" area adjacent to Strøget, on streets like Læderstræde and Studiestræde; **Carmen & Fantasio** is one of the best. For vintage frocks and clever accessories, head to Nansensgade or try **Glam Vintage** in Silkegade 7. The collection of high-end 1960–70s glad rags is particularly pleasing.

Jewellery

Danish jewellery has a reputation for fine design and attention to detail. The city's most famous jewellery shop is silversmith **Georg Jensen**, but Julie Sandlau (stocked at **Magasin du Nord**), who creates pretty gold designs, is the name on many a celebrity's lips. Similarly trendy (and expensive) are the gold and silver creations at **Marlene Juhl Jørgensen Fine Jewellery**. For jewellery fit for Denmark's Queen, visit **Peter Hertz**. Amber washed up on Denmark's west coast makes its way into jewellery at **The Amber Specialist** and branches of **House of Amber**, which also has an amber museum.

Interior of a shop selling Bodum kitchenware, a popular Danish product

Royal Shopping

Historic royals have left their mark on Copenhagen's architecture, and fans of today's popular royal family can follow in their footsteps to the shops. The Queen can be seen shopping in the city centre while several family members frequent Copenhagen's two big department stores, **Illum** and **Magasin du Nord**.

Grand stores carrying the coveted words "Purveyors to her Majesty, the Queen of Denmark" cluster together on the Amagertorv section of Strøget – the great silversmith **Georg Jensen**, **Royal Copenhagen**, which also boasts a charming tea room, and **Illums Bolighus**, a shrine to modern design.

Crown Princess Mary is a fashion and style icon in Denmark. Among her favourite clothes designers are Julie Fagerholt at **Heart Made**, known for her subtle detailing, and the sexy and sophisticated look of **By Malene Birger**, and the innovative yet classic lines of Baum und Pferdgarten, stocked at **Urban Factory**.

Should you wish to take home wine bottled on Prince Henrik's estate in France, visit **Kjaer & Sommerfeldt**.

Markets

Hours can be spent bargain hunting in Copenhagen's outdoor flea markets that pop up around the city between April or May and mid-October. The flea market on **Thorvaldsens Plads**, in front of the museum, sells antiques, Danish design, posters, paintings and ceramics. It is particularly popular with its canalside setting and outdoor cafés.

Torvehallerne København (KBH), the purpose-built covered food market on Israel Plads, offers more than 60 stands, from fresh produce to meat and fish, and from handmade chocolate to gourmet ready meals.

Copenhagen Street Food on Papirøen is the city's first street food market with over 39 stalls serving both regional and international cuisine. You can reserve a table in the hall or eat outside on the canals.

Flea market in one of Copenhagen's picturesque squares

Art and Antiques

Bredgade, in the financial district, and Ravnsborggade in Nørrebro are packed with antiques shops, bric-a-brac sellers and collectibles, especially modern Danish classics and funky retro designs. Come here for pieces by the great names in 20th-century Danish design, such as Arne Jacobsen, famed for his Egg, Ant and Swan chairs, Hans J Wegner, Kaare Klint and lighting by Poul Henningsen. Out of town but worth the trek, **Dansk Møbelkunst**, in Østerbro, and **Green Square**, out on Amager, are essential browsing territory for collectors of modern Danish classics. Great furniture and style from the 1950s, 1960s and 1970s can be found at **Klassik**, while **Lysberg** is popular for the timeless quality of its designs. Bredgade is also the home of traditional auction houses. Sotheby's have a house here as do the long-established Danish auction houses, such as **Bruun Rasmussen**.

In vibrant Vesterbro, the side streets off Istedgade and the meat-packing district of Kødbyen are the places to look for galleries displaying work by up-and-coming artists. The small streets in the Islands Brygge area are a hotbed of galleries specialising in experimental art. Among the cluster of antiques shops there are specialists in porcelain and china, vintage watches and books, prints and comics. For

the finest porcelain, silver and crystal, visit **Royal Copenhagen**.

Specialist Shops

The array of individual and innovative little shops make strolling Copenhagen's streets a pleasure. They are also a great way to find gifts and souvenirs to take home from the city. Buy specialist teas in one of Europe's oldest teashops, **A.C. Perch's Thehandel**, which dates from 1834. Having retained its original interior, the shop and tearoom are a highlight on fashionable Kronprinsensgade. **Sømods Bolcher** is an old-fashioned sweet shop where you can watch traditional treats being made in time-honoured fashion. For the finest foods, take a look at the delicious pastries at **Lagkagehuset** and the specialist breads at **Meyers Bakery**, or explore Vaernedamsvej in Vesterbro, a great street for gourmets, with specialist cheese, wine, fish and chocolate shops, as well as cafés and grocers.

Buy a posy, or just soak up the colour and scent of **Bering Flowers**, who not only provide the flowers for the Royal Theatre but for royal weddings.

Craft Beer

The Danes are among the top beer drinkers worldwide. Although the mainstream brands Carlsberg and Tuborg are perennially popular, there's a growing market for distinctive craft beers. Carlsberg has its own craft brewery, **Jacobsen Brewhouse**, named after the Carlsberg founder. You can experience Jacobsen at the Carlsberg Brewery (see p96).

Renowned Copenhagen brewer Mikkel Borg Bjergsø, owns Mikkeller, one of the world's most creative small breweries, exporting to over 40 countries. The **Mikkeller Barrel Room** in København has a 16-tap bar of Mikkeller beers.

At **Nørrebro Bryghus**, award-winning brewer Anders Kissmeyer has 10 different brews available on tap each day, best tasted with the restaurant's Danish dishes.

DIRECTORY

Department Stores and Shopping Centres

Fields
Arne Jacobsens Allé 12.
Tel 70 20 85 05.
w fields.dk

Fisketorvet
Kalvebod Brygge 59.
Map 3 A5. Tel 33 36 64 00.
w fisketorvet.dk

Illum
Østergade 52. Map 3 C1.
Tel 33 14 40 02.
w illum.dk

Magasin du Nord
Kongens Nytorv 13.
Map 4 D1. Tel 33 11 44 33.
w magasin.dk

Design and Interior Decoration

Bang & Olufsen
Østergade 18. Map 4 D1.
Tel 33 11 14 15.
w bang-olufsen.com

Bolia
Christian IX Gade 7.
Map 1 C5. Tel 70 10 00 55.
w bolia.com

Casa Shop
Store Regnegade 2.
Map 1 C3. Tel 33 32 70 41.
w casashop.dk

Danish Design Centre
H C Andersens Blvd 27.
Map 3 B2.
Tel 33 69 33 69.
w danskdesigncenter.dk

Designer Zoo
Vesterbrogade 137. Tel 33
24 94 93. w dzoo.dk

Hay Cph
Pilestræde 29–31. Map 3
C1. Tel 42 82 08 20.

Hay House
Østergade 61, 2nd/3rd
Floors. Map 3 C1.
w hay.dkIllums
Bolighus
Amagertorv 10. Map 3 C1.
Tel 33 14 19 41.
w illumsbolighus.com

Louis Poulsen
Gammel Strand 28. Map
3 C1. Tel 70 33 14 14.
w louispoulsen.com

Normann Copenhagen
Østerbrogade 70. Map 1
C1–C2. Tel 35 27 05 40.
w normann-
copenhagen.com

Paustian
Kalkbrænderiløbskaj 2.
Tel 39 16 65 65.
w paustian.dk

Clothes and Accessories

Bruuns Bazaar
Kronprinsensgade 8–9.
Map 3 C1. Tel 33 32 19
99. w bruunsbazaar.dk

Carmen & Fantasio
Larsbjørnsstræde 11.
Map 3 B1. Tel 33 14 30 36.

Day Birger et Mikkelsen
Pilestræde 16. Map 3 C1.
Tel 33 45 88 80. w day.dk

Designers Remix
Pilestræde 8D. Map 3 C1.
Tel 33 14 33 00.
w designersremix.com

Glam Vintage
Silkegade 7. Map 3 C1.
Tel 35 38 50 41.

Holly Golightly
Gammel Mønt 2. Map 1 C5.
Tel 33 14 19 20.
w hollygolightly.dk

Munthe plus Simonsen
Grønnegade 10. Map 2
D5. Tel 33 32 00 12.
w munthe.com

Jewellery

The Amber Specialist
Frederiksberggade 28.
Map 3 B2. Tel 33 11 88 03.

Marlene Juhl Jørgensen Fine Jewellery
Store Regnegade 2.
Map 1 C3. Tel 33 93 09 92.

Georg Jensen
Amagertorv 4. Map 3 C1.
Tel 33 11 40 80.
w georgjensen.com

House of Amber
Kongens Nytorv 2. Map 4
D1. Tel 33 11 67 00.
w houseofamber

Magasin du Nord
(See Department Stores)

Peter Hertz
Købmagergade 34.
Map 3 C1.Tel 33 12 22 16.
w phertz.dk/en

Royal Shopping

By Malene Birger
Antonigade 10. Map 3 C1.
Tel 35 43 22 33.
w bymalenebirger.com

Georg Jensen
(See Jewellery)

Illum
(See Department Stores)

Illums Bolighus
(See Design and Interior
Decoration)

Heart Made
Pilestræde 45. Map 3 C1.
Tel 33 38 08 80.
w heartmade.dk

Kjaer & Sommerfeldt
Gammel Mønt 4. Map 1
C5. Tel 70 15 65 00.
w kogs.dk

Magasin du Nord
(See Department Stores)

Royal Copenhagen
Amagertorv 6. Map 3 C1.
Tel 33 13 71 81.
w royalcopenhagen.com

Urban Factory
Store Regnegade 2. Map
1 C3. Tel 33 91 70 75.

Markets

Thorvaldsens Plads Antique Market
Bertil Thorvaldsens Plads
2 (in front of Thorvaldsens
Museum). Map 3 C2.
Open May–Oct: Fri & Sat

Torvehallerne København
Frederiksborggade 21.
Map 1 B5. Tel 70 10 60 70.
w torvehallernekbh.dk

Copenhagen Street Food
Hal 7 & 8 Papirøen,
Trangravsvej 14. Map 4 F4.
Tel 33 93 07 60.
w copenhagen-
streetfood.dk

Art and Antiques

Bruun Rasmussen
Bredgade 32. Map 2 E5.
Tel 88 18 11 11.
w bruun-rasmussen.dk

Dansk Møbelkunst
Aldersrogade 6C. Tel 33
32 38 37. w dmk.dk

Green Square
Strandlosvej 11B.
Tel 32 57 59 59.
w greensquare.com

Klassik
Bredgade 3. Map 2 D5. Tel
33 33 90 60. w klassik.dk

Lysberg
Bredgade 77. Map 2 E4.
Tel 33 14 47 87.

Royal Copenhagen
(See Royal Shopping)

Specialist Shops

A.C. Perch's Thehandel
Kronprinsensgade 5. Map
3 C1. Tel 33 15 35 62.
w perchs.dk

Bering Flowers
Landemærket 12. Map 1
C5. Tel 33 15 26 11.
w beringflowers.com

Lagkagehuset
Torvegade 45. Map 4 D2.
Tel 32 57 36 07.
w lagkagehuset.dk

Meyers Bakery
Store Kongensgade 46.
Map 2 D5. Tel 25 10 75 79.
w meyersmad.dk

Sømods Bolcher
Nørregade 36B. Map 1 B5.
Tel 33 12 60 46.
w soemods-bolcher.dk

Craft Beer

Jacobsen Brewhouse
Gamle Carlsberg Vej 11,
Vesterbro. Tel 33 27 12 82.
w visitcarlsberg.com

Mikkeller Barrel Room
Refshalevej 169B, København. Tel 51 25 61 65.
w mikkeller.dk

Nørrebro Bryghus
Ryesgade 3, 2200 København. Tel 35 30 05 30.
w noerrebrobryghus.dk

ENTERTAINMENT IN COPENHAGEN

Copenhagen offers a seasonal range of entertainment. In summer you can find locals and visitors outside, strolling through Tivoli gardens, enjoying nostalgic rides or watching world-class concerts. Other options include enjoying a performance at the Copenhagen Jazz Festival, watching open-air theatre, and packing a picnic and cycling to the nearest urban beach. In autumn, cultural events such as CPH PIX Film Festival fill the agenda, while winter sees the Det Kongelige Teater and Opraen put on an impressive programme of theatre, dance and opera, and Tivoli offers a wonderfully festive Christmas market for all ages. Come spring, museums such as SMK and Louisiana launch cutting-edge exhibits. The annual opening of Tivoli in April marks the official end of winter. For more information about entertainment across Denmark, see pp280–81.

Stylish and modern interiors at the DR Koncerthuset

Practical Information

The first place to look for up-to-date information is the free magazine *Copenhagen This Week* (which despite its name comes out monthly) for the latest news on cultural events and club listings. It also has its own website: www.ctw.com.

Booking Tickets

Tickets for theatre, opera, concerts, festivals and sport events can be booked via **Billetnet**, by phone, online, or at a post office. The **Royal Theatre/Opera Box Office** on Kongens Nytorv opens at 4pm for the sale of half-price tickets for that day's performances. Get there early, as queues can be long. Under-25s and over-65s are eligible for half-price tickets when booking for shows more than a week in advance.

Cinema tickets tend to be cheaper for matinee and weekday performances; these can be booked online at www.biobooking.dk.

Opera and Classical Music

Opera fans should not miss a performance of the Royal Opera at the striking **Operaen** *(see p93)* which also hosts classical music concerts. From early June until late August, **Det Kongelige Teater** (The Royal Theatre) has an open-air stage Ofelia Beach, on the waterfront outside Skuespilhuset. It hosts free cultural events, including opera performances by the Royal Danish Opera Academy. For eight days in late July and early August, the **Copenhagen Opera Festival** organizes shows at several venues across the city. Many events are free and take place outside, while others are produced specially for children. National broadcaster Danmarks Radio's world-class **DR Koncerthuset** houses a number of concert halls, the largest of which can seat 1,800 people.

Those who enjoy classical music will be thrilled by the concerts given at the **Tivoli Koncertsal**. Throughout the summer season, Danish and international conductors and soloists join the 80-strong Tivoli Symphony Orchestra for the **Tivoli Festival**'s varied programme. During the winter months, the orchestra becomes the Copenhagen Philharmonic. For a less formal occasion, students from the Royal Danish Academy of Music give free concerts on Wednesday afternoons during spring and autumn in various venues. See www.onsdagskoncerter.dk for more details.

Ballet and Contemporary Dance

Det Kongelige Teater is home to the Royal Danish Ballet, whose season runs August–June, finishing with a free open-air performance in the grounds of Kastellet *(see p58)*.

The main venue for contemporary dance is **Dansescenen**, located in Northern Europe's largest centre for modern dance, the vast Dansehallerne complex, in the Carlsberg Brewery *(see p96)*. With a large stage (Store Carl) and the smaller Lille Carl, this venue is devoted to the best in Danish and international dance, as well as hosting a number of festivals to showcase young dance companies and choreographers. Dansehallerne is also home to **Dansk Danseteater**, an experimental dance company founded in 1981 by the British dancer and choreographer Tim Rushton. Every August the company presents its popular

Performers at the Copenhagen Jazz Festival

festival Copenhagen Summer Dance, with free performances in the colonnaded courtyard of the Copenhagen City Police headquarters.

Jazz Clubs and Live Music

International performers are regulars at the atmospheric **Copenhagen Jazzhouse** and at the legendary **Jazzhus Montmartre**. At **The Standard** you can experience an intimate jazz performance of the highest international level. Many bars host their own jazz sessions – like gritty **La Fontaine**, the oldest jazz venue in Copenhagen, which has live sessions every weekend. In July, the **Copenhagen Jazz Festival** fills the streets and venues all over the city, attracting some of the world's finest jazz musicians. Many of the 800 or so performances are free.

For blues fans, there is live music every night at **Mojo Blues Bar** and, in September, the **Copenhagen Blues Festival**.

For up-and-coming bands as well as international acts, **VEGA**, in Copenhagen's rejuvenated Vesterbro district, is a popular venue housed in a 1950s trade union building. The large hall (Store Vega) has seen many international bands, while the smaller room (Lille Vega) is ideal for more intimate, acoustic concerts. A great place to see the best young indie bands is **Loppen**, in alternative Christiania.

Last but by no means least is **Tivoli** *(see pp80–81)*, where in summer, world-famous rock and pop acts perform on the open-air stage.

Nightlife Venues

Copenhagen's clubs start getting lively only after midnight, so many people head first to a pre-club bar, such as the trendy **Zoo Bar** or Ideal Bar in **VEGA**. **Rust**, in the vibrant Nørrebro district, has club nights from midweek on three floors; indie rock and hip hop dominate the live music, while in the basement DJs play indie, punk and electro. **Culture Box** is a purist techno club. The converted warehouses and cattle stalls of the former meat-packing district in Kødbyen come alive on weekend nights. The vast **KB3** attracts the hippest locals, as well as visiting DJs, to its dance nights.

For something completely different, head to **Wallmans Saloner**, where you can enjoy a seated dinner show with artists performing on different stages around the restaurant.

Theatre

Most theatre in Copenhagen is performed in Danish, and while there are a number of English-language theatre companies,

none have venues of their own. The best known of these is **London Toast**, whose pre-Christmas pantomime in Tivoli's Glassalen is a tradition.

Most of the drama performed by the Royal Danish Theatre is now staged at the company's playhouse Skuespilhuset *(see p75)*. Housed in an 1807 listed building in the Latin Quarter, **Københavns Musikteater** is a lively venue for experimental musical theatre and avant-garde opera.

Cinema

There are scores of cinemas in and around Copenhagen, ranging from art-house theatres to huge multiplexes. Most films are shown in their original language, with Danish subtitles.

To catch the latest block-busters, the big **Cinemaxx**, part of the Fisketorvet shopping centre down by the harbour, shows all the major releases on ten screens. The **Imperial** is used for all the Danish premieres. Around the corner, the **Dagmar** has a diverse programme and a pleasant atmosphere, while the independent **Empire Bio**, in a former locomotive factory, is popular with locals for its late-night shows.

To get away from the main-stream, the long-established **Grand Teatret**, with its repertoire of European films, and **Cinemateket**, which is attached to the Danish Film Institute, are traditional art-house cinemas. For off-circuit and low-budget films, try **Vester Vov Vov**, in the Vesterbro district, or the tiny **Gloria** on Rådhuspladsen.

Entrance to Cinemaxx, one of Copenhagen's main cinemas

Gay and Lesbian

Copenhagen is a city with a long tradition of openness and acceptance: the city's first gay bar, **Centralhjørnet**, opened its doors in the 1930s and is still going strong. Famed for its annual Gay Pride Parade in August and for Mix, a well-established gay, lesbian, bi-sexual and transgender film festival in October, the city has a stream of other events year-round, including the Sankt Hans midsummer bonfire and beach party on Amager Island in June.

The gay club, bar and restaurant scene in the city centre is concentrated in quite a small area, so everything is pretty much within walking distance. **Club Cristopher** is Copenhagen's biggest gay club, with several dance floors, resident as well as visiting DJs and an open bar. **Jailhouse** is a popular concept bar and restaurant with booths kitted out as prison cells and staff dressed in police uniforms. On Friday evenings, DJs and a good atmosphere are available at the lounge-style **Oscar Bar & Café**. Young gay men favour **Masken Bar**, where the shows span live music and drag. **Mens Bar** is for the leather-clad contingent. For the really late night scene, head on to the aptly named **Never Mind**, open daily until 6am, or the darker, dingier **Dunkel**, where closing time is when the manager feels like closing. **Café Intime** is a piano bar near Frederiksberg Have that attracts theatrical types.

For up-to-date listings of gay events in the city, see the **Copenhagen Gay Life** website.

Beaches

Clean and spacious harbour swimming pools, with beaches and sports activities, are a great summer feature and only a short walk from the centre of Copenhagen. The harbour area has been revitalised with apartments, hotels and restaurants and the water really is clean enough for swimming. The pools are open from June until early September. **Havnebadet**, just across the

Bright lights and rides at Tivoli amusement park

ramparts from Christianshavn at Islands Brygge, has five pools and a large grassy bathing "beach". The smaller **Copencabana** pool is by the Fisketorvet shopping centre and comes complete with sand beach and palm trees.

Further afield, the north end of **Bellevue Strand**, at Klampenborg, is a short train or bike ride from town. It's a gay-friendly place with a nudist area at the top end. **Amager Strandpark** (see pp100–101) on Amager Island is divided into two parts: an "urban" beach with a range of fitness activities, bars, food stalls, even a Bedouin tent; and a "wild" section with wide sandy beaches and small sand dunes. A lagoon between the island and the mainland has child-friendly shallow water.

Children's Entertainment

No child visiting Copenhagen should miss **Tivoli** amusement park (see pp80–81), which has enough rides and attractions to keep even the most demanding young person happy. **Bakken** (see p124) in a wooded area north of the city near Klampenborg, claims to be the oldest fun park in the world and has over 100 rides. **Zoologisk Have** (see pp96–7) is the city's zoo and includes a mini zoo for smaller children and a large play area. **Den Blå Planet** (see p99) allows children to see weird and wonderful marine life up close.

Several museums in or near Strøget are especially suitable

for children, including **Ripley's Believe It or Not!** (see p77), **Hans Christian Andersen's Wonderful World** and **Guinness World Records Museum** (see p73). These are all part of the same group, and it's possible to pay a joint entry price. There is also the **Experimentarium** (see pp98–9), a science-based museum with plenty of hands-on fun; or the chance to be dazzled by a 3D movie in the IMAX Space Theatre of the **Tycho Brahe Planetarium** (see p96). The **Nationalmuseet** (see pp88–9) has a separate children's wing, and families and children have their own exhibitions and guided tours at the **Statens Museum for Kunst** (see pp66–7).

Children's theatre is very popular in Denmark, with a number of international festivals held annually or bi-annually. Kids even have their own theatres, with child-size seats or centrally placed stages. **Zebu** in Amager has performances for kids aged one and upwards; most of them are virtually wordless.

Free puppet shows take place from June to mid-August at the **Marionet Teatret** at the foot of Kongens Have (see p62), a lovely green space in front of the fairytale Rosen-borg Palace. There are plenty of other playgrounds, including many in natural settings, like the one in Naturcenter Vestamager (see p101). The harbour swimming pools (see Beaches) have areas reserved for kids and events during July's summer holidays.

DIRECTORY

Booking Tickets

Billetnet
Tel 70 15 65 65.
W billetnet.dk

Royal Theatre/ Opera Box Office
Kongens Nytorv. **Map** 4 D1. W kglteater.dk

Opera and Classical Music

Copenhagen Opera Festival
W copenhagenopera festival.com/en

Det Kongelige Teater
August Bournonvilles Passage, Kongens Nytorv. **Map** 4 D1. Tel 33 69 69 69. W kglteater.dk

DR Koncerthuset
Emil Holms Kanal 20, Ørestad. Tel 35 20 62 62. W dr.dk/koncerthuset

Operaen
Ekvipagemestervej 10. **Map** 2 F5. Tel 33 69 69 69. W operahus.dk

Tivoli Festival
W tivolifestival.dk/en

Tivoli Koncertsal
Vesterbrogade 3. **Map** 3 A3. Tel 33 15 10 12. W tivoli.dk

Ballet and Contemporary Dance

Dansescenen
Pasteursvej 20. Tel 33 88 80 00. W dansehallerne.dk

Dansk Danseteater
Tel 35 39 87 87. W danskdanseteater. dk

Det Kongelige Teater
(See Opera and Classical Music)

Jazz Clubs and Live Music

Copenhagen Blues Festival
W copenhagenblues festival.dk

Copenhagen Jazz Festival
W jazz.dk

Copenhagen Jazzhouse
Niels Hemmingsens Gade 10. **Map** 3 C1. Tel 33 15 47 00. W jazzhouse.dk

Jazzhus Montmartre
Store Regnegade 19A. **Map** 1 C5. W jazzhusmontmartre. dk

La Fontaine
Kompagnistræde 11. **Map** 3 C1. Tel 33 11 60 98. W lafontaine.dk

Loppen
Bådsmandsstræde 43, Christianshavn. **Map** 4 E2. Tel 32 57 84 22. W loppen.dk

Mojo Blues Bar
Løngangstræde 21. **Map** 3 B2. Tel 33 11 64 53. W mojo.dk

Tivoli
(See Opera and Classical Music)

VEGA
Enghavevej 40. Tel 33 25 70 11. W vega.dk

Nightlife Venues

Culture Box
Kronprinsensgade 54. **Map** 1 C5. Tel 33 32 50 50. W culture-box.com

KB3
Kødboderne 3, Kødbyen. W kb3.dk

Rust
Guldbergsgade 8. Tel 35 24 52 00. W rust.dk

The Standard
Havnegade 44. **Map** 4 E1. Tel 72 14 88 08. W thestandardcph.dk

VEGA
(See Jazz Clubs and Live Music)

Wallmans Saloner
Wallmans Cirkusbygningen, Jernbanegade 8. **Map** 3 A2. Tel 33 16 37 00. W wallmans.dk

Zoo Bar
Sværtegade 6. **Map** 3 C1. Tel 33 16 37 00. W zoobar.dk

Theatre

Københavns Musikteater
Kronprinsensgade 7. **Map** 3 C1. Tel 33 32 55 56. W kobenhavns musikteater.dk

London Toast
Tel 33 22 86 86. W londontoast.dk

Cinemas

Cinemateket
Gothersgade 55. **Map** 1 C5. Tel 33 74 34 12. W dfi.dk/filmhuset

Cinemaxx
Kalvebod Brygge 59. **Map** 3 A5. Tel 70 10 12 02. W cinemaxx.dk

Dagmar
Jernbanegade 2. Tel 70 13 12 11. W nfbio.dk

Empire Bio
Guldbergsgade 29F. Tel 35 36 00 36. W empirebio.dk

Gloria
Rådhuspladsen 59. **Map** 2 A2–B2. Tel 33 12 42 92. W gloria.dk

Grand Teatret
Mikkel Bryggersgade 8. **Map** 3 B2. Tel 33 15 16 11. W grandteatret.dk

Imperial
Ved Vesterport 4. Tel 70 13 12 11. W nfbio.dk

Vester Vov Vov
Absalonsgade 5. Tel 33 24 42 00. W vestervovvov.dk

Gay and Lesbian

Café Intime
Allegade 25, Frederiksberg. Tel 38 34 19 58.

Centralhjørnet
Kattesundet 18. **Map** 3 B2. Tel 33 11 85 49. W centralhjornet.dk

Club Christopher
Knabrostræde 3. **Map** 3 B1. Tel 60 80 71 76. W clubchristopher.dk

Copenhagen Gay Life
W copenhagen-gay-life.dk

Dunkel
Vester Voldgade 10. **Map** 3 B2. Tel 33 14 13 30.

Jailhouse
Studiestræde 12. **Map** 3 B1. Tel 33 15 22 55. W jailhousecph.dk

Masken Bar
Studiestræde 33. **Map** 3 A1. Tel 33 91 09 37. W maskenbar.dk

Mens Bar
Teglgårdsstræde 3. **Map** 3 A1. Tel 33 12 73 03. W mensbar.dk

Never Mind
Nørre Voldgade 2. **Map** 3 A1. W nevermindbar.dk

Oscar Bar & Café
Rådhuspladsen 77. **Map** 3 B2. Tel 33 12 09 99. W oscarbarcafe.dk

Beaches

Bellevue Strand
Strandvejen 340, Klampenborg.

Copencabana
Kalvebod Brygge. **Map** 3 A5.

Havnebadet
Islands Brygge. **Map** 3 C3.

Children's Entertainment

Hans Christian Andersen's Wonderful World
Rådhuspladsen 57. Tel 33 32 31 31. W topattractions.dk

Marionet Teatret
Tel 33 12 12 29. W marionetteatret.dk

Zebu
Øresundsvej 4, Amager. Tel 38 77 38 77. W zebu.nu

STREET FINDER

The map references given for all of Copenhagen's sights, hotels, restaurants, bars, shops and entertainment venues included in this guide refer to the maps in this section. All major sights, famous historic buildings, museums, galleries, railway, bus, metro and suburban train stations have been marked on the map. Other features are indicated by symbols explained in the key below. The names of streets and squares contained on the map are given in Danish. The word *gade* translates as street; *plads* means square, *allé* translates as avenue and *have* means park or garden.

Key to Copenhagen Street Finder

Major sight	Police station
Place of interest	Church
Other building	Synagogue
M Metro station	Railway line
S S-tog station	Pedestrianized street
Railway station	
i Tourist information	**Scale of Maps 1–4**
A&E hospital	**1:11 500**

0 kilometres   1
0 miles   1

0 metres   200
0 yards   200

Street Finder Index

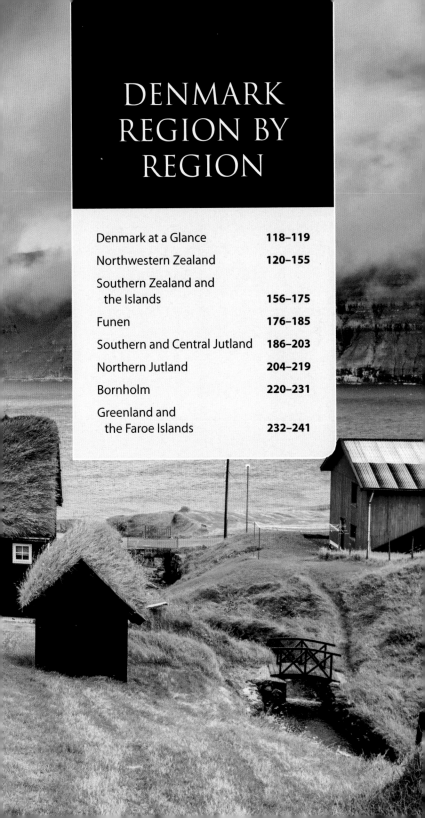

DENMARK REGION BY REGION

Denmark at a Glance

Denmark has a host of attractions for visitors. Small rural farms, rolling fields of wheat, lush woodlands and fine beaches are just some of the things that make the country especially popular with nature lovers. Those favouring outdoor activities will enjoy the many trails and cycle routes, many of which are themed and designed to take in some of the country's best historic churches, castles and palaces. For sightseers, there are Neolithic ruins, Viking remains and medieval villages to explore, while the various delights on offer at amusement parks such as Bakken or LEGOLAND® will thrill most children.

Northern Jutland has some beautiful beaches, as well as fine buildings such as Voergård Slot. The works on display in the Skagens Museum perfectly capture the shimmering Nordic light found in this part of the country.

Southern Jutland is famous for towns such as Ribe, which survived flood and fire, and retains some of the best-preserved medieval architecture in Denmark. The level to which the waters of the Ribe Å River rose during a flood in 1634 are marked on a wooden column.

Funen has been nicknamed the "Garden of Denmark". The charm of this island resides mainly in its scenery, which includes flower-filled fields and meadows, ancient castles and half-timbered houses.

◄ Charming village of Saksun on the Faroese island of Streymoy

Map labels:
Ska
Hirtshals
Frederiksh
Brønderslev
Hanstholm
Aalborg
Thisted
NORTHERN JUTLAND
(see pp204–19)
Nykøbing Mors
Hobro
Skive
Lemvig
Viborg
Randers
Holstebro
Silkeborg
Århus
Ringkøbing
Skanderborg
SOUTHERN & CENTRAL JUTLAND
(see pp186–203)
Horsens
Vejle
Varde
Kolding
Esbjerg
Odense
Ribe
FUNEN
(see pp176–
Haderslev
Faabor
Åbenrå
Tønder

BORNHOLM
(see pp220–31)

Bornholm is sometimes described as "Scandinavia in a nutshell" because it combines many typically Scandinavian features, such as rocky shores, picturesque villages and peaceful forests.

Northwestern Zealand is known for its royal castles and palaces. Among these is the magnificent Kronborg Slot on the Øresund coast, which was used by William Shakespeare as the setting for *Hamlet*. The castle now contains a museum.

Grenå

ltoft

Helsingør

Hillerød

Holbæk

Copenhagen
(København)

andborg

NORTHWESTERN
ZEALAND
(see pp120–55)

Roskilde

Køge

Slagelse

Ringsted

yborg

Næstved

dborg

SOUTHERN ZEALAND
& THE ISLANDS
(see pp156–75)

Nakskov

Nykøbing F.

Rødbyhavn

Gedser

Copenhagen is Denmark's capital and its largest city. It has many sights, both modern and old, including the magnificent Marmorkirken, which offers splendid views from its grand dome *(see pp50–115)*.

Southern Zealand is a mix of farmland, woodland and glorious coastal scenery. There is much to see, including a 1,000-year-old Viking fortress at Trelleborg and the 12th-century Sankt Bendts Kirke, which is the oldest brick church in Denmark.

0 km   30
0 miles   30

NORTHWESTERN ZEALAND

Zealand is the largest of the Danish islands and has an area of 7,500 sq km (2,895 sq miles). On its eastern shore lies Copenhagen (*see pp50–115*) – the country's capital city as well as its cultural and commercial centre. Away from the city, there is much to enjoy, from mighty castles and historic towns to sandy beaches, rural villages and beautiful countryside.

The island's landscape is typical of the lowland regions: idyllic meadow scenery broken here and there by beech forests and coastal fjords that cut deep into the land. Much of the region's wildlife can be seen around Arresø, Denmark's largest lake.

Most of the port towns were once Viking settlements. A reconstructed 10th–11th-century Viking camp can be visited in Trelleborg, while Viking ships can be seen at Roskilde's Viking Ship Museum. A visit to Sagnlandet Lejre, an open air tourist attraction with hands-on, authentic activities from both Iron Age and Viking eras offers a glimpse into the past, as do the Viking plays staged at Frederikssund.

Northwestern Zealand has played an important part in the history of Denmark. Lejre was one of the first centres of Danish administration; later on this function was assumed by Roskilde, which in 1020 became a bishopric and the capital of Denmark. This lasted until 1443 when the role of the country's capital was taken over by Copenhagen. Traditionally, this area has been favoured by wealthy Danes and some of the most impressive royal castles can be found here including Kronborg, Fredensborg and Frederiksborg. In addition, there are a variety of more modest establishments that make for an informative visit, such as Ermitagen, a royal hunting lodge a short way west of Klampenborg.

Hundested's popular beach

◄ Neptune's Fountain, Frederiksborg Slot, symbolizing Denmark's power in the 17th century

Exploring Northwestern Zealand

Most visitors to Zealand never stray beyond the limits of Copenhagen. There are, however, many other parts of the island that are not to be missed. The list of sacral buildings includes Roskilde Domkirke (Cathedral) and Vor Frue Kirke, in Kalundborg, a 12th-century church with five spires. The region also has several areas that are conducive to carefree holidays. The northern shores, washed by Kattegat's waters, are famous for their beautiful sandy beaches, while the forests, criss-crossed with a network of trails, are perfect for cyclists and hikers.

A statue of Esbern Snare, 12th-century founder of Kalundborg

Getting Around

Denmark's capital, served by Copenhagen International Airport, is a good starting point for exploring Zealand. Central Station in Copenhagen is the island's main railway hub. Northwestern Zealand has a well-developed network of motorways and major roads, which make getting around by car straightforward.

Havnebjen ODSHERRED

35

Sejerø

Sejerø Bugt

225

Asnæs

34 DRAGSHOLM

Hørve

RØSNÆS

Ulstrup **32**

Saltbæk Vig

33 SVINNINGE

155

KALUNDBORG **31**

23

Asnæs

Svebølle   Jyderup

NØRRE JERNLØ MØL

23

22

225

Tissø

Gørlev 255

Stenlil

Dianalund

Høng

225

Bj

22

E20 SORØ **2**

TRELLEBORG

30

Slagelse

STOREBÆLT BRIDGE

29

27 TÅRNBORG

22

Næstved

Odense **28** KORSØR

265

Key

━━━ Motorway
━━━ Major road
╌╌╌ Minor road
━━━ Scenic route
╌━╌ Main railway
──── Minor railway
▬▬▬ Regional border

Roskilde Domkirke's impressive nave

For hotels and restaurants in this area see pp250–51 and pp266–8

Sights at a Glance

1. Jægersborg Dyrehave
2. Bakken
3. Frilandsmuseet
4. Rungstedlund
5. *Louisiana Museum pp126–7*
6. *Helsingør pp128–9*
7. *Kronborg Slot pp130–31*
8. Hornbæk
9. Gilleleje
10. Fredensborg Slot
12. *Frederiksborg Slot pp136–7*
13. Grønnesse Skov
14. Hundested
15. Nordskoven
16. Jægerspris Slot
17. Frederikssund
18. Selsø Slot
19. Skibby
20. *Roskilde pp144–7*

21. Lejre
22. Ledreborg Slot
23. Holbæk
24. Tveje Merløse Kirke
25. Nørre Jernløse Mølle
26. Sorø
27. Tårnborg
28. Korsør
29. Storebælt Bridge
30. Trelleborg
31. Kalundborg
32. Røsnæs
33. Svinninge
34. Dragsholm

Tours

11. Esrum Sø and Arresø
35. Odsherred

Stately Dutch Renaissance entrance to Frederiksborg Slot

For keys to symbols *see back flap*

❶ Jægersborg Dyrehave

Road map: F4. 🚇 🚌

The beech forests and parkland that cover an area between the motorway running from Copenhagen towards Helsingør and the shore of the Øresund (Sound) is a favourite place for weekend forays out of Copenhagen. This area, which is criss-crossed with paths and cycle routes, was established as a royal hunting ground in 1669. The park still supports a herd of some 2,000 deer. A good vantage point from which to view them is the Ermitagen hunting lodge at the centre of the park, which was built in 1736 for Christian VI.

Among the park's other attractions are Bakken amusement park *(see below)*, Kirsten Pils Kilde (a holy spring that was a pilgrimage destination in the 16th century) and, nearby, Bellevue (one of the area's best beaches). Horse-drawn carriages offer rides through the park and there is also a golf course and a horse-racing track just to the south of Dyrehaven.

Ermitagen hunting lodge

❷ Bakken

Road map: F4. Dyrehavevej 62. Ⓢ Klampenborg. **Tel** 39 63 35 44. **Open** Apr–Aug. Opening hours vary; consult the website before visiting. 🚇 🌐 **bakken.dk**

Bakken was founded in 1583 and is considered to be the world's oldest amusement park. Located just a short way out of Copenhagen, it is on

One of the many rides to be enjoyed at Bakken

the edge of the Jægersborg Dyrehave deer park.

The present amusement park has 100 or so rides, including rollercoasters and merry-go-rounds, as well as circus shows and a cabaret-style revue. There are 40 cafés and restaurants on site, although people can bring their own supplies for a picnic. Entrance to the park is free though rides must be paid for. Bakken opens on 1 May and closes on 31 August; both occasions are cause for a huge motorcycle parade up to the park from north Copenhagen.

❸ Frilandsmuseet

Road map: F4. Kongevejen 100, 2800 Lyngby. 🚇 🚌 **Tel** 41 20 64 55. **Open** May–Oct: 10am–4pm Tue–Sun (Jul–mid-Aug: to 5pm). 🚇 🌐 **natmus.dk/frilandsmuseet**

This open-air museum, founded in 1897, contains virtually every kind of Danish country dwelling imaginable. Originally situated near Rosenberg Slot in Copenhagen, it was relocated to its present site in 1901 and is now run as part of the Nationalmuseet. Over 100 buildings are arranged into 40 groups and include many examples of rural architecture from cottages to grand manor houses, many of which are furnished and decorated in keeping with the period in which they were built. Visitors should allow a day to look round the collection, which includes fishermen's cottages,

windmills, peasant huts, a post mill (still with working sails) and a smithy (kitted out with irons and a hearth). Many of the staff dress in traditional costume and demonstrate such fading arts as turning clay pots and weaving cloth. The ticket also allows entry to Brede Værk, by the northern entrance of Frilandsmuseet. This textile mill, which closed in 1956, is preserved as an industrial village complete with cottages, a school, an "eating house" and the owner's country house.

A meticulously reconstructed house interior, Frilandsmuseet

❹ Rungstedlund

Road map: F4. Rungsted Strandvej 111. 🚇 🚌 **Tel** 45 57 10 57. Karen Blixen Museum: **Open** May–Sep: 10am–5pm Tue–Sun; Oct–Apr: 1–4pm Wed–Fri, 11am–4pm Sat–Sun. 🚇 🌐 **karen-blixen.dk**

Made famous by Karen Blixen, author of *Out of Africa*, Rungstedlund is the author's birthplace and was where she grew up and wrote most of her works under the pen name Isak Dinesen.

Karen Blixen's house was built around 1500 and was first used as an inn. In 1879 her father bought the property. It is now maintained by a foundation established by the writer, and in 1991 was converted into a museum devoted to Blixen's life and work. The rooms remain little changed from the period when she lived here, and manuscripts, photographs and personal belongings are on display. Blixen's grave is in the surrounding park.

Karen Blixen

Karen Blixen was born in 1885. The most colourful period in the Danish writer's life was her stay in Africa. Blixen left for Kenya at the age of 28 with her Swedish husband, Baron Bror von Blixen-Finecke, to establish a coffee plantation. While in Kenya she wrote *Seven Gothic Tales,* a collection of stories that launched her career. Safari expeditions, the raptures and miseries of her affairs, the breakdown of her marriage and the eventual failure of the plantation are all themes of her best-known work, *Out of Africa,* which established her reputation. The author returned to Rungsted in 1931 and lived here until her death in 1962. Among Blixen's other famous stories is *Babette's Feast,* which was made into a film in 1987.

Karen Blixen's House
Only part of the original house is still standing; two wings burned down when Blixen was 13 years old.

Blixen's Grave
The park behind the house contains a beech tree, with a modest gravestone underneath. This is the final resting place of Karen Blixen, who died at the age of 77.

African Room
Displayed in the room are Masai shields and spears as well as other mementos brought back from Africa.

Karen Blixen
Karen von Blixen-Finecke was also known by her pen name Isak Dinesen. Other pen names she wrote under were Tania Blixen, Osceola and Pierre Andrézel.

The Film Version
The screen version of *Out of Africa* stars Robert Redford and Meryl Streep. It was directed by Sydney Pollack (above) and departs markedly from the novel.

Out of Africa
Out of Africa was first published in 1937. It was originally written by the author in English and then translated by Blixen herself into Danish. The cover seen here is of the rare first Danish edition.

❺ Louisiana Museum

This striking museum was established in 1958 to house a collection of modern Danish art. The museum's remit has expanded considerably since then and the collection now concentrates on modern American and European paintings, graphic art and photography. The location and architecture are equally impressive – light-filled galleries form a semi-circle round a 19th-century villa, and open out onto a tranquil sculpture park offering stunning views of the Øresund. Among the many artists represented here are Giacometti, Henry Moore, Picasso and Warhol.

★ **Big Thumb** (1968)
The French artist César was fascinated by the shape of his thumb. This bronze image is 185 cm (73 inches) high.

L'Homme qui marche I (1961) This edition of Alberto Giacometti's Walking Man was one of the original six versions that had been created by the artist, and is one of his most famous works.

Sculpture garden

Exit

★ **Vénus de Meudon** (1956)
This work by the French sculptor and painter Jean Arp depicts a woman's body reduced to its simplest form.

Asger Jorn Room
This gallery is dedicated to the abstract works of Asger Jorn (1914–73), an important figure in 20th-century Danish art.

Main entrance

Key

▨ Exhibition space

☐ Cinema

▨ Giacometti collection

☐ Children's wing

NORTHWESTERN ZEALAND | 127

VISITORS' CHECKLIST

Practical Information
Road map: F4. Humlebæk Gl. Strandvej 13. **Tel** 49 19 07 19.**Open** 11am–10pm Tue–Fri, 11am–6pm Sat, Sun & hols.
W **louisiana.dk**

Transport
Humlebæk.

Café
On sunny days you can eat outside, enjoying coastal views and the works in the sculpture garden.

Gleaming Lights of the Souls (2008)
One of the most popular exhibits in the museum, Yayoi Kusama's installation consists of a small space which is covered with reflecting surfaces and hundreds of lamps, giving it a look of the night sky.

Two Piece Reclining Figure No. 5 (1963–64)
This Henry Moore bronze is in the sculpture garden, in keeping with the artist's intention to blend the female figure with the landscape.

The Graphics Wing, opened in 1991, was built underground to protect its displays from daylight.

Ground floor

★ South Wing
The south wing of the museum was added in 1982 and is half buried in a hillside facing the Øresund. It houses temporary and special exhibitions.

Gallery Guide
Single-storey galleries are connected by a corridor to the south wing and underground galleries. Works are on rotation apart from a room devoted to Giacometti and Japanese artist Kusama. A children's wing has workshops, art materials and computers for kids and their families.

6 Helsingør

Helsingør owes its prosperity to its location on the sound that links the North Sea with the Baltic. The town was a centre of international shipping during the 1400s, when Erik of Pomerania levied a tax on every ship passing through its local waters. In 1857 the dues were abolished, causing a temporary economic decline in the town's fortunes. This downturn was reversed in 1864 with the opening of a railway line and ferry services to Sweden. Today, most people visit Helsingør to see Kronborg Slot *(see pp130–31)*, a late-16th-century castle that was used by William Shakespeare as the setting for *Hamlet*.

Old apothecary on display in the town museum

Exploring Helsingør

When sightseeing in Helsingør it is a good idea to start with a visit to the Carmelite Monastery and the Municipal Museum, and then continue with a walk along Biergegade promenade, turning occasionally into side streets (Stengade in particular). Further south is the tourist information centre in Havnepladsen and, a little further on, the ferry terminal.

Gothic cloisters surrounding the Karmeliterklosteret's courtyard

🏠 Karmeliterklosteret Sankt Mariæ Kirke

Sankt Anna Gade 38. **Tel** 49 21 17 74. **Open** mid-May–mid-Sep: 10am–3pm Tue–Sun; mid-Sep–mid-May: 10am–2pm Tue–Sun. 🅿 🆆 **sctmariae.dk**

This Gothic building once belonged to the Carmelites and was erected in the second half of the 15th century. It is considered to be one of the best-preserved medieval monasteries anywhere in Scandinavia and was described by H.C. Andersen as "one of the most beautiful spots in Denmark". Among its many features are the chapterhouse with its barrel vault and the "Bird Room" decorated with ornithological frescoes. Christian II's mistress, Dyveke, who died in 1517, is believed to be buried in the grounds.

🏛 Helsingør Bymuseum

Sankt Anna Gade 36. **Tel** 49 28 18 00. **Open** noon–4pm Sun–Fri, 10am–2pm Sat.

The building that currently houses the town museum was erected by friars from the neighbouring monastery, who used it as a hospital for sailors arriving at the local harbour. Some of the instruments once used by the friars for brain surgery in the hospital are on display together with other exhibits relating to the town's past including a model of Kronborg Slot as it was in 1801. Visitors to the museum can also learn about the origin of the region's name: Øresund refers to the levy demanded by Erik of Pomerania which translates as "Penny Sound" (an "øre" is a Danish penny, and "sund" is Danish for "channel" or "sound").

🏙 Axeltorv

Helsingør's main square has a number of restaurants and bars. On Wednesday and Saturday mornings there is a colourful local market here that sells flowers, vegetables, fresh fish, handicrafts, cheese and souvenirs.

The statue in the centre depicts Erik of Pomerania – the Polish king and nephew of Margrethe I who occupied the throne of Denmark between 1397 and 1439. Following the break-up of the Kalmar Union and his subsequent dethronement in 1439 in favour of Christoffer III of Bavaria, the ex-monarch moved to the Swedish island of Gotland. Here, he began to occupy himself with piracy and he is sometimes referred to as "the last Baltic Viking".

In his old age Erik returned to Pomerania and is buried in the Polish seaside town of Darlowo. One legend has it that Darlowo's castle still

Monument to Erik of Pomerania in Axeltorv

contains hidden treasure plundered from Denmark.

🏚 Stengade

Helsingør's medieval quarter includes Stengade, a pedestrianized street that is linked by various alleyways to Axeltorv. Many of the colourful half-timbered houses once belonged to merchants and ferrymen and date from the 17th and 18th centuries. Oderns Gård, at Stengade 66, was built around 1460.

⛪ Sankt Olai Kirke

Sankt Anna Gade 12. **Tel** 49 21 04 43. **Open** May–Aug: 10am–4pm Mon–Fri; Sep–Apr: 10am–2pm Mon–Fri. 🅿

This building was consecrated around 1200 and served for centuries as a parish church. It was elevated to the rank of cathedral in 1961. Numerous elaborate epitaphs can be seen commemorating the many rich merchants and distinguished citizens of Helsingør who are buried here. The church's present-day appearance dates from 16th-century modifications

Statue of the Virgin Mary, Skt Olai's Kirke

when it also acquired its current furnishings. Among its most precious possessions are a 15th-century Gothic crucifix, a Renaissance pulpit (1568) and a carved wooden altar.

🏛 Museet for Søfart

Ny Kronborgvej 1. **Tel** 49 21 06 85. **Open** Jul & Aug: 10am–5pm daily; Sep–Jun: 11am–5pm Tue–Sun. 🅿 ♿ 📷 🖥
w mfs.dk

The spectacular Maritime Museum of Denmark was built around an old dry dock in front of Kronborg Castle by the internationally acclaimed architecture company BIG – Bjarke Ingels Group.

Leaving the over 60-year-old dock walls untouched, the galleries are located below ground and arranged in a continuous loop around the dry dock walls, making the dock the centrepiece of the exhibition. Visitors can experience the scale of ship building, and follow the sloping bridges down to an underground maritime world that traces the story of Denmark as one of the world's leading shipping nations.

VISITORS' CHECKLIST

Practical Information
Road map: F4. 🏙 60,000.
ℹ Havnepladsen 3. Tel 49 21 13 33. **w** visitnorthsealand.com

Transport
🚉 Helsingør.

🦑 Øresundakvariet

Strandpromenaden 5. **Tel** 35 32 19 70. **Open** Jun–Aug: 10am–5pm daily; Sep–May: 10am–4pm Mon–Fri, 10am–5pm Sat & Sun. 🅿
w oresundsakvariet.ku.dk

In addition to a colourful collection of tropical fish from around the world, Helsingør's aquarium contains many species taken from the waters of the Øresund (Sound). These local varieties include Baltic jellyfish and seahorses.

A model ship at the Maritime Museum

Helsingør Town Centre

① Karmeliterklosteret
② Helsingør Bymuseum
③ Axeltorv
④ Stengade
⑤ Sankt Olai Kirke
⑥ Museet for Søfart
⑦ Øresundakvariet

0 metres 300
0 yards 300

For keys to symbols *see back flap*

❼ Kronborg Slot

Hamlet's "Castle of Elsinore" was originally built by Erik of Pomerania in the early 15th century. It was remodelled by Frederik II and later by Christian IV but still retains an eerie quality that makes it perfect for the many productions of Shakespeare's play performed here. Among the most impressive rooms are the 62-m (203-ft) Great Hall, the King's Chamber, which has a ceiling painted by the Dutch artist Gerrit van Honthorst, and the "Lille Sal" containing 16th-century silk tapestries by the Flemish painter Hans Knieper. The castle was added to UNESCO's World Heritage List in 2000.

Exterior
Originally constructed using red brick, in 1580 the castle was remodelled on the orders of Frederik II and faced with attractive sandstone.

Viking Chief
The dungeons contain a sleeping statue of Holger Danske, a Viking chief. According to legend he will wake up should Denmark find itself in peril.

★ **Ballroom**
Once the longest hall in northern Europe, it was completed in 1582 and is decorated with paintings from Rosenborg Slot. The chandeliers date from the 17th century.

Hamlet

Shakespeare probably never visited Kronborg, but it is here that he set one of his best-known plays. The prototype for the fictional Danish prince was Amleth, whose story is recounted by the 12th-century Danish chronicler Saxo Grammaticus in his *Historia Danica* (Danish History). Shakespeare may have encounted this classic tale of murder and revenge via Francois de Belleforest's *Histoires Tragiques* (Tragic Histories), published in 1570. A festival is held in the castle each year in August during which *Hamlet* and other works by Shakespeare are performed.

★ King's Tapestries
The "small hall" has seven tapestries depicting Danish kings with verses describing their various achievements.

VISITORS' CHECKLIST

Practical Information
Road map: F4. Kronborg 2C,
DK 3000, Helsingør.
Tel 49 21 30 78. Fax: 49 21 30 52.
Open Apr, May, Sep & Oct:
11am–4pm daily; Jun–Aug:
10am–5:30pm daily; Nov–Mar:
11am–4pm Tue–Sun.
W kongeligeslotte.dk

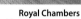

Royal Chambers
These rooms contain ornate ceiling decorations and marble fireplaces. At one time the walls would have been lined with gold-embossed leather.

★ Chapel
The chapel has a beautiful altar, oak benches with intricately carved ends, a royal balcony and an organ dating from the early 18th century.

KEY

① **Trumpeter's Tower**

② **King's Tower,** built during 1584–5, was also known as the "Turner's Tower" because one of its rooms housed Frederik II's turnery containing lathes.

③ **The North Wing** was completed in 1585. Its western section contained the castle offices.

④ **The Queen's Chambers** at the corner of the north wing had direct access to the chapel, via the east wing.

⑤ **The Pigeon Tower** housed birds that were used for sending important royal messages.

Clean sandy beaches of Hornbæk

❽ Hornbæk

Road map: F4. 🚌 🚃 ℹ️ Vestre
Stejlebakke 2A. **Tel** 49 70 47 47.
🌐 **visitnorthsealand.com**

The northern shore of Zealand
is famous for its pleasant sandy
beaches, clean water and the
small town of Hornbæk, which
has for years been a favoured
resort. A large number of
visitors come from Copenhagen,
many of whom have built
holiday homes here. In
summer the resort fills
with holiday-makers
enjoying various
outdoor pursuits,
including sailing
and swimming.

Environs
Esrum, situated
southwest of
Hornbæk, is
famous mainly for its Cistercian
monastery, Esrum Kloster.
Founded in 1151, it was regarded
as one of the most important
monasteries in Denmark during
the Middle Ages. Its prominence
was acknowledged even by
the monarchy: in 1374 Queen
Helvig, wife of Valdemar IV,
was buried here. Even the fires
that plagued the establishment
(in 1194 and 1204) did not
prevent the monastery from
becoming one of the largest
buildings in Scandinavia. During
the Lutheran Reformation in
the 16th century much of the
church was demolished and
the materials were used to build
Kronborg Slot (see pp130–31).

Former Cistercian
monastery buildings

What remained of the buildings
passed into the hands of the
monarch and the premises
were used first as a hunting
base and later as warehouses
before being turned into
army barracks. In the 20th
century they were used as
offices, as a post office and
then as an orphanage. During
World War II they became an
air-raid shelter and a fireproof
store for valuable documents
brought here from the National
Archives, and for the Royal
Library collection. This
chequered history
came to an end
when a decision
was reached to
renovate the
ancient walls
and in 1997 the
former mon-
astery opened
to visitors. Its main building
now houses an exhibition
devoted to the Cistercian
order while the vaults have
been transformed into a café.
Also open to visitors is the
herb garden, where medicinal
plants are grown and used, as
they once were when the
monastery flourished. Some
of the plants are used to
produce a flavoured beverage,
which is on sale in the shop.
Not far from the monastery is
Esrum Møllegard, a 400-year-
old mill. The mill was first
used to grind grain, and
later to generate electricity.
Today, it houses a centre for
environmental awareness.

❾ Gilleleje

Road map: F4. 🚏 6,000. 🚌
ℹ️ Peter Fjelstrup Vej 12. **Tel** 49 21 13
33. 🌐 **visitnorthsealand.com**

The northernmost town in
Zealand is also one of the oldest
Danish fishing ports and
contains the island's largest
harbour. From historical records
it has been established that the
local inhabitants were engaged
in fishing here as early as the
mid-14th century. Today,
Gilleleje is an attractive town
with thatched houses, a busy
harbourside fishing auction and
a colourful main street that has
been turned into a promenade.
Rising above the fisherman's
cottages is the town's church –
Gilleleje Kirke. During the
German occupation locals used
the church as a hiding place for
Danish Jews who were then
smuggled into neutral Sweden
aboard fishing boats under
cover of darkness.
Other places focus on
Gilleleje's history as a fishing
centre. At **Skibshallerne**,
fishing boats from several
centuries are on display; in the
same building is **Det Gamle
Hus**, an old fisherman's house
that illustrates the realities of
everyday life for a mid-19th-
century fishing family. A coastal
trail from the town centre leads
east to the Nakkehoved Østre
Fyr lighthouse. Built in 1772, it is
one of a very few coal-fuelled
lighthouses in the world to have
survived to this day. This historic
building is now open to visitors.

Nakkehoved Østre Fyr, a coal-fired
lighthouse near Gilleleje

Fishing boats in Gilleleje's harbour, the largest in Zealand

Environs

The Gilbjergstien is a 2.5-km (1.5-mile) foot- and cycle path leading from Vesterbrogade, in Gilleleje, all the way to Gilbjergshoved, Zealand's northernmost point. The path offers splendid views across the water to Sweden from the cliffs. En route you can admire the Gilbjergstenen rock, which has a natural seat and back support, and a monument to the Danish philosopher Søren Kirkegaard.

Skibshallerne/Det Gamle Hus
Hovedgade 49, Gilleleje. **Tel** 72 17 02 40. **Open** mid-Jun–mid-Aug: 11am–4pm Tue–Sun; mid-Aug–mid-Oct: 11am–4pm. 🅿 Includes a visit to the lighthouse.

⑩ Fredensborg Slot

Road map: F4. **Tel** 33 40 31 87. Palace, Chapel, Orangery and Herb Garden: **Open** July and 1st week of Aug: 1–4:30pm daily. 📷 compulsory; every 15 mins (duration about 35 mins). 🅿 Palace and Baroque Gardens: **Open** 9am–5pm daily. 🅆 **kongeligeslotte.dk**

Frederik IV decided to build Fredensborg Castle in order to commemorate the 1720 peace treaty between Denmark and Sweden at the end of the Nordic Wars (Fredensborg means "Palace of Peace"). The building was originally used as a hunting lodge. Nowadays the castle is one of the main residences of the Danish royal family and is often used to receive VIPs from all over the world. According to tradition, guests who spend the night at the palace must sign their name on a glass pane using a diamond pen.

The original design was modelled on French and Italian castles and the long list of contributors who influenced its final shape includes renowned architects such as Niels Eigtved, Lauritz de Thurah and Caspar Frederik Harsdorf. The present-day complex consists of 28 separate buildings. At its centre is the Dome Hall (Kuppelsalen), surmounted by a dome crowned with a lantern. The magnificent room is encircled by a gallery, which divides the hall into two levels. It is used for formal royal family occasions and also for entertaining special guests.

One of the most interesting rooms in the palace is Havesalen, or the Garden Room, which features a wide door leading to the castle gardens. Its ceiling is decorated with a painting by Hendrik Krock depicting

Fredensborg's gardens decorated with numerous statues

Denmark and Norway begging the Olympian gods for help against Sweden.

Fredenborg Slot's ornate Chinese Dining Room (Kinesisk Spisesalon) is another notable room. It is decorated in yellow and red and houses a collection of Chinese porcelain.

The palace garden was established in the 1760s, and contains a lane decorated with a sculpted group of 70 figures, created by J.G. Grund, of fishermen and farmers from Norway and the Faroe Islands. Plants sensitive to cold, including a 250-year-old myrtle shrub, are shielded from low temperatures in a greenhouse built in 1995.

Fredensborg Slot, used as a residence by the Danish royal family

⓫ A Tour Around Esrum Sø and Arresø

These beautiful lakes are the two largest in Denmark and attract a great many visitors, especially in summer. Gribskov, on the west bank of Esrum Sø, is a forested area where marked paths and bicycle trails lead through thick clusters of ancient beech and spruce trees. Arresø, to the east of Esrum Sø, is Denmark's largest lake and reaches depths of 22 m (72 ft). Ospreys and cormorants can occasionally be spotted diving for fish. As well as being perfect for anglers, bathers and enthusiastic sailors, a tour around the area takes in lush farmland, ancient church ruins, picturesque towns and historic medieval villages.

③ **Ramløse**
Situated on Arresø's north bank, the town's most interesting feature is its Dutch-style windmill (1908) that can be seen working on traditional "Mill Days".

② **Asserbo**
Scenic ruins surrounded by a wind-blown forest are all that remains of this former fortress, built in 1100 on the orders of Bishop Absalon.

① **Frederiksværk**
Frederiksværk, built alongside a canal, is Denmark's oldest industrial town. A museum in a former gunpowder factory has exhibits on the town's industrial past.

⑩ **Æbelholt Kloster**
This 12th-century Augustinian abbey was once a hospital. Today, as well as viewing the ruins, visitors can examine the museum's collection of surgical instruments.

⑤ **Esrum**

The restored build-ings of this former Cistertian monastery house a museum devoted to the community that lived here, giving visitors an idea of the monk's day-to-day life *(see p132)*.

④ **Annisse Nord**

Annisse Nord is a sleepy village but was strategically important for the surrounding area in medieval times; at that time numerous watchtowers were erected along the fjord.

Tips for Drivers

Length: about 100 km (62 miles).
Stopping-off points: There is a large choice of restaurants and accommodation in Fredensborg.
W **visitdenmark.com**
W **visitnorthsealand.com**

⑥ **Fredensborg Slot**

The castle gardens are arranged in a Baroque style and are open to the public all year round *(see p133)*.

Gilleleje

Langesø ●

Gurre Sø

Esrum Sø

Helsingør

Copenhagen

⑦ **Fredensborg**

This historic town has a long tradition of hunting and holds regular demon-strations of falconry.

Copenhagen

⑨ **Gribskov**

Growing along the undulating western shoreline of Esrum Sø, Gribskov is the second largest forest in the country.

Key

▦ Suggested route
▬ Scenic route
═ Other road
═ River, lake
 Viewpoint

0 km   2
0 miles   2

⑧ **Nødebo**

The tiny village of Nødebo is on the banks of Esrum Sø (left) and surrounded by Gribskov. The pretty village church is decorated with 15th-century frescoes.

For keys to symbols *see back flap*

⓬ Frederiksborg Slot

The first royal residence was constructed on this site by Frederik II in 1560. A fire in 1859 destroyed most of the castle, which may well have remained a ruin were it not for Carlsberg boss J C Jacobsen who restored the building and helped found a national history museum shortly after the fire. The museum now takes up 80 or so of the palace rooms. Jacobsen also donated many of his own paintings which, along with others, are arranged chronologically to chart Denmark's history. Period furnishings and some magnificent architecture help to conjure up a feel for the country's past.

★ Slotskirken
From 1671 until 1840 the castle chapel was used to crown Denmark's monarchs. Its ebony altar dates from 1606 and is the work of Jakob Mores, a German goldsmith.

★ Riddersalen
The Knights' Hall has a carved wooden ceiling. The gilded ornaments, a 19th-century black marble fireplace and intricate tapestries add to the splendour.

Audienssalen
The Audience Chamber was completed in 1688. Among the paintings lining the walls is a portrait of a proud-looking Christian V, depicted as a Roman emperor surrounded by his children.

Chapel Portal
The oak door, set within a sandstone portal in the shape of a triumphal arch, survived the fire of 1859 and looks as it would have done in Christian IV's day.

Queen Sophie's Room
During the reign of Christian IV this room was used by the king's mother. When the palace became a museum, it was hung with paintings associated with Frederik III.

VISITORS' CHECKLIST

Practical Information
Road map: F4. 3400 Hillerød, Slotsgade 1.
Tel 48 26 04 39.
Open Apr–Oct: 10am–5pm daily; Nov–Mar: 11am–3pm daily.
Baroque gardens: **Open** 10am–sunset daily.
W dnm.dk

The Royal Wing has a gallery of statues symbolizing the influence of planets on human life and is an excellent example of Dutch Mannerism.

Room 42
This example of over-blown Baroque is typical of the taste associated with Denmark's era of absolute monarchy *(see pp42–3)*. The bed with silk draperies was made in France in 1724.

Room 46
All the items in this room, such as this ornate wall clock, are in perfect accord with the colours and Rococo excess of the overall design.

Gardens
The castle gardens were established in the 1720s and restored in 1996. The carefully trimmed shrubs create a symmetrical pattern typical of a Baroque garden.

⓭ Grønnesse Skov

Road map: E4.

The ancient forest of Grønnesse Skov is about 5 km (3 miles) east of Hundested, on the shores of Roskilde Fjord. Archaeological excavations indicate that during the Neolithic era this area was one of the more important sites of early culture in Zealand and the site now attracts thousands of visitors every year.

One of the most important relics of Denmark's Neolithic past is an extraordinary burial chamber known as a dolmen. It is one of many such tombs in Denmark and consists of a huge flat stone resting on three chunky pillars. The dolmen is referred to locally as Carlssten ("Carl's Stone") and is one of the biggest and best preserved of its type anywhere in Denmark. It must be reached on foot but the forest car park is only a short distance away.

Carlssten, a prehistoric dolmen in Grønnesse Skov

⓮ Hundested

Road map: E4. 🚌 ℹ️ Havnegade 20. **Tel** 49 21 13 33.
🌐 visitnorthsealand.com

This small town lies on a slender peninsula. Its name translates literally as "dog's place" and derives from a species of local seal commonly known as a sea dog because of its canine-like barking. The main reason to come to Hundested is to take a look around **Knud Rasmussens Hus**, which is situated on a high cliff close to Spodsbjerg lighthouse. The house was built in 1917 by the intrepid Arctic explorer, Knud Rasmussen, and now houses a museum devoted to his life and travels. Close by is a monument to him erected in 1936 made of stones brought over from Greenland.

Environs

A short way northeast is Kikhavn, the oldest fishing village on the Halsnæs peninsula, which dates back to the 13th century. In the 18th century there were many small farms here, some of which were partly destroyed by a fire in 1793. The remaining farms and buildings have been preserved, and form a picturesque village. Kikhavn is also the starting point of a footpath, Halsnæsstien,

Knud Rasmussen's house, now a popular museum

that links the shores of Isefjord and Kattegat.

Another place worth visiting is Lynæs, just south of Hundested. The local church, built in 1901 from granite blocks, serves as a navigational guide for returning fishermen. A monument standing by the church commemorates those who lost their lives at sea.

🏛️ **Knud Rasmussens Hus**
Tel 47 72 06 05. **Open** Easter–Oct: 11am–4pm Tue–Sun. 🅿️
🌐 knudrasmus.dk

Kongeegen, believed to be the oldest living oak tree in Europe

⓯ Nordskoven

Road map: F4.

The peninsula that separates Roskilde Fjord from Isefjord contains one of Denmark's most beautiful beech forests. The forest has two sections, known as Fællesskoven and Studehaven. Running between them is a 15-km- (9-mile-) long bicycle trail with views over Roskilde Fjord. At its highest

Knud Rasmussen

Knud Rasmussen was born in 1879. Part Inuit himself, Rasmussen was fascinated by Inuit culture and language and resolved to become a polar explorer at an early age. He took part in his first scientific expedition in 1902 and soon began organizing them himself. In 1910, together with Peter Freuchen, he founded the Thule settlement in the north of Greenland. Between 1921 and 1924 Rasmussen completed a grand expedition from Greenland to the Bering Strait, covering 18,000 km (11,185 miles) by dog-sleigh. From each of his expeditions the explorer brought back many artefacts; most of these are now in the Nationalmuseet in Copenhagen (see pp88–9). In the course of his seventh expedition Rasmussen fell seriously ill. He died in 1933, aged 54.

The explorer's house, full of reminders of his expeditions

Statue of a deer in front of Jægerspris Slot

point, called Frederikshøj, is a hunting pavilion built by Frederik VII in 1875. A number of ancient trees can be found in the forest including three famous oaks: Kongeegen, Storkeegen and Snoegen, which have inspired many artists. Kongeegen, the most ancient of the three trees, is believed to be 1,500–1,900 years old. In 1973 its last bough broke away, leaving only the vast trunk, which has a circumference of 14 m (46 ft).

⑯ Jægerspris Slot

Road map: F4. ![i] Jægerspris Slot, Slotsgården 20. **Tel** 47 53 10 04. **Open** Easter–Oct: 11am–4pm Tue–Sun. ![park] Park: **Open** all year round. **W** kongfrederik.dk

This medieval castle, situated about 6 km (4 miles) west of Frederikssund, has been used by Danish royalty since the early 14th century and is open to the public. The first royal building, known as Abrahamstrup, still exists although it has been swallowed by the north wing of the present complex. A life-size statue of a deer standing before the entrance to the castle is by Adelgund Vogt, a pupil of Bertel Thorvaldsen.

In the mid-19th century Frederik VII made the palace his summer residence. After his death in 1863 the monarch's widow, Countess Danner,

turned part of the palace into a refuge for poor and unwanted girls. The centre became the first children's home in Denmark. A special exhibition illustrates the often austere way of life in an early 20th-century Danish orphanage.

Much of the house retains its royal character, and visitors can take a look at magnificent rooms arranged by Frederik VII. There is also an exhibition of archaeological finds reflecting one of Frederik VII's abiding passions.

The gardens stretching to the rear of the castle include Zealand's largest collection of rhododendrons; standing among them are 54 obelisks with busts of famous Danish personages. The tomb of countess Danner is also in the castle gardens. The forests around Jaegerspris offer walking and cycling opportunities.

⑰ Frederikssund

Road map: F4. ![] 15,700. ![]
![i] Havnegade 5A. **Tel** 47 31 06 85.
![] Viking Festival (late Jun–mid-Jul).
W visitfrederikssund.dk

This town was founded in 1655 on the orders of Frederik III. The choice of site was not accidental, as it overlooks the narrowest part of the Roskilde Fjord and was used for many years by boats crossing to the other side.

In the town centre is the **J F Willumsens Museum**. Willumsen (1863–1958), a prominent Danish Symbolist painter, donated his paintings, sculptures and drawings to Frederikssund on condition that a suitable building be erected to display them. The museum also contains works by other artists that were collected by Willumsen.

Frederikssund is primarily known, however, for its reconstructed Viking Village, located near the town's harbour. The village is open to visitors from April to October but the best time to visit is during the summer Viking Festival, when events are held that involve the whole town. The most popular are the evening Viking plays that feature more than 250 actors, many of them local residents and children; the final night is celebrated with a grand banquet.

▥ J F Willumsens Museum
Jenriksvej 4. **Tel** 47 31 07 73.
Open 10am–5pm Tue–Sun. ![]
W jfwillumsensmuseum.dk

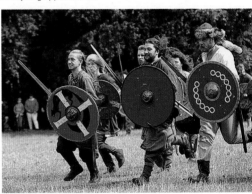

Danes dressed as Vikings during Frederikssund's summer festival

Selsø Slot, built in 1578

⑱ Selsø Slot

Road map: F4. ℹ️ Selsøvej 30A, 4050 Skibby. **Tel** 52 17 20 60. **Open** May–mid-Sep: 11am–4pm Tue–Sun. 📷
🌐 **selsoe.dk**

This property's history dates back to the 12th century. According to records, Bishop Absalon became interested in the site in about 1170 and by 1228 a sumptuous residence had been built here.

The present castle was built in 1578. It was reworked in 1734 and much of its original Renaissance style was replaced with Baroque details. The castle is now a museum and gives visitors an idea of what aristocratic life was like in the 1800s. The castle's stern, simple exterior hides a richer interior, including the "Grand Ballroom". With original marble panels and a decorated ceiling, it is used as a venue for classical music concerts. Wine-tasting sessions are held in the castle vaults. The castle church has an altarpiece dating from 1605.

The property owes much of its charm to its location on the banks of Selsø lake. A bird reserve established in the gardens is one of the premium places for birdwatching in Denmark. A viewing tower standing in the garden was built specifically for this purpose.

⑲ Skibby

Road map: F4. 🚌 ℹ️ Havnegade 5A, 3600 Frederikssund. **Tel** 47 31 06 85.
🌐 **visitfrederikssund.dk**

The main town of the peninsula between Roskilde Fjord and Isefjord, Skibby is known mainly for its early 12th-century church, which is decorated with some well-preserved frescoes. The oldest of these were found in 1855 in the Romanesque apses and date from the second half of the 12th century. Similar decorations can be found in other churches in the district, including some at nearby Dråby. In 1650 a manuscript, known as the *Skibby Chronicle*, was found buried behind the altar. The work, written in Latin, recounts the history of Denmark between 1046 and 1534. It is uncertain why the chronicle was found here. Its style points to the authorship of Paul Helgsen, a Carmelite monk and orator. Helgsen was a native of Helsingør, however, and since the work is unfinished, its discovery has provoked debate as to the fate of its author. Skibby's other claim to fame is as the location of Scandinavia's first nudist swimming pool.

Environs
Northeast of Skibby, in the town of Skuldelev, is a doll museum with a 6,000-strong collection. Also on display are antique baby carriages, dolls' prams and a working model railway from 1940 (runs from March to October).

⑳ Roskilde

See pp144–7.

Visitors trying out a dugout canoe at Sagnlandet Lejre

㉑ Lejre

Road map: F4. Sagnlandet Lejre: Slangealleen 2, 4320 Lejre. **Tel** 46 48 08 78. **Open** May–Jun: 10am–4pm Tue–Fri, 11am–5pm Sat & Sun; end Jun–mid-Aug: 10am–5pm daily. 📷
🌐 **sagnlandet.dk**

A reconstructed village that takes visitors back through 10,000 years of Danish history is the main attraction of Lejre, which is situated 8 km (5 miles) to the southwest of Roskilde. In summer Sagnlandet Lejre ("Land of Legends") is an authentic open air museum dedicated to Stone Age, Iron Age and Viking eras where museum staff,

Dråby Kirke, situated near Skibby

 The chapel at Frederiksborg Slot, with stunning decor dating back to Christian IV

Ledreborg Slot, surrounded by beautiful, well-kept gardens

dressed in the clothing of the period, show visitors how to use traditional tools and carry out chores such as chopping firewood and making clay pots.

The village is popular with children, especially in summer, when it is possible for them to take part in activities such as archery, dying clothes and paddling a dugout canoe. The centre also has a 19th-century cottage farm that re-creates the lives of Danish farmers of that period.

Lejre was one of the earliest centres of government in Denmark. Legend has it that it was the seat of a royal Stone-Age clan, the Skjoldungs, although the building shown to the visitors, once home of the supposed sovereign, is an 18th-century re-creation. It is quite likely, however, that the nearby gravemound dates from the Stone Age period. The **Lejre Museum** has displays on the Skjoldung clan and artifacts from Viking times, as well as from the Stone and Iron ages.

🏛 **Lejre Museum**
Orehøjvej 4B. **Open** Apr–Oct: 11am–4pm Tue–Sun (Nov–Mar: Sun only).

㉒ Ledreborg Slot

Road map: F5. Ledreborg Alle 2, 4320 Lejre. **Tel** 46 48 00 38. **Open** only for events. Park: **Open** 11am–4pm daily (all year round). 🚻 🎫 can be pre-booked in summer.
🌐 **ledreborg.dk**

Elegant on the outside and opulent on the inside, Ledreborg Slot is one of the foremost examples of Baroque architecture in northern Europe.

It was built in 1739 on the orders of Count Johan Ludvig Holstein. In 1745 this exclusive residence acquired a chapel, which until 1899 served as a parish church.

The palace is closed to the public, but the gardens are open and house Scandinavia's longest zipline course. The neatly trimmed hedges make it one of the most enchanting Baroque gardens in Scandinavia. The grounds host a lifestyle exhibition in May and an outdoor chamber music concert in August.

㉓ Holbæk

Road map: E4. 🏙 27,000. 🚉
ℹ Ahlgade 1C **Tel** 59 43 11 31.
🌐 **visitholbaek.com**

An important port, Holbæk is also the main commercial town for the area. It serves as a good starting point for people wishing to visit Øro island, which lies just 7 km (4 miles) away. The area has several bicycle trails, and Holbæk itself is popular with cyclists.

Holbæk was granted municipal privileges in the late 13th century, making it one of the oldest of Zealand's towns. At that time it was the site of a dynamic Dominican monastery, although the oldest surviving remains are those of a Franciscan monastery, which is located next to the Neo-Gothic Sankt Nicolaj Kirke in the medieval part of the town.

Not far from this church is **Holbæk Museum**, which consists of a dozen or so period houses dating from 1660 to 1867. Their interiors include typical items and furnishings from rural and urban dwellings of the 17th and 18th centuries. There is also a reconstructed grocery shop, a merchant's yard, café, toy shop and pottery exhibition. The tiny market square between the houses is a venue for numerous events staged during summer months, which often feature people dressed in period costumes.

Holbæk has some good local parks, such as Østre Anlæg and Bysøparken, which has a charming fountain. Just ouside the city is **Andelslandsbyen Nyvang**, an open-air museum that re-creates country life as it was from the 1870s to the 1950s.

🏛 **Holbæk Museum**
Klosterstræde 18. **Tel** 59 43 23 53. **Open** 10am–4pm Tue–Fri, noon–4pm Sun. **Closed** Jan. 🚻
🌐 **vestmuseum.dk**

🏛 **Andelslandsbyen Nyvang**
Oldvejen 25. **Tel** 59 43 40 30. **Open** mid-Apr–mid-Oct: 10am–4pm Tue–Thu, Sat & Sun. 🌐 **adlbn.dk**

Period interior in Holbæk Museum

⑳ Roskilde

Founded in the 10th century by the Vikings, Roskilde was Denmark's first capital. In AD 980 Harald I (Bluetooth) built Zealand's first church here, and from the 11th century it was a bishopric. In the Middle Ages Roskilde had a population of 10,000 and was one of the largest towns in northern Europe. When Erik of Pomerania moved the capital, the town lost much of its status. Still a thriving town, it is popular with tourists drawn to the cathedral and Viking ships, as well as the summer rock festival and modern museum of rock and pop culture, Ragnarock.

Exploring Roskilde

All of the town's attractions are within easy reach. The most prestigious streets, lined with shops and cafés, are Skomagergade and Algade. The Vikingeskibsmuseet (Viking Ship Museum) is by the harbour, while Ragnarock Museum is in Musicon, a short walk or bus ride south of the station.

Fountain in front of the town hall in Stændertorvet

⚲ Roskilde Domkirke
See pp146–7.

▦ Stændertorvet

This small square situated by the town's main promenade has for centuries been the heart of Roskilde. In the Middle Ages it was the site of fairs. Sankt Laurence, a Romanesque church, was demolished in the mid-16th century to provide more space for the growing market. A few remaining parts of the church can be seen today including the tower, which now adorns the town hall (built in 1884) and what remains of the church foundations. The foundations are open to the public and are in the town hall's vaults. In the square is a monument depicting Roar and his brother Helge. King Roar is often credited with the founding of Roskilde.

⚲ Roskilde Palace and the Museum of Contemporary Art

Stændertorvet 3. **Tel** 46 31 65 70. Art Museum: **Open** noon–4pm Tue–Sun (to 8pm Wed).
ⓦ samtidskunst.dk

Built in 1733 by the Danish architect Laurits de Thurah, this yellow Baroque palace is the former seat of Roskilde's bishops. It is linked to the neighbouring cathedral by the Arch of Absalon. Part of the palace houses the Museum of Contemporary Art (Museet for Samtidskunst), which organizes temporary exhibitions of Danish and foreign artists. Another wing is used by a local art association.

▥ Roskilde Museum

Sankt Ols Gade 18. **Tel** 46 31 65 29. **Open** 11am–4pm Tue–Sun. 🅿
ⓦ roskildemuseum.dk

The municipal museum in Roskilde is an excellent place for anyone interested in the town's history, and includes both permanent and changing exhibits. The museum also includes a building in Ringstedgade, Lützhøfts Købmandsgård, which is furnished in the style of a 19th century shop.

⚲ Roskilde Kloster

Sankt Peder Stræde 8. **Tel** 46 35 02 19. **Open** for tours only. 🗓 Easter & July: 11am & 2pm Wed (in Danish; book in advance for tours in English). 🅿
ⓦ roskildekloster.dk

In the Middle Ages Roskilde had about 20 churches and monasteries, not counting the cathedral. Their sacral functions ceased as the Reformation swept through the country in 1536. This brick-built monastery, which stands in its own grounds, was built in 1560 and, in 1699, became Denmark's first refuge for unmarried mothers from well-to-do families. It has some fine interiors including a chapel, and a banquet hall.

Hussar's uniform, Roskilde Museum

♣ Gråbrødre Kirkegård

The former cemetery, where prominent and wealthy citizens of the town were buried during the Middle Ages, is now used as a park and is located near the railway station. The station was built in 1847 to serve the Copenhagen–Roskilde line and is one of the oldest train stations in Denmark.

Brick monastery buildings of Roskilde Kloster

🏛 Hestetorvet

The landmark of the market square, used in medieval times for horse trading, are the three 5-m (16-ft) tall jars. Engraved on one of the jars are verses from a poem written by Henrik Nordbrandt, dedicated to Roskilde and to Margrete I. The jars' creator, Peter Brandes, intended them to symbolize life and death.

Roskilde Jars commemorating the city's 1,000-year anniversary

🏛 Vikingeskibsmuseet

Vindeboder 12. **Tel** 46 30 02 00. **Open** Jul & Aug: 10am–5pm daily; Sep–Jun: 10am–4pm daily. 🅿
W vikingeskibsmuseet.dk

About 1,000 years ago the ships now exhibited at the Viking Ship Museum were filled with stones

and sunk in the fjord in order to block the passage of enemy ships. In 1962 five of the vessels were recovered. Although they had been underwater for so long, they are in remarkably good condition and give a good indication of Viking boat-building skills. The largest of them is a 30-m (98-ft) long warship with the capacity to carry a crew of 70 to 80 Vikings. The best preserved is a 14-m-(46-ft-) long merchant ship, which sailed around the Baltic and Danish sounds. The other ships are a deep-sea trader, a longship and a fishing boat.

🏛 Ragnarock Museum for Pop, Rock & Youth Culture

Rabalderstræde 16, Musicon. **Tel** 46 31 68 54. **Open** 10am–5pm Tue, Fri–Sun, 10am–9pm Wed & Thu. 🅿
W museumragnarock.dk

Denmark's national rock museum opened in 2015 and is based in the Musicon quarter, a culture district that also includes a skate park, café and a modern dance theatre. Set in a striking gold cube, visitors enter the museum via a long red carpet, giving a feeling

VISITORS' CHECKLIST

Practical Information
Road map: F4. 🚗 50,000.
🛈 Stændertorvet 1. **Tel** 46 31 65 65. 🎵 Roskilde Rock Festival (late Jun–early Jul).
W visitroskilde.com

Transport
🚉 Roskilde.

of celebrity. The museum's range of interactive exhibits chart music's influence on youth culture from the 1950s onwards. Alongside temporary exhibits, the museum hosts several permanent shows, which explore fancultures and music genres, as well as the creation of dance-based music. Visitors are also invited to participate in a continuously growing digital choir.

Historic boat at Vikingeskibsmuseet

Roskilde Town Centre

① Roskilde Domkirke
② Stændertorvet
③ Roskilde Palace
④ Roskilde Museum
⑤ Roskilde Kloster
⑥ Gråbrødre Kirkegård
⑦ Hestetorvet
⑧ Vikingeskibsmuseet
⑨ Ragnarock Museum for Pop, Rock & Youth Culture

0 metres   400
0 yards   400

Roskilde Domkirke

The twin towers of this magnificent brick cathedral, begun in the 12th century on the orders of Bishop Absalon, are a landmark of Roskilde. The cathedral is an organic mix of styles. For centuries it was used as the burial site of Danish monarchs, 39 of whom are interred here. The remains of Harald I (Bluetooth), a 10th-century Viking king, are said to be inside one of the columns to the side of the main altar. In view of its historic value the cathedral has been declared a UNESCO World Heritage Site.

★ **Christian IV's Chapel**
Christian IV supervised the construction of his own final resting place. The grand chapel contains a painting of the king in combat and a bronze statue by Bertel Thorvaldsen.

St Birgitta's Chapel
In 1511, frescoes were painted inside the chapel, including this small demon in the corner and another of Mary Magdalene washing the feet of Jesus.

KEY

① **The Royal Column** indicates the height of several Danish kings. Christian I is recorded as 2.19 m (7 ft 2 inches), although his skeleton is 1.88 m (6 ft 2 inches).

② **The South Tower** has a unique clock with tiny moving figures including one of St Jørgen chasing a dragon.

③ **The storm bell** is the oldest medieval bell in Denmark.

④ **Margrete's Spire** replaced a tower destroyed by fire in 1968.

⑤ **Chapter House** contains a crucifix made from two bells that melted in the 1968 fire.

Main entrance

Pulpit
The pulpit was ordered by Christian IV in 1610. Its ornate carvings in marble, alabaster and sandstone were made by Hans Brokman of Copenhagen.

Stalls
Set near the altar these wooden pews are beautiful examples of Gothic carving.

★ Altarpiece
The altar, depicting scenes from the life of Christ, was produced in Antwerp in the 1500s.

★ Sarcophagus of Margrete I
The sarcophagus bearing an alabaster effigy of Margrete I as a young girl is considered to be the most beautiful sculpture in the cathedral.

Interior
The cathedral has been rebuilt several times, acquiring features typical of the styles that were then in fashion. The last major works were carried out following a fire in 1968.

㉔ Tveje Merløse Kirke

Road map: E4. ℹ️ Holbæk, Tveje Merløse 14. **Tel** 59 43 24 53. **Open** 8am–3:30pm daily. 🔲 tvejemerloesekirke.dk

As a miniature version of Roskilde's original 12th-century cathedral, the church in Tveje Merløse, south of Holbæk, is one of the most interesting Romanesque sacral buildings in Denmark. Its most distinctive features are the two almost identical square towers. The history of the site as a place of worship is believed to date back to the Viking era; some records suggest it was used for worship in the 3rd century.

The church's interior has an altarpiece by Joakim Skovgaard. At one time the church contained some colourful 13th-century frescoes depicting, among other things, the devil and the motif of God's Majesty, a typical medieval theme found particularly in the region of Øresund. These have been removed and are now on display in Copenhagen's Nationalmuseet (see pp88–9). A small cemetery is in the church grounds.

㉕ Nørre Jernløse Mølle

Road map: E4. Windmill: Møllebakken 2, Regstrup. **Tel** 23 40 30 03. **Open** Apr–Oct: 2–4pm 1st Sun of each month. 🔲 nrjernlosemolle.dk

The small village of Nørre Jernløse, located some 25 km (16 miles) west of Roskilde, has a 12th-century church containing 16th-century frescoes. The town is best known, however, for its 19th-century windmill, which is set on a sturdy octagonal base surrounded by a distinctive gallery.

The Dutch-style windmill was built in 1853 in Nørrevold, near Copenhagen, where it was known as Sankt Peders Mølle. When financial difficulties forced its owners to sell the mill it was bought by Niels Peter Rasmussen, a miller, who dismantled it and transported it in pieces on a horse cart to Jernløse, 70 km (43 miles) away. In 1899 the windmill was bought by Ole Martin Nielsen, whose family used and maintained it for the next 60 years. Finally, in 1979 the windmill was handed over to the parish of Jernløse. Built on a stone base, the Nørre Jernløse

mill has a timber structure with a shingled roof crowned with a wooden, onion-shaped cupola. Its sails were once cloth covered and could be operated directly from the gallery. The mill, which is no longer used to grind flour, now has an information centre where visitors can learn about the mill's history and about early methods of flour production.

Well in front of the monastery in Sorø

㉖ Sorø

Road map: E5. 🚋 7,000. **Tel** 70 25 22 06. 🔲 visitwestzealand.com

Located on the banks of the Tuel and Sorø lakes, Sorø is one of the most beautiful towns in Zealand. In 1142 Bishop Absalon, the founder of Copenhagen, began to build a monastery here. When it was complete, the Klosterkirke was the largest building of its kind in Scandinavia and one of the first brick structures ever to be built in Denmark. This 70-m (230-ft) long Romanesque-Gothic church contains the remains of Bishop Absalon in a tomb at the rear of the main altar. The church also contains the sarcophagi of Christian II, Valdemar IV and Oluf III.

Attractions in Sorø include the **Museum Vestsjælland** (Museum of Southwest Zealand), which displays exhibits from the Stone Age right up to the present time. Next to the museum is the Bursers Apotekerhave (Apothecary Garden), with

Dutch-style windmill in Nørre Jernløse

plants from the herbarium of Joachim Burser, a pharmacist linked to the Danish royal family in the 1600s.

Sorø is perhaps best known for its Akademiet, which is set in a picturesque spot on Lake Sorø. This establishment, dedicated to the education of the sons of the nobility, was founded in 1623 by Christian IV in the monastery buildings left empty as a consequence of the Reformation. The Akademiet is surrounded by a park which contains a monument depicting the writer Ludwig Holberg, who bequeathed his considerable fortune and library to the school after his death in 1754. The school still operates though it is no longer reserved only for the country's nobility.

Environs
Tystrup-Bavelse is a national wildlife reserve with two connected freshwater lakes that attract a variety of birdlife; more than 20,000 water birds winter here. The forests contain many prehistoric grave-mounds, including Kelleroddysen, Zealand's largest megalithic stone formation, which is over 120 m (394 ft) in length. Bjernede, near Sorø, has the only surviving round church in Zealand. Constructed of stone and brick, it is quite unlike Bornholm's round churches *(see p225)* and was built around 1175 by Sune Ebbesøn, a provincial governor to Valdemar I (The Great).

Bjernede Rundkirke – the only round church in Zealand

🏛 **Museum Vestsjælland**
Storgade 17. **Tel** 57 83 40 63.
Open 1–4pm Tue–Thu & Sun, 11am–2pm Sat.

㉗ Tårnborg

Road map: E5.

This ancient parish on the shores of Korsør bay, with the rising outline of a white 13th-century church, was once occupied by a castle and settlement.

Distinct white exterior of the 13th-century church in Tårnborg

Tårnborg appeared as a place name for the first time in a royal land survey completed in the first half of the 13th century, though it is likely that a strong-hold existed at least one hundred years prior to this and that, together with the forts at Nyborg and Sprogø, it controlled the passage across the Store Bælt *(see pp150–51)*. From the 13th century it was also a major centre of commerce and in the 14th century Tårnborg forged links with neighbouring estates, helping to intensify foreign trade. The castle was demolished in the 15th century following a financial crisis.

Archaeological excavations suggest that Tårnborg's original stronghold measured approxi-mately 30 m (98 ft) in diameter, with an 8-m (26-ft) high tower at its centre.

㉘ Korsør

Road map: E5. 🚉 15,000. **Tel** 70 25 22 06. 🔲 visitwestzealand.com

The earliest records of this town date from 1241. The most prominent building in Korsør is a 13th-century fortress (Korsør Fæstning), which played a crucial role in the town gaining control of the Storebælt. In 1658 the constantly enlarged fortress was captured by the Swedes, but returned to Danish control a year later. Its 25-m- (82-ft-) high tower now houses the **Korsør By-og Overfarts-museet** (Town and Ferry Service Museum), which has a collection that includes models of ships that once sailed across the Storebælt.

Clusters of historic buildings, mainly from the 18th century, can be seen in the environs of Algade, Slottensgade and Gavnegade. The Rococo mansion at No. 25 Algade dates from 1761 and was built by Rasmus Langeland, a shipowner. It was originally used as an inn for sailors who were waiting for the right conditions to cross the Storebælt. Its front is adorned with allegories of the four seasons. Inside is a small art museum displaying, among other things, sculptures by artist Harald Isenstein who died in 1980.

🏛 **Korsør By-og Overfartsmuseet**
Søbatteriet 7. **Tel** 58 37 47 55. **Open** Apr–Nov: 11am–4pm Tue–Sun. 🔲 byogoverfartsmuseet.dk

Cannons outside Korsør Fæstning (Fortress)

㉙ Storebælt Bridge

Until the late 20th century, the only way of travelling to Zealand was by air or ferry across the Storebælt (Great Belt). In 1998, after 12 years of construction work, the two biggest Danish islands – Zealand and Funen – were joined together in the largest construction project in Danish history. The link consists of two bridges with an artificial island in between and has cut the journey time to 10 minutes. Of the two bridges, the Østbro (Eastern) suspension bridge is the most impressive, and remains one of the most ambitious engineering projects ever. The bridge is open 24 hours a day, weather permitting. A toll charge of around 240–365 Dkr, depending on the size of your vehicle, is payable at the toll station on the Zealand side.

VISITORS' CHECKLIST

Practical Information
Road map: E5. **Tel** 70 15 10 15.
🗺️ 🆆 storebaelt.dk

Bridges
The Østbro is 7 km (4.4 miles) long and carries cars (trains run in a tunnel). The Vestbro is 6.6 km (4.1 miles) long and carries cars and trains.

These pylons, at 254 m (833 ft), are the highest man-made structures in Scandinavia.

85-m- (279-ft-) long cables

The bridge is 48.2 m (158 ft) wide.

This railway tunnel is located 75m (246 ft) underground.

Sprogø
This small island in the middle of the Storebælt is the junction where the Østbro motorway and the railway track meet.

The Storebælt

Key
▬ Motorway
▬ Major road
▬ Other road

Slagelse
Langeskov
Nyborg
Tamborg
Korsør
Skælskør
Agersø

0 km   15
0 miles   15

Tunnel
An 8-km- (5-mile-) long rail tunnel, measuring 7.7 m (25 ft) in diameter, descends 75 m (246 ft) below the surface. It is the second largest underwater tunnel in Europe.

A display of Viking archery in Trelleborg

⑳ Trelleborg

Road map: E5. 7 km (4 miles) east of Slagelse. Tower: Trelleborg Allé 4, 4200 Slagelse. **Open** Jun–Aug: 10am–5pm Tue–Sun; Apr–May & Sep–Oct: 10am–4pm Tue–Sun. 🖼
W **natmus.dk**

The best-preserved of Denmark's Viking fortresses was founded in the 10th century by Harald I (Bluetooth). At the height of its power it was manned by an estimated force of 1,000 warriors. Of the reconstructed buildings, the longhouse is the most impressive. It is built of rough oak beams and furnished with benches on which the Vikings slept.

Originally, there were 16 buildings in the main section of the fortress. Outside the fortress was a small cemetery, where archaeologists have counted about 150 graves.

In summer visitors can participate in fun and games. Some of the staff are dressed in Viking costume and are on hand to demonstrate such workaday jobs as grinding corn and sharpening tools. Daily workshops provide children with the opportunity to try their hand at archery and even dress up as Vikings.

A small museum exhibits finds excavated from the grounds such as jewellery and pottery. It also screens a 20-minute film about the history of Trelleborg.

㉛ Kalundborg

Road map: E4. 🏛 16,000. 🚉
ℹ Klosterparkvej 7. **Tel** 70 25 22 06. Museum: Adelgade 23.
Tel 59 51 21 41. **Open** 10:30am–4pm Tue–Sun. 🖼
W **visitwestzealand.com**

Kalundborg is one of Zealand's oldest towns and was populated by the Vikings as early as the 9th century. The town was also once used as a base by pirates but in 1168 a castle was built here and control of the fjord's waters was assumed by the crown.

The ruins in Volden square are all that remains of the castle. Its builder was Esbern Snare, the brother of Bishop Absalon. Snare was also the creator of the well-preserved 12th-century Vor Frue Kirke (Church of Our Lady), which has five octagonal towers and a Byzantine design based on a Greek crucifix.

Kalundborg's medieval quarter surrounds the church and includes cobbled streets and 16th-century buildings. One of these now houses the town museum. Most of the exhibits are devoted to local history and include a collection of costumes and the skeletons of two beheaded Vikings. Standing in the museum courtyard is a model of Kalundborg, providing a view of the town's 17th-century layout.

㉜ Røsnæs

Road map: E4. ℹ Kalundborg.

The Røsnæs peninsula, as well as the Asnæs peninsula that flanks the Kalundborg Fjord on the other side, were created by a continental glacier some 20,000 years ago. In the Middle Ages the Røsnæs peninsula, which thrusts into the Storebælt, was covered with thick forest, making it one of the favourite areas for royal hunting trips. One hunt, in 1231, organized at the request of Valdemar the Victorious, ended in a bitter tragedy when a stray arrow killed the king's son (who was also named Valdemar).

The peninsula's tip is the westernmost point of Zealand and is marked by a lighthouse erected in 1845. The light from its lantern, mounted 25 m (82 ft) above sea level, can be seen up to 40 km (25 miles) away. A short way before the lighthouse, in the village of Ulstrup, is a Dutch-style windmill built in 1894. It was still being used in the 1950s to grind flour but is now purely a visitor attraction.

At the base of the Asnæs peninsula is Lerchenborg Slot, a Baroque castle built in 1753 by General Christian Lerche. H.C. Andersen stayed here in 1862 and some of the rooms contain items relating to the famous writer.

The unusual five-towered church in Kalundborg

❸ Svinninge

Road map: E4. 🚉 **Tel** 59 91 08 88.

The main reason people come to this town, located at the base of the Odsherred peninsula, is to visit its model electric railway, which is one of the longest in Europe. **Svinninge Modeljernbane** is housed in a building measuring 8 m by 14 m (26 ft by 46 ft) and contains over 550 model railway coaches and nearly 90 locomotives. All of the rolling stock, as well as the convincing reconstructions of many Danish stations (including Svinninge, Hilbæk, Lisebro, Hjortholm and Egaa), are built to a scale of 1:87. The creators of this extraordinary display have meticulously and painstakingly recreated entire railway routes, including the link from Holbæk to Oxneholm.

The model railway was originally a private affair and was opened to the public after it was donated to the town by its original creator. The building of this impressive display involved a great deal of work by many people including model makers, carpenters, joiners and electricians. More than 80 m (262 ft) of cable were laid in order to supply current to over 2 km (1.3 miles) of track. The display continues to grow with new sections of track and locomotives added yearly.

🏛 **Svinninge Modeljernbane**
Stationen 2, 4520 Svinninge.
Tel 59 21 60 09. **Open** end Apr–end Oct: 10am–4pm Fri–Sun. 🚉
w svmjk.dk

Section of the model railway in Svinninge

Dragsholm Slot, seen from the courtyard

❸ Dragsholm

Road map: E4. Dragsholm Allé, 4534 Hørve. **Tel** 59 65 33 00. 🚶 tours only: call to book a tour in English or German. 🚉 **w** dragsholm-slot.dk

The castle in Dragsholm was once a fortress and later a royal residence. It is now used as a luxurious hotel and restaurant, but has lost none of its historical grandeur.

Situated on the shores of Nekselø bay, at the foot of Zealand's third highest hill – Vejrhøj (121 m/397 ft above sea level) – Dragsholm Slot is one of Denmark's oldest castles. Its origins date back to the beginning of the 13th century, when the Bishop of Roskilde decided to build a palace, which would also serve as a military fortress. The bishops owned the castle until 1536, when the king took possession of it following the Reformation. The king established a prison at the castle. The most famous prisoner was James Hepburn, the 4th Earl of Bothwell. He was married to the Scottish queen, Mary Stuart, but had to flee from Scotland. He was captured in Bergen and later sent to Dragsholm, where he was imprisoned for five years. Hepburn died in 1578, and his mummified body is located in the church in Fårevejle.

In 1657 Denmark declared war on Sweden. When Sweden won, the Swedish soldiers blew

Heraldic arms from Dragsholm Slot

up parts of the castle. The castle was then given to Henrik Müller, who rebuilt the southern wing in 1675. In 1694 the castle was bought by Frederik Christian Adeler and his wife Henriette Margrethe von Lente. They rebuilt the rest of the castle as the Baroque building seen today. The Adeler family owned the castle until 1932, when the state had to take over. Since 1937 the property has been owned by the Bøttger family, who today run it as a hotel with a spa and two restaurants. The castle contains 34 rooms, all with unique and contemporary furnishings. Some rooms overlook the park, with others offering views of the fields, moat or beautiful cobblestone castle yard. The 1-m (3-ft) thick walls, high ceilings and sumptuously decorated interiors enhance the historic aura of the place. The most interesting rooms include the magnificent Banqueting Hall (Riddersalen) and Hunting Room (Jagtværelset).

The castle and its moat are surrounded by a large expanse of parkland that contains, among other plants, a collection of rhododendrons. Like all great castles, Dragsholm is reputed to be haunted. The three ghosts that are most frequently spotted are the White Lady, the Grey Lady and, of course, Lord von Bothwell.

㉟ Odsherred

Surrounded by the waters of the Kattegat, Isefjord and Sejerø bay, the Odsherred peninsula is one of the most popular holiday destinations in Denmark, visited annually by sun-seekers and water sport enthusiasts. Its wide sandy beaches, the lure of the sea and the varied landscape also make this region popular with artists, some of whom have established galleries here.

③ **Sommerland Sjælland**
This amusement park (open mid-May–Sep only) provides a good day out for families with kids. Among the many attractions are a mini train, a roller coaster and giant water slides ending in splash pools.

⑤ **Havnebyen**
Cutters in the harbour and the aroma from the local smokehouses make this fishing village a memorable place.

④ **Lumsås Mølle**
This restored mill dates from the 19th century and is open to the public. Flour ground on site can still be bought.

② **Højby Sø**
The banks of this small lake are inhabited by a wide variety of birds. The lake is also popular with anglers.

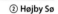

Klint · Overby · Ebbeløkke · Tengslemark · Stenstrup · Nyrup · Gudmindrup · Vig

⑥ **Gniben**
The narrow strip of land stretching westwards has wide sandy beaches and is excellent for sunbathing. Gniben, situated furthest to the west, affords magnificent views of the sea.

0 km   2
0 miles   2

Key

▬ Suggested route
▬ Scenic route
═ Other road

Tips for Drivers

Length of route: 50 km (31 miles). 🚹 Holtets Plads 1. **Tel** 59 91 08 88.
🅆 visitodsherred.com

① **Højby**
The interior of the local church is decorated with frescoes depicting, among others, Sankt Jørgen.

SOUTHERN ZEALAND AND THE ISLANDS

The lowlands of southern Zealand are characterized by cultivated fields and beautiful lakes. Many visitors see only Vordingborg and Køge, two towns that have played a significant part in Denmark's history, but the islands of Lolland, Falster and Møn to the south are attractive holiday destinations and offer miles of sandy beaches, woodland and awe-inspiring views of coastal cliffs.

Southern Zealand (Sjælland) is an important region for the Danes. Vordingborg was the capital of the Valdemar dynasty and in the 12th century was used by Bishop Absalon as a staging post for his military expeditions to eastern Germany. The market town of Ringsted, in central Zealand, was for many years the venue of the *landsting*, a regional government assembly that formed the basis of the present-day parliament. In 1677, Køge Bay was the scene of a major naval engagement in which the Danish Admiral Niels Juel became a national hero when he dealt a crushing blow to the Swedish fleet.

The islands to the south of Zealand are more rural in character. Lolland is Denmark's third biggest island (1,243 sq km/ 480 sq miles) and also its flattest (at its highest point it is a mere 22 m/72 ft above sea level). The island has some pretty beaches and is popular with hikers in summer. Falster is only slightly smaller and is visited mainly for its wide beaches. Møn is the smallest of the islands and the hardest to reach. The journey is worth it, however, as Møn has rustic scenery, spectacular white cliffs, good beaches and some interesting sights including Neolithic burial places and a number of medieval churches containing some spectacular frescoes.

Tree-lined beach on the island of Møn

◀ Vallø Slot, an impressive Renaissance castle in Southern Zealand

Exploring Southern Zealand and the Islands

The largest town in southern Zealand is Næstved, which has been a prominent market town since the Midde Ages. Equally worth a visit, however, are the region's other market towns: Køge, Ringsted and Vordingborg. This part of Denmark is particularly attractive to families because it has a slow, relaxed pace and a number of child-friendly attractions such as BonBon-Land, Knuthenborg Safari Park on Lolland and, on Falster, a recreated medieval village. Falster benefits from some of Denmark's best beaches; Lolland has a popular resort complex.

Brick-built Holsted Kirke, Næstved

Getting Around

Getting from southern Zealand to Falster and Lolland presents few problems thanks to the toll-free bridges. The main arterial road – the E47 motorway – runs from Copenhagen via southern Zealand to Falster and Rødbyhavn on Lolland. Most places are easily accessible from Copenhagen by train except for Møn, which has no railway.

Key

- ▭▭▭ Motorway
- ▬▬▬ Major road
- ▭▭▭ Minor road
- ▬▬▬ Scenic route
- ▬▪▬ Main railway
- ▬▬▬ Minor railway

Neolithic burial site on the Knudshoved Odde peninsula

Sights at a Glance

For keys to symbols see back flap

Vaulted interior of Sankt Bendts
Kirke, Ringsted

① Agersø

Road map: E5. 🚢 🚌 agersoe.com
Agersø Mølle: **Tel** 58 19 81 03.
Open Jul–early Aug: 2–4pm Fri–Sun.
🚲 🚌 agersoe-moelle.dk

A 15-minute ferry trip from
Stigsnæs, a small port 7 km
(4.3 miles) southwest of
Skælskør, takes visitors to the
lovely island of Agersø. This strip
of land is just 3 km (1.8 miles)
wide and 7 km (4.3 miles) long,
and it is home to a community
of about 240 people.

Despite its small size, Agersø
has a lot to offer, starting with
the pretty harbour, which plays
host to all manner of vessels,
from ferries and yachts to
fishing boats. There is also a
comprehensive network of
walking and cycling routes
starting from the harbour and
covering a length of 20 km
(12.4 miles). The north of
the island features several
unspoiled beaches with good
bathing opportunities.

The island's main attraction,
however, is probably the Agersø
Mølle, a mill built in 1892.
Farmers from the surrounding
areas would come here to grind
their corn. Resting on a stone
base, the octagonal upper mill
is made of wood and covered
with shingle. The mill was in use
until 1959, when its owner, a
baker called Erik Thomsen,
gifted it to the people of
Agersø. A bench was placed
next to the mill in his honour.

② Ringsted

Road map: E5. 🚗 21,000. 🚌
ℹ️ Tvær Allé 1–3. **Tel** 57 62 66 00.
🇼 visitringsted.dk

Owing to its location at the
crossroads of two trading routes,
Ringsted was once an important
market town. It was the venue
for regional government
assemblies – the *landsting* –
which took decisions and
passed laws on major national
issues. The three stones standing
in the market square were used
hundreds of years ago by
members of the *landsting*.

Ringsted gained notoriety in
1131 when Knud (Canute)
Laward, duke of southern
Zealand, was murdered in the
neighbouring woods by his
jealous cousin Magnus. He is
buried in Ringsted's Sankt Bendts
Kirke (St Benedict's Church)
along with a number of Danish
kings and queens. Sankt Bendts
Kirke was erected in 1170 and is
believed to be the oldest brick
church in Scandinavia. Its main
altarpiece dates from 1699; its
baptismal font is believed to be
12th century and was for a time
used as a flower pot in a local
garden until it was discovered
quite by chance. The
magnificent frescoes were
painted in about 1300 and
include a series depicting Erik IV
(known as Ploughpenny for his
tax on ploughs).

In the 17th century it was
decided to open some of the
coffins. The items found in them
are on display in one of the
chapels. The Dagmar Cross,
dating from about AD 1000, is

a copy. The original is on display
in the Nationalmuseet in
Copenhagen (*see pp88–9*). The
famous cross once belonged to
Queen Dagmar, the first wife of
Valdemar II. Depicted on its
enamelled surface is a figure of
Christ with his arms outstretched.
On the other side of the cross,
Christ is pictured with the Virgin
Mary flanked by John the
Baptist, St John and St Basil.

③ Suså

Road map: E5.

At nearly 90 km (56 miles) long,
Suså is one of Denmark's
longest rivers. From its source
near the town of Rønnede it
flows through two lakes, Tystrup
Sø and Bavelse Sø, to end its
journey in Karrebæk Bay, near
Næstved. The picturesque
surroundings and slow-flowing
current make the river particularly popular with canoeists.
Canoe trips are usually taken
over the final stretch of the river,
where a canoe or a kayak can
be hired for an hour or two.
River traffic gets quite busy in
summer, and many large family
groups enjoy picnicking along
the river banks.

Environs
Near Haslev are two magnificent
properties. **Gisselfeld Kloster**,
completed in 1575, is one of
the finest Renaissance castles
in northern Europe and is
surrounded by gardens
containing about 400 species
of trees and shrubs. The castle
was often visited by Hans

Suså – Zealand's longest river

Canoeing on the Suså past the Gunderslev Kirke in Skelby

Christian Andersen – it was here that he got his idea for *The Ugly Duckling*. The name Gisselfeld can be traced back to the year 1370, but the red castle as it appears today was built during the period 1547–75 by Peder Oxe, the mightiest High Chancellor of Denmark. There has been a garden park around the castle since then. The present castle park of about 40 hectares (99 acres) was laid out towards the end of the 19th century by H.E. Millner, the famous English landscape architect. The English landscape garden with its beautiful oases and botanic rarities is definitely worth a visit. The grounds are open to the public for opera concerts, classic car shows and market days. On the latter, there are also guided tours of the house.

Bregentved Slot, on the outskirts of Haslev, was erected in the 1650s; however, the property was substantially modified in the late 1880s.

🏠 Gisselfeld Kloster
Godskontoret, Gisselfeldvej 12 A, 4690 Haslev. **Tel** 56 32 60 32. **Open** variable; check website before visiting. 🧒
W gisselfeld-kloster.dk

❹ Glumsø
Road map: E5. 🚇

Glumsø is a good base from which to embark upon a canoeing trip along the Suså. Located about 10 km (6 miles)

south of Ringsted, its other main attraction is the **Dansk Cykel & Knallert Museum** (Museum of Bicycles and Motorbikes), which has a huge collection of two- and three-wheeled transportation, from vintage cycles to trendy modern scooters. Some bikes can even be ridden by visitors.

Environs
South of Glumsø, on the banks of the Suså, is Skelby. The main point of interest here is Gunderslev Kirke, a 12th-century church. Its sumptuously furnished interior was paid for by the former owners of the nearby Gunderslevholm estate.

🏛 Dansk Cykel & Knallert Museum
Sorøvej 8. **Tel** 57 64 77 94. **Open** May–Sep: 11am–5pm Wed, Sat & Sun. 🧒
W dckm.dk/cykelmuseum

❺ BonBon-Land
Road map: E5. Holme-Ostrup, Gartnervej 2. **Tel** 55 53 07 00. **Open** end Apr–late Oct. Opening hours vary; check the website before visiting. 🧒 children up to 90 cm (3 ft) tall are admitted free.
W bonbonland.dk

This nostalgic amusement park attracts large numbers of visitors in the warmer summer months. The entrance fee covers all of the 100 or so attractions. The greatest thrill is undoubtedly provided by a ride on the giant roller coaster, which races along at speeds up to 70 km/h (43 mph) and rises to a height of 22 m (72 ft) before hurtling back down again. A similar surge of adrenaline can be felt when dropping from the 35-m (115-ft) high tower. Gentler amusement for younger children can be had on the park's merry-go-rounds or mini racetracks.

The queues lengthen for the water slides when the temperature rises, as do those for a raft trip down some white-water rapids. BonBon-Land has lots of attractions for toddlers too, including an adventure playground.

BonBon-Land is attractively situated in woodland a short walk from Holme-Ostrup train station. There are a number of picnic benches, so visitors can bring lunch into the amusement park. Expect queues in the summer, at the snack bars.

The beautiful grounds of Gisselfeld Kloster

❻ Næstved

Road map: E5. 🗺 42,500. 🚏 ℹ
Sankt Peders Kirkeplads 4. **Tel** 55 72 08
07. 🌐 **visitsouthzealand-mon.com**

Southern Zealand's largest
town, Næstved has been an
important centre of trade since
medieval times. The 15th-
century town hall in Axeltorv,
the main square, is one of the
oldest in Denmark. The town
has two Gothic churches. The
14th-century frescoes in Sankt
Peder Kirke (St Peter's Church)
depict Valdemar IV and his wife
Helvig kneeling in prayer. Sankt
Mortens is 13th century and has
a beautiful altarpiece that was
completed in 1667.

Other notable buildings
include Kompagnihuset, a half-
timbered guildhall (1493) and
Aposteluset (Apostles' House),
built in the early 16th century.
Its name derives from the figures
of Christ and his 12 disciples
placed between the windows.

Næstved's oldest building,
however, is Helligåndhuset
(House of the Holy Spirit), which
dates from the 1300s and was
used as a hospital and
almshouse. It now houses part
of the **Næstved Museum**, with
a collection of medieval and
contemporary woodcarvings.
Another annex of the museum,
in the Boderne houses near
Sankt Peder Kirke, displays
local handicrafts from the
Holmegaard glass factory and
nearby potteries (dating 1839–
1970). The Løveapoteket
(Pharmacy), on Axeltorv, dates
back to 1640 – a herb garden is

English-style castle garden in Gavnø

situated in the courtyard.
Munkebakken Park (not far from
Axeltorv) contains statues of
seven monks which have been
carved out of tree trunks.

🏛 **Næstved Museum**
Sankt Peders Kirkeplads 14. **Tel** 70 70
12 36. **Open** 10am–2pm Tue–Sat,
10am–4pm Sun.

❼ Gavnø

Road map: E5. **Tel** 55 70 02 00.
Open late Apr–Sep: 10am–4pm daily.
♿ 🌐 **gavnoe.dk**

Located a little way from
Næstved and linked to Næstved
by road, this tiny island had a
castle used by pirates in the
12th century. In 1398 it was
purchased by Queen Margrete
I, who established a convent
here for unmarried women
of noble rank. The convent
church is said to
be the most
colourful church
in Scandinavia.

Gavnø Castle is
one of Denmark's
finest Rococo castles
with plenty to inter-
est visitors. The
art collection is
the largest privately
owned collection
of paintings in
Scandinavia. Also
worth seeing are
the Great Dining
Room with its
stunning French

chandelier and the beautifully
furnished guest rooms dating
from the 1750s. The rooms are
still used on special occasions.

Gavnø Castle Garden has
been referred to as the most
beautiful garden in Denmark.
The grounds look spectacular
in spring when there are
displays of tulips and narcissus.
The floral splendour continues
into the autumn with a
succession of summer flowers,
rhododendrons, begonias,
lilies and the beautifully
landscaped rose garden at
the northern end of the castle
garden. In the centre of the
garden is the "Skjærsommer"
playhouse, which was built for
the little Baroness Julie Reedtz-
Thott in 1846. A part of the
private doll collection is
exhibited here. The gardens
also have a butterfly house, a
pirate-themed nature playground and a treasure hunt
for both children and adults.

❽ Vordingborg

Road map: F6. 🗺 12,000. 🚏
ℹ Slotsruinen 1. **Tel** 55 37 52 43.
🌐 **visitsouthzealand-mon.com**

Vordingborg is on the strait
between Zealand and Falster that
leads to the Baltic, and was once
Denmark's most important town.
It was the royal residence of
Valdemar I (The Great) who came
to the throne in 1157 and built a
castle here, ushering in a period
of relative peace in the country's
history. In 1241 Valdemar II

Former Benedictine abbey in Næstved

sanctioned the Jutland Code in Vordingborg, which gave Denmark its first written laws. Subsequent monarchs from the Valdemar dynasty also took a liking to the castle and enlarged it over the years. The final length of its defensive wall was 800 m (2,625 ft) and its imposing appearance was emphasized by nine mighty towers.

Most of the towers are now in ruins except for the 14th-century **Gåsetårnet** (Goose Tower). This 36-m (118-ft) high tower has walls that are 3.5 m (11.5 ft) thick in places. Its name dates back to 1368 when Valdemar IV placed a golden goose on top of the tower in order to express his belief that the Hanseatic League's declaration of war was no more threatening than the cackling of geese. Though it has been modified, Gåsetårnet is important as the only intact building to remain from the Valdemar era. The building opposite the tower houses the remodelled **Danmarks Borgcenter** (Danish Castle Centre), which has displays on the castle's history and the three kings who lived there.

Algade is Vordingborg's main street and has been pedestrianized. It leads to Vor Frue Kirke (Church of Our Lady), a 15th-century church which contains a Baroque altarpiece dating from 1642.

Environs
The **Kalvehave Labyrintpark** features several exciting outdoor mazes and an area with brain-teasers and puzzles.

The 14th-century Gåsetårnet in Vordingborg

🏛 **Gåsetårnet – Goose Tower & Danmarks Borgcenter**
Open Apr–Jun: 10am–5pm Tue–Sun; Jul–Aug: 10am–5pm daily; Sep–Oct: 10am–4pm Tue–Sun. 🌐
W danmarksborgcenter.dk

🅿 **Kalvehave Labyrintpark**
Hovvejen 12, Kalvehave. **Tel** 55 34 47 71. **Open** late Apr–Jun: 11am–4pm Mon–Fri, 10am–5pm Sat & Sun; Jul: 10am–6pm daily; Aug: 10am–4pm daily.
🌐 **W** kalvehave-labyrintpark.dk

❾ Knudshoved Odde

Road map: E5. The peninsula can be reached by car, from Oreby. 🚗

The narrow strip of the Knudshoved Odde peninsula is 20 km (12 miles) long and only 1 km (half a mile) at its widest point. The peninsula is owned by the Rosenfeldt Estate, which has managed to preserve the unique landscape. There are no towns or villages here, and the only road is closed to motor traffic after about 10 km (6 miles). This inaccessibility makes the Knudshoved Odde peninsula popular with people who wish to get away from it all and relax by indulging in simple activities such as sitting on the seashore, gathering blackberries and exploring the woods (which can be reached by foot from the car park halfway along the peninsula where the trail begins). The wood's marked walking trails are not taxing and range in distance from a short stroll to one that is just under 4 km (2 miles).

The peninsula is also known for its Neolithic burial mounds. One of these historic graves, which was dug about 5,500 years ago, can be seen close to the car park. Excavations have established that its ancient occupant was provided with all possible necessities for the after-life, including plenty of food and drink.

❿ Sakskøbing

Road map: E6. Lolland. 🚆 4,700. 🛈 Torvet 4. **Tel** 54 70 56 30 (Jun–Sep).

One of Lolland's oldest settlements, Sakskøbing has few historic remains other than a Romanesque church (13th century). However, in view of the town's location on the E47, the main road linking Zealand to Falster and Lolland, it is a popular stopping-off point. The town's most striking feature is a water tower that resembles a smiling face. A distinctive landmark in the market square is the monument erected in 1939 for the Polish men and women who worked in the local fields. The town's links with Poland date back to the end of the 19th century when many Poles came here in search of work. Many settled permanently and some local Catholic churches still celebrate mass in Polish.

Monument to Polish workers in Sakskøbing

Shores of the Knudshoved Odde peninsula

⓬ Knuthenborg Safari Park

Knuthenborg Safari Park provides the chance to see such exotic creatures as zebras, camels, antelopes and giraffes. The parkland itself has been in the hands of the same family since the 17th century. It was land-scaped in an English style in the 19th century and the first animals were transported by ship from Kenya in 1969. Today there are more than 1,000 animals. The park's botanical garden contains many rare trees and shrubs, and there is an attractive lake area that is ideal for picnics.

Exit

Bandholm Huset

Bandholm-porten

AUSTRALIA & REST OF WORLD

Egebæk Pla

Knuthenborg

ASIA

Skovridergar

Skovr Pla

ASIA

Nordre Snapind

Tiger Res

Søndre Snapind

★ **Knuthenborg**
The house is surrounded by English-style parkland and was designed by Edward Milner. It bears clear signs of a Victorian influence. The main building is still inhabited by the Knuth family and closed to the public.

★ **Tiger Reserve**
The pride of the park are the Siberian tigers, the largest of all tigers. They enjoy bathing, which is unusual for cats. The deep marks visible on the trees in the reserve have been left by the tigers' sharp claws.

Congo Splash ride
The exhilarating Congo Splash ride allows visitors to experience the park from 16 m (52 ft) up in the air then take the plunge on Denmark's highest waterslide. Riders are guaranteed to get wet so towels and spare clothes are recommended.

Zebras

The zebras are allowed to roam freely and mingle with other animals in the park. They can run at speeds of up to 60 km/h (40 mph) when startled.

VISITORS' CHECKLIST

Practical Information
Road map: E6. Knuthenborg Alle, 4930 Maribo. **Tel** 54 78 80 89. **Open** end Apr–early Sep: daily; early Sep–early Oct: Sat & Sun; for opening hours, visit the website.
W **knuthenborg.dk**

Key

▇▇▇ Main route
▇▇▇ Car route only
═══ Pedestrian route

Pheasant Woods

AMERICA

Bird Paradise

P
♿

Swan Lake

Deer Park

Wolves Wood

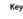
P

uset

Savannah

Limpopo House

♿ ♿
🔄 ℹ P

nkey est

AFRICA

Safari Grill

Limpopoland

Giraffes

The giraffe can grow up to 5.5 m (18 ft) in height. The park's giraffes can sometimes be seen bending, with legs wide apart, to drink water.

Limpopoland

This park for children in the old orchard features a water playground with geysers, water cannons and much more. There are also climbing courses, swings, playhouses and a formidable suspension bridge.

Maglemer Slottet

Maglemerporten

Cape Baboons

Take a free ride on a bus through the baboons' area, and watch them jump on and off the ride with you.

Entrance

0 metres   250
0 yards   250

Half-timbered houses in Maribo

⑪ Maribo

Road map: E6. Lolland. 🚍 6,000. 🚉
ℹ️ Torvet 1, Det Gamle Rådhus. **Tel** 54
78 04 96. 🌐 **visitlolland-falster.com**

Situated on the northern shore
of Maribo Søndersø, the largest
of four inland lakes, Maribo is
Lolland's commercial centre.
The town was founded in 1416
by Erik of Pomerania and soon
acquired a Gothic cathedral. All
that remains of an original
convent and monastery complex
are the cathedral's bells (that toll
six times a day) and a gallery
where the nuns used to pray.
The convent was dissolved
following the Reformation.

The cathedral is located a
short way from Torvet, the
town's main square, which
contains a 19th-century Neo-
Classical town hall and several
half-timbered houses.

Maribo has two museums,
which offer separate, as well as
joint admission fees. The
Lolland-Falster Stiftsmuseet
has a collection of church art
and displays relating to Polish
workers. **Frilandsmuseet**, a
short way southwest of Maribo,
is an open-air museum with a
number of period cottages, as
well as other buildings,
including a windmill, a school
and a smithy.

🏛 **Lolland-Falster Stiftsmuseet**
Banegårdspladsen 11. **Tel** 54 84 44 00.
Open 11am–4pm Thu–Sat. 🖼

🏛 **Frilandsmuseet**
Meinckesvej. **Tel** 54 84 44 00. **Open**
May–Sep: 10am–4pm Tue–Sun. 🖼

⑫ Knuthenborg Safari Park

See pp164–5.

⑬ Nakskov

Road map: E6. Lolland.
🚍 12,600. ℹ️ Axeltorv 3.
Tel 54 92 21 72.

Nakskov's origins
date back to the 13th
century. A reminder
of its medieval past is
the tower of Sankt
Nikolai Kirke (Church),
which rises above
the old quarter. One
of Nakskov's oldest houses is
Dronningens Pakhus, a quayside
warehouse from 1590. Also on
the quay is the Skibs og Søfarts
Museum (Maritime and Ship
Museum), which has various
exhibits highlighting Nakskov's
shipbuilding past.

Most of Denmark's sugar beet
is grown on Lolland. Housed in
a former factory, **Denmark's
Sugar Museum** tells the story
of the crop and the Polish
immigrants who arrived to work
in the fields.

There are 20 small islands in
Nakskov Fjord, some of them
inhabited. Post and other goods
are still delivered using the
Postbåden, a small boat that
also welcomes tourists on its
route (Jun–Aug). The route
varies, but it always stops for a
1-hour lunch break at Albuen
(The Elbow), an area with
numerous natural attractions.
It is well worth paying a little
extra and bringing a bike; after
cycling around one of the
islands, you can catch another
boat back to Nakskov. In
addition to the daily morning
excursions, there are also trips
just before sundown.

Environs
Købelevhaven, about 6 km
(4 miles) north of Nakskov, is a
Japanese-style botanical garden.
Established in 1975, it has a
large rhododendron collection,
a Japanese garden and some
rare magnolia and Asian trees.

🏛 **Denmark's Sugar Museum**
Løjtoftevej 22. **Tel** 54 92 36 44.
Open Oct–May: 1–4pm Sat; Jun–Sep:
1–4pm Tue–Sun. 🖼
🌐 **sukkermuseet.dk**

Postbåden
Havnegade 27. **Tel** 54 93 12 36.
Open Jun–Aug: 9am daily. 🖼

🌿 **Købelevhaven**
Oddevej 116, Købelev. **Tel** 54 93 20 87.
Open May–Aug: 10am–5pm Tue–Sun;
Sep: 10am–4pm Fri–Sun. 🖼
🌐 **koebelevhaven.dk**

⑭ Lalandia

Road map: E6. Lolland. 🚍 ℹ️ Rødby,
Lalandia Centret 1. **Tel** 54 61 05 00. 🖼
🌐 **lalandia.dk**

Many families come to Lalandia
– Denmark's largest holiday
centre – for a short break. The
resort is on the southern coast
of Lolland and offers numerous
attractions to visitors. The local
beach competes for children's
attention with the aquapark
where swimming pools and
slides are surrounded by
artificial lakes and tropical
vegetation. Regardless of the
outside temperature, the water
in the pools never falls below
28° C (82° F). For sports
enthusiasts, there are tennis
courts, a golf course, mini-golf
and, in the case of bad weather,

Palm trees enliven the aquapark area at Lalandia

Display in Polakkasernen, Tågerup

a vast leisure complex that includes a gymnasium, bowling alleys, amusement arcades and indoor tennis.

Visitors to Lalandia can stay in apartments that sleep up to eight people. All of the apartments have their own bathrooms and kitchens. There are also numerous restaurants and bars spread around the holiday complex.

⓮ Tågerup

Road map: E6. Lolland. 🚌

The main attraction of Tågerup, a small village situated a short way south of Maribo, is its Romanesque-Gothic church, which contains some fine 15th- century frescoes. At the entrance to the church is a runic stone. Many visitors are surprised to find a building displaying the Polish flag. This is **Polakkasernen**, or the Polish Barracks, and contains documents, fragments of diaries and various items left by Polish immigrants who from 1893 began arriving in Lolland in great numbers. Many Poles were on the move for political reasons as the Soviet Union had taken control of Poland. There were also economic reasons, however, and immigrants arrived from Poland between 1870 and 1920 in a bid to escape a feudal system that gave them few legal rights. Once they arrived, most Poles found employment as labourers in the local sugar-beet fields. A short way from Polakkasernen

is **Lungholm Gods**, an early 15th-century residence with English-style landscaped grounds. The house is now used as a conference centre and spa. The footpaths around it are ideal for a pleasant ramble.

🏛 **Polakkasernen**
Højbygårsvej 34. **Tel** 54 78 23 30. **Open** Easter, Whitsun, Jul–Aug: 2–4pm Tue–Sun. 🅿

🏠 **Lungholm Gods**
Rødbyvej 24. **Tel** 54 60 02 53.

⓯ Nysted

Road map: E6. Lolland. 🚹 1,500. 🚌

This small harbour town situated on the Rødsand bay was founded in the 13th century. Nysted's main historic monuments are a large Gothic church dating from the early 14th century, and a much later 17th-century tower. There are also a number of half-timbered houses and a

water tower, which now serves as a viewpoint.

Environs
Ålholm Slot (Castle) is on the outskirts of Nysted and dates from the 12th century. It was crown property for many years and the rooms contain many royal furnishings. In 1332 Christian II was held prisoner in the dungeons here on the orders of his half-brother. The castle is now in private hands and is not open to the public.

About 3 km (2 miles) north of Nysted is Kettinge, a small village with an old Dutch windmill and a church containing magnificent frescoes dating from around 1500.

⓰ Fuglsang Kunstmuseum

Road map: E6. Nystedvej 71, Toreby, Lolland. **Tel** 54 78 14 14. **Open** Apr– Oct: 11am–5pm daily (until 8pm on Wed); Nov–Mar: 11am–4pm Wed– Sun. 🅿 ♿ 🆆 aabne-samlinger.dk

Located in the grounds of Fuglsang Manor, between Nysted and Nykøbing F, this art museum was designed by the British architect Tony Fretton. The modern white building provides a stark contrast to the green rural landscape. Inside is a collection of Danish art from the 18th century onwards, with a focus on art from 1850 until 1950. Golden Age painters such as P C Skovgaard and Kristian Zahrtmann are represented, as are the Funen artists, painters from the Skagen School and the CoBrA group *(see pp30-31)*.

Ålholm Slot seen from the water

Woman dressed in period costume at Middelaldercentret

⓲ Middelalder-centret

Road map: E6. Lolland. ⓘ Ved Hamborgskoven 2. **Tel** 54 86 19 34. **Open** May & Sep: 10am–4pm Tue–Sun; Jun & Aug: 10am–4pm daily; Jul: 10am–5pm daily. 🅿 🅦 middelaldercentret.dk

Lolland's Middle Ages Centre is a recreated medieval settlement that provides an insight into what life was like in the 14th century. Crafts and games from medieval times are displayed and explained by staff wearing costumes from the period, while the local inn serves a range of "medieval" food. A replica sailing ship lies in the harbour and a huge wooden catapult is ready for firing. Jousting tournaments are a regular feature in summer, and visitors can also try their hand at archery. A marked walking trail in the nearby forest explains medieval customs and includes a site where charcoal is made. Along the walk, visitors

are warned about woodland spirits and are invited to throw a ghost-repelling stick at an appropriate spot – just in case.

The centre can easily be reached from Nykøbing F by crossing the bridge that connects Lolland and Falster.

⓳ Nykøbing F

Road map: F6. Falster. 🅰 16,500. 🚌 🅑 ⓘ Færgestræde 1 A. **Tel** 54 85 13 03. 🅦 visitlolland-falster.com

Falster's largest town and capital city was a busy commercial centre in medieval times and was granted municipal status in the early 13th century by Valdemar II. In order to distinguish it from two other Danish towns of the same name, this Nykøbing is followed by the letter F (standing for Falster).

Nykøbing F's main historic sight is a 15th-century brick church, which once formed part of a Franciscan monastery. Its richly decorated interior includes an eye-catching series of portraits of Queen Sophie (wife of Frederik II) together with her family, which were commissioned in 1627. Another notable sight is the half-timbered Czarens Hus (Tsar's House), which is one of the oldest buildings in town. In 1716 the Russian Tsar, Peter the Great, stopped here overnight on his way to Copenhagen. Today, the

building is used as a restaurant and also houses a local history museum – **Falsters Minder**. Among the museum's exhibits are some reconstructed interiors including an 18th-century peasant cottage and a 19th-century burgher's house.

A wonderful panoramic view of Nybøking F can be found from the early 20th-century yellow water tower. The town's **Guldborgsund Zoo** is a little way east of the train station and has a variety of animals including deer, monkeys, donkeys and goats.

🏛 Falsters Minder
Falsters Minder Færgestræde 1a. **Tel** 54 85 13 03. **Open** 10am–4pm Tue–Fri, 10am–2pm Sat (Jul–Sep: 10am–4pm Mon–Fri, 10am–2pm Sat). 🅿

🐾 Guldborgsund Zoo
Østre Alle 97. **Tel** 54 73 27 00. **Open** May–mid-Oct: 9am–5pm daily; mid-Oct–Apr: 10am–4pm daily. 🅿 🅦 guldborgsundzoo.dk

⓴ Eskilstrup

Road map: F6. Falster. 🚌 🚌

This small town is situated a short distance from the E47 motorway and has two rather unusual museums. The **Traktormuseum** is housed in a multi-storey brick building

Statue of a bear in Nykøbing F

and contains over 200 tractors and engines dating from 1880 to 1960. Alongside a wide selection of vintage Fiats, Fords, Volvos and

Nykøbing F, as seen from the river

◀ A 13th-century fresco in the cupola of Sankt Bendts Kirke, Ringsted

Beautiful white beaches around Marielyst

Fergusons are rare Czecho-slovakian and Romanian tractors. The oldest tractor in the museum is American and was built in 1917. There is also a steam traction engine built in England in 1889. Until 1925 it was still being used as a threshing machine. A number of small pedal-tractors are also provided for the amusement of children.

About 3 km (2 miles) from the town centre is the **Krokodille Zoo**. This is the largest collection of crocodiles in Europe and includes 21 of the 23 species of these sharp-toothed reptiles that exist worldwide. The smallest among them is the dwarf cayman, which grows up to 159 cm (62 in) in length. At the other end of the scale, the zoo's giant Nile crocodile Sobek is currently the largest crocodile in Europe.

As well as the many croc-odiles, the zoo also contains a variety of other species including a green anaconda (the world's largest snake), turtles, tortoises and a number of rare clouded leopards. The zoo donates a percentage of the admission price to an international programme of scientific research and protection associated with crocodiles living in the wild.

Traktormuseum
Nørregade 17B. **Tel** 54 43 70 07.
Open May–Jun & Sep: 10am–4pm Sat–Mon Jul & Aug: 10am–4pm daily.
traktormuseum.dk

Krokodille Zoo
Ovstrupvej 9. **Tel** 54 45 42 42. **Open** mid-Jun–Aug: 10am–5pm daily; Sep–mid-Jun: noon–4pm Tue–Sun. **Closed** Jan, Dec. **krokodillezoo.dk**

⑳ Marielyst

Road map: F6. Falster. Marie-lyst Strandvej 54. **Tel** 54 13 62 98.
visitlolland-falster.com

Situated on the eastern end of the island, Marielyst gets its revenue mainly from its many summer visitors and is one of the foremost holiday resorts in the whole of Denmark. One of the main attractions is the fine white sand beach, which is a good length and easily accessible. It also benefits from clean and fairly shallow waters. The dunes running parallel to the coastline are an additional attraction and are fringed by an ancient beech forest. There

are plenty of shops, restau-rants and bars. Along with camp sites, guesthouses and hotels the town also has about 6,000 summer cottages.

If you feel like taking time off from the beach, **Marielyst's Marielyst Gokart Paintball Center** has both an adult and children's go-cart course, as well as electric cars for the under-6s. Both track and karts are of professional quality and there is also a paint-ball and bow-tag field at the same location.

Environs
Just south of Marielyst is the Bøtø Nor bird sanctuary where a variety of birds can be spotted including cranes, ospreys and plovers. An important place for spotting migratory birds in the autumn, the observation tower here offers spectacular views.

Situated a little way south of Nykøbing F, the small town of Væggerløse has an 18th-century windmill, which now houses a glass-blowing workshop, and ceiling paintings from the late-Middle Ages in the church, which itself dates from the late-Romanesque period.

Marielyst Gokart and Paintball Center
Godthåbs Alle 3B, 4873 Væggerløse.
Tel 54 17 44 04. Different opening times for summer and winter; check website for more details.
gokart.dk

The Church of Væggerlose with the surrounding cemetery and gardens

Lime-based paintings in Fanefjord Kirke, painted around 1500–1520

❷ Fanefjord Kirke

Road map: F6. Fanefjord Kirkevej 49, Askeby. **Open** 8am–6pm daily.
Ⓦ fanefjordkirke.dk

The small church of Fanefjord stands on top of an isolated hillock surrounded by green fields. It provides an excellent viewpoint and from here it is possible to look out over the Baltic and the island of Falster. Local folklore tells that the Gothic church derives its name from the Fanefjord bay, whose waters come close to the building. The fjord was in turn named after Queen Fane, wife of King Grøn Jæger, local rulers in the late Stone Age.

Built about 1250, the church was at that time far too big for the needs of the 300 or so parishioners, but its builders took into account worshippers from ships anchoring in the bay as this was a busy harbour in the Middle Ages. According to records it was probably here that Bishop Absalon gathered his fleet before embarking on his raids against the Wends on the south coast of the Baltic Sea.

Fanefjord Kirke is famous in Denmark for its frescoes. The oldest of them date from around 1350 and include an image of St Christopher carrying the infant Jesus. The later paintings date from the mid-15th century and include frescoes painted in warm colours by the Elmelunde master, an artist about whom virtually nothing is known. His

mark, which is an arrow with a cross line, can be seen on one of the ribs of the first arch in the northeastern vault. A collection of votive ships hangs in the church. The oldest is a barquentine hanging above the entrance which commemorates a tragic shipwreck off the north coast of Møn.

❸ Kong Asgers Høj

Road map: F6. Møn.

King Asgers mounds, located in a farmer's field near the village of Røddinge, are all that remain of Denmark's largest passage grave.

The Stone Age corridor consists of an 8-m (26-ft) long underground passage that leads to a large chamber, 10 m (33 ft) long by 2 m (6.5 ft) wide. It is dark inside, so it is advisable to take a torch.

Corridor leading to the burial chamber of Kong Asgers Høj

Environs

A short way south of Kong Asgers Høj stands yet another burial mound – the Klekkendehøj, which has two entrances placed side by side. The chamber is 7 m (23 ft) long. The mound has been restored and is now illuminated.

At the south end of Møn is Grønjægers Høj, another highly unusual tomb that is estimated to be about 4,000 years old. The burial site is one of the largest dolmens in Denmark and consists of 134 weighty stones arranged in an oval shape. According to one local legend, the site is the final resting place of Queen Fane and her husband, Grøn Jæger.

Chalk crags of Møns Klint, rising from the waters of the Baltic

❹ Møns Klint

Road map: F6. Møn.

The white chalk cliffs soaring above the Baltic are one of Møn's main attractions. The cliffs are about 70 million years old and are formed mostly of calcareous shells. Stretching over a distance of about 7 km (4 miles), the crags reach 128 m (420 ft) in height to form a striking landscape. The highest point is near Dronningestolen (Queen's Throne). At one time these cliffs were mined for chalk but they are now a legally protected zone. **Geocenter Møns Klint**, a visitors' centre close to the cliffs, comprises geological exhibitions and hands-on activities. There is also a 3D-cinema and café.

After a clifftop hike many people head inland to explore Klinteskoven (Klint Forest), where about 20 types of orchid can be seen flowering from May to August.

Klintholm Havn is a port south of the cliffs. In the 19th century it was a private estate and later taken over by the local authorities. Small pleasure boats leave for 2-hour cruises from here and are a good way to take in the stunning coastal scenery.

One of Stege's quieter shopping streets

🏛 **Geocenter Møns Klint**
Stengårdsvej 8, Borre. **Tel** 55 86 36 00. **Open** Apr–Oct: 11am–5pm daily (Jul–mid-Aug: 10am–6pm). 🅿 ♿
🌐 moensklint.dk

㉕ Liselund Slot

Road map: F6. Møn. Palace: Langebjergvej 4. **Tel** 55 81 21 78. 📷 May–Sep: 10:30am, 11am, 1:30pm & 2pm Wed–Sun. 🅿 free admission to the park. 🌐 natmus.dk

The diminutive palace of Liselund was once crown property. A subsequent owner gave the building its present name in honour of his wife. The house is set in a large park, and its whitewashed walls are reflected in the waters of a small lake. The fairytale atmosphere is enhanced by the immaculate thatch on the building's roof (locals joke that this is the world's only thatched-roof palace). Liselund Ny Slot (New Castle), a 19th-century building in the midst of the estate, is now a hotel.

Sun dial at Liselund Slot

㉖ Elmelunde

Road map: F6. Møn. Elmelunde Kirke: Leonora Christines Vej 1; Keldby Kirke: Præstegårdsstræde 6 🚌 Churches in Elmelunde and Keldby: **Open** May–Sep: 8am–5pm daily; Oct–Apr: 8am–4pm daily. 🌐 keldbyelmelundekirke.dk

Along with its famous cliffs, Møn boasts a number of churches with highly original frescoes.

One of them can be visited in Elmelunde; another in Keldby, a little to the west. Built around 1075, the church in Elmelunde is one of the oldest stone churches in Denmark. The frescoes date from the 14th and 15th centuries and were whitewashed during the Reformation. Ironically this only served to preserve the paintings from fading. They were restored in the 20th century under the guidance of Copenhagen's Nationalmuseet (National Museum).

The frescoes depict scenes from the Old and New Testaments and include images of Christ and the saints as well as lively portrayals of demons and the flames of hell. Most of them are attributed to one artist, known simply as the Elmelunde Master. The paintings served to explain biblical stories to illiterate peasants and are characterized by their quirky

Medieval fresco in Stege Kirke

static figures with blank faces devoid of any emotion. More frescoes can be seen in Keldby Kirke, which also has a sumptuously carved 16th-century pulpit.

㉗ Stege

Road map: F6. Møn. 🚶 4,000. 🚌 ℹ Storegade 75. **Tel** 70 70 12 36. 🌐 visitsouthzealand-mon.com

Møn's commercial centre, Stege grew up around a castle built in the 12th century and reached the height of its power in the Middle Ages, when it prospered thanks to a lucrative herring industry. A reminder of those days is Mølleporten (Mill Gate), which spans the main street of the town and once served as Stege's principal entrance. Ramparts belonging to the fortress walls are another medieval relic. **Empiregården**, Stege's museum, is a short way from Mølleporten and has local history exhibits.

Stege Kirke is in the town centre. This Romanesque church was built by Jakob Sunesen, who ruled Møn in the 13th century. Its ceiling frescoes were painted over during the Reformation and exposed again in the 19th century.

🏛 **Empiregården**
Storegade 75. **Tel** 70 70 12 36. **Open** varies; check website. 🅿
🌐 moensmuseum.dk

Nyord island's meadows, with marshland beyond

㉘ Nyord

Road map: F5.

Until the late 1980s, the only way to reach the small island of Nyord was by boat. A bridge, built in 1986, now links Nyord with Møn and has made the island more accessible and so increasingly popular with visitors. Nevertheless, both the island and the pretty hamlet of the same name have changed little since the 19th century. Nyord is particularly favoured by bird-watchers – its salt marshes attract massive flocks of birds, especially in spring and autumn, when the island is used as a stopping-off place for winged migrants. The most numerous among them include arctic terns, curlews and swans. The birds can be best viewed from an observation tower situated near the bridge.

㉙ Fakse

Road map: F5. 🚌 🚆 **Tel** 56 71 60 34.
🅦 visitsouthzealand-mon.com

References to Fakse (also known as Faxe) can be found in late 13th-century records when it was an important area for limestone mining. Today the town is best known for its local brewery, Faxe Bryggeri, which produces over 130 million litres (28.6 million gallons) of beer each year.

The town's most historic building is the 15th-century Gothic church, which has a number of wall paintings dating from around 1500. **Geomuseum Faxe** has a collection of over 500 types of fossils including some 63 million-year-old remains of plants and animals found in the Faxe Kalkbrud

quarry about 2 km (1 mile) outside the town. Visitors can collect their own fossils from the quarry.

🏛 **Geomuseum Faxe**
Kulturhuset Kanten, Østervej 2.
Tel 56 50 28 06. **Open** Jul–Aug:
10am–5pm daily; Apr–Jun:
10am–5pm Fri–Sun; Sep–Mar:
10am–5pm Sat & Sun **Closed** Mon in Jul.

Fakse's brewery, producing millions of gallons of beer a year

㉚ Stevns Klint

Road map: F5. 🛈 Rødvig, Havnevej 21. **Tel** 56 50 64 64. 🅦 visitsouth-zealand-mon.com

Although Denmark's most famous cliffs are found on Møn, the limestone peninsula of Stevns Klint (a UNESCO World Heritage site) is just as impressive. There is a footpath starting and ending in Rødvig that leads you to Bøgeskov Harbour on the Gjorslev estate, site of a 15th century castle. The cliffs are especially picturesque when the sun glints against the white chalk surface.

The area was for centuries known for its limestone quarries, which supplied building

material for the first castle built by Bishop Absalon in Copen-hagen; this castle became the nucleus of the royal residence, which in later times was given the name of Christiansborg Slot *(see pp90–1)*. Large-scale limestone quarrying was abandoned in the 1940s.

The strip of coastal cliffs is about 15 km (9 miles) long and 22 m (72 ft) tall. The best view-point can be found next to the old church of Højerup (Højerup Kirke). Legend has it that this 13th-century edifice, built close to the cliff's edge, moves inland each Christmas Eve by the length of a cockerel's jump.

Another local myth recounts a story about a king of the cliffs who lives in a cave in a crag south of the church. The king of the cliffs failed, however, to save the church from the destructive forces of nature. Over the years, due to constant erosion, the sea has advanced closer and closer towards the church and in 1928 the presbytery collapsed and crashed into the water.

A short distance from the church is the small town of Højerup. Here, the **Stevns Museum** has a local-history collection that includes workshops, Stone-Age tools, antique toys and a collection of fire-fighting equipment from the past including pumps and fire engines. There is also an exhibition dealing with the geology of the local cliffs.

Limestone cliffs of Stevns Klint on Zealand's east coast

Environs

A few kilometres inland is Store Heddinge, with one of Zealand's best Romanesque churches. The 12th-century church is made from limestone excavated in the nearby quarries. Its octagonal shape probably made it easier to defend.

🏛 **Stevns Museum**
Højerup Bygade 38, 4660 Store Heddinge. **Tel** 56 50 28 06. **Open** May, Jun, Aug, Sep: 11am–5pm Tue–Sun; Jul: 11am–5pm daily. 🖼

Vallø Slot, a moated 16th-century castle

➌ Vallø Slot

Road map: F5. **Tel** 56 26 05 00. Castle: **Closed** to visitors, but it is possible to explore the courtyard 10am–6pm daily. Garden: 8am–sunset daily. 🖼

The secluded castle of Vallø is one of the most impressive Renaissance buildings in Denmark. As early as the 15th century the islet was surrounded by a moat and featured a complex of defensive buildings. The castle owes its present shape to the influence of two enterprising sisters, Mette and Birgitte Rosenkrantz, who in the 16th century owned the surrounding land. The sisters divided the estate in equal shares between themselves – the east part was managed by Birgitte, while the western section belonged to Mette.

In 1737 the castle was taken over by a trust that provided a home for unmarried daughters of noble birth during their later years.

The castle is closed to visitors. The large park is open, however, as is the former stable block, which houses a museum containing a mix of agricultural implements and equestrian accessories.

➌ Køge

Road map: F5. 🏙 36,500. 🚊 🚌
ℹ Vestergade 1. **Tel** 56 67 60 01.
🖥 **visitkoege.com**

One of Denmark's best-preserved medieval towns, Køge was granted a municipal charter in 1288 and grew quickly thanks to its large natural harbour at the mouth of a navigable river. Køge Bay entered the annals of Danish history in 1677, when the Danish fleet, led by Admiral Niels Juel, crushed a Swedish armada heading for Copenhagen. The battle and the victorious Admiral Niels Juel are commemorated by a 9-m (30-ft) tall obelisk by the harbour.

The heart of the town is its market square, which contains a monument to Frederik VI. The town hall standing in the cobbled square is the longest-serving public building of its kind in Denmark. The cobbled streets leading from the market square are lined with half-timbered houses for which Køge is famous. The most interesting street in this respect is Kirkestræde. The small house at No. 20, with only

Kirkestræde 10, now part of Køge library

two windows, is the oldest dated half-timbered house in Denmark; the beam under its front door gives the year of construction as 1527.

Another impressive historic building is Sankt Nicolai Kirke, which dates from 1324. Its tower served for many years as a lighthouse and is now used as a viewpoint.

Køge Museum is located along Nørregade and occupies two early-17th-century buildings. Its exhibits include historic furniture, costumes and, as a reminder of the town's bloody past, the local executioner's sword. By the harbour is Kjøge Mini-by, an exact miniature version of Køge as it was in 1865.

🏛 **Køge Museum**
Nørregade 4. **Tel** 56 63 42 42. **Open** Jul–Aug: 10am–5pm daily; Sep–Jun: 11am–4pm Tue–Sun. 🖼

The Aristocratic Ladies of the Castle

In 1737, Vallø's owner, Queen Sophie Magdalene, donated the castle to the Royal Vallø Foundation. From then on the castle become a home for unmarried women from noble families. The famously religious queen ensured the typically cloistral character of the place and promoted a lifestyle true to Christian principles. Initially it housed 12 women, some of whom were as young as 15. The convent was run by a prioress of high birth, and the mother superior was also descended from an aristocratic family. The male staff, an administrator, doctor and servants, lived opposite the castle. Some unmarried ladies still reside in Vallø Slot.

The imposing twin towers of Vallø Slot

FUNEN

Funen (Fyn in Danish) is Denmark's second largest island and occupies an area of about 3,000 sq km (1,158 sq miles). It has some of Denmark's best scenery including wide, sandy beaches, steep cliffs and lush pasture land and orchards. A number of neighbouring islands are considered to be part of Funen including Ærø and Tåsinge, which are themselves popular destinations.

Funen is separated from Zealand by the Store Bælt (Great Belt) and from Jutland by the Lille Bælt (Little Belt). Nearly half of Funen's inhabitants live in Odense, which is the island's capital, a lively cultural centre and the birthplace of Hans Christian Andersen. Aside from Odense there are no large towns on Funen and the island is sometimes described as the "garden of Denmark" because of the large amount of produce that grows in its fertile soil.

Thanks to the fact that the island has escaped most of Denmark's wars with other nations, Funen has an exceptionally high number of well-preserved historic buildings and palaces. The best-known of these is Egeskov Slot, a Renaissance castle encircled by a moat.

The relatively small distances, gently rolling landscape and the many interesting places to visit, make Funen an ideal area for cycling trips. The south-western part of the island features a range of wooded hills. The highest of these, rising to 126 m (413 ft), are found near the town of Faaborg. Central Funen is mostly flat and only becomes slightly undulated in the northeastern region. The south has most of the island's harbours and towns, while the northern and western parts are sparsely populated.

An archipelago of southern islets includes Langeland, Ærø and Tåsinge as well as a number of tiny islands inhabited only by birds. This area is popular with Danish yachtsmen and it is possible to explore the archipelago by joining an organized cruise on board a wooden sailing ship. Some of the islands can be reached by ferry.

The imposing façade of Egeskov Slot, one of Denmark's finest castles

◀ Picturesque Dukkehuset (Dolls' House) in Ærøskøbing, on the island of Ærø

Exploring Funen

Funen is known as the garden of Denmark and for its windy roads and cosy half-timbered houses. Throughout the centuries the Danish aristocracy built their opulent residences on the island, and Funen has over 120 beautifully preserved mansions, castles and palaces. The most impressive are Egeskov Slot and, on Tåsinge, Valdemars Slot. Funen's coastline is 11,000 km (6,800 miles) long and has some beautiful beaches. The lovely island of Ærø is a picturesque place with tiny villages and ancient farms. Odense, Denmark's third-largest city, is a university town and the birthplace of Hans Christian Andersen.

Den Gamle Gaard, a merchant's house in Faaborg

Key

═══ Motorway

──── Major road

········ Minor road

──── Scenic route

┈┈┈ Main railway

──── Minor railway

0 kilometres   10

0 miles   10

Sights at a Glance

1 Assens

2 *Odense pp182–3*

3 Kerteminde

4 Hindsholm

5 Nyborg

6 Egeskov Slot

7 Faaborg

8 Svendborg

9 Tåsinge

10 Langeland

11 Marstal

12 Ærøskøbing

Traditional wooden boat moored in Svendborg harbour

For hotels and restaurants in this area see pp251–2 and pp269–270

Imposing turrets and high walls of
Egeskov Slot

Getting Around

Funen is linked by bridge to Jutland
and Zealand. There is a frequent
(almost hourly) rail service from
Copenhagen and Jutland. The island's
main transport artery is the E20
motorway running from east to west (a
railway line runs roughly parallel to this).
The most important roads that lead from
Odense towards other major towns are
the No. 9 road to Svendborg and the No.
43 to Faaborg. Ferries sail to Ærø, while
Langeland can be reached via a bridge.

For keys to symbols *see back flap*

Quiet yacht marina in Assens

❶ Assens

Road map: C5. 🚇 6,000. 🚌
ℹ️ Tobaksgaarden 7. **Tel** 23 37 84 66.
🌐 visitassens.dk

Situated on the shores of the Store Bælt (Great Belt), Assens was for centuries a busy harbour for ferries on the route between Funen and Jutland. Following the construction of a bridge across the strait, far north of the town, it lost importance. Assens contains numerous historic buildings including 18th- and 19th-century merchants' houses, as well as the 15th-century Vor Frue Kirke (Church of Our Lady).

The best-known citizen of Assens was Peter Willemoes (1783–1808), a war hero who, in 1801, fought against Admiral Nelson during the Napoleonic Wars and distinguished himself during Nelson's bombardment of Copenhagen. Willemoes' birthplace, **Willemoesgården**, now houses a museum of cultural history. A monument to Willemoes has been erected near the harbour. A house by the monument was once a sailors' kitchen.

The museum complex also includes a silver and glass collection, Ernsts Samlinger (open for guided tours only), and Toldbodhus at Nordre Havnevej 19, which hosts changing exhibits in the town's old customs building.

🏛️ **Willemoesgården**
Østergade 36. **Tel** 64 71 31 90.
Open Easter, May–mid-Oct: 10am–4pm Tue–Sun; mid-Oct–Apr: 10am–4pm Wed & Sat. 🎭

❷ Odense

See pp182–3.

❸ Kerteminde

Road map: D5. 🚇 6,000. 🚌
ℹ️ Hans Schacksvej 5. **Tel** 65 32 11 21.
🌐 visitkerteminde.dk

Much of this pretty seaside town is clustered around the 15th-century Sankt Laurentius Kirke (Church). One of the town's main attractions is **Fjord&Bælt**, a sea-life centre built in 1997. A 50-m long tunnel with large windows allows visitors to walk beneath the fjord and enjoy the underwater view. The famous Danish painter Johannes Larsen (1867–1961) once lived in Kerteminde and the **Johannes Larsen Museum** contains many of his paintings.

Environs
Four kilometres (2 miles) southwest of Kerteminde is the **Ladbyskibet**, a 22-m (72-ft) long Viking ship that dates from the 10th century

Statue of St Laurentius, in Kerteminde

and was used as the tomb of a Viking chieftain.

🚢 **Fjord&Bælt**
Margrethes Plads 1. **Tel** 65 32 42 00.
Open Jul–Aug: 10am–5pm daily; Sep–Nov & Feb:–Jun 10am–4pm Tue–Sun. **Closed** Jan, Dec. 🎭
🌐 fjord-baelt.dk

🏛️ **Johannes Larsen Museum**
Møllebakken 14. **Tel** 65 32 11 77.
Open Jun–Aug: 10am–5pm daily; Sep–May: 10am–4pm Tue–Sun. 🎭
🌐 johanneslarsenmuseet.dk

❹ Hindsholm

Road map: D5. 🚌

Rising at the far end of the Hindsholm peninsula are 25-m (82-ft) high cliffs, which provide a splendid view over the coast and the island of Samsø. A little way inland is Marhøj Jættestue, a 2nd-century BC underground burial chamber.

The small town of Viby, north of Assens, has a 19th-century windmill and an Early-Gothic church. According to legend, Marsk Stig, a hero of Danish folklore, was buried here in 1293. Before setting off for war, Marsk Stig is said to have left his wife in the care of the king, Erik Klipping. The king took the notion of "care" somewhat too far and when the knight returned he killed the king and was outlawed. Even his funeral had to be held in secret.

Crops growing on the Hindsholm peninsula

Royal painting and suits of armour in the Knights' Hall, Nyborg Slot

❺ Nyborg

Road map: D5. 🏔 16,000. 🚗 🚌
ℹ Torvet 2B. **Tel** 63 33 80 90.
🌐 visitnyborg.dk

The castle of **Nyborg Slot** was built around 1170 by Valdemar the Great's nephew as part of the fortifications that guarded the Store Bælt. For nearly 200 years the castle was the scene of the Danehof assemblies (an early form of Danish parliament). As a result, the city is considered to have been Denmark's capital from 1183 to 1413. The castle was also the venue of the signing, in 1282, of a coronation charter that laid down the duties of the king. Nyborg grew up around this fortress. Over the centuries the castle gradually fell into ruin; it was only after World War I that it was restored and turned into a museum. A number of rooms are open to the public including the royal chambers and the Danehof room. The castle ramparts and moat are now a park.

Nyborg Church, built in the late 14th century, has just one artifact from this time: a Gothic crucifix that is decorated to represent the Tree of Life.

During July and August, on Tuesdays at about 7pm, the Tappenstreg regiment marches through the streets of Nyborg. This regiment upholds an 18th-century tradition of checking whether all the town's entertainment venues have closed on time.

🏰 **Nyborg Slot**
Slotsgade 34. **Tel** 65 31 02 07.
Open Apr, May, Sep & Oct: 10am–3pm Tue–Sun; Jun–Aug: 10am–4pm daily. 🖼 🌐 nyborgslot.dk

❻ Egeskov Slot

Road map: D5. Egeskov Gade 18, Kværndrup. **Tel** 62 27 10 16. **Open** May–mid-Jun & late Aug–mid-Oct: 10am–5pm daily; mid-Aug–Sep: 10am–6pm daily; end Jun–mid-Aug: 10am–7pm daily. 🖼 🌐 egeskov.dk

This magnificent castle was built in the mid-16th century and is one of Denmark's best-known sights. Egeskov means "oak forest" and the castle was built in the middle of a pond on a foundation of oak trees. The interior has some grand rooms containing antique

Coat of arms from Egeskov Slot

furniture and paintings, and a hall full of hunting trophies that include elephant tusks and tiger heads.

Much of the grounds were laid out in the 18th century and include a garden adorned with various fountains, as well as a herb garden. Other additions to the layout are a bamboo maze and a vintage car museum.

❼ Faaborg

Road map: D5. 🏔 7,000. 🚌
ℹ Torvet 19. **Tel** 72 53 18 18.
🌐 visitfaaborg.com

Faaborg is a picturesque place with cobbled streets and half-timbered houses. The market square contains the town's most famous monument, Ymerbrønden, produced by the Danish painter and sculptor Kai Nielsen in the early 1900s. Its main figure is Ymer, a giant who according to Nordic mythology was killed by Odin.

The view from the 31-m (102-ft) tall Klokketårnet (Belfry) embraces the bay. The tower is all that remains of a medieval church.

Den Gamle Gaard is a wealthy merchant's house that dates from 1725. **Faaborg Museum**, designed by Carl Petersen, has a number of works by the "De Fynske Malere" group of Danish artists, which included the likes of Peter Hansen, Johannes Larsen and Fritz Syberg.

🏛 **Den Gamle Gaard**
Holkegade 1. **Tel** 63 61 20 00.
Open check website for latest information on opening hours. 🖼
🌐 ohavsmuseet.dk

🏛 **Faaborg Museum**
Grønnegade 75. **Tel** 62 61 06 45.
Open Apr–Oct: 10am–4pm Tue–Sun; Jul & Aug: 10am–4pm daily (until 6pm Wed); Nov–Mar: 10am–3pm Tue–Sun. 🖼
🌐 faaborgmuseum.dk

Collection of Danish art in Faaborg Museum

❷ Odense

One of the oldest cities in Denmark, Odense derives its name from the Nordic god Odin who was worshipped by the Vikings. In medieval times it was an important centre of trade and from the 12th century on it was a major pilgrimage destination. Since the 19th century, when a canal was built linking Odense with the sea, the city has been a major port. Odense has a rich cultural life and plenty to see including a cathedral and a museum devoted to the city's most famous resident, Hans Christian Andersen.

Childhood home of Hans Christian Andersen

Exploring Odense

Most attractions lie within the boundaries of the medieval district. Getting around Odense is made easy by the Citypass, which entitles the holder to free travel, free admission to museums and cut-price tickets for boat cruises.

🏛 Brandts

Brandts Torv 1. **Tel** 65 20 70 10. **Open** 10am–5pm Thu–Tue; noon–8pm Wed. **Closed** Mon (except for weeks 7, 8 & 42). 🅿 **W** brandts.dk

For more than fifty years Brandt's textile factory was the biggest company in Odense. After its closure in 1977 it stood empty for a number of years until it was renovated and transformed into a cultural centre. Today it houses museums, a cinema, art galleries, shops, restaurants and cafés. The museum gallery is divided into various sections: the Mediemuseet has displays on the history of print production and the latest electronic media. The Museet for Fotokunst exhibits works by Danish and international photographers, while the Kunsthallen Brandts shows contemporary art, craft, design and performance.

🏛 H C Andersens Barndomshjem

Munkemøllestræde 3–5. **Tel** 65 51 46 01. **Open** Jan–Jun & Sep–Dec: 11am–4pm Tue–Sun; Jul & Aug: 10am–5pm daily. 🅿 **W** museum.odense.dk

The Andersen family moved to this small house close to the cathedral when Hans was two years old. Andersen lived here until the age of 14. The museum has only a few rooms, furnished with basic period household objects, but manages to conjure up what life was like for a poor Danish family in the early 19th century.

⛪ Sankt Knuds Kirke

Klosterbakken 2. **Tel** 66 12 03 92. **Open** Apr–Oct: 10am–4pm Tue–Sat, noon–4pm Mon, noon–4pm Sun & holidays; Nov–Mar: 10am–5pm Tue–Sat, noon–5pm Mon, noon–4pm Sun & holidays. **W** odense-domkirke.dk

Odense cathedral is named after Canute (Knud) II, who ruled Denmark from 1080–86. The king's skeleton is on public display in a glass case down in the basement. The present cathedral is one of Denmark's most beautiful examples of Gothic architecture. It stands on the site of an earlier Romanesque structure, which was destroyed by fire in 1248. The cathedral's ornate gilded altar is a masterpiece of 16th-century craftmanship by Claus Berg of Lübeck. The triptych is 5 m (16 ft) high and includes nearly 300 intricately carved figures within its design.

🏚 Flakhaven

Flakhaven derives its name from an old Danish word meaning an area surrounded by meadows and gardens. For centuries the square was used as a market venue and attracted merchants and farmers from all over Funen. The main building standing in the square is the Rådhus (city hall), which has a west wing dating from the 19th century. The remainder of the building is 20th century. Guided tours are available on Tuesdays and Thursdays in the summer and include access to the Wedding Room, the Town Council Chamber and a wall commemorating citizens who have made major contributions to the city's history.

🏛 Brandts 13

Jernbanegade 13. **Tel** 65 20 70 00. **Open** 10am–5pm Thu–Tue, noon–8pm Wed. 🅿 **W** brandts.dk

This museum has a very large collection of Danish art, though

The nave and altar at Sankt Knuds Kirke in Odense

Paintings in the Memorial Hall, H C Andersens Hus

VISITORS' CHECKLIST

Practical Information
Road map: D5. 193,000.
Vestergade 2. Tel 63 75 75 20.
visitodense.com

Transport
Odense.

only a fraction of it is on display at any one time. The Classical building is adorned on the outside with a frieze depicting scenes from Danish history and mythology. The interior is filled with paintings, etchings and sculptures by Danish artists spanning a period of 250 years. One section of the museum contains works by local Funen artists, collectively known as Fynboerne.

H C Andersens Hus
Bangs Boder 29. Tel 65 51 46 01. Open Jan–Jun & Sep–Dec: 10am–4pm Tue–Sun; Jul & Aug: 10am–5pm daily.
museum.odense.dk

Denmark's most famous writer was born in this house in 1805.

It is now a museum, and it was greatly extended and modernized to celebrate the 200th anniversary of Andersen's birth. The exhibition includes a recreation of the author's study and numerous items belonging to Andersen, including his notes and letters. There is even an old rope – apparently Andersen was terrified by the thought of a fire and carried this with him wherever he went in readiness for an emergency evacuation. Hanging on one of the walls is a world map indicating the countries in which Andersen's tales have been published in translation. A special collection includes copies of his works in 120 languages.

Close to the museum is Fyrtøjet (the Tinderbox), a children's cultural centre based on Andersen's stories.

Den Fynske Landsby
Sejerskovvej 20, 5260 Odense S. Tel 65 51 46 01. Open Jul–mid-Aug: 10am–6pm daily; mid–late Aug: 10am–5pm daily; Sep–late Oct, Apr–Jun: 10am–5pm Tue–Sun. Closed late Oct–Mar. museum.odense.dk

The 'Funen Village' is an open air museum located in a pleasant woodland just south of Odense city centre. Here, you can imagine what life would have been like during Hans Christian Andersen's childhood 200 years ago. In summer, open air theatre events and acts are also held here. You can take a riverboat tour from Munkemose near H C Andersens Barndomshjem to Fruens Bøge, next to the museum.

Odense City Centre

① Brandts
② H C Andersens Barndomshjem
③ Sankt Knuds Kirke
④ Flakhaven
⑤ Brandts 13
⑥ H C Andersens Hus
⑦ Den Fynske Landsby

❽ Svendborg

Road map: D5. 🏛 27,000. 🚌 🚆
ℹ️ Havnepladsen 2. **Tel** 62 23 69 52.
🎭 Fyn Rundt Regatta (Jul).
W visitsvendborg.com

Funen's second largest town, Svendborg is a busy port and has strong links with ship-building. In the 19th century its boatyards produced half of all Danish vessels.

Most of Svendborg's sights are within easy reach of Torvet, the market square. Closest to hand is the 13th-century Vor Frue Kirke, which has a carillon consisting of 27 bells. Sankt Nicolai Kirke is slightly older, though also 13th century. A short distance west of Vor Frue Kirke is Anne Hvides Gård, a half-timbered building dating from 1560. **SAK Kunstbygningen** (SAK Art Exhibitions) displays works by the Danish sculptor Kai Nielsen (1882–1924), who was born in Svendborg. Other museums include Naturama, a natural history museum, and **Forsorgsmuseet**, built in 1872 as a "poor farm". In 1906 there were 450 such institutions in Denmark; this, the only extant one, houses a museum telling the story of the country's poor.

🏛 SAK Kunstbygningen

Vestergade 27. **Tel** 62 22 44 70.
Open 11am–4pm Tue–Sun. 📷

🏛 Forsorgsmuseet

Viebæltegård Gruppemøllevej 13.
Tel 62 21 02 61. **Open** mid-Feb–late Dec: 10am–4pm Tue–Sun.
📷 ♿ 🚻 🍴 📷 **W** svendborg-museum.dk

Kattesund, a scenic alley in Svendborg

An elegant apartment in Valdemars Slot, Tåsinge

❾ Tåsinge

Road map: D6. 🏛 6,000. 🚆

The island of Tåsinge is linked by bridge to Funen and Langeland. The major local attraction is **Valdemars Slot**, built by Christian IV for his favourite son Valdemar and completed in 1644.

The castle's architect was Hans van Steenwinckel, who was also responsible for Rosenborg Slot in Copenhagen (see pp64–5). In the 1670s the king gave the castle to Admiral Niels Juel in recognition of his successful command of the Danish fleet during the Battle of Køge Bay (see p175). The castle has remained in the hands of the Juel family ever since. The royal apartments, the reception rooms and the kitchens are open to the public. In the attic there is a collection of items including trophies from African safaris. The domestic quarters, arranged around a lake, house a small museum.

Environs

Near the castle, heading for Svendborg, is the fishing port of Troense. Its most attractive street, Grønnegade, is lined with half-timbered houses. In Bregninge, the Tåsinge Museum illustrates life at sea; it also tells of the ill-fated love affair between circus performer Elvira Madigan and Swedish lieutenant Sixten Sparre.

🏰 Valdemars Slot

Slotsalléen 100, Troense. **Tel** 62 22 61 06. **Open** Apr–Oct: 10am–5pm, days vary; see website for details. 📷
W valdemarsslot.dk

Statue of Hans Christian Ørsted in Rudkøbing

❿ Langeland

Road map: D6. 🏛 13,000. 🚆 🚆
ℹ️ Rudkøbing Torvet 5. **Tel** 62 51 35 05. **W** langeland.dk

Langeland is located off the southeast coast of Funen and can be reached by bridge or from Lolland by ferry. The island has a number of good beaches and marked cycling paths. Windmills are dotted here and there, along with quaint hamlets and farms.

Rudkøbing is the capital and the island's only sizeable town. Its most famous citizen was Hans Christian Ørsted (1777–1851), a physicist who made major advances in the field of electromagnetism. The house in which the scientist was born is known as **Det Gamle Apotek** (The Old Pharmacy) and has been arranged to re-create an 18th-century pharmacist's shop and herb garden. In front of it stands a statue of Ørsted. From here it is only a short distance to the market square, which contains a 19th-century town hall and a much older church with an inscription giving its year of founding as 1105.

About 10 km (6 miles) north of Rudkøbing is Tranekær, whose main attraction is Tranekær Slot, a pink-coloured castle that dates from around 1200. The castle is normally closed to visitors, but there are some guided tours in July, and the grounds can also be visited. Part of the estate now serves as a botanical garden which has a number of rare trees including some Californian sequoias. An open-air gallery exhibits sculptures and installations by Danish and international artists. About 30 km (18 miles) south of Rudkøbing is the **Koldkrigsmuseum** (Cold War Museum), where you can explore a submarine, a mine-sweeper and a bunker.

🏛 **Det Gamle Apotek**
Brogade 15, Rudkøbing. **Tel** 63 51 63 00. **Open** for guided tours (Jul). 🚫

🏛 **Koldkrigsmuseum**
Vognsbjergvej 4B, Bagenkop. **Tel** 62 56 27 00. **Open** May–Sep: 10am–5pm daily; Apr & Oct: to 4pm.
🌐 **langelandsfortet.dk**

Colourful façade of Tranekær Slot, Langeland

Picturesque 17th-century houses in Marstal

⑪ Marstal

Road map: D6. Ærø. 🚗 2,300. 🚌 🚢
Tel 62 52 13 00.

Marstal is the largest town on the island of Ærø. Its history has long been associated with the sea and in the 18th century it was a busy port with about 300 ships arriving here every year. The **Søfartmuseum** (Maritime Museum) occupies four buildings near the harbour and contains many items connected with the sea including model schooners and seafaring paintings.

The dependence of the local population on the sea is also apparent in the local church on Kirkestræde, which was built in 1738. The altarpiece in the church depicts Christ calming the rough waves, and hanging in several places within the building are votive sailing ships. Outside in the cemetery there are numerous gravestones of local sailors. The church clock was created by Jens Olsen, who also produced the World Clock in the Rådhus in Copenhagen (*see p78*).

🏛 **Søfartmuseum**
Prinsensgade 1. **Tel** 62 53 23 31. **Open** 16 Apr–31 May: 10am–4pm daily; Jun–Aug: 9am–5pm daily; Sep & Oct: 10am–4pm daily; 1 Nov–15 Apr: 11am–3pm Mon–Sat. 🚫

Exhibit from Marstal's Søfartmuseum

⑫ Ærøskøbing

Road map: D6. Ærø. 🚗 900. 🚢 🚌 ℹ️ Ærøskøbing Havn 4. **Tel** 62 52 13 00.

Many of the 17th-century houses lining the cobbled streets are a reminder of a time when Ærøskøbing was a prosperous merchant town. The oldest house dates from 1645 and can be found at Søndergade 36. The town's most picturesque dwelling is Dukkehuset (Dolls' House) at Smedegade 37. Also in Smedegade is **Flaske-Peters Samling**, a museum devoted to Peter Jacobsen, who first went to sea at the age of 16. Known as "Bottle Peter", he created about 1,700 ships-in-a-bottle before he died in 1960. Also in the museum is a cross he made for his own grave. **Ærø Museum** has displays on the history of the island and its people, including a collection of 19th-century paintings.

🏛 **Flaske-Peters Samling**
Smedegade 22. **Tel** 61 75 49 80. **Open** Jul & Aug: 10am–4pm daily; Sep, May & Jun: 11am–3pm Mon–Sat. 🚫

🏛 **Ærø Museum**
Brogade 3–5. **Tel** 62 52 29 50. **Open** May & Jun: 11am–3pm daily; Jul & Aug: 10am–4pm Mon–Fri, 11am–3pm Sat & Sun; Sep–late Oct: 11am–3pm Mon–Sat; Nov–Apr: 11am–2pm daily. 🚫

SOUTHERN AND CENTRAL JUTLAND

As well as the scenic lowlands and undulating hills and meadows found on the eastern side of central Jutland, this region has much to recommend it. Attractions include beautifully preserved medieval towns, traditional hamlets, parks, castles and ancient Viking burial grounds. No one travelling with children should miss a trip to famous LEGOLAND®.

Jutland derives its name from the Jutes, a Germanic tribe that once inhabited this peninsula. When the Vikings, who occupied the islands to the east, began to encroach on this territory, the mixing of the two tribes gave rise to the Danes as a distinct people.

After Denmark's defeat during the Schleswig Wars in 1864, Jutland was occupied by Prussia, and subsequently, as part of Schleswig, remained under German control. It was not until a plebiscite in 1920 that it once more became part of the kingdom of Denmark. After the final resolution of this Danish-German border dispute, many families decided to remain on the "other" side. The expatriate minorities are still active on both sides of the border.

On the islands of Fanø and Rømø the influence of the nearby Netherlands can be seen in the tiles decorating some of the houses. The Wadden Sea around these islands makes for excellent exploration, either on a seal or oyster safari. The milder east coast features wealthy borough towns with fine museums.

The top attraction for families with children is LEGOLAND®, where millions of plastic LEGO® bricks are used to create Denmark's best-known amusement park. The cities of Aarhus and Silkeborg offer a more cultural option.

Carved Viking figures and replica Viking ship in Vejle Fjord

◀ Terrace café at the Glass Museum (Glasmuseet), Ebeltoft

Exploring Southern and Central Jutland

Jutland is the only part of Denmark that is not an island. The bottom section of the peninsula is cut across by a 69-km- (43-mile-) long national border with Germany. The most popular attraction of southern and central Jutland is LEGOLAND®. However, this region has much more to offer, including four national parks; several historically significant centres – such as Ribe, Denmark's oldest town, and Jelling, which is famous for its ancient burial mounds; and the delightfully arty town of Silkeborg, splendidly located in the heart of a Lake District.

Aarhus, Denmark's second city, is famous for its restaurants and nightlife, fuelled by the students at its university.

Sights at a Glance

1. Ebeltoft
2. Aarhus pp192–3
3. Moesgård
4. Horsens
5. Silkeborg Lake District
6. Silkeborg
7. Herning
8. Ringkøbing Fjord
9. Givskud Zoo
10. Jelling
11. LEGOLAND® pp196–7
12. Vejle
13. Esbjerg
14. Ribe
15. Rømø
16. Tønder
17. Sønderborg
18. Haderslev
19. Kolding
20. Fredericia

Ramparts around the town of Fredericia in central Jutland

For hotels and restaurants in this area see pp252–3 and pp270–72

Key

- Motorway
- Motorway under construction
- Major road
- Minor road
- Scenic route
- Main railway
- Minor railway
- International border
- Regional border
- △ Summit

Restored cutter in front of Esbjerg's maritime museum

Getting Around

Jutland is almost three times larger than the rest of Denmark put together and distances between towns can be significant. The E45 runs from the German border all the way to northern Jutland along the eastern coast of the peninsula, connecting to Esbjerg from Kolding, and to Silkeborg and Herning from Aarhus. The fastest route from Copenhagen is the E20, which joins with the E45 at Fredericia. It is also possible to take a ferry to either Aarhus or Ebeltoft from Copenhagen.

The 15th-century Koldinghus in Kolding

For keys to symbols *see back flap*

Fregatten Jylland in Ebeltoft, now serving as a museum

❶ Ebeltoft

Road map: D3. 🔼 7,500. 🚌 ℹ️ S.A. Jensens Vej 3. **Tel** 86 34 14 00.

Boasting the smallest rådhus (town hall) in Denmark, Ebeltoft, part of the Mols Bjerge national park, is over 700 years old. Many of the town's cobbled streets, including Adelgade, are lined with half-timbered houses from the 17th century.

In the harbour is **Fregatten Jylland**, a large restored wooden ship that took part in the Battle of Helgoland in 1864. Groups of visitors can arrange overnight stays on board, sleeping in a hammock and experiencing the life of a sailor. A large museum annex focuses on maritime history and will interest all ages.

Bell from Fregatten Jylland

The nearby **Glasmuseet** has many items of contemporary glass art on display, including pieces by Dale Chihuly and Harvey Littleton.

🏛 Fregatten Jylland
S.A. Jensen Vej 2–4. **Tel** 86 34 10 99. **Open** Nov–Mar: 11am–4pm Wed–Sun; Apr–Oct: 10am–5pm daily (Jul & Aug until 6pm); during school holidays: 10am–6pm. 🅰️
W fregatten-jylland.dk

🏛 Glasmuseet
Strandvejen 8. **Tel** 86 34 17 99. **Open** Jan–Mar, Nov & Dec: 10am–4pm Tue–Sun; Apr–Jun, Sep & Oct: 10am–5pm Tue–Sun; Jul & Aug: 10am–6pm Tue–Sun. 🅰️ **W** glasmuseet.dk

❷ Aarhus

See pp192–3.

❸ Moesgård

Road map: D4. 7 km (4 miles) south of Aarhus. **Tel** 87 16 10 16. 🎪 Vikingetræf (Jul). **W** moesmus.dk

Formerly located in a manor house, Moesgård is a large prehistoric museum that is due to reopen to the public in purpose-built premises in 2014–15. Situated on a hill known as Hill of the Elves, a short drive south of Aarhus, the museum has several highlights, ranging from its collection of runic stones, the largest in Scandinavia, to a hoard of votive offerings – swords, axes, shields and other items – found at Illerup Ådal, near Skanderborg, and dating to about 200 AD. Its star exhibit, however, is the Graauballe Man. This mummified body, discovered in 1952 in a bog, had been preserved thanks to a combination of acids and iron in the soil. He is believed to have been about 40 years old when he died in 80 BC. A slash across his throat indicates that he was probably murdered.

Each year in late July, Moesgård becomes the venue for a lively and entertaining Viking festival, Vikingtræf, which features battles, a Viking marketplace and performing Icelandic horses.

Lichtenberg Palace, Horsens, once a residence for the tsar's family

❹ Horsens

Road map: C4. 38 km (24 miles) south of Aarhus. 🔼 55,000. 🚉 🚌 ℹ️ Fussingsvej 8. **Tel** 75 60 21 20. 🎪 Medieval Festival (late Aug). **W** visithorsens.dk

Horsens is the birthplace of Vitus Bering (1681–1741), the explorer who discovered Alaska and the straits that separate it from Siberia (these were subsequently named after him). The guns from Bering's ship now stand in the town's main park. Mementos from his expeditions are on display in **Horsens Museum**.

The Danish Romanesque Vor Frelsers Kirke (Our Saviour's Church) is 13th century. Nearby, Lichtenberg Palace was used by the tsar's family after they fled Russia. The **Horsens Kunst Museum** has contemporary Danish art.

🏛 Horsens Museum
Sundvej 1A. **Tel** 76 29 23 50. **Open** Jul–Aug: 10am–4pm daily; Sep–Jun: 11am–4pm Tue–Sun. 🅰️ **W** horsensmuseum.dk

🏛 Horsens Kunst Museum
Carolinelundsvej 2. **Tel** 76 29 23 70. **Open** Jul & Aug: 10am–4pm daily (to 5pm Sat & Sun); Sep–Jun: 11am– 4pm Tue–Sun (to 5pm Sat & Sun). 🅰️ **W** horsenskunstmuseum.dk

Reconstructed burial chamber at Moesgård

Silkeborg harbour, in Denmark's Lake District

❺ Silkeborg Lake District

Road map: C4.

The stretch between Silkeborg and Skanderborg and the area slightly to the north of it is a land of lakes and hills known as Søhøjlandet. Here, visitors find Jutland's largest lake – the Mossø, as well as Denmark's longest river, the Gudenå (176 km/ 109 miles). The Lake District also has some of the country's highest peaks. In summer it is a favourite destination for canoeists and cyclists, as well as hikers, all of whom make the most of the lakeland scenery.

Gjern has a vintage car museum (with about 70 models, the oldest dating from the early 20th century), while Tange Sø boasts Elmuseet, an electricity museum situated next to the country's largest power station.

Other places worth visiting include the church in Veng, which was built around 1100 and is thought to be the oldest monastery in Denmark, and, on the shores of Mossø, the ruins of Øm Kloster, the best-preserved Cistercian monastery in Denmark.

❻ Silkeborg

Road map: C4. 42,000.
Torvet 2A. **Tel** 86 82 19 11.
Jazz Festival (Jun), Country Music Festival (Aug). **W** silkeborg.com

Silkeborg owes much of its past prosperity to the paper factory, built in 1846, that was at one time powered by the local river. The popular **Museum Silkeborg** occupies a former manor built in 1767. Most visitors head straight

for the Tollund Man, one of the best-preserved prehistoric bodies in the world.

The city is also famous for its art galleries, such as **Silkeborg Bad**, which focuses on contemporary art, and **Museum Jorn**, with works by the Danish artist Asger Jorn and other members of the CoBrA movement.

In summer a 19th-century paddle steamer travels the 15 km (9 miles) to Himmel-bjerget, where a 25-m- (82-ft-) high tower offers great views.

Tollund Man

Museum Silkeborg
Hovedgårdsvej 7. **Tel** 86 82 14 99.
Open 10am–5pm daily.
W museumsilkeborg.dk

Silkeborg Bad
Gjessøvej 40. **Tel** 86 81 63 29.
Open noon–4pm Tue–Fri, 11am–5pm Sat & Sun (May–Sep: 10am–5pm Tue–Sun). **W** silkeborgbad.dk

Museum Jorn
Gudenåvej 7–9. **Tel** 86 82 53 88. **Open** 11am–5pm Tue–Fri, 10am–5pm Sat & Sun. **W** museumjorn.dk

❼ Herning

Road map: C4. 30,000.
Østergade 21. **Tel** 96 27 22 22.
W visitherning.dk

The town of Herning was established in the late 19th century following the arrival of the railway. Herning has twice been named Denmark's 'city of the year' due to its economic importance to the country. The **Frilandsmuseet** tells the story of the town as well as the history and archaeology of the region. **HEART Herning Museum of Contemporary Art** exhibits works by artists such as Carl-Henning Pedersen, a representative of the CoBrA movement. Housed in a building designed by the US architect Steven Holl, HEART is a museum of Danish and international contemporary art. The **Danmarks Fotomuseum** has a large collection of cameras and photographic displays.

Frilandsmuseet
Museumgade 32. **Tel** 96 26 19 00.
Open 10am–4:30pm Tue–Fri, 11am–4:30pm Sat & Sun (Jul: also Mon).
W museummidtjylland.dk

HEART Herning Museum of Contemporary Art
Birk Centerpark 8. **Tel** 97 12 10 33.
Open 10am–5pm Tue–Sun.
W heartmus.dk

Danmarks Fotomuseum
Museumsgade 28. **Tel** 97 22 53 22.
Open noon–4:30pm Tue–Sun (Jul & Aug: 11am–4:30pm daily).
W fotomuseum.dk

One of Herning's tranquil streets

② Aarhus

Denmark's second-largest city, and a European Capital of Culture in 2017, dates back to Viking times. It was originally named Aros, meaning "at the mouth of the river", and due to its location on Jutland's eastern coast it became a major seaport. After the Reformation Aarhus grew into an important trading centre, and the 19th century saw the development of the harbour. A university was founded here in 1928, and today Aarhus boasts a vibrant cultural life, with some fine museums and venues, as well as lively cafés and bars. The city is also a major centre for wind energy and the home of many wind turbine manufacturers.

City panorama from the Rådhus tower

Exploring Aarhus

Most of the town's attractions are concentrated within a fairly small area; the only site located more than 1 km (0.6 mile) away is Den Gamle By. Sightseeing is made easier by the Aarhus Card, which gives free admission to some museums and free use of public transport.

🎼 Musikhuset

Thomas Jensens Allé 2. **Tel** 89 40 40 40. **Open** 11am–6pm daily.
🇼 **musikhusetaarhus.dk**

The city's concert hall opened in 1982 and is one of Denmark's foremost cultural centres. The glass-fronted building is home to the prestigious Jutland Opera Company and Aarhus Symphony Orchestra, which holds concerts most Thursday evenings. The building is worth visiting if only to see its vast glazed hall, planted with luxuriant palm trees. The centre features its own café, which often has concerts, and a restaurant, the Richter, named after Johan Richter, the main architect of the building.

🏛 Rådhus

Rådhuspladsen. **Tel** 87 31 50 10. 📷
🇼 **aarhus.dk/Aarhus-Raadhus**

The modern city hall was designed by Arne Jacobsen and Erik Møller and completed in 1941. The building is a prime example of Danish Modernism. It is clad on the outside with dark Norwegian marble and topped with a rectangular clock tower, which affords a good view of the city. The interior has a lighter feel. The large council chamber and Civic Room are worth seeking out.

The modernist Rådhus, designed by Arne Jacobsen

🏛 ARoS Kunstmuseum

Aros Allé 2. **Tel** 87 30 66 00. **Open** 10am–5pm Tue, Thu–Sun, 10am–10pm Wed. 🚻 ♿ ✏ 🇼 **aros.dk**

This gallery is housed in a ten-storey building topped by a circular rainbow-coloured walkway; designed by Olafur Eliasson, called *Your Rainbow Panorama* it offers breathtaking views of the city. The art collection presents works spanning from the Danish Golden Age to the present day.

🏛 Vikingemuseet

Sankt Clemens Torv. **Open** 10:15am–4pm Mon–Wed, Fri, 10:15am–5pm Thu. 🇼 **vikingemuseet.dk**

In a building across from the cathedral, next to the Nordea Bank, is a museum devoted to the Viking era. The prime exhibit is a section of archaeological excavation that was carried out in Clemens Torv. Fragments of the original Viking ramparts, discovered in 1964, are on display along with items dating from 900 to 1400 including a skeleton, a reconstructed house, wood-working tools, pottery, and runic stones. Similar discoveries at nearby Store Torv have confirmed the importance of Aarhus as a major centre of Viking culture.

🏠 Domkirke

Store Torv. **Tel** 86 20 54 00. **Open** May–Sep: 9:30am–4pm Mon–Fri; Oct–Dec: 10am–3pm Mon–Sat (10:30am–2pm Tue). 🇼 **aarhus-domkirke.dk**

Aarhus's main place of worship is at the heart of the city's oldest district. The cathedral was built in 1201 but destroyed by fire in the 14th century. It was rebuilt in the late 15th century in a Gothic style, and is easily Denmark's longest cathedral with a nave that spans nearly 100 m (328 ft). Until the end of the 16th century most of the cathedral walls were covered with frescoes. During the Reformation these were whitewashed over, but many have since been restored. The five-panel altarpiece dates from 1479 and is the work of Bernt Notke of Lübeck. The Baroque pipe organ dates from 1730.

�🏛 Kvindemuseet

Domkirkeplads 5. **Tel** 86 18 64 70. **Open** 10am–5pm daily (to 8pm Wed).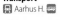
W kvindemuseet.dk

The Women's Museum has made a name for itself with its imaginative temporary exhibitions relating to women's issues – past and present. Since 1984 the museum has been collecting objects, photographs and documents illustrating the many changes that have taken place over the centuries in the lives of women in Danish society.

⚑ Vor Frue Kirke

Frue Kirkeplads. **Tel** 86 12 12 43. **Open** May–Sep: 10am–4pm Mon–Fri; Oct–Apr: 10am–2pm Mon–Fri, 10am–noon Sat.
W aarhusvorfrue.dk

Figure from Bernt Notke's altarpiece

Vor Frue Kirke is a complex of three churches in a former Dominican monastery. The oldest section of this complex is the 11th-century Romanesque stone crypt. The highlight here is a replica of an early crucifix featuring a Christ with Viking plaits. The star adornment inside the church is a 16th-century wooden altarpiece carved by Claus Berg.

The 11th-century crypt of Vor Frue Kirke

🏛 Den Gamle By

Viborgvej 2. **Tel** 86 12 31 88. **Open** year-round opening but check website for current times prior to your visit. 🖼 **W** dengamleby.dk

This open-air museum has exhibits from the 17th, 18th and 19th centuries, as well as from 1927 and 1974. One exhibit is a typical Danish town the way it would have looked in the 19th century, at the time of Hans Christian Andersen. The atmosphere is especially vibrant during the Living History season (Easter–Dec), when actors play key characters in the town, such as the vicar and the town crier.

Aarhus City Centre

① Musikhuset
② Rådhus
③ ARoS Kunstmuseum
④ Vikingemuseet
⑤ Domkirke
⑥ Kvindemuseet
⑦ Vor Frue Kirke
⑧ Den Gamle By

0 metres 200
0 yards 200

Harbour with Ringkøbing Fjord in the background

❽ Ringkøbing Fjord

Road map: B4. 🛈 Ringkøbing, Torvet
22; Hvide Sande, Nørregade 2B. **Tel** 70
22 70 01. 🎨 Sand Sculpture Festival
(Søndervig, mid-Jun–Nov).
🅦 visitvest.dk

A thin strip of land some 35 km
(22 miles) long separates
Ringkøbing Fjord from the
North Sea. This sandy spit is
about 1 km (half a mile) wide
and has many summer cottages
tucked among the dunes. The
only water access between the
sea and Ringkøbing Fjord is
through a channel and lock in
the town of Hvide Sande.
Ringkøbing Fjord is popular
with windsurfers and the calm
waters of the bay are suitable
for novices; the North Sea, on
the other side of the spit, offers
more challenging conditions.

On the bay's northern shore
is **Ringkøbing**, the largest town
in this region. Ringkøbing was
once a seaport but over the
centuries the entrance from
the bay to the sea shifted southwards and the town became
an inland harbour. Standing in
Torvet, the town's main square,
are some of the most historic
buildings including Hotel
Ringkøbing, a timbered building that dates from 1600.
The local **museum** has
alternating exhibitions.

The locality includes many
attractions. **Fiskeriets Hus** (House
of Fisheries) at Hvide Sande
contains an aquarium with fish
and shellfish from the North Sea
and fjord waters as well as
displays on the area's fishing
industry. A paved footpath,

suitable for wheelchair users,
leads from the museum to
Troldbjerg, Hvide Sande's main
viewpoint. The mast at the top
was once used by sailors to
warn them about water levels.
Another good view is from the
60-m- (197-ft-) high lighthouse
on the Nørre Lyngvig dune, 5 km
(3 miles) north of Hvide Sande.

A different kind of scenery
can be found on the
southern shores of
Ringkøbing Fjord, where
the marshes form
Tipperne Nature Reserve,
one of Denmark's most
important sites for
waterfowl. Access is
restricted to a few
hours on Friday or
Sunday mornings so
as not to disturb the
migrating birds. The reserve
contains an observation tower.

🏛 Ringkøbing Museum
Herningvej 4. **Tel** 97 32 16 15.
Open 11am–5pm Mon–Fri, 10am–
3pm Sat & Sun. 🅿️
🅦 levendehistorie.dk

🐟 Fiskeriets Hus
Nørregade 2B, Hvide Sande. **Tel** 97 31 26
10. **Open** 10am–5pm daily (Nov–Easter:
to 4pm). 🅿️ 🅦 fiskerietshus.dk

❾ Givskud Zoo

Road map: C4. Løveparken Givskud
Zoo: **Tel** 75 73 02 22. **Open** Apr–mid-
Oct: from 10am daily. Closing times
vary; check the website for details. 🅿️
🅦 givskudzoo.dk

A short way north of Jelling is
Givskud Zoo (sometimes
referred to as Zootopia), home
to the largest pride of lions in

Scandinavia. When the park was
established in 1969 the pride
had 29 members; today it has
over 40. In addition to the lions,
Givskud has about 700 other
animals representing 70
species. Givskud is part-zoo,
part-safari park, and many of
the animals are left to wander
freely. Car drivers can travel
along marked routes. Visitors
on foot can enjoy a safari
by bus.

The lions are the
most popular sight,
but there is no
denying the appeal
of the giraffes, zebras,
buffalos, ostriches and
other species that
inhabit the park.
One of the zoo's
other attractions

Bust of Jacob Hansen,
Givskud Zoo's founder

is the Western Lowland gorillas
enclosure; the family of apes
was brought over from
Copenhagen's zoo in 2001.

Fenced-off areas provide
children with the opportunity
to stroke some of the park's
more domesticated animals or
have fun feeding the camels.

Small herd of zebra wandering freely in
Givskud Zoo

Ancient burial mound in Jelling

Givskud Zoo is not only a family attraction but also a major scientific establishment. There are 50 endangered species at the park. One of Givskud's programmes resulted in deer and antelope reared at the park being re-introduced into the wilds of Pakistan in the late 1980s.

⑩ Jelling

Road map: C4. 🏔 2,500. 🚌
ℹ Gormsgade 23. **Tel** 75 87 23 50.
📷 Viking Fair (Aug). 🅦 visitvejle.com

For the Danes Jelling is a special place: this unassuming village served as the royal seat of Gorm the Old, a 10th-century Viking who conquered Jutland and then Funen and Zealand to create a new state. The dynasty he established has ruled Denmark continuously to this day.

Although few traces are left of the old royal castle, **Jelling Kirke** and the two burial mounds beyond it have revealed much of Denmark's ancient history. The church was built in about 1100, but it is now known that the site was occupied far earlier than this by at least three wooden churches. The first of these was, according to legend, built by Gorm's son, Harald Bluetooth, who came to the throne around 958 and adopted Christianity a short time afterwards. For a long time it was believed that the two knolls outside the church contained the remains of Denmark's first ruler, but when they were excavated in the 19th century nothing was found. In the late 1970s, however, archaeologists began a series of digs inside Jelling Kirke and found the remains of the three earlier wooden churches, along with Viking jewellery and human bones. Forensic examinations, conducted at Copenhagen's Nationalmuseet, concluded that the bones could indeed be those of Gorm and in the year 2000, in the presence of the current royal family, the remains were reburied under the floor of Jelling Kirke. Today the place is marked with a silver sign. Close to the church are two runic stones. The larger one, known as the "Danes' baptism certificate", was erected in 965 by Harald in memory of his parents – Gorm and Thyra. Still visible on the stone is a picture of Christ – the oldest representation of Christ in Scandinavia. The stone's inscription proclaims that "Harald king ordered this monument to be erected to Gorm his father and Thyra his mother for the glory of Denmark", and that he converted the Danes to Christianity. This inscription is considered to be the first written record in which the word "Denmark" appears. In 1994 the entire complex was declared a UNESCO World Heritage Site. The stones have been placed under glass cases in order to preserve archaeological finds in as authentic a setting as possible.

Kongernes Jelling, an exhibition centre opposite the church is devoted to the history of the Vikings and the establishment of the Danish monarchy.

Runic stone in Jelling

The atmosphere of Jelling can best be enjoyed during the annual Viking Fair. This weekend-long event is popular with many Danes, some of whom take it as an opportunity to dress up as Vikings and parade through the streets of the town. Another reminder of Denmark's past can be found at Fårup lake where a full-scale replica of a Viking ship takes visitors on cruises of the lake.

🏛 **Jelling Kirke**
Open 8am–5pm Mon–Sat (to 8pm May–Aug), noon–5pm Sun.
🅦 jellingkirke.dk

🏛 **Kongernes Jelling**
Gormsgade 23. **Tel** 41 20 63 31.
Open 10am–3pm Mon–Fri. 📷
🅦 natmus.dk/museerne/kongernes-jelling

Runic writing including the oldest record of the name "Denmark"

⑪ LEGOLAND®

LEGO® bricks, known and loved by children throughout the world, were invented in the 1930s by Danish toymaker Ole Kirk Christiansen. This popular amusement park opened in 1968. Its attractions include amazingly detailed miniature versions of cities, as well as famous landmarks, constructed entirely from plastic LEGO® bricks. In addition there are thrilling rides, miniature trains and water chutes.

★ Toyota Traffic School
Children aged 7 to 13 can learn to dr... here. This is one of the park's most popular attractions, so book ahead.

Atlantis by SEA LIFE ™
At this underwater attraction, visitors are able to get up close and personal with sharks and tropical fish. There are also submarines and shipwrecks.

LEGO® Studios
Musical Fountain
DUPLO® Playhouses
DUPLO® Express
LEGONDOL®
LEGC NINJAGO Wor...
Monorail
Hotel LEGOLAND®
Mine Train
LEGOTOP®
Timber...
LEGO® Safari
The Lighth...
Cater...
Frog Hoppe...
Mini Boats

LEGO® Train
Miniland can be explored aboard a train or viewed from a revolving platform that gradually ascends to the top of a tower.

Entrance

★ Miniland
Over 20 million LEGO® bricks were used to construct famous buildings, airports, trains and even entire cities.

The Dragon
Shaped like its namesake, this roller coaster hurtles through the majestic King's Castle and is great fun for children and adults alike.

★ Polar Land
Hop aboard the hair-raising Polar X-plorer, a roller coaster that travels through a frozen polar landscape filled with LEGO® animals.

- Ice Pilots School
- Polar X-plorer
- X-treme Racers
- Knight's Kingdom
- Penguin Bay
- Jungle Racers
- Falck Fire Brigade
- Adventure Land
- Pirate World ②

| 0 metres | 20 |
| 0 yards | 20 |

The Temple
Re-creating a large Egyptian archaeological dig, The Temple allows young visitors to go on an exciting treasure hunt.

Pirate Splash Battle
Board a pirate ship and take your position behind a water cannon. See how long you can stay dry in this playful re-creation of a sea battle.

KEY

① **DUPLO® Land** is for the youngest children.

② **Vikings River Splash** is an aquatic roller coaster ride sending rafts splashing down wild water rapids and waterfalls through a world of dragons and Vikings.

Vindmølle, a Vejle landmark with a flour-milling museum

⑫ Vejle

Road map: C4. 🚗 53,000. 🚃 🚌
ℹ️ Banegårdspladsen 6. **Tel** 75 81 19 25. 🌐 visitvejle.com

The fjord town of Vejle is famous for being the place where the beech trees (Denmark's national tree) are first to burst into leaf and announce the arrival of spring. Vejle makes a good base for visiting LEGOLAND® *(see pp196–7)* and the burial mounds at Jelling *(see p195)*. Its main point of interest is Sankt Nicolai Kirke, a Gothic church dating from the 13th century. A curiosity of the church, though they can't be seen, are the 23 skulls hidden in its walls, which belonged to 23 robbers executed in 1630.

Rådhustorvet, Vejle's main square, contains the town hall. It stands on the site of a Dominican monastery and its medieval bell can be heard ringing each day from the tower. The **Vejle Museum** is spread over a number of locations in town. A modern interactive venue displays the mummified body of a woman known as Queen Gunhild. The body was found in 1835 in a peat bog; forensic tests have revealed that the woman lived during the Iron Age, around 450 BC. The exhibition in Den Smidtske Gard, an early 19th-century burgher's residence, covers 800 years of Vejle's history. On the edge of town, Vejle Vindmølle is also part of the museum. Built in 1890

and operational until 1960, the windmill houses an exhibition devoted to flour milling.

While in Vejle it is also possible to visit the Ecolarium, a centre that aims to raise awareness of environmental issues and the potential of alternative energy, and Ravninge Broen, a Viking-era bridge in Ravninge Enge (Meadows) exhibition centre.

🏛️ **Vejle Museum**
Tel 76 81 31 00. **Open** see the website. 🌐 vejlemuseerne.dk

⑬ Esbjerg

Road map: B5. 🚗 83,000. 🚃 🛳️ 🚌
ℹ️ Skolegade 33. **Tel** 75 12 55 99.
🎸 Rock Festival (mid-Jun); Esbjerg Festival Week (mid-Aug), Chamber Music (Aug). 🌐 visitesbjerg.dk

In 1868, the former fishing village of Esbjerg began to develop into a harbour from which Jutland's farmers and producers could export goods. Today it is one of Denmark's largest commercial ports and a centre for North Sea oil operations.

Despite lacking a medieval district, Esbjerg has several places worth visiting. For years the town's main symbol was its **Vandtårnet** (Water Tower), which was

Seals, a favourite sight at Esbjerg's aquarium

erected in 1897. Today, it serves as an observation platform, from which there is a panoramic view of the town. Close to the tower is the Musikhuset (Concert Hall) designed by Jørn Utzon and built in 1997.

Esbjerg Art Museum contains one of Denmark's finest collections of contemporary Danish art. The **Fiskeri-og Søfartsmuseet** (The Fisheries and Maritime Museum), 4 km (2 miles) northwest of Esbjerg's centre, contains a large aquarium and various marine-related displays. Most of the sea life in the aquarium comes from the North Sea. Its most popular inhabitants are the seals, most of which have been rescued. This vast museum complex also features a collection of navigation instruments and model vessels, a number of fishing boats placed outside the building and a reconstructed coastal lifeboat station. Outside the museum grounds, on the seashore, are four 9-m- (30-ft-) tall snow-white stylised figures of seated men, which are entitled *Man Meets the Sea* and were created by Svend Wiig Hansen to mark the city's centennial in 1995. The maritime theme continues in Esbjerg harbour where the 20th-century **Horns Rev Lightship** is moored.

Exhibition room in Esbjerg's Fiskeri-og Søfartsmuseet

For hotels and restaurants in this area see pp252–3 and pp270–72

🏛 Vandtårnet
Havnegade 22. **Tel** 76 16 39 39.
Open Jun–mid-Sep: 10am–4pm
Tue–Sun. ♿

🏛 Esbjerg Art Museum
Havnegade 20. **Tel** 75 13 02 11.
Open 10am–4pm daily. ♿

🏛 Fiskeri-og Søfartsmuseet
Saltvandsakvariet Tarphagevej 2–6.
Tel 76 12 20 00. **Open** Sep–Jun:
10am–5pm daily; Jul–Aug: 10am–6pm
daily. ♿

🏛 Horns Rev Lightship
Tel 21 62 11 04. **Open** May–Aug:
11am–4pm Mon–Fri. ♿

🔴 Ribe

Road map: B5. 🚂 18,000. 🚗 🚌 ℹ️
Torvet 3, 75 42 15 00. 🌐 **visitribe.com**

Scandinavia's oldest town is also
one of the best preserved and
contains many fine buildings
including a medieval cathedral
and a 16th-century schoolhouse.
The medieval centre features a
maze of cobbled streets lined
with crooked, half-timbered
houses with beautifully painted
and ornamented doors.

Ribe was once a seaport.
With the passage of time the
mouth of the river that flows
through it became silted up, and
now the town is quite a way
from the seashore.

In 856 the missionary Ansgar,
known locally as the
Apostle of
Scandinavia, built
a small wooden
church here. In the
10th century Ribe
became a bishopric,
and in the mid-12th
century it acquired
an impressive cathe-
dral, which still stands
today. **Ribe Domkirke**
is built of a soft porous
rock called tufa that
was quarried near
Cologne. The most
prominent entrance, used
by the bishops, is on the south
side of the church. This entrance
features a 13th-century "Cat's
Head" doorway that got its name
from the knocker made in the
shape of a lion's head. Another
feature of the portal is the pediment portraying Jesus and

Nave of Ribe Domkirke

The night watchman in Ribe

Mary – positioned at their feet
are the images of Valdemar II and
his wife Dagmar, who died in
childbirth in 1212. To this day at
noon and 3pm the cathedral
bells chime the tune of a folk
song dedicated to the queen.
The most notable features of
the church's interior are the 16th-
century frescoes and the modern
mosaics by Carl-Henning Pedersen. The left wing of the transept
contains a marble floor slab
from the tomb of Christoffer I,
who died in 1259 and is laid in
the adjacent sarcophagus. It is
thought to be the oldest royal
tombstone in Scandinavia.
Stunning views of the flat lands
and the Wadden Sea can be
had from the top of the 14th-
century tower. **Det Gamle
Rådhus**, opposite the
cathedral's southeast
corner, was built in 1496.
The town hall's
museum has a small
collection of torture
instruments and
executioners'
swords. From here it
is not far to the river,
where the Stormflods-
søjlen (Flood Column)
indicates the floods
that have submerged
the town.

Ribe has two Viking museums.
Standing opposite the railway
station on Odin square is **Ribes
Vikinger**, where the market
town atmosphere of late 8th-
century Ribe is re-created. The
Vikingecenter, 3 km (2 miles)
south of the town centre, is an

open-air museum
that offers a portrait of
Ribe in the Viking era.
Ribe Kunstmuseum, the
local art gallery, houses a
collection of Danish art
from 1750 until 1950,
including examples from
the Skagen School and
the Danish Golden Age.

Environs
At the **Vadehavscentret**,
you can learn more
about the Wadden Sea
and arrange safari tours.

🏛 Ribe Domkirke
Torvet. **Tel** 75 42 06 19. **Open** daily.
Oct–Apr: 11am–3pm (Apr & Oct: to
4pm); May–Sep: 10am–5pm (Jul–mid-
Aug: to 5:30pm). ♿

🏛 Det Gamle Rådhus
Von Støckens Plads. **Tel** 76 16 88 10.
Open check webiste for times. ♿
🌐 **detgamleraadhusiribe.dk**

🏛 Ribes Vikinger
Odin Plads 1. **Tel** 76 16 39 60.
Open Jul–Aug: 10am–6pm (until 9pm
Wed) daily; Sep, Oct & Apr–Jun: 10am–
4pm daily; Nov–Mar: 10am–4pm
Tue–Sun. ♿ 🌐 **ribesvikinger.dk**

🏛 Ribe Vikingecenter
Lustrupvej 4. **Tel** 75 41 16 11.
Open May–mid-Oct; see website for
times. ♿ 🌐 **ribevikingecenter.dk**

🏛 Ribe Kunstmuseum
Sankt Nicolaigade 10. **Tel** 75 42 03 62.
Open Jul & Aug: 11am–5pm daily (to
8pm Wed); Sep–Jun: 11am–4pm Tue–
Sun. ♿ 🌐 **ribekunstmuseum.dk**

🏛 Vadehavscentret
Okholmvej 5, Vester Vedsted. **Tel** 75
44 61 61. **Open** mid-Feb–Nov: 10am–
4pm daily (May–Sep: to 5pm).
🌐 **vandehavcentret.dk/en**

Half-timbered houses, adding to the charm
of Ribe

Palisade by Rømø dyke

⓰ Rømø

Road map: B5. 🚗 750. 🚌 ℹ️ Nørre
Frankel 1. **Tel** 74 75 51 30.
🌐 **romo.dk**

The largest Danish island in
the North Sea, Rømø was a
prosperous whaling base in
the 18th century. Its western
shores are fringed with wide
stretches of beach. The island
is connected to Jutland by a
causeway that passes through
marshland rich in birdlife.

In the village of Toftum is
the Kommandørgården
(Captain's House), which dates
from 1748. The house, which
now serves as a museum,
has a thatched roof and
some original interior decor,
including wall coverings
consisting of 4,000 Dutch tiles.
Close by is an 18th-century
school. A short distance further
north, in the hamlet of Juvre,
is a whale jawbone fence
constructed in 1772.
In Kirkeby, next to
the walls that
surround the Late-
Gothic church, are
whalers' gravestones
that were brought
back from
Greenland. The
histories of captains
and their families
have been carved
by local artists.

The main point
of interest at the
south end of the
island is Havneby,
which has a labyrinth
park. A ferry goes
from here to the
tranquil island of
Sylt, in Germany, just
to the southwest.

⓱ Tønder

Road map: B6. 🚗 8,200. 🚌 🚌
ℹ️ Torvet 1. **Tel** 74 72 12 20. 🎭 Tønder
Festival (Aug). 🌐 **romo.dk**

In the Middle Ages Tønder was
a major fishing port. During
subsequent centuries it
became the centre of a lace-
making industry, which is now
commemorated by a lace-
makers' festival held every three
years. Examples of fine lace and
the sophisticated
tools used in its
production are on
display in the **Tønder
Museum**. In the 17th
and 18th centuries
Tønder also produced
ceramics that were
used as wall tiles,
some of which can be
seen in the museum.
The Tønder Museum is
part of the **Museum of
Southern Jutland**, which shows

Font in Haderslev
Domkirke

a collection of modern art,
including chairs by Danish
designer Hans J. Wegner.

Tønder's town centre is a
pleasant place to explore and
the narrow streets contain
many houses with decorative
doorways and picturesque
gables and window shutters.
The best-known house is Det
Gamle Apotek (The Old
Pharmacy), at Østergade 1,
which has a Baroque doorway
dating from 1671. The market
square contains a 16th-century
Rådhus (town hall). Also in the
square is the 16th-century
Kristkirken, which has some
fine paintings and carvings.

🏛️ **Tønder Museum & Museum
of Southern Jutland**
Kongevejen 51. **Tel** 74 72 89 89.
Open Jun–Aug: 10am–5pm daily;
Sep–May: 10am–5pm Tue–Sun. 🅿️
🌐 **museum-sonderjylland.dk**

⓲ Sønderborg

Road map: C6. Als. 🚗
30,000. 🚌 🚌 ℹ️ Rådhus-
torvet 7. **Tel** 74 42 35 55.
🌐 **visitsonderborg.com**

Sønderborg, meaning
"South Castle", is on
the island of Als. It
owes its name to a
castle fortress built
by Valdemar I in 1170.
Over the centuries the castle
served a variety of purposes.
Christian II was held prisoner here
for 17 years in the early 16th
century. Later on it was used in
turns as a warehouse, a hospital,
a prison and military barracks.

The town's turbulent history is
brought to life at the **Historiecenter Dybbøl Banke**, situated
near Sønderborg, close to the
village of Dybbøl. In the spring
of 1864 this area was the scene
of a fierce battle between Danish
and Prussian forces. Dybbøl
Mølle, a windmill that was
damaged during the fighting,
is now regarded as a national
symbol. As a result of Denmark's
defeat, Sønderborg was nearly
destroyed and southern Jutland
incorporated into Prussia and
later into Germany (the territory
was returned in 1920).

Doorway of a house in Østergade, Tønder

Environs

About 16 km (10 miles) to the west is the royal castle of **Gråsten**; the garden can be visited when the queen is not in residence.

🏠 Sønderborg Castle
Sønderbro 1. **Tel** 74 42 25 39. **Open** Apr, May & Oct: 10am–4pm Tue–Sun; Jun–Sep: 10am–5pm daily; Nov–Mar: 1–4pm Tue–Sun. 🅿 🌐 **museum-sonderjylland.dk**

🏛 Historiecenter Dybbøl Banke
Dybbøl Banke 16. **Tel** 74 48 90 00. **Open** early Apr–mid-Oct: 10am–5pm daily. 🅿 🌐 **museum-sonderjylland.dk/dybbol-banke.html**

⑱ Haderslev

Road map: C5. 🚗 21,000. 🚌
ℹ Nørregade 52, 73 54 56 30.
🌐 **visithaderslev.dk**

The present-day capital of southern Jutland is situated between a narrow fjord and a lake that was formed by the construction of a dam. A market town in the 13th century, Haderslev contains many period buildings.

During the Reformation Haderslev was a major centre of Protestantism and in 1526 it became the site of the first Protestant theological college. The town's main place of worship, Haderslev Domkirke, was built in the 13th century but has been remodelled many times. It boasts a magnificent altarpiece featuring a 14th-century crucifix and

Interior of the 13th-century cathedral in Haderslev

Interior courtyard with a fountain at Koldinghus castle

alabaster statues of the apostles. The most enchanting of the town's buildings are found on Torvet, a square flanked by half-timbered houses. The nearby **Haderslev Museum** has exhibits on the archaeological history of the area, a local-history collection and its own mini open-air museum.

🏛 Haderslev Museum
Dalgade 7. **Tel** 74 52 75 66. **Open** Jun–Aug: 10am–4pm Tue–Sun; Sep–May: 1–4pm Tue–Sun. 🅿

⑲ Kolding

Road map: C5. 🚗 56,000. 🚌 🚌
ℹ Akseltorv 8. **Tel** 76 33 21 00.
🌐 **visitkolding.dk**

Kolding's most important historic building is Koldinghus – a mighty castle that has a distinctive square tower with a flat roof (called the Heroes' Tower). The first fortress on this site was built in 1268, but the oldest surviving walls date from about 1440. More of the castle's history can be learned at the **Museet på Koldinghus**, which also hosts temporary exhibitions on decorative art and design. Kolding's main square is Akseltorv, which contains the beautiful Renaissance Borchs Gård dating from 1595. The **Kunstmuseet Trapholt** on the town's eastern outskirts

has a large collection of Danish modern art.

Every August, an outdoor concert by the National Opera Ensemble draws large crowds to the hill of Skamlingsbanken.

🏛 Museet på Koldinghus
Markdanersgade 11. **Tel** 76 33 81 00. **Open** 10am–5pm daily. 🅿
🌐 **koldinghus.dk**

🏛 Kunstmuseet Trapholt
Æblehaven 23. **Tel** 76 30 05 30. **Open** 10am–5pm daily (to 8pm Wed). 🅿
🌐 **trapholt.dk**

⑳ Fredericia

Road map: C5. 🚗 40,000. 🚌 🚌
ℹ Vendersgade 30D. **Tel** 72 11 35 11.
🌐 **visitfredericia.dk**

Frederik III decided to build Fredericia on this strategic section of the Lille Bælt (Little Belt) – the narrowest point between Jutland and Funen – in 1650. In 1657 the fortress town was captured by the Swedes who slaughtered the entire garrison stationed here. In 1849, during the Schleswig conflict, it was the scene of a battle between the Danes and the Prussian army. The Landsoldaten monument by the Prince's Gate commemorates that event. The town ramparts remain from the original fortress. The best section is by Danmarksgade, where the grassy embankments reach 15 m (49 ft) in height. The nearby water tower dates from 1909 and provides the best view of the surrounding area. **Fredericia Museum** has displays relating to the town's military

Coat of arms on gate in Fredericia

and civilian history. Madsby Park, a short way outside the old town, contains a miniature version of Fredericia.

🏛 Fredericia Museum
Jernbanegade 10. **Tel** 72 10 69 70. **Open** noon–4pm Tue–Sun (mid-Jun–mid-Aug: daily). **Closed** Jan. 🅿
🌐 **fredericiahistorie.dk**

NORTHERN JUTLAND

Visitors to northern Jutland can enjoy beautiful, pristine scenery and peace in this region of farmland and fields, heathland and dunes. The university town of Aalborg is the area's only large city, but in the summer months, the seaside resorts of Skagen and Løkken-Blokhus can also get very busy. There are a number of places to visit, including a Viking burial ground at Lindholm Høje.

The least populated and the wildest part of this region is its northern end, which is shaped by its proximity to the sea. This area provides excellent nesting grounds for a variety of birds. On the northwestern side, facing Skagerrak, the scenery is dominated by dunes, which display the clear effects of frequent sea breezes that shift the sand by up to 10 m (33 ft) each year.

Many visitors embark on trips to Grenen, Denmark's northernmost point, which is washed over by the waters of the Baltic and the North Sea. This area is sometimes referred to as the "Land of Light" and enjoys more hours of sunshine than anywhere else in Denmark. The extraordinary light has long been appreciated by artists, who came here in search of inspiration in the 19th century. Many settled around Skagen, which became a magnet for prominent painters and writers who formed the Skagen School.

Another distinct feature of northern Jutland's landscape are its heathlands. As recently as the mid-19th century they covered one third of this region; now they can be seen only here and there. Northern Jutland also boasts Rold Skov, Denmark's largest forest. Numerous coves make up the Limfjord straits, where you can find traditional inns and little wooden ferries.

The most important of the area's historic sights are the Lindholm Høje prehistoric burial ground and the 1,000-year-old Viking fortress at Fyrkat, which includes a replica Viking farmstead.

Some of Denmark's best beaches can also be found in northern Jutland and there are many holiday cottages and camp sites in the area.

Renaissance manor in Voergård

◀ Boat-shaped grave at Lindholm Høje – the largest Viking burial ground in Scandinavia

Exploring Northern Jutland

Aalborg makes a good base for exploring this part of the country, while smaller towns such as Thisted, Løgstør, Mariager or Skagen can also serve as good jumping-off points. When heading north, it is best to travel by car, since many of the most attractive areas are some distance from each other, and there may be problems with finding suitable public transport. Even when travelling by car it pays to allow plenty of time as many roads are fairly minor and pass through villages. The advantage of travelling on these minor routes is that the scenery is varied and offers a portrait of Denmark quite different from any seen from motorways.

Viking enthusiast sharpening a blade in the village of Fyrkat

View of the cathedral from the shore of the lake in Viborg

Sights at a Glance

1. Fårup
2. Hirtshals
3. Grenen
4. Frederikshavn
5. Sæby
6. Voergård Slot
7. Lindholm Høje
8. Aalborg pp212–13
9. Limfjorden pp214–15
10. Holstebro
11. Hjerl Hedes Frilandsmuseum
12. Kongenshus Mindepark
13. Mønsted
14. Viborg
15. Rebild Bakker
16. Mariager
17. Fyrkat
18. Randers
19. Gammel Estrup

Getting Around

The major transport artery of the region is the E45 motorway, running from the German border to Frederikshavn. The larger towns of the region are all accessible by train. The main ferry harbours are in Frederikshavn and Hirtshals.

Key

━━ Motorway
━━ Major road
╌╌╌ Minor road
━━ Scenic route
╌╌╌ Main railway
──── Minor railway
▭▭▭ Regional border

Former Carmelite monastery in Sæby

One of the rides at Fårup Sommerland, a vast amusement park

❶ Fårup

Road map: C2. Pirupvejen 147. **Tel** 98 88 16 00. **Open** May & early Sep: from 10am Sat & Sun; early Jun–late Aug: from 10am daily. Always consult the website before visiting. 🏖 **W faarup sommerland.dk**

Fårup Sommerland is an amusement park set deep in the forest close to the beach, between Saltum and Blokhus. Among the thrills and spills on offer are wild roller coasters and Denmark's largest and wettest water world. There are also gentler attractions for younger visitors in the children's theme park. Once the splashing is over, visitors can cook a meal in the grill area, jump on the trampolines or take in a film at the 4-D cinema.

❷ Hirtshals

Road map: C1. 🏙 15,000. 🚢 🚌 *i* Dalsagervej 1. **Tel** 98 94 22 20. **W visithirtshals.dk**

Towards the end of the 19th century Hirtshals was no more than a small fishing hamlet; now it is one of Jutland's major ports. Regular ferry links with the Norwegian towns of Kristiansand, Oslo and Moss make this small town an important bridge with Denmark's Scandinavian neighbours on the other side of Kattegat. The town has a thriving fishing harbour and every day, at 7am, it

becomes the venue for auctioning the night's catch.

The greatest attraction is the **Nordsøen Oceanarium**, a sea-life centre that is situated about 1 km (half a mile) east of the town centre. Since it opened in 1984, the oceanarium has attracted thousands of visitors every year. Its vast tank contains 4.5 million litres (990,000 gallons) of sea water, making it one of Europe's biggest aquariums. The aquarium includes an amphitheatre that looks onto a huge glass pane that is 8 m (26 ft) high and 41 cm (16 in) thick. The fish include schools of herring and mackerel as well as sharks. A diver enters the tank every day at 1pm (and also at 4pm in summer) to feed the fish.

As well as the aquarium, the Nordsøen Oceanarium has numerous displays that explain about the issues surrounding fishing in the North Sea and the ecology of the region. Outside is a seal pool, which has regular feed times at 11am and 3pm.

Hirtshals also offers an extensive network of walking and cycling trails, including

Aquarium at Nordsøen Oceanarium, Hirtshals

one leading to a 57-m- (187-ft-) tall lighthouse and also to Husmoderstrand – a beach with many safe places for children to play and swim.

Hirtshals Museum is in a former fishermen's cottage that dates from 1880. This has an exhibition of everyday objects illustrating the significance of the sea to the local population in the early 20th century.

🐟 **Nordsøen Oceanarium**
Willemoesvej. **Tel** 98 94 41 88. **Open** Jan–Mar & Nov: 9am–4pm daily (to 5pm Sat, Sun & hols); Apr–Jun, Sep & Oct: 10am–5pm daily; Jul & Aug: 9am–6pm daily. 🏖 **W nordsoenoceanarium.dk**

Grenen, where the Baltic meets the North Sea

❸ Grenen

Road map: D1. 🚌 *i* Vestre Strandvej 1, Skagen. **Tel** 98 44 13 77. **W skagen-tourist.dk**

Grenen is the northernmost point of Denmark. Standing by the car park, from which a 2-km (1-mile) trail leads to the point, is the Skagen Odde Naturcenter. Designed by the Danish architect Jørn Utzon, the centre aims to enable visitors to appreciate the natural environment of this region through a series of imaginative displays utilizing sand, water, wind and light.

The environs of Grenen consist of vast sand dunes, here and there overgrown with heather. This wild landscape captivated the Danish writer Holger Drachmann (1846–1908) to such an extent that he made it his wish to be buried in the sands of Grenen. His grave can be found on one of the nearby dunes.

Skagen Artists

The former fishing port of Skagen is now a fashionable resort, full of brightly painted yellow houses and a good number of restaurants and shops. The town's character is accurately represented by its coat of arms, which features a painter's palette in the shape of a flounder. In the late 19th century many artists flocked here in order to "paint the light" and formed what is now known as the Skagen School. Its members included the writer Holger Drachmann, and painters Anna and Michael Ancher, Peder Severin Krøyer, Laurits Tuxen, Carl Locher, Christian Krogh and Oscar Björk. The Skagens Museum exhibits many of their works and it is also possible to visit the former home of the Anchers and that of Drachmann.

The extraordinary light, produced by the reflection of the sun's rays in the waters surrounding Skagen and the dunes, was the inspiration for the 19th-century artists arriving here from all over Denmark, as well as from Sweden and Norway.

The Skagens Museum houses a huge collection of works. Most of the paintings are of local scenes and all of the Skagen School of artists are well represented.

The fishing harbour is crowded with cutters as Skagen is still one of the major centres of fishing in northern Denmark, although much of the town's income now derives from tourism.

Brøndums Hotel, founded by Erik Brøndum in 1859, is charmingly old-fashioned. The hotel was popular with artists, who often met in the bar at night. The Skagens Museum is located in the grounds.

The Skagen artists' work is often characterized by vibrant seascapes and naturalistic portraits. The painting above, by P.S. Krøyer, depicts Anna Ancher and the artist's wife, Marie.

Michael Ancher lived for four years in Brøndums Hotel. Ancher married Anna Brøndum, step-sister of the hotel's owner, who was herself a talented artist. This 1886 portrait of Ancher is by P S Krøyer.

❹ Frederikshavn

Road map: D1. 🏠 23,000. 🚇 🚢 🚌
ℹ️ Skandiatorv 1. **Tel** 98 42 32 66.
🎭 Tordenskiold Festival (Jun).
Ⓦ **visitfrederikshavn.dk**

The main international ferry
port of Jutland has a number of
historical sights. The Krudttårnet
(Gunpowder Tower) is all that
remains of a 17th-century
citadel that once guarded the
port. Today the tower houses a
small military museum.
Frederikshavn Kirke dates from
the 19th century and contains
a painting by Michael Ancher,
one of the best-known of the
Skagen School *(see p209)*. The
Kystmuseet Bangsbo is about
3 km (2 miles) south of the
centre. This 18th-century manor
house has an eclectic collection
that includes objects relating
to the town's history and the
Danish Resistance during World
War II. There is also a display of
artefacts made from human
hair. Perhaps the best exhibit is
a reconstructed 12th-century
Viking merchant ship.

🏛 **Kystmuseet Bangsbo**
Dronning Margrethes Vej 6. **Tel** 98 42
31 11. **Open** check website for times.
🅿️ Ⓦ **kystmuseet.dk**

❺ Sæby

Road map: D1. 🏠 18,000. 🚇 🚌
ℹ️ Algade 14. **Tel** 98 46 12 44.
Ⓦ **visitsaeby.dk**

The town skyline is dominated
by the tower of Vor Frue Kirke
(Church of Our Lady), which
once formed part of a
15th-century Carmelite

Opulent dining room in Voesgård Slot

monastery. The church is richly
decorated with frescoes. Its
beautiful Late-Gothic altarpiece
dates from around 1520. Next to
the church is the grave of Peter
Jakob Larssøn, a 19th-century
buccaneer who went on to
become Sæby's mayor.

Sæby has a compact centre
with half-timbered houses and
an attractive harbour. In
summer a trumpeter heralds
the end of each day, which is
followed by the ceremonial
lowering of a flag. **Sæby
Museum**, housed in the 17th-
century Ørums Consul's House,
contains a 1920s schoolroom
and a violinmaker's workshop.

Environs
A short distance north of
town is Sæbygård, a beautifully
preserved 16th-century
manor house set in a small
beech forest.

🏛 **Sæby Museum**
Algade 1–3. **Tel** 98 46 10 77. **Open** see
website for times. 🅿️ Ⓦ **kyst
museet.dk /saeby-saebygaard**

❻ Voergård Slot

Road map: D2. Voergård 6,
Dronningelund. **Tel** 98 86 71 08.
Open 11am–4pm on certain days
from Easter to Oct; variable times so
check website for latest information
before visiting. 📷 compulsory. 🅿️
Ⓦ **voergaardslot.dk**

This Renaissance castle is one
of Denmark's most stylish
buildings. Its splendid portal
was intended originally for
the royal castle of Fredensborg.
Initially the estate was part of
a religious complex, but after
the Reformation it passed into
private hands. The main wing
has a large collection of
paintings that includes works
by Raphael, Goya, Rubens and
Fragonard. Also on display are
many fine pieces of furniture
and porcelain (including a
dinner set made for Napoleon I).

❼ Lindholm Høje

Road map: C2. Burial ground:
Open until dusk. Museum: Vendilavej
11. **Tel** 99 31 74 40. **Open** Apr–Oct:
10am–5pm daily; Nov–Mar: 10am–
4pm Tue–Sun. 🅿️ Ⓦ **nordmus.dk/
lindholm-hoje-museet**

Denmark's largest Iron Age
and Viking burial ground has
survived so well due to a thick
layer of sand that blew over it.
The sand deposit kept the
site hidden until 1952, when
archaeologists unearthed nearly
700 graves. The oldest ones are
triangular; others are circular.
The Viking-era graves have been
made to resemble ships. Other
finds discovered in the vicinity

Half-timbered house in one of Sæby's picturesque streets

indicate that between the 7th and 11th centuries this was an important Viking trading centre. Lindholm Høje comes to life each year during the last week of June, when a Viking festival is held here. Throughout the rest of the year it is possible to visit a museum and try Viking-era food in its restaurant.

❽ Aalborg

See pp212–13.

❾ Limfjorden

See pp214–15.

❿ Holstebro

Road map: B3. 🗺 31,000. 🚆 🚌
ℹ Jeppe Schous Gade 14. **Tel** 96 11 70 86. 🌐 **visitholstebro.dk**

The earliest records of Holstebro can be found in 13th-century documents. The town was often plagued by fire, however, and has few historic sights. Continuing a centuries-old tradition the town bells chime every day at 10pm reminding citizens to put out fires for the night.

In front of the mid-19th-century town hall in the centre of town is a sculpture by Alberto Giacometti. The nearby Neo-Gothic church is 20th century and contains the remains of a 16th-century altar.

The **Holstebro Kunstmuseum** has a sizeable collection of paintings (including works by Picasso and Matisse), as well as sculpture and ceramics, mainly by contemporary Danish

Façade of the Holstebro Kunstmuseum

Village house in Hjerl Hedes Frilandsmuseum

artists. It also houses interesting temporary exhibitions.

Environs
The **Strandingsmuseet St George**, 45 km (28 miles) to the west of Holstebro, tells the story of a shipwreck that took place in 1811.

🏛 **Holstebro Kunstmuseum**
Museumsvej 2. **Tel** 97 42 45 18.
Open Jul–Aug: 11am–5pm Tue–Sun; Sep–Jun: noon–4pm Tue–Fri, 11am–5pm Sat–Sun. 🌐 **holstebrokunstmuseum.dk**

🏛 **Strandingsmuseet St George**
Vesterhausgade 1E, Thorsminde.
Tel 97 49 33 66. **Open** Jan–Mar: 11am–4pm daily; Apr–Oct: 10am–5pm daily; Nov: 11am–3pm daily. 🖼

⓫ Hjerl Hede Frilandsmuseum

Road map: B3. Hjerl Hedevej 14.
Tel 97 44 80 60. **Open** Opening hours vary; consult the website for details.
🖼 🖼 🌐 **hjerlhede.dk**

A short distance northeast of Holstebro is an open-air museum that re-creates the development of a Danish village from 1500

to 1900. The collection of buildings includes an inn, a school, a smithy and a dairy. In summer, men and women wear period clothes and demonstrate traditional skills such as weaving and bread-making.

The uncultivated Kongenshus Mindepark heathland reserve

⓬ Kongenshus Mindepark

Road map: C3. Vestre Skivevej 142, Daugbjerg, Viborg. **Tel** 86 66 13 78.
Open all year round. 🖼
🌐 **kongenshus.dk**

A small section of Denmark's uncultivated heathland, of which just 800 sq km (309 sq miles) remains, can be explored at Kongenhus Mindepark. For many years early pioneers attempted to cultivate this windswept and inhospitable area. In the 18th century an army officer from Mecklenburg leased the land from Frederik V, intending it for cultivation. Assisted by the king's generosity, he built a house, which he named Kongenshus (King's House). However, after 12 years the officer abandoned the project and returned to Germany. Today the scenery of Kongenshus Mindepark can be experienced from an observation tower next to the café.

❽ Aalborg

North Jutland's capital city is situated on the south bank of the Limfjorden. It was founded by the Vikings in the 10th century and rapidly acquired a strategic significance as a hub of trade and transport. It prospered in the 17th century thanks to a thriving herring industry and many of its finest buildings date from this time. Aalborg remains a commercial centre and is the seat of the regional government and a university town. The local industry includes the country's leading producer of Danish schnapps, *akvavit*.

Coat of arms from Jens Bangs Stenhus

Panoramic view of Aalborg, capital of northern Jutland

Exploring Aalborg

Most of the historic buildings in Aalborg are clustered around the compact medieval quarter. Jomfru Ane Gade has restaurants and bars and is the centre of the city's nightlife.

🔼 Vor Frue Kirke

Niels Ebbesens Gade. **Open** 9am–2pm Mon–Fri, 9am–noon Sat. 🆆 vorfrue.dk

The Church of Our Lady dates back to the 12th century. In the 16th and 17th centuries it was the main place of Christian worship in Aalborg. The west portal deserves a closer look.

🔼 Aalborghus Slot

Slotspladsen 1. **Open** 8am–9pm daily. Dungeons: **Open** May–Sep: 8am–3pm Mon–Fri. Underground passages: **Open** 8am–9pm daily. 🆆 kongeligeslotte.dk

This modestly sized half-timbered castle was built on the orders of Christian III and completed in 1555. The dank castle dungeons and underground passages leading off them make for an eerie walk.

🏛 Utzon Center

Slotspladsen 4. **Tel** 76 90 50 00. **Open** 10am–5pm Tue–Sun (until 9pm Thu). 🆆 utzoncenter.dk

The Utzon Center, a powerhouse of architectural and design exhibitions, is the last building created by the late Jørn Utzon, in collaboration with his son Kim. Utzon, the man responsible for the Sydney Opera House, grew up in Aalborg. The centre also features a restaurant, library and an auditorium. It is located by the waterfront, next to the harbour pool, where you can go for a swim.

🏛 Jens Bangs Stenhus

Østerågade 9. **Closed** to the public.

A Dutch Renaissance-style house, this five-storey edifice, decorated with gargoyles and floral ornaments, was built in 1624 for Jens Bang, a wealthy merchant. Its façade facing the Rådhus (city hall) includes a stone figure of a satyr sticking its tongue out – this was intended to symbolize the owner's attitude towards the city's councillors who refused to admit him into their ranks. The cellars house a wine bar that also serves traditional Danish food.

🏛 Rådhuset

Gammel Torv 2. **Closed** to the public.

The yellow-painted Baroque city hall was completed in 1762 and stands on the site of a demolished Gothic town hall. The motto written above the main door translates as "Wisdom and Determination" and was used by Frederik V, who was on the throne when the city hall was built.

Soldiers preparing for a parade, Aalborghus Slot

For hotels and restaurants in this area see pp253–4 and pp272–3

⛪ Budolfi Domkirke

Algade 40. **Tel** 98 12 46 70. **Open** Jun–Aug: 9am–4pm Mon–Fri, 9am–2pm Sat; Sep–May: 9am–3pm Mon–Fri, 9am–noon Sat. 🌐 **aalborgdomkirke.dk**

With a distinctive Baroque cupola, this white-plastered Gothic cathedral from around 1400 is an important Aalborg landmark. Among the notable interior features are portraits of wealthy merchants, a gilded Baroque altarpiece and 16th-century frescoes. The church's patron, St Budolfi, is the patron saint of sailors whose cult was propagated by English missionaries.

Delightfully simple interior of Budolfi Domkirke

🏛 Historiske Museum

Algade 48. **Tel** 99 31 74 00. **Open** 10am–5pm Tue–Sun. 🌐 **nord jyllandshistoriskemuseum.dk**

Just west of the cathedral is the local history museum. Its varied collection includes archaeological finds from Lindholm Høje *(see pp210–11)* and rare glassware and ancient coins. The museum's star exhibits include a reconstructed drawing room from an early 17th-century merchant's house. Most interesting of all, perhaps, is the skeleton of a 40-year-old female discovered in a peat bog who died around AD 400.

⛪ Helligåndsklostret

Kloster Jordet 1, C.W. Obels Plads. **Tel** 98 12 02 05. 🕒 late Jun–mid-Aug: 2pm Mon–Fri. 🌐

This convent was founded in 1431 and is one of the best-preserved buildings of its type in Scandinavia. The only original part is the west wing; the north and the east wings are 16th century. Guided tours allow visitors to look at the frescoes in the hospital chapel, step into the refectory with its starry vault and listen to the story of a nun who was buried alive for having a relationship with a monk.

VISITORS' CHECKLIST

Practical Information
Road map: C2. 🔲 201,000.
🛈 Nordkraft, Kjellerups Torv 5. **Tel** 99 31 75 00. 🎭 Aalborg Carnival and Regatta (May).
🌐 **visitaalborg.com**

Transport
🚉 Aalborg. 🚌

Helligåndsklostret

🏛 Kunsten Museum of Modern Art Aalborg

Kong Christians Allé 50. **Tel** 99 82 41 00. **Open** 10am–5pm Tue–Sun (until 9pm Wed). 🌐 **kunsten.dk**

Designed by Alvar Aalto in conjunction with Danish architect Jean-Jacques Baruël, this striking museum has a great collection of Danish and European modern art.

Aalborg Historic Centre

① Vor Frue Kirke
② Aalborghus Slot
③ Utzon Center
④ Jens Bangs Stenhus
⑤ Rådhuset
⑥ Budolfi Domkirke
⑦ Historiske Museum
⑧ Helligåndsklostret

⑨ Limfjorden

Limfjorden is Denmark's largest body of inland water. Although narrow inlets connect it to both the Kattegat and the North Sea, Limfjorden resembles a lake. In summer, ferries offer trips to the smaller islands and other areas. The significance of this area can be deduced from the many Bronze Age burial mounds, churches and castles. The shape of the island of Mors resembles Jutland. According to legend, when God created Jutland he first built a model. It was so good that he placed it at the centre of Limfjorden. The Hanklit Cliffs on the northern tip of Mors have particularly stunning views.

★ **Jesperhus Park**
This park is planted with half a million flowers. Some are planted to form figures of animals found in the park zoo, such as a crocodile.

Spit
A narrow 10-km (6-mile) spit leads from Thyborøn to Harboøre. The east side is flanked by the fjord, the western side by the North Sea.

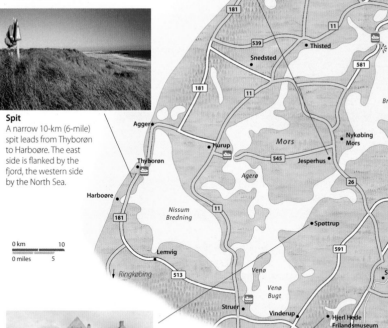

Hjerl Hede Frilandsmuseet
Among the many historic buildings at this open-air museum are an inn, a smithy, a dairy, a school, a vicarage and a grocer's shop (*see p211*).

★ **Spøttrup Borg**
Protected against attack by a moat and high ramparts, this medieval castle has changed little since it was built in 1500.

Fjerritslev
Situated between the fjord and the North Sea, Fjerritslev is surrounded by beautiful scenery. The town brewery, a red-brick building, has been preserved as a museum.

VISITORS' CHECKLIST

Practical Information
Road map: B2–C2. Thisted.
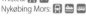 Store Torv 6. **Tel** 97 92 56 04.
Havnen 4. **Tel** 97 72 04 88.
W **visitmors.dk** W **visitthy.dk**
W **visitskive.dk**

Transport
Thisted:
Nykøbing Mors:

Aalborg
Northern Jutland's capital city has many interesting sights, including the superb Kunsten Museum of Modern Art *(see p213)*.

Nibe
This idyllic Limfjord town used to be famous for its herring markets, which would supply fish for the royal table.

Key

⬛ Motorway

⬛ Major road

⬛ Other road

Lovns Bredning
This section of Limfjorden, which has some enchanting coves, is a protected area because of the rich diversity of birdlife found here.

Mønsted's limestone mine

⓭ Mønsted

Road map: C3. Mønsted Kalkgruber, Kalkværksvej 8. **Tel** 86 64 60 11. **Open** Apr–Oct: 10am–5pm daily. 🖼 **W** monsted-kalkgruber.dk

As far back as the 10th century the area around Mønsted was famous as a centre of limestone mining. The mine, which was still in operation in the 20th century, is now an unusual local attraction. Although only 2 km (1 mile) of the entire 60 km (37 miles) of its tunnels are open, a walk through the underground maze is an unforgettable experience. Visitors can wander at their own pace through the galleries, but they must wear safety helmets. For those who prefer more comfort, there is a mine train, which travels into the pit, past limestone columns and underground lakes. In view of the mine's steady humidity and temperature, which stays at 8° C (46° C), some of the caves situated 35 m (115 ft) below the surface are used for ripening cheese.

⓮ Viborg

Road map: C3. 🚹 35,000. 🚌 🚂 🛈 Nytorv 9. **Tel** 87 87 88 88. 🖼 Marching Festival (Jun). **W** visitviborg.dk

Viborg is scenically located on the shores of two lakes. Its history dates back to the 8th century and it became one of Denmark's bishoprics in 1060. The 12th-century cathedral was used for coronation ceremonies by the Danish monarchy until the 17th century. The present twin-towered **Domkirke** (cathedral) was completed in 1876. This huge granite building has some valuable relics as well as a crypt dating from 1130, which is all that remains of the original cathedral. Other features include a gilded altarpiece and a vast 15th-century candelabra. The cathedral's frescoes form an illustrated Bible and were created

Figures from Viborg's Domkirke

by the Danish artist Joakim Skovgaard (1901–06). Other works by the artist can be seen in the **Skovgaard Museet**, which is next to the cathedral. The **Viborg Museum** contains a variety of exhibits relating to the town's history, including some items that date from the Viking era. Viborg's city hall, located on the outskirts of the town, in the middle of a park, is a modern and fully sustainable building designed by the architect Henning Larsen.

🏛 Domkirke
Domkirkepladsen, Sankt Mogensgade 4. **Tel** 87 25 52 50. **Open** opening hours vary so see website for latest information befor visiting. 🖼 **W** viborgdomkirke.dk

🏛 Skovgaard Museet
Domkirkstræde 4. **Tel** 86 62 39 75. **Open** Jun–Aug: 10am–5pm Tue–Sun; Sep–May: 11am–4pm Tue–Sun. 🖼

🏛 Viborg Museum
Hjultorvet 4. **Tel** 87 87 38 38. **Open** Jul–mid-Aug: 11am–5pm Tue–Sun; mid-Aug–Jun: 1–4pm Tue–Fri, 11am–5pm Sat & Sun. 🖼

⓯ Rebild Bakker

Map C2. 🛈 VisitRebild – RebildPorten, Rebildvej 25A, Rebild. **Tel** 99 88 90 00. **W** rebildporten.dk

Rebild Bakker is part of Rold Skov, the largest forest in Denmark. In 1912, after fund-raising among the Danish expatriate community in the USA, a section of it was purchased and turned into this park. Covering 77 sq km 30 sq miles), an array of wildlife lives in the park, including foxes, deer, squirrels, martens, badgers and numerous birds. Close to Rebild Bakker is the **Fiddlers Museum**, where every Sunday afternoon visitors are encouraged to participate in a lively square dance. The museum also explores the way in which the surrounding forest has shaped the economy of the area and the lives of the local people by looking at various forest trades, including hunting and poaching.

🏛 Fiddlers Museum
Cimbrervej 2. **Tel** 98 39 16 04. **Open** Oct–Apr: 1–5pm Sun; May–Aug: 10am–5pm daily; Sep: 11am–4pm daily. 🖼 📷 🎦 **W** spillemandsmuseet.dk

⓰ Mariager

Road map: D3. 🚹 2,500. 🚌 🛈 Torvet 1B, 70 27 13 77. **W** visitmariagerfjord.dk

In the Middle Ages Mariager was a major centre of pilgrimages, owing to the nunnery that was established here in 1410. Today, it is a quiet fjord town, with cobbled streets and picturesque houses engulfed in roses. The main reminder of the convent is the church standing on a wooded hill. Though it is much smaller than the original

Banks of Limfjorden, near Mariager

14th-century building it is possible to imagine what the convent would have been like from a scale model in **Mariager Museum**, which is housed in an 18th-century merchant's house.

At **Mariager Saltcenter** visitors can learn about methods of salt production, make their own crystals and take a bath in Denmark's version of the Dead Sea, which has pools filled with warm water so salty that it's quite impossible to dive beneath the surface. Bring a swimsuit.

Small bag of salt from Mariager Saltcenter

🏛 **Mariager Museum**
Kirkegade 4A. **Tel** 99 31 74 60. **Open** mid-May–mid-Sep: noon–4pm daily.
🌐 **nordmus.dk/mariager**

🏛 **Mariager Saltcenter**
Ny Havnevej 6. **Tel** 98 54 18 16. **Open** 10am–4pm daily (to 5pm Sat, Sun & hols). 🌐 **saltcenter.com**

⓱ Fyrkat

Road map: C3. Fyrkatvej 37B, Hobro. **Tel** 99 82 41 75. **Open** May: 10am–4pm daily; Jun–Aug: 10am–5pm daily; Sep: 10am–3pm daily. 🌐 **nordmus.dk/vikingecenter-fyrkat**

In 1950 the remains of a Viking settlement dating from around AD 980 were discovered in fields 3 km (2 miles) from the town of Hobro. A modern visitor centre has since been built around the site.

The entire settlement was surrounded by ramparts 120 m (394 ft) in diameter. The entry

gates to the fortress, aligned strictly with the points of the compass, were linked with each other by two intersecting streets. An ancient burial site containing 30 graves was discovered outside the main camp. A Viking-style farmstead north of the settlement re-creates many aspects of Viking life. Visitors can try on a Viking tunic and bake bread over an open fire.

⓲ Randers

Road map: D3. 🏘 60,000. 🚉 🚌 ℹ Rådhustorvet 4. **Tel** 86 42 44 77. 🌐 **visitranders.com**

Jutland's fourth largest city was already a major market town in the Middle Ages. Its most important historic sight is the 15th-century Sankt Mortens Kirke. Hanging inside is a model of a ship dating from 1632. The three-storey Paaskesønnernes Gård nearby is late 15th century and one of the city's oldest houses. The most popular attraction is **Randers Regnskov**, an unusual tropical zoo that houses 200 animal species and 450 species of plants in a tropical rain forest environment. Here, regardless of the time of the year, the temperature remains at a constant 25° C (77° F), accompanied by very high

humidity. Among the many animals kept at the zoo are crocodiles, gibbons, colourful butterflies, tapirs and snakes. There is also an area focusing on old breeds of Danish farm animals.

🦎 **Randers Regnskov**
Tørvebryggen 11. **Tel** 87 10 99 99. **Open** 10am–4pm Mon–Fri, 10am–5pm Sat & Sun. 🌐 **regnskoven.dk**

⓳ Gammel Estrup

Road map: D3. Randersvej 2–4. **Tel** 86 48 30 01. **Open** Opening hours vary; check the website prior to your visit. 🌐 **gammelestrup.dk**

One of the region's major attractions is the Gammel Estrup estate, near the village of Auning on the Djursland peninsula. The estate's 15th-century manor house is partially surrounded by a moat and now houses a museum. Its interiors, complete with period furniture, paintings and tapestries, include reception rooms, bedrooms, a chapel and an alchemist's cellar. An agricultural museum, the Dansk Landbrugs-museum, focuses on Denmark's agricultural past and includes farm machinery and tools.

Environs
Rosenholm Slot, near Hornslet, is a 16th-century castle built on a small island in the middle of a lake. It was here that Count Rosenkrantz, immortalized in Shakespeare's *Hamlet*, lived.

Façade of Gammel Estrup's manor house

BORNHOLM

Far out in the Baltic, the idyllic island of Bornholm has an atmosphere all of its own. For years it remained relatively unknown to outsiders but the beauty of the island's sprawling beaches, its rugged coastal cliffs and distinctive architecture have made it a popular holiday destination. Tourism remains a low-key affair, however, and the villages and towns have changed little over the years.

Bornholmers are proud of their ancestry and have their own flag and, among the older generation, a distinctive dialect that is as unique to the island as the *rundkirke* (round churches) that are found here.

The discovery of ancient burial mounds and engravings suggest that the island was inhabited by 3000 BC. At one time Bornholm was an important centre for trade, and coins have been unearthed from as far afield as Rome and the Near East. The name "Bornholm" appeared for the first time in AD 890 at a time when the island was inhabited by the Vikings.

From the mid-12th century much of Bornholm became the property of the Archbishop of the city of Lund, which at that time belonged to Denmark. For a period in the 17th century it was controlled by Sweden but the islanders'

strong allegiance to Denmark resulted in a rapid withdrawal of Swedish forces. Following the surrender of Germany in May 1945 Bornholm was occupied by the Soviets until the Danish army established a permanent garrison.

Bornholm has developed a reputation for its regional cuisine and boasts local delicacies and a thriving fishing industry. Don't leave without sampling its smoked herring, known as *røget bornholmer*.

A wide variety of natural habitats is found here ranging from secluded forests and pasture land to rugged cliffs and long, sandy beaches. Another of the island's assets is its climate, with mild winters and Denmark's highest percentage of sunny days. The local flora features many species typical of the Mediterranean, including orchids, figs, grapes and mulberry trees.

Svaneke's yacht marina

◀ Myreagre Mølle windmill on the island of Bornholm

Exploring Bornholm

Bornholm has some good cycle paths and exploring by bicycle is both convenient and enjoyable. The northern shore is marked by steep cliffs while sandy beaches are the main feature of the south and southeast coasts. Bornholm is known for its round churches and for the atmospheric ruins at Hammershus Slot. Rønne, the island's main town, has some well-preserved quarters, as do many of the smaller harbour ports. Children will enjoy a visit to Joboland Park, which includes an aquapark and a small zoo, and Østerlars' history centre where they can see what life was like in a medieval village.

One of Rønne's many colourful half-timbered houses

Getting There

Bornholm's airport is 5 km (3 miles) southeast of Rønne. A flight from Copenhagen takes half an hour. Many visitors arrive by ferry. The journey from Køge takes six to seven hours (overnight ferries are an option). As an alternative, visitors can take a three-hour journey by train to Ystad in Sweden, and pick up a ferry from there to Rønne. Buses are also available from Copenhagen to Ystad and cost a little less.

Modern power-generating windmills north of Hasle

For keys to symbols *see back flap*

The scenic coast of Bornholm

Key

— Major road

····· Minor road

— Scenic route

Christiansø
19 km (12 miles)

GUDHJEM
Melsted

ØSTERLARS
KIRKE

158

Bølshavn Listed
Østermarie
JOBOLAND SVANEKE

Ibsker Årsdale

B O R N H O L M

Almindingen

KIRKEBY

158

Øle Å

38

Bodilsker Neksø

Balka

Pedersker Snogebæk
Povlsker
erne

Dueodde

Sights at a Glance

1. Hammershus Slot
2. Allinge
3. Olsker
4. Hasle
5. Nyker
6. Rønne
7. Nylars
8. Aakirkeby
9. Svaneke
10. Joboland
11. Østerlars Kirke
12. Gudhjem

One of Bornholm's fortified 12th-century round churches

Picturesque ruins of Hammershus Slot

❶ Hammershus Slot

Castle: **Open** all year round. Hammershus Exhibition: Langebjergvej 128, Allinge. **Open** mid-Apr–mid-Oct: 10am–4pm daily; (Jun–Aug: 10am–5pm daily).

The atmospheric ruins of Hammershus Slot are the largest in northern Europe and stand on a 70-m- (230-ft-) high cliff. The castle was built in the 13th century on the orders of the Archbishop of Lund. Legend has it that Hammershus was originally to be built at a different site, but the walls erected during the day vanished each night. A change of location was thought necessary and horses were let loose; the spot where they finally stopped was chosen as the new site.

The entrance to the castle leads over a stone bridge that was once a draw-bridge. The ruins also include what remains of a brewery, a granary and a bakery.

The impressive square tower, Manteltårnet, was used in the Middle Ages for storing the country's tax records and later served as the quarters of the castle commander and also as a prison. In 1660 Leonora Christina, daughter of Christian IV, and her husband were

imprisoned in the tower, accused of collaboration with the Swedes. Technological improvements in artillery eventually diminished the castle's defensive capabilities as its walls became vulnerable to attack from powerful cannons. It was abandoned in 1743 and much of the castle was used as building material for local homes. An exhibition includes a model of Hammershus Slot as it was at the peak of its might.

❷ Allinge

🏠 1,600. 🚌 ℹ️ Sverigesvej 11. **Tel** 56 59 95 00.

Allinge and nearby Sandvig, 2 km (1 mile) to the north-west, are treated as one town though the two have slightly different characters. Allinge has the majority of commercial facilities while Sandvig is quieter, with walking trails and neatly-tended gardens. Allinge's church is mostly 19th century, although the church itself grew out of a chapel erected five centuries earlier. Inside is a painting that once adorned the chapel in Hammershus Slot as well as tomb-stones of the castle's past commanders. On the outskirts of Allinge there is a well-kept cemetery for Russian soldiers, with a granite obelisk proudly displaying the Soviet star at the top. This is a

Granite obelisk at Allinge Cemetery

reminder of the Red Army, who occupied Bornholm from the end of World War II until March 1946.

On the outskirts of Allinge is Madsebakke Helleristininger – the biggest and the most precious set of rock carvings to be found in the whole of Denmark. These simple enigmatic Bronze Age drawings, depicting ships, boats and the outlines of feet, are thought to be 4,000 years old. Another local curiosity is the Moseløkken quarry, where between May and September visitors can learn all about the excavation of granite on Bornholm and even have a go at splitting a piece themselves.

12th-century three-storey round church in Olsker

❸ Olsker

🏠 1,700. 🚌

The village of Olsker, south of Allinge, has one of the best known of Bornholm's distinctive round churches. Historians once believed they were of pagan origin. This hypothesis has now been discarded and the current theory is that they were intended for defensive purposes, as well as being used for storage. This three-storey granite building is the slenderest of Bornholm's four round churches and has nine windows. It was erected in the mid-12th century in honour of St Olaf, a Norwegian king who died in 1031, and who is revered in Denmark. The hill on which the church stands affords a beautiful view of the surrounding countryside.

Round Churches

Bornholm's four sparkling-white *rundkirke* (round churches) are each dedicated to a different saint. They were built between 1150 and 1200 at a time when pirate attacks were a constant threat to the island and have 2-m (7-ft) thick granite walls. Apart from the one at Nyker, all are three-storey buildings. The bottom level was used mainly for worship. The first floor served as a supply warehouse and also stored the church's valuables and donations received from the faithful. In times of danger the first floor also provided shelter for women and children, while the third, top level was used for surveillance and was an ideal place from which to shoot and throw stones at the advancing enemy below.

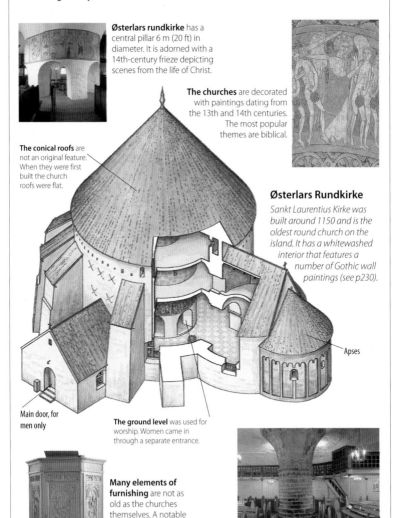

Østerlars rundkirke has a central pillar 6 m (20 ft) in diameter. It is adorned with a 14th-century frieze depicting scenes from the life of Christ.

The churches are decorated with paintings dating from the 13th and 14th centuries. The most popular themes are biblical.

The conical roofs are not an original feature. When they were first built the church roofs were flat.

Østerlars Rundkirke

Sankt Laurentius Kirke was built around 1150 and is the oldest round church on the island. It has a whitewashed interior that features a number of Gothic wall paintings (see p230).

Apses

Main door, for men only

The ground level was used for worship. Women came in through a separate entrance.

Many elements of furnishing are not as old as the churches themselves. A notable feature of Olsker's church is its richly ornamented 16th-century pulpit.

Top floors were accessed by a stairway leading through narrow passages knocked out of the thick walls.

❹ Hasle

🗺 1,600. 🚌 ℹ️ Storegade 64. **Tel** 56 96 44 81. 🌐 **hasleroegeri.dk**

One of Bornholm's oldest towns, Hasle is mentioned in records as early as 1149. The herring industry has long been the town's main source of revenue although many locals were once also employed in excavating brown coal until the mine closed in 1946. The town is popular with visitors, many of whom come to sample the smoked herring. Hasle Smokehouse is the last smokehouse in Bornholm where smoking takes place in the traditional way in open chimneys with alder fire wood. There are smoking sessions every day from May to October and it is possible to follow the smoking process from early morning to about 10:30pm, when the herring and other fish products are finished and ready to be eaten.

In the centre of town stands an interesting 15th-century church with a lovely two-winged altarpiece made in Lübeck in 1520. According to one local story the altar was a gift from a sailor who miraculously escaped from a sinking ship.

A monument in the town square commemorates Peder Olsen, Jens Kofoed and Poul Anker who became the local heroes of an uprising against the Swedes that erupted in Bornholm in 1658.

On the outskirts of the town, on the road leading towards Rønne, is a huge runic stone – the largest one on the island.

Nykirke's pillar with scenes from the Stations of the Cross

❺ Nyker

🗺 700. 🚌

The smallest of Bornholm's historic round churches (see p225) is in Nyker. It is only two storeys high and lacks external buttresses. In keeping with its name (Nykirke or New Church) it is also the most recently built of the churches. A Latin inscription found on the Late-Gothic chalice kept in the church proclaims that the church is dedicated to All Saints. Other items to look out for include the frescoes that decorate the main pillar of the church, which depict the Stations of the Cross, and a stone laid in the portico with a Resurrection scene that dates from 1648. Another interesting object is an 18th-century tablet carved with the names of the local inhabitants who died in two plagues that devastated the area in 1618 and 1654.

❻ Rønne

🗺 13,600. ✈️ 🚌 ℹ️ Nordre Kystvej 3. **Tel** 56 95 95 00. 🛒 Wed, Sat. 🌐 **bornholm.info**

One third of Bornholm's population live in Rønne. The town has grown up around a natural harbour and two of the first buildings that can be seen when approaching from the sea are the 19th-century lighthouse and Sankt Nicolai Kirke.

Rønne has two main squares – Store Torv and Lille Torv (Big Market and Little Market). Store Torv was originally used for military parades but is now the venue for a twice-weekly market.

The Tinghus at Store Torv 1 dates from 1834 and was once used as the town hall, courthouse and jail. A number of picturesque cobbled streets lead off from Store Torv and many of the early 19th-century houses are still standing, despite a series of bombing raids carried out by the Soviets in May 1945. One of Rønne's most unusual buildings is in Vimmelskaftet – its width allows for one window only. Standing at the corner of Østergade and Theaterstræde is the restored Rønne Theatre, one of the oldest theatres in Denmark, dating from 1823. **Bornholms Museum** has a good local-history section that includes archaeological finds, a small collection of paintings and a selection of 6th-century golden tablets known as *goldgubber*. Over 2,000 of these tablets engraved with small figures have been found on the island. The **Forsvarsmuseet**

Distinctive white chimneys of a smokehouse in Hasle

Harbourside smithy in Rønne

(Military Museum) is housed in a citadel south of the town centre that was built around 1650. The defensive tower houses a large collection of weapons, ammunition, uniforms and one of the oldest cannons in Denmark.

🏛 Bornholms Museum

Sankt Mortensgade 29. **Tel** 56 95 07 35. **Open** Jan–mid-May & mid-Oct–Dec: 1–4pm Mon–Fri, 11am–3pm Sat; mid-May–Jun & Sep–mid-Oct: 10am–5pm Mon–Sat; Jul & Aug: 10am–5pm daily. 🅿

🏛 Forsvarsmuseet

Arsenalvej 8. **Tel** 51 33 00 33. **Open** Apr–Oct: 10am–4pm Mon–Fri. 🅿

❼ Nylars

Situated some 7 km (4 miles) east of Rønne, Nylars Rundkirke is one of Bornholm's four well-preserved round churches *(see p225)*. It was built in 1150 and is dedicated to St Nicholas, the patron saint of sailors. To climb the stairs to the upper levels it is necessary to squeeze through narrow passages knocked through thick walls. For invaders trying to reach the upper floor this presented a big obstacle. The frescoes that adorn the distinctive pillar that rises through all three levels of the building depict biblical scenes including Adam and Eve's expulsion from the Garden of Eden.

❽ Aakirkeby

🏘 2,000. 🚌 ℹ Torvet 30. **Tel** 56 95 95 00.

During the Middle Ages this was the most important town on the island and the seat of Bornholm's church and the lay authorities. As a result, the 12th-century Aa Kirke is Bornholm's largest church. The Romanesque building contains a number of treasures including a 13th-century baptismal font and an early 17th-century pulpit. Climbing to the top of the church's high bell tower affords great views of the town. Another, more modern attraction is **NaturBornholm**, a state-of-the-art natural history museum situated on the southern outskirts of town. A trip to the museum takes visitors back 2,000 years and provides an entertaining and

Denmark's national emblem, Åkirke

informative way to learn about the flora and fauna of the island. Behind this centre is a gigantic natural fault in the bedrock created some 400 million years ago, which marks the geological boundary between the continental plates of Europe and Scandinavia.

🏛 NaturBornholm

Grønningen 30. **Tel** 56 94 04 00. **Open** Apr–Oct: 10am–5pm daily. 🅿 🌐 **naturbornholm.dk**

❾ Svaneke

🏘 1,100. 🚌 ℹ Peter F. Heerings Gade 7. **Tel** 56 95 95 00. 🛍 Sat.

In the 1970s this appealing town won the European Gold Medal preservation award and Svaneke continues to maintain its unspoilt historic character. A short distance south of the town centre is Svaneke Kirke. A majestic swan adorns the spire of this 14th-century church (Svaneke translates as "Swan Corner"), and the image of a swan is also included in the town emblem.

In the local glass factory, Pernille Bulow, visitors can watch as skilled workers produce glassware. As well as being known as one of the most photogenic towns on Bornholm, Svaneke is also famous for its windmills. These can be seen standing by each of the town's exit roads. The best preserved is the Årsdale Mølle (1877) on the road leading to Nexø. The mill is open to visitors and also sells its own flour.

Horse-drawn tram in Svaneke, a popular way to see the town

⑩ Joboland

3 km (2 miles) from Svaneke,
Højevejen 4. **Tel** 56 49 60 76.
Open May–Jun & mid-Aug–mid-Sep:
11am–5pm Tue–Thu, Sat & Sun; Jul–
early Aug: 10am–6:30pm daily; early
Aug–mid-Aug: 11am–5pm daily.
W joboland.dk

This amusement park has
enough entertainment to last an
entire day. Its greatest attraction
is the aquapark with pools of
water kept at a constant 25° C
(77° F). The aquapark contains
five water slides and a 125-m-
(410-ft-) long Wild River, which
adventurous visitors can ride on
a rubber tyre. It is also possible to
sail a boat, whizz down a "death
slide" and walk across a rope
bridge. During high season the
park lays on additional shows
and games for children, such as
treasure hunts. Joboland also has
its own small zoo with a variety
of animals including peacocks,
goats, monkeys and exotic birds.

Climbing frames at Joboland amusement park

Østerlars Kirke, the largest of the island's
round churches

⑪ Østerlars Kirke

Vietsvej 25. **Tel** 40 38 42 06. **Open**
mid-Apr–mid-Oct: 9am–5pm Mon–Sat;
Nov–Mar: 9am–2:45pm Tue–Sat.

The largest of Bornholm's round
churches *(see p225)* is Østerlars
Kirke, which is scenically
located in the middle of wheat
fields. The church dates from
1150 and is dedicated to Sankt
Laurentius (St Laurence). The
sturdy buttresses and conical
roof are later additions. Inside,
the central pillar is decorated
with 14th-century frescoes.
A rune stone at the entrance
dates from 1070 and bears
the inscription: "Edmund

and his brother erected this
stone to the memory of their
father Sigmund. May Christ,
St Michael and St Mary help
his soul."

Near the church is Middelaldercenter, a re-created village
where staff in medieval dress
work in the smithy, grind corn
and tend sheep. There are daily
demonstrations of medieval
skills such as making clay pots
and archery.

🏛 **Middelaldercenter**
Stangevej 1. **Tel** 56 49 83 19.
Open Apr–Jun & mid-Aug–late Oct:
10am–4pm daily; Jul–mid-Aug: 10am–
5pm daily. **W** bornholms-
middelaldercenter.dk

⑫ Gudhjem

🚌 700. 🚏 ℹ Ejnar Mikkelsens Vej
17. **Tel** 56 95 95 00.

The village of Gudhjem ("God's
Home") is built on a steep hill
overlooking the sea. The
picturesque harbour, cobbled
streets and brightly painted
half-timbered houses with

red-tiled roofs make it a popular
spot with visitors in summer.

The village has long been
associated with the fishing
industry and in 1893 Gudhjem
acquired the first proper
smokehouse in Bornholm. The
famous "Sun over Gudhjem", a
herring smoked in its skin and
served with egg yolk, is well
worth trying.

In the centre of the village is a
late 19th-century church. Close
by are the remains of a much
older chapel dating from the
13th century. The **Oluf Høst
Museet** has a large selection of
paintings by the Bornholm artist
Oluf Høst who died in 1966. The
collection is housed in the artist's
home, which he built in 1929. An
old railway station houses the
Gudhjem Museum, which has
displays on local history.

🏛 **Oluf Høst Museet**
Løkkegade 35. **Tel** 56 48 50 38. **Open**
Apr–May, Sep–Oct: 11am–5pm Wed–
Sun; Jun–Aug: 11am–5pm daily.

🏛 **Gudhjem Museum**
Stationsvej 1. **Tel** 61 22 33 65. **Open**
10am–5pm Mon–Sat, 2–5pm Sun.

Half-timbered houses in Gudhjem

◀ Rock formations leading into the sea at Bornholm

Cycling on Bornholm

The best way to explore Bornholm is by bicycle and cycle groups are a common sight. The island has 235 km (146 miles) of well signposted cycling routes, many of which connect to the main towns. The routes provide an ideal way to enjoy Bornholm's meadows, fields and forests, particularly as most are far away from busy roads. Rønne, Allinge, and Gudhjem are good places to start. An English language brochure entitled *Bicycle Routes on Bornholm* is available at tourist information centres. Be aware that cycling on Bornholm requires a reasonable level of fitness due to the numerous hills.

Aakirkeby's church contains a 14th-century stone font created by Sigraf, a master stonemason from Gotland in Sweden.

Gudhjem is a pretty harbourside village. The Sankt Anna chapel dates from the 13th century.

Key (km/miles)
- 1. Rønne–Allinge (21/13)
- 2. Rønne–Helligdommen (17/11)
- 3. Rønne–Gudhjem (21/13)
- 4. Rønne–Aarsdale (31/19)
- 5. Rønne–Nexø (26/16)
- 6. Rønne–Svaneke (42/26)
- 7. Allinge–Aakirkeby (28/17)
- 8. Gudhjem–Helligdommen (7/4)

Rønne is Bornholm's capital and an important port. The distinctive lighthouse is 19th century.

Bornholm's harbours are used by fishing boats throughout the year and by visiting yachts in summer.

GREENLAND AND THE FAROE ISLANDS

These two far-flung territories of Denmark offer spectacular adventure and some of the world's most stunning scenery. Greenland's vast frozen glaciers and wondrous northern lights, and the remote settlements and varied birdlife on the Faroe Islands, are ideal for visitors attracted by solitude and natural beauty.

Denmark's two distant island territories enjoy a particular status. Greenland was granted home rule in 1979; the Faroe Islands in 1948. Both have their own government but, due to the fact that Denmark retains responsibility for matters such as defence, both are represented in the Danish parliament.

Native Greenlanders share a common heritage with the Inuit of Alaska and northern Canada. Denmark's links with the island began in the 10th century when Viking settlers arrived here and began trading with the Greenlanders. The island was named by Erik the Red, a Viking chief who reached the southern end of Greenland around AD 985.

Early settlers on the Faroe Islands were from Norway. When Norway came under Danish rule in the 14th century, the islands also became part of Denmark. Denmark ceded Norway to Sweden in 1814 under the Treaty of Kiel but the Faroes continued under the Danish crown until demands for independence led to eventual home rule. The local name for the Faroes is Føroyar, which translates as "sheep island". The Faroes are aptly named and there are currently almost twice as many sheep as people.

Both Greenland and the Faroe Islands are perfect for nature lovers. A boat tour through parts of Greenland, for instance, takes visitors through crystal-clear waters teeming with marine life including seals and whales. Dog-sled tours across frozen lakes are possible during the winter. The Faroe Islands are a paradise for hikers and ramblers and have a huge variety of birdlife.

Typical Faroe Islands scenery with rocky islets jutting out into the sea

◀ Atlantic puffins on Mykines, the Faroe Islands

Exploring Greenland

Greenland is the world's largest island (assuming Australia is a continent) and has a total area of 2,175,600 sq km (840,000 sq miles) and 40,000 km (25,000 miles) of coast. About 80 per cent of the land mass is covered by a huge ice-sheet that is up to 3 km (2 miles) thick. Despite its great size, the island has a population of a little over 56,000, who are primarily from Inuit and European backgrounds. For much of the year Greenland is a snow-covered wilderness, though Greenlanders live there, and tourists visit, year round. During spring and summer, the coastal regions thaw and the temperature can rise to as much as 21° C (70° F) in the south of the country and most of the inland areas. Many towns and villages have had both Greenlandic and Danish names since the 1980s.

Greenlanders in colourful national costumes

A modern Inuit hut at the edge of Amitsorsuaq Lake, Greenland

For keys to symbols see back flap

Lincoln Sea

Knud Rasmussen Land

6 QAANAAQ (THULE)

Savissivik

Qimusseriarsuaq

Baffin Bay

Upernavik

UUMMANNAQ (UMANAK) 5

Disko Øer

Qeqertarsuaq (Godhavn)

Aasiaat (Egedesminde)

4 ILULISSAT (JAKOBSHAVN)

Sisimiut (Holsteinsborg)

3 KANGERLUSSUAQ (SØNDRE STRØMFJORD)

Maniitsoq

Labrador Sea

NUUK (GODTHÅB) 2

Paamiut (Frederikshåb)

Ivittuut

Narsarsuaq

QAQORTOQ (JULIANEHÅB) 1

Kap Farve

Key

Ice-free areas

Permafrost

Greenland huskies, sled dogs north of the Arctic Circle and in East Greenland

Kap Morris Jesup

Nord

Kong Frederik VIII Land

GREENLAND SEA

Danmarks
Havn

Daneborg

Kong Christian X Land

Ymers Øer

Traill Øer

Scoresby Land

Ittoqqortoormiit
(Scoresbysund)

Kong Christian IX Land

Aputiteeq

Arctic Circle

ATLANTIC OCEAN

 **⑦ TASIILAQ
(AMMASSALIK)**

Getting There & Around

Kangerlussuaq, just north of the Arctic Circle, has Greenland's main airport. It lies 370 km (230 miles) north of Nuuk and serves international traffic from Denmark, as does Narsarsuaq in South Greenland. Ilulisaat, Kulusuk, Naarsarsuaq, Nerlerit Inaat and Nuuk serve international traffic from Iceland. Nuuk also serves international traffic from Canada. All domestic inland services are handled by Air Greenland. These flights tend to be expensive. Domestic travel by coastal ferry is possible, and all are handled by Arctic Umiaq Line. Sailing times are vulnerable due to adverse weather conditions.

Sights at a Glance

① Qaqortoq (Julianehåb)
② Nuuk (Godthåb)
③ Kangerlussuaq (Søndre
   Strømfjord)
④ Ilulissat (Jakobshavn)
⑤ Uummannaq
⑥ Qaanaaq (Thule)
⑦ Tasiilaq (Ammassalik)

0 km   200

0 miles   200

Ilulissat Icefjord, part of the UNESCO World Heritage site near Ilulissat

The 19th-century church of St Saviour in Nuuk

❶ Qaqortoq (Julianehåb)

🏙 3,300. **Tel** (+299) 64 24 44.
W sagalands.com

The town of Qaqortoq was established in 1775. Traces of earlier, 10th-century Viking settlers can be seen in nearby Hvalsey where the remains of a local settlement and church are the best-preserved Nordic ruins in Greenland.

Other local attractions include the hot springs in Uunartoq and the research station in Upernaviarsuk which grows the only apple trees in Greenland.

Qaqortoq was the site for Greenland's Stone and Man programme, a 1990s open-air sculpture project that used natural rock formations as base material for a variety of abstract shapes and figures.

❷ Nuuk (Godthåb)

🏙 16,500. 🛈 Hans Egedesvej 29.
Open 8am–4pm Mon–Fri. **Tel** (+299) 34 28 20. W greenland.com

Greenland's capital was founded in 1728 by Hans Egede, a Danish missionary who established a year-round trading post here. Nuuk is the largest and oldest town on the island and the seat of Greenland's government. Egede's monument is on a hill, close to the cathedral.

More information about the history of Nuuk can be found at the **National Museum**, which has a collection of Inuit costumes as well as other Greenland artefacts.

According to some traditions Santa Claus lives in Nuuk and even has his own post box number (Box 785, 3952 Ilulissat). Next to the post office is a huge letterbox for Santa's letters.

The best time to visit is summer – in June humpback whales can be seen in the bay.

🏛 **National Museum**
Hans Egedesvej 8. **Tel** (+299) 32 26 11.
Open Jun–mid-Sep: 10am– 4pm daily; mid-Sep–May: 1– 4pm Tue–Sun.
📷 W en.nka.gl

❸ Kangerlussuaq (Søndre Strømfjord)

🏙 500. 🛈 World of Greenland – Polar Lodge & Old Camp Mitaarfit Aqq Arctic Circle, P.O. Box 1009. **Tel** (+299) 84 16 48. W wogac.com

Situated near the fjord of the same name, Kangerlussuaq was until 1992 home to Blue West 8, a US base. A museum, located in the former HQ building, contains memorabilia from the base's history including a replica of the commander's hut.

This area is an excellent venue for hiking, biking, camping and fishing and is inhabited by large herds of reindeer as well as musk ox, arctic foxes and polar hares. A popular day-trip is to Russells Glacier, part of the Greenland ice sheet some 25 km (16 miles) away. Rising about 10 km (6 miles) from Kangerlussuaq is Sugarloaf Mountain, which has a wonderful view of the Greenland ice sheet from its peak.

Gently sloping green coastline near Kangerlussuaq

➍ Ilulissat (Jakobshavn)

🏔 4,500. ℹ Destination Avannaa, Fredericap aqq 7A. **Tel** (+299) 94 33 37. 🅦 **northgreenland.com**

The town of Ilulissat looks out over Disko Bay, which is full of floating icebergs. It has been calculated that almost 10 per cent of the icebergs floating on Greenland's waters come from the nearby 40-km (25-mile) long glacial fjord, where the ice can be up to 1,100 m (3,600 ft) thick. The glacier can be reached by boat from Ilulissat.

The most famous inhabitant of Ilulissat was the polar explorer Knud Rasmussen. His former house contains objects associated with Inuit art and the everyday life of Greenlanders.

Other museums include the Museum of Hunting and Fishing and the so-called Cold Museum (it has no heating), which has a selection of tools and machinery from a former trading settlement.

➎ Uummannaq

🏔 1,300. ℹ c/o Hotel Uummannaq Box 202. **Tel** (+299) 95 15 18. 🅦 **icecaphotels.gl**

Despite its location 600 km (373 miles) north of the Arctic Circle, this place enjoys more days of summer sunshine than anywhere else in Greenland. Such favourable conditions have for a long time been a magnet for hunters and whalers. The charm of this town, situated on a small island, is due in part to its colourful houses set on a rocky shore against the backdrop of the 1,175-m (3,855-ft) high Hjertetjeldet ("Heart Shaped") mountain. The old stone cottages with turf roofs date from 1925. The nearby museum, housed in a late 19th-century hospital, contains hunting implements, kayaks and a display devoted to German scientist Alfred Wegener's expedition across the inland ice in 1930 on propeller-driven sledges. Nearby is the Inuit village

Children dressed in colourful Greenlandic national costumes

of Qilakitsoq, where some mummified bodies were discovered in a cave in 1972. The mummies can be seen in Nuuk's National Museum.

In winter it is possible to take an exhilarating dog-sled trip across the frozen fjord.

➏ Qaanaaq (Thule)

🏔 700. ℹ P.O. Box 75. **Tel** (+299) 97 14 73.

Greenland's northernmost town was built in the 1950s. Its inhabitants follow a traditional way of life hunting for seals, walruses and polar bears. Visitors can participate in hunts, which involve sleeping in igloos and travelling by sled. Hunts such as these are an important means of survival in this area and not for the squeamish.

About 500 km (311 miles) from Qaanaaq is the vast North and East Greenland National Park. The park is mostly covered by an inland ice cap and contains musk ox, polar bears and, in summer, walruses. Permission to enter must be obtained from the Expedition Office of the Government of Greenland (*exp@nanoq.gl*).

➐ Tasiilaq (Ammassalik)

🏔 2,000. ℹ P.O. Box 506, Skæven Ujuaap Aqqulaa 48. **Tel** (+299) 98 15 43. 🅦 **eastgreenland.com**

Situated on the shores of a fjord, surrounded by high mountains, Tasiilaq is one of eastern Greenland's larger towns. The first Europeans arrived here about 100 years ago, and tourism is becoming increasingly important. From here, visitors can go whale watching, visit the nearby "Valley of Flowers" (in summer this is a splendid opportunity to enjoy the Arctic flora) or climb the mound that towers over the town (it was raised in 1944 to celebrate the 50th anniversary of Tasiilaq), from which there are some stunning views.

The town's other points of interest include a modern church dating from 1985 and decorated with Greenland artefacts. The oldest of Tasiilaq's houses dates from 1894 and was built by a Danish missionary.

Uummannaq, built on the rocks of a small island

Exploring the Faroe Islands

This cluster of 18 islands, sandwiched between the Atlantic and the Norwegian Sea, is home to about 48,000 people, almost half of whom live in the capital Tórshavn on Streymoy. The Faroes have a total area of 1,399 sq km (540 sq miles) and are 450 km (280 miles) from the Shetland Islands and 1,500 km (900 miles) from Copenhagen. Many of the islands are interlinked by a network of tunnels and causeways. The Faroes are perfect for ramblers, and marked trails cover many routes. This is rough terrain and the right equipment, including maps and a compass, should always be carried. The island's seafaring past is evident in the busy harbours, while the town museums have displays on island customs and folklore. Sea cruises are an ideal way to explore the Faroes.

Gjógv

Eiði

Tjørnuvík   Oynadarfjø

Fuglafjørður

Saksun

6

EYSTU

STREYMOY 🛥️🏛️ **2**

Vestmanna

Kollafjørður

MYKINES   **VÁGAR**   Kvívík

Mykines **4** 🚶   Bøur   **3**

Sørvágur ✈️   Sandavágur

Miðvágur

Syðradulur

Koltur

Hestu

H

Skopur

Sa

Sk

* Skr*

Garden gate made from a ship's wheel

Sandvík

Hvalba

Tvø

Famjin

SUÐUROY 🛥️

Steel sheep sculpture in Tórshavn

For keys to symbols *see back flap*

0 km 10
0 miles 10

Viðareiði
Múli
dalur *Viðoy*
Kunoy Hvannasund *Fugloy*
Kunoy Svinoy Kirkja
OY *Svinoy*
Klaksvík
Borðoy
Leirvik

Saltangará
Tóftir

RSHAVN
Nólsoy
Nólsoy
bøur

oy
Skálavik

Dalur

ra Dímun

Litla Dímun

Sumba

Norwegian Sea

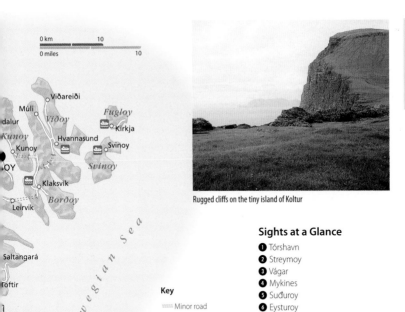
Rugged cliffs on the tiny island of Koltur

Sights at a Glance

1 Tórshavn
2 Streymoy
3 Vágar
4 Mykines
5 Suðuroy
6 Eysturoy
7 Kalsoy

Key

=== Minor road
: : : Tunnel

Getting There & Around

The Faroe Islands Smyril Line ferry service operates regularly between Tórshavn, the island's capital, and Hanstholm in northern Jutland. In summer there are additional services from Seyðisfjörður in Iceland. Atlantic Airways serves routes from Copenhagen in Denmark, Oslo in Norway, the UK, Spain and Italy. The Faroe Islands' international airport is near the town of Sørvágur, on the island of Vágar, about 70 km (43 miles) from Tórshavn. A bus connects the airport with Tórshavn. Most of the towns and villages are connected by road, while local ferries cater for the more outlying settlements.

Fishing boats in Klaksvik's harbour

Brightly coloured houses lining Tórshavn harbour

❶ Tórshavn

🏘 19,000. 🚢 🚌 ℹ Niels Finsens gøta 17. **Tel** (+298) 30 24 25. 🅦 **visittorshavn.fo**

The Faroe Islands' capital is a lively and picturesque place with a well-preserved old centre, although much of the town is fairly modern. Tórshavn was granted municipal status in 1909, but its history stretches back much further.

In the 11th century Tórshavn became a venue for annual Viking gatherings known as the Althings, an early form of the Faroese parliament. The meetings were held in summer and were used to settle quarrels and as an opportunity to trade. A permanent settlement developed around the annual event, and eventually became Tórshavn.

Some of the Faroes' earliest inhabitants were Irish friars, and Tórshavn's oldest building is the 15th-century Munkastovan, or Monks' House, which is one of the few buildings to survive a fire in 1673.

The ruins of Skansin Fort, which was built in 1580 to defend the village from pirates, can still be seen. The fort acquired its present shape in 1780 and was used by British troops during World War II. Today, it provides a good viewpoint for surveying the town's busy harbour, which is crammed with fishing boats, ferries and pleasure craft.

Søvn Landsins (Historical Museum) has a wide-ranging collection tracing the Faroes' seafaring history, including boats and fishing equipment, as well as some religious artefacts and items dating back to the Viking era.

🏛 **Søvn Landsins**
Brekkutún 6, Hoyvík. **Tel** (+298) 34 05 00. **Open** mid-May–mid-Sep: 10am–5pm daily (from 2pm Sat & Sun); mid-Sep–mid-May: 2–5pm Thu & Sun. 🅿 🅦 **savn.fo**

❷ Streymoy

🏘 22,000. 🚢 🚌 ℹ Niels Finsens gøta 17. **Tel** (+298) 30 24 25.

The largest of the Faroe Islands has a varied terrain and is crisscrossed by ancient paths that were once used to travel between settlements.

Saksun is a small village on the shores of an inlet that leads into Pollur lake – a fine spot to

fish for trout and salmon. The **Dúvugarðar Museum**, located in an old turf-roofed farmhouse, has exhibits on island life from medieval times to the 1800s.

Traces of a group of 8th-century Irish friars have been found in the village of Kirkjubøur, at the south end of Streymoy. Written records show that Kirkjubøur was a busy place in medieval times. A reminder of those days is the 12th-century church of St Olaf, the archipelago's oldest historic site.

Southwest from Tórshavn are the Vestmannabjørgini (Bird Cliffs) where hundreds of sea birds inhabit the 640-m- (2,100-ft-) high cliff face.

🏛 **Dúvugarðar Museum**
Saksunarvegur 31, Saksun. **Tel** (+298) 59 44 55. **Open** 2–5pm daily during the summer. 🅿

❸ Vágar

🏘 3,000. ✈ 🚌 ℹ Flogvøllurin 2, Sørvágur. **Tel** (+298) 33 34 55. 🅦 **visitvagar.fo**

The Faroe Islands' modern airport is on Vágar and was originally used as a landing strip by the RAF. This mountainous island has some of the region's most stunning sights including the 313-m (1,027-ft) tall needle rock called "Trollukonufingur" ("Troll Woman's Finger"). Lake Sorvagsvatn is a little way from Midvagur, Vágar's largest town, and is a great place for fishing. Sandavagur, a nearby village, is the birthplace of Venceslaus Ulricus Hammershaimb (b. 1819), creator of the Faroese alphabet.

House hugging the cliff on Streymoy

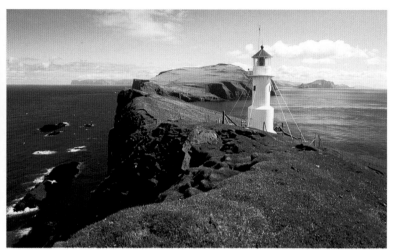

Lighthouse standing on the cliffs of Mykines

❹ Mykines

🏠 20. 🚢 ℹ️ Flogvøllurin 2, Sørvágur. **Tel** (+298) 33 34 55.

On this tiny island of only 10 sq km (4 sq miles), the inhabitants are vastly outnumbered by the birds, including thousands of puffins. All the islanders live in the same village, which is a pretty place with colourful houses topped by turf roofs. This is one of the hardest islands to reach but the trip is worth it, especially for keen hikers. Mykineshólmur, a tiny islet, is a good spot from which to view gannets, as well as large colonies of puffins. It is connected to the island by a footbridge that has been built 24-m (79-ft) above the sea.

❺ Suðuroy

🏠 4,500. 🚢 ℹ️ Tvørávegur 37, Tvøroyri. **Tel** (+298) 61 10 80.
🌐 visitsuduroy.fo

The largest town on Suðuroy, the Faroes' southernmost island, is Tvøroyri, which has a population of 1,800. The little village of Famjin, on the west coast, is more historically important, however, as its church contains the original Faroe Islands' flag. The red-and-blue cross on a white background was designed by two students and accepted as the national ensign in 1940. A short hike above the village is

Kirkjuvatn ("Church Lake"), one of the Faroes' largest lakes.

The village of Sandvík, at the northern end of the island, has an isolated and expansive beach. In AD 1000 Sigmund Bresterson, an early Norwegian settler and hero of the Faroe Sagas, was murdered here while preaching Christianity. On the way from Sandvík to Hvalba are two stones that, according to legend, were brought here by Bresterson. Passing between them is believed to be unlucky and can spell misfortune or even death.

❻ Eysturoy

🏠 11,000. ℹ️ Heiðavegur 26, Runavík. **Tel** (+298) 41 70 60.
🌐 visiteysturoy.fo

The second largest island of the archipelago is connected to Streymoy by a road bridge, which is often jokingly described by locals as the only bridge across the Atlantic.

Eysturoy has a number of unique features. At 882 m (2,894 ft), Slættaratindur is the Faroes' highest point. The summit can easily be reached by climbing the mountain's

eastern ridge – the views from the peak are breathtaking.

Close to Fuglafjørður are the Varmakelda hot springs. Their water remains at a constant 18° C (64.4° F) and is believed to have medicinal properties. Further north is the village of Oynadarfjordur.

Just beyond its shore are the Rinkusteinar, or rocking stones, two huge blocks that constantly rock, moved by the motion of the sea.

At nearby Gjógv there is a 200-m- (656-ft-) long gorge that with time has eroded to become a sea-filled bay.

Goat on one of the islands' rural smallholdings

❼ Kalsoy

🏠 100. 🚢 ℹ️ Tingstøðin, Klaksvík. **Tel** (+298) 45 69 39.

Nicknamed the "flute" because of its elongated shape, this rugged island is ideal for hikes. Many walkers head towards Kap Kallur, at the island's northern tip, where the lighthouse makes an excellent point from which to view the cliffs. Puffins are a frequent sight. The sea stacks at Eysturoy's northern tip can be seen on a clear day.

TRAVELLERS' NEEDS

WHERE TO STAY

Denmark knows design and its holiday accommodation, whether simple or upscale, urban or rural, reflects this. Stay on board boutique canal boats, at sleek Scandi-style hotels or functional and comfortable hostels in Copenhagen. Outside of the capital are countless historic and characterful inns, beachfront hotels frequented by the Skagen Painters and idyllic rural retreats that offer outdoor activities as well as their own restaurants. Those seeking something more outlandish might choose to stay in a quirky manor house B&B, or on one of the farms taking part in Denmark's agritourism scheme. Whether in a city or in the countryside, the Danes are accustomed to travelling with children so there are many family-friendly solutions within apartments, hotels and camp sites. For more inspiration, see pp248–55.

Main entrance to a hotel in Sandvig, Bornholm

Choosing a Hotel

Travellers in Denmark have a wide choice of hotel accommodation. Information is readily available and details of hotels found in brochures and on websites is generally both up to date and accurate. Most of Denmark's hotels are of 3-star standard or higher, and are aimed at holiday-makers as well as business travellers. The majority offer rooms with a private bathroom, telephone and TV.

Be clear when booking a room if a bath is specifically required, as most hotels have showers rather than baths in rooms. Visitors should be able to use their laptops as rooms usually have Internet access, but it is wise to check.

Cheaper hotels tend to be rather plain, but even these are generally clean and well run. An all-you-can-eat breakfast, consisting of pastries, bread, cereal, coffee/tea and fruit, is often included in the price of a room, although bigger city hotels may offer breakfast for an additional cost (usually around 100 Dkr).

When planning a journey to Denmark by car, take into account the cost of parking in town centres. It is worth finding out in advance whether the hotel has its own car park or off-street parking.

Hotels on Greenland and the Faroe Islands tend to be rather spartan in design and costly, particularly outside the capital cities, although ecotourism is growing in popularity.

How to Book

During peak season, hotels are often booked up in Denmark so it pays to reserve a room in advance. Prices vary immensely according to both demand and season, and pre-booking online offers the best rates, often directly via the hotel's own website. Information on hotels in the area, as well as links for booking, can be found at www.dkhotellist.com or www.visitdenmark.com. Alternatively, bookings can be made by phone or e-mail. Local tourist offices can also provide accommodation lists for their towns.

Hotel Prices

Hotel prices in Denmark can be rather high. There are many hotels at the lower end of the scale, however, which charge about 600 to 700 Dkr per night; the most expensive ones may quote up to 10,000 Dkr for a luxury suite. The majority of room prices fall into the 900–1,400 Dkr bracket. Many hotels offer discounted rates at weekends, while those that cater for tourists rather than business travellers may offer special reduced winter rates.

Chain Hotels

Many hotels in Denmark belong to large hotel chains including First & Clarion, Hilton, Radisson and Scandic. Some chains, such as Best Western, have their own schemes whereby visitors can get discounted rooms at weekends or during the holiday period. It is best to book in advance for these, though deals can sometimes be struck on the spot.

Historic Houses

A number of Denmark's manor houses offer accommodation, especially in connection with conferences

A guest room in the Admiral Hotel, Copenhagen *(see p248)*

and weddings. These historic buildings, while privately managed, are typically affiliated with the **Danske Slotte & Herregaarde** (The Danish Association of Castles and Manor Houses). They are usually located in the countryside, surrounded by nature, and having a car is essential for guests. The venues are undeniably romantic, but they can be rather expensive.

Inns

Outside larger towns, it is possible to stop for a night in an inn, known as *kro* in Denmark. The variety on offer ranges from modern roadside inns to meticulously restored period houses and *badehoteller* – traditional beachside inns offering old-fashioned seaside relaxation. Some country inns have retained much of their 18th or 19th- century rusticity; others are downright luxurious. Many *kro* offer a family atmosphere, and it is not unusual for inns to be used for family gatherings and big occasions such as weddings. **Danske Kroer & Hoteller** is an association of country inns that manages over 100 inns, castles and manor houses.

Bed & Breakfasts

Denmark's bed and breakfasts offer good quality and value, and usually charge about 600 Dkr for a double room per night. B&Bs can usually be booked from local tourist offices. Alternatively, a list is available from **Dansk Bed & Breakfast** and **Airbnb** offers extensive options at various rates. Some Danish B&Bs quote a price that only includes accommodation. Breakfast usually costs extra, or it may not be available at all.

Cottages and Holiday Centres

Cottages are available to rent – usually on a weekly basis (from Saturday to Saturday). Weekend mini-breaks are also possible out of high season (which runs from July through to mid-August). Many places are let out by private owners but managed by professional rental agencies. Others are run purely as commercial ventures. Either way, a cottage must be booked well in advance.

Holiday centres, which have purpose-built accommodation, children's playgrounds, swimming pools and other family-friendly amenities, have lots of space for children to play. Prices vary widely.

Farm Holidays and Home Exchanges

Spending time on a farm is becoming an increasingly popular activity in Denmark. There are now more than 100 Danish farms where a stay is possible, and most are far away from busy resorts. Such rural retreats provide a chance to relax in pastoral surroundings and, in some cases, to muck in with the chores. Farm stays can be booked via **Landsforeningen for Landboturisme**. A holiday of this sort can be arranged in several ways. You can choose B&B or full-board accommodation. Cottages, a simple apartment with a kitchen, or a room can be rented. Alternatively, visitors can pitch a tent or park a caravan on farm land.

Regardless of what type of vacation is on offer, visitors can be sure of a clean room and warm rural atmosphere. Prices start from 200 Dkr per adult (for bed and breakfast).

A home exchange allows participants to swap their home with that of a family in Denmark, offering an authentic Danish experience. Visit **Home Link** for more information on it.

A traditional furnished room in the historic Dragsholm Slot, Hørve *(see p250)*

Historic hotel room in Liselund Ny Slot, Møn

Hostels

Most of Denmark's 95 or so hostels or *vandrehjem* are incorporated into the **Danhostel** association, which registers its hostels in five categories marked by stars. Along with communal dormitories, most hostels have private "family" rooms, which usually sleep four to six and must be booked in advance. Blankets and pillows are usually provided, but it is generally the case that visitors supply their own bed linen and towels (though these are available for a fee). In all hostels it is possible to buy breakfast; many also offer dinner or even packed lunches, and charge half-price for children up to the age of 12.

The prices of family rooms can vary, but the maximum price of a bed in a communal dormitory is fixed each year for the entire country. Prices vary between high and low seasons. From September until May a place in a provincial hostel must be booked at least three days ahead. During peak season all hostels should be booked as early as possible.

It is not necessary to have a Youth Hostel Association (YHA) card to stay at a hostel, but card-holders enjoy reduced rates. For visits that exceed five days it is worth buying membership.

Danhostel's website has telephone numbers and website addresses for all of its hostels, where additional information can be found.

In the cities, independent hostels offer more specialised lodging, such as Generator Hostel Copenhagen, for a more luxurious hostel experience.

Camp Sites

Denmark has hundreds of camp sites, 460 of them approved by the Danish Camping Union. Of these, around 100 are open all year round, providing relatively inexpensive accommodation, often in areas of outstanding natural beauty. Campsites are rated by the Dansk Camping Union using a system of stars from one to five. Prices depend on the number of stars, which reflect not only comfort and a site's attractiveness, but also specific facilities, such as whether the site has a playground and the distance to the nearest grocery store. The cost per night generally includes a charge for pitching a tent or parking a caravan, plus a charge for each occupant. One-star sites will have little more than basic facilities, such as fresh drinking water and toilets. Sites rated three stars and above will have a TV room, on-site shop and a café or restaurant. Whatever the rating and the amenities on offer, it is rare to find a Danish camp site that is not efficiently run.

Most of Denmark's camp sites also feature chalet accommodation, or cabins that can sleep four to six.

Many cabins have cooking facilities, but visitors usually have to supply their own linen, including towels. Most cabins do not have private washing or toilet facilities.

Anyone wishing to camp in Denmark will need a Visitor's Pass. These annual permits are readily available and can be purchased on the spot at any of the official camp sites.

Denmark also offers the chance to pitch a tent, at "primitive nature camp sites". These are designated areas with basic facilities such a public toilet, running water and sometimes a place to make a fire. About one-third of the sites also have a primitive shelter to use for overnight sleeping.

Wild camping, while not actually encouraged, should be done with respect for both nature and neighbours. Guidelines and regulations for wild camping in Denmark can be obtained at the website of the **Danish Nature Agency**.

Travellers with Disabilities

Many hotels can accommodate disabled guests, especially the newer and larger ones, although it is best to check when booking. The majority of multi-storey hotels have lifts. The **God Adgang** scheme, which also provides classification for restaurants, provides a list of hotels with disabled access.

Entrance to one of Denmark's converted manor houses

Comfortable and sophisticated rooms at the Babette Guldsmeden *(see p248)*

and budgets. **Value** establishments include unfussy inns and affordable hostels, while **B&B** options offer a personable experience and hearty breakfast. **Family-friendly** hotels provide facilities and entertainment for all the family. **Rural retreat** options include charming remote cabins and yurts near the sea. There are a number of **historic** establishments based in fascinating buildings of note, while **character** options promise fun and often eccentric design elements. **Boutique** hotels are generally small and high end with a limited number of rooms, while **luxury** hotels encompass the finest establishments and the very best service. Entries labelled DK Choice draw attention to establishments that stand out in some way or another.

Travelling with Children

Taking children on holiday to Denmark is not a problem. Many hotels and hostels, particularly establishments aimed at holiday-makers, offer family rooms for three to four people. Hotels belonging to the Scandic group are also ready to receive young guests; many of these have playrooms.

Hotel restaurants provide high chairs for babies and toddlers and also offer special menus that will satisfy all but the most picky children.

Recommended Hotels

The hotels on pp248–255 offer a wide variety of accommodation options to suit all tastes

DIRECTORY

Information on Accommodation & Reservations

W **hotel.dk**
W **visitdenmark.com**

Copenhagen Right Now Information and Booking Service
Vesterbrogade 4A.
Tel 70 22 24 42.
Fax 70 22 24 52.
W **visitcopenhagen.com**

Holiday Centres

Danland & DanCenter
Lyngbyvej 20, 2100 Copenhagen Ø.
Tel 33 63 02 00.
Fax 70 13 70 71.
W **danland.dk**

Dansk Folkeferie
Hedegaardsvej 88, 2300 Copenhagen.
W **folkeferie.dk**

Historic Houses

Danske Slotte & Herregaarde
L. Sct. Mikkelsgade 7, 1, 8800 Viborg.
Tel 86 60 38 44.
W **slotte-herregaarde.dk**

Inns

Danske Kroer & Hoteller
Vejlevej 16, 8700 Horsens.
Tel 75 64 87 00.
W **smalldanishhotels.com**

B&Bs

Airbnb
W **airbnb.dk**

Dansk B&B
Sankt Peders Stræde 41, 1453 Copenhagen K.
Tel 39 61 04 05.
W **bedandbreakfast.dk**

Cottages

Dansommer
Voldbjergvej 16, 8240 Risskov. **Tel** 86 17 61 22.
Fax 86 17 68 55.
W **dansommer.dk**

Novasol
Rygårds Alle 104, 2900 Hellerup.
Tel 70 42 44 24.
W **novasol.co.uk**

Sol & Strand
Ilsigvej 21, Hune, 9492 Blokhus.
Tel 99 44 44 44.
Fax 99 44 44 45.
W **sologstrand.com**

Farm Holidays and Home Exchanges

Home Link
W **homelink.org**

Landsforeningen for Landboturisme
Føllevej 5, 8410 Ronde.
W **bondegaardsferie.dk**

Hostels

Danhostel Danmarks Vandrehjem
Vesterbrogade 39, 1620 Copenhagen V.
Tel 33 31 36 12.
W **danhostel.dk**

Camp Sites

Campingrådet
Mosedalvej 15, DK-2500 Valby.
Tel 39 27 88 44.
Fax 39 27 80 44.
W **campingraadet.dk**

Danish Nature Agency
Haraldsgade 53, 2100 Copenhagen Ø.
Tel 72 54 30 00.
W **naturstyrelsen.dk**

Dansk Camping Union

Korsdalsvej 135, 2605 Brøndby.
Tel 33 21 06 00.
W **dcu.dk**

DK-CAMP 2002

Industrivej 5, Bredballe, 7120 Vejle Ø.
Tel 75 71 29 62.
Fax 75 71 29 66.
W **dk-camp.dk**

FDM Camping

Firskovvej 32. 2800 Kgs. Lyngby.
Tel 45 27 07 07.
W **fdmcamping.dk**

Travellers with Disabilities

God Adgang
W **godadgang.dk**

Where to Stay

Copenhagen

North Copenhagen

Generator Copenhagen Ⓚ
Value Map 2 D5
Adelgade 5–7, 1304 Cph K
Tel *78 7 754 00*
W generatorhostels.com/en/
destinations/copenhagen
A six-storey design hostel placed
a short walk from Kongens
Nytorv square. The chain caters
for luxury-seeking backpackers,
with private rooms and modern
features as well as dorms.

DK Choice

Babette Guldsmeden ⓀⓀ
Boutique Map 2 E4
Bredgade 78, 1260 Cph K
Tel *33 14 15 00*
W guldsmedenhotels.com/
Home/GuldsmedenHotels.aspx
Formerly the Hotel Esplanden,
Babette Guldsmeden opened
in 2014 and is centrally situated
opposite Churchillparken. An
eco-friendly boutique hotel,
guests can enjoy Balinese-style
furnishings, four-poster beds and
original artwork in their rooms.
In addition the hotel offers
luxurious, organic breakfasts.

**Wakeup Copenhagen –
Borgergade** ⓀⓀ
Family Friendly Map 2 D5
Borgergade 9, 1300 Cph K
Tel *44 80 00 00*
W wakeupcopenhagen.com
The second Wakeup Copenhagen
hotel provides budget accom-
modation that rises in price the
higher up the building you stay.
Modern features include air
conditioning and Wi-Fi.

71 Nyhavn ⓀⓀⓀ
Historic Map 4 E1
Nyhavn 71, 1051 Cph K
Tel *33 43 62 00*
W 71nyhavnhotel.com
Part of the citywide Arp Hansen
Group, and located in a
renovated 1880s warehouse,
this hotel overlooks the
waterfront. Rooms are rather
small but charming.

Admiral Hotel ⓀⓀⓀ
Boutique Map 2 E4
Toldbodgade 24–28, 1253 Cph K
Tel *33 74 14 14*
W admiralhotel.dk
An 18th-century granary, this
expansive waterfront hotel has
been carefully restored with a

maritime theme. It features
exposed beams and has uniquely
designed rooms. There is also an
excellent restaurant, SALT.

Central Copenhagen

Hostel Downtown Ⓚ
Value Map 3 B2
Vandkunsten 5, 1467 Cph K
Tel *70 23 21 10*
W copenhagendowntown.com
This lively, central hostel on one
of the city's most attractive streets
offers dorm accommodation as
well as doubles and triples.
Guests can eat in the cafeteria or
cook in the communal kitchen.

Sømandshjem Hotel Bethel Ⓚ
Value Map 4 D1
Nyhavn 22, 1051 Cph K
Tel *33 12 60 00*
W hotel-bethel.dk
The old seaman's hostel on Nyhavn's
quieter side operates as a budget
hotel with basic rooms and good
service. Free tea and coffee as
well as a breakfast buffet.

Ascot Hotel & Apartments ⓀⓀ
Historic Map 3 A1
Studiestræde 61, 1554 Cph K
Tel *33 12 60 00*
W ascot-hotel.dk
A former public baths, this 4-star
hotel has retained many original
features. Guests can stay in hotel
or apartment accommodation, and
there are spa and fitness facilities.

First Hotel Kong Frederik ⓀⓀ
Historic Map 3 A1
Vester Voldgade 25, 1552 Cph K
Tel *33 12 59 02*
W firsthotels.com
A short walk from the
Rådhuspladsen, this elegant

Chill out area at the stylish hostel
Generator Copenhagen

19th-century townhouse has
been refurbished in classic
English style, with plenty of
dark wood.

Grand Hotel ⓀⓀ
Historic Map 3 A3
Vesterbrogade 9
Tel *33 27 69 00*
W grandhotelcopenhagen.com
An elegant and classic hotel,
built in 1892, the Grand Hotel
has small, simple rooms. It offers
good facilities and service, and
is located close to Tivoli.

Radisson Blu Royal ⓀⓀ
Historic Map 3 A2
*Hammerichsgade 1,
1611 Cph K*
Tel *33 42 60 00*
W radissonblu.com/royalhotel-
copenhagen
Designed by Danish architect
Arne Jacobsen in the 1950s,
the 20-storey Royal was the
world's first design hotel. Today,
only room 606 remains as
Jacobsen left it but you can still
marvel at Jacobsen's striking
spiral staircase and sleek decor
including reproductions of his
famed swan and egg chairs.

The Square ⓀⓀ
Boutique Map 3 A2
Rådhuspladsen 14, 1550 Cph V
Tel *33 38 12 00*
W thesquarecopenhagen.com
This trendy, modern six-storey
hotel overlooks the central
location of Rådhuspladsen.
It boasts stylish design features
and modern facilities in all rooms
as well as an expansive lobby.

Hotel Alexandra ⓀⓀⓀ
Boutique Map 3 A1
*H C Andersens Boulevard 8,
1553 Cph V*
Tel *33 74 44 44*
W hotelalexandra.dk/
Situated close to the town
hall, this classic building dates
from the early 19th century
and was furnished by notable
20th-century Danish designers,
including Finn Juhl and Vernor
Panton. Along with providing
all necessary comforts, the
hotel is also known for being
eco-friendly.

Hotel D'Angleterre ⓀⓀⓀ
Luxury **Map** 4 D1
Kongens Nytorv 34, 1050 Cph K
Tel 33 12 00 95
Ⓦ dangleterre.dk
A landmark on Kongens Nytorv
since 1755, the D'Angleterre
remains synonymous with
luxury, its celebrity guests
ranging from Winston Churchill
to Robbie Williams.

Hotel Sankt Petri ⓀⓀⓀ
Boutique **Map** 3 B1
Krystalgade 22, 1172 Cph K
Tel 33 45 91 00
Ⓦ sktpetri.com
In a former department store, this
modern design hotel has a
rooftop terrace, trendy wine bar
and air conditioning in all rooms,
plus a fantastic location in the
historic Latin Quarter.

Nimb Hotel ⓀⓀⓀ
Luxury **Map** 3 A3
Bernstorffsgade 5, 1577 Cph K
Tel 88 70 00 00
Ⓦ nimb.dk
An expensive, luxury boutique
hotel in the Moorish Nimb
building with views over Tivoli
Gardens. No two rooms are the
same, and the attention to detail
is exquisite.

DK Choice

Palace Hotel ⓀⓀⓀ
Historic **Map** 3 B2
Rådhuspladsen 57, 1550 Cph K
Tel 33 14 40 50
Ⓦ scandichotels.com/hotels/
denmark/copenhagen/scandic-
palace
Declared a historic landmark in
1985, the Palace overlooks
Rådhuspladsen almost as
majestically as the adjacent
Town Hall. It was built in 1910
by Anton Rosen as one of the
city's grandest hotels. Famous
guests such as Danish King
Frederik VII and Audrey
Hepburn have added to the
glamour. Following extensive
refurbishment, the Palace has
found a more modern glory.

South Copenhagen

Danhostel Copenhagen City Ⓚ
Boutique **Map** 3 C3
H C Andersens Boulevard 50, 1553 Cph V
Tel 33 11 85 85
Ⓦ danhostelcopenhagencity.dk
Huge design hostel with 192
modern rooms that is as popular
with families as it is with young
groups. Includes a playroom and
private rooms for four, six and
eight people.

Riverside deck on the floating Hotel CPH Living

Hotel Amager Ⓚ
Family Friendly **Map** 4 F4
Amagerbrogade 29, 2300 Cph S
Tel 32 54 40 08
Ⓦ hotelamager.dk
Small, independent hotel in a
residential building in the suburb
of Amager, with good transport
connections into the centre.
Cheap four-bed rooms are
available for families and there's
a ground floor café.

Hotel Copenhagen Ⓚ
Family Friendly **Map** 3 C4
Egilsgade 33, 2300 Cph S
Tel 32 96 27 27
Ⓦ hotelcopenhagen.dk
Family-friendly, budget hotel in
the rejuvenated waterfront
Islands Brygge district. Options
include basic rooms sleeping
up to four in bunks, as well as
studio apartments.

Hotel CPH Living ⓀⓀ
Boutique **Map** 3 C3
Langebrogade 1C, 1411 Cph K
Tel 61 60 85 46
Ⓦ cphliving.com
Copenhagen's floating boutique
hotel offers designer double
rooms on a boat moored in
Copenhagen's harbour,
overlooking Slotsholmen and
Den Sorte Diamant. The price
includes breakfast and use of
the sundeck.

Radisson Blu Scandinavia ⓀⓀ
Modern **Map** 4 D4
*Amager Boulevard 70, |
2300 Cph S*
Tel 33 96 50 00
Ⓦ radissonblu.com/
scandinaviahotel-copenhagen
With 26 storeys, this hotel rises
high above Copenhagen's
skyline. A modern hotel with
spotless rooms, it offers
impeccable service, upmarket
restaurants and a casino. It is
popular with business guests.

DK Choice

STAY Apartment Hotel
Copenhagen ⓀⓀⓀ
Boutique
*Islands Brygge 79,
2300 Cph S*
Tel 72 44 44 34
Ⓦ staycopenhagen.dk
STAY Apartment Hotel is set
in a converted 1960s office
building, housing spacious
designer apartments with up
to three bedrooms. Facilities
include a gym, bakery,
grocery shop, washing
machines, balconies and
waterfront views. STAY makes
a great (though not cheap)
alternative to traditional
hotel accommodation.

Further Afield

Woodah Hostel Ⓚ
Value **Road Map** F4
*Abel Cathrinesgade 1–3,
1654 Cph V*
Tel 23 90 55 63
Ⓦ woodah-hostel.com
Small, independent hostel in
Vesterbro with focus on eco-
accommodation in bunks in
8- and 12-bed dorms and
private doubles. Provides
organic breakfast, bedding,
vegetarian snacks and morning
yoga sessions.

AC Bella Sky Comwell ⓀⓀ
Boutique **Road Map** F4
Center Boulevard 5, 2300 Cph S
Tel 32 47 30 00
Ⓦ acbellaskycopenhagen.dk
Architecturally noteworthy and
23 floors high, the four-star Bella
Sky is located in Ørestad, near
the airport. Its modern facilities
include a wellness centre, spa,
meeting rooms and BASALT,
their fine dining restaurant. Pet-
friendly hotel.

For more information on types of hotels *see pages 244–5*

Andersen Boutique Hotel ⓦⓦ
Boutique   **Map** 3 A3
Helgolandsgade 12,
1653 Cph V
Tel *33 31 46 10*
ⓦ andersen-hotel.dk
Personal service and colourful
designer rooms set in an old
building packed with character.
Located close to the Central
train station.

Axel Guldsmeden ⓦⓦ
Boutique   **Map** 3 A3
Helgolandsgade 11, 1653 Cph V
Tel *33 31 32 66*
ⓦ guldsmedenhotels.com/
Part of the Guldsmeden chain,
Vesterbro's Axel Guldsmeden
offers luxurious boutique accommodation focusing on eco-friendly
products. The courtyard garden
and spa are pleasant surprises in
the urban setting.

Hotel Kong Arthur ⓦⓦ
Historic   **Map** 1 A5
Nørre Søgade 11, 1370 Cph K
Tel *33 45 77 77*
ⓦ arthurhotels.dk/hotel-kong-arthur
Built in 1882, this historic hotel is
surprisingly quiet for its central
location, facing the lakes and with
a secluded courtyard. Includes
Copenhagen's oldest spa, Ni'mat.

Hotel Tiffany ⓦⓦ
Family Friendly   **Map** 3 A3
Colbjørnsensgade 28, 1652 Cph V
Tel *33 21 80 50*
ⓦ hoteltiffany.dk
Small, family-run hotel close to
Central Station. Rooms feature a
kitchenette with a fridge, microwave
and toaster; breakfast is delivered
to your room at the time you choose.

Savoy Hotel ⓦⓦ
Historic   **Road Map** F4
Vesterbrogade 34, 1620 Cph V
Tel *33 26 75 00*
ⓦ savoyhotel.dk
This independent hotel in
the Art Nouveau "Løvenborg"
building dates from 1905 on
bustling Vesterbrogade. Wide
range of room sizes available, all
facing the rear courtyard.

Northwestern Zealand

CHARLOTTENLUND:
Skovshoved Hotel ⓦⓦⓦ
Historic   **Road Map** F4
Strandvejen 267,
2920 Charlottenlund
Tel *39 64 00 28*
ⓦ skovshovedhotel.com
A coaching inn with old world
atmosphere dating from 1660.

Located on the Øresund coastal
road, it features an upmarket
restaurant and offers sea views
from many of the bedrooms.

GILLELEJE: Gilleleje
Badehotel ⓦⓦⓦ
Boutique   **Road Map** F4
Hulsøvej 15, 3250 Gilleleje
Tel *48 30 13 47*
ⓦ gillelejebadehotel.dk
A nostalgic spa hotel, this classic
white and blue painted establishment dates back to 1895 and is
set high on a cliff with views over
to Sweden.

HELSINGØR: Hotel Skandia ⓦ
Value   **Road Map** F4
Bramstræde 1, 3000 Helsingør
Tel *49 21 09 02*
ⓦ hotelskandia.dk
Rather basic, old-fashioned hotel
with personal service and a
handy location within walking
distance of all Helsingør's
attractions. Breakfast is included
in the price.

HOLBÆK: Hotel Sidesporet ⓦ
Value   **Road Map** F4
Ahlgade 1B, 4300 Holbæk
Tel *59 44 29 19*
ⓦ sidesporet.dk/hotel/
information.php
Previously going by the name
Holbæk Vandrehjem, this low-
cost hotel is located on the
harbour and has rooms for up to
four people, as well as its own
Turkish baths and restaurant.

DK Choice

HORNBÆK: Hotel
Hornbækhus ⓦⓦ
Character   **Road Map** F4
Skovvej 7, 3100 Hornbæk
Tel *49 70 01 69*
ⓦ hornbaekhus.com
Unashamedly romantic,
Hornbækhus was a popular
retreat for wealthy
Copenhageners in the 1920s
and 1930s. Tastefully
modernised and furnished in
Swedish 18th-century
Gustavian style, many of the
rooms have balconies. Guests
can relax in the hotel's elegant
living room, which opens onto
a large garden.

HØRVE: Dragsholm Slot ⓦⓦⓦ
Historic   **Road Map** E4
Dragsholm Alle, 4534 Hørve
Tel *69 65 33 00*
ⓦ dragsholm-slot.dk
One of Denmark's oldest castles,
13th century Dragholm oozes
historical atmosphere. Its
luxurious, period-furnished

Traditional decor at Dragsholm Slot
in the 'Himmilseng' room

rooms look out onto the moat
or the grounds; the restaurant
meanwhile is world class.

KALUNDBORG: Debbie's Bed
and Breakfast ⓦ
B&B   **Road Map** E4
Hovvejen 114, 4400 Kalundborg
Tel *29 92 29 28*
ⓦ debbiesbedandbreakfast.dk
In a building dating from 1886,
Debbie's B&B is a working farm
3 km (2 miles) from Kalundborg
centre. It offers rooms with and
without en suite bathrooms, and
a small kitchen is available for
guests to use.

ROSKILDE: Svogerslev Kro ⓦⓦ
Character   **Road Map** F4
Svogerslev Hovedgade 45, 4000 Roskilde
Tel *46 38 30 05*
ⓦ svogerslevkro.dk
This coaching inn, dating back to
the 1700s, is located a few miles
west of Roskilde in the pleasant
countryside. Guests can enjoy the
rustic decor, including thatched
roof and beamed ceilings.

ROSKILDE: Zleep Hotel
Roskilde ⓦⓦ
Historic   **Road Map** F4
Algade 13, 4000 Roskilde
Tel *70 23 56 35*
ⓦ zleephotels.com
A late 17th century inn, centrally
placed on Roskilde's walking
street and close to all necessary
amenities. Formerly the Prindsen,
it is now part of a Danish chain
of hotels.

SORØ: Hotel Postgården ⓦⓦ
Historic   **Road Map** E5
Storgade 25, 4180 Sorø
Tel *57 83 22 22*
ⓦ hotelpostgaarden.dk
This small, historic hotel is
housed in a building, dating back
some 300 years, on Sorø's main

shopping street. It offers friendly service, elegant rooms and makes a great base from which to explore the local attractions.

Southern Zealand

KØGE: Centralhotellet ⓚⓚ
Value   Road Map F5
Vestergade 3, 4600 Køge
Tel *56 65 06 96*
ⓦ centralhotellet.dk
Inexpensive accommodation at Køge's oldest hotel, which dates from the 1800s and has a good central location. Rooms are clean, though fairly basic, with a choice of en suite or shared bathrooms.

DK Choice

MØN: Liselund Ny Slot ⓚⓚ
Historic   Road Map F6
Langebjergvej 6, 4791 Borre, Møn
Tel *55 81 20 81*
ⓦ liselundslot.dk
A romantic atmosphere is assured at this doll-sized castle built in 1887 and located some 5 km (3 miles) from Møns Klint. Each of the 17 individual, tastefully decorated rooms are named after H C Andersen's fairy tales. At the very top is the Tower Room, which affords splendid views over the surrounding area. The castle also has its own restaurant and summertime outdoor café.

NÆSTVED: Hotel Kirstine ⓚⓚ
Character   Road Map E5
Købmagergade 20,
4700 Næstved
Tel *55 77 47 00*
ⓦ hotelkirstine.dk
Privately owned hotel in a quaint, half-timbered farmhouse from 1745 that was once a mayoral residence, with upmarket restaurant and antique furnished rooms. A popular venue for wedding parties.

NYKØBING F: Ny Kirstineberg Bed & Breakfast ⓚ
B&B   Road Map F6
Ny Kirstinebergvej 7,
4800 Nykøbing Falster
Tel *70 27 92 79*
ⓦ nykirstineberg.com
This 19th-century country villa just north of Nykøbing Falster is more manor house than B&B. It offers elegantly furnished singles, doubles and triples, plus a shared kitchen and large garden for guests to use.

NYSTED: Hotel Nysted Havn ⓚⓚ
Character   Road Map E6
Strandvejen 73, 4880 Nysted
Tel *54 87 16 07*
ⓦ hotelnystedhavn.dk
Located directly on the harbour, all of the brightly decorated, maritime themed rooms at this small hotel enjoy sea views and en suite bath. Ask for a room with balcony.

RINGSTED: Sørup Herregaard ⓚⓚ
Rural Retreat   Road Map E5
Sørupvej 26, 4100 Ringsted
Tel *57 64 30 02*
ⓦ sorup.dk
Relax in 4-star comfort at this 14th-century manor house located a short drive south of Ringsted. It sits in 400 hectares (990 acres) of land and features a lake plus facilities for crazy golf, petanque and swimming.

SAKSKØBING: Hotel Sakskjøbing ⓚⓚ
Historic   Road Map E6
Torvet 9, 4990 Sakskøbing
Tel *54 70 40 39*
ⓦ hotel-saxkjobing.dk
Dating from 1835, this hotel on Sakskøbing town square is co-owned by culinary guru Claus Meyer, who has injected new life into both the restaurant and rooms.

VORDINGBORG: Hotel Kong Valdmar ⓚ
Value   Road Map F6
Algade 101, 4760 Vordingborg
Tel *55 31 12 10*
ⓦ hotelkongvaldemar.dk
Ideal for visiting Vordingborg Slot, the hotel's most immediate neighbour, this hotel is friendly enough if rather lacking in character. Doubles and triples are available, and there's a small petanque terrain in the garden.

Funen

ÆREØSKØBING: Pension Vestergade 44 ⓚⓚ
Character   Road Map D6
Vestergade 44, 5970 Ærøskøbing
Tel *62 52 22 98*
ⓦ vestergade44.com
Built in 1784, this charming guesthouse's beautifully furnished rooms have a romantic feel. It has a lovely garden and cosy sitting room.

FAABORG: Danhostel Faaborg ⓚ
Value   Road Map D5
Grønnegade 71, 5600 Faaborg
Tel *62 61 12 03*
ⓦ danhostelfaaborg.dk
This atmospheric hostel is located in a 19th-century poorhouse in central Faaborg, 10 minutes' walk from a sandy beach. Guests have access to a garden courtyard and a shared kitchen.

FAABORG: Hotel Faergegaarden ⓚⓚ
Historic   Road Map D5
Chr IX's Vej 31, 5600 Faaborg
Tel *62 61 11 15*
ⓦ hotelfg.dk
Close to the harbour, this small hotel dates back to the late 19th century. There are sea views from many rooms and a traditional Danish restaurant on the premises.

KERTEMINDE: Tornøes Hotel ⓚⓚ
Historic   Road Map D5
Strandgade 2, 5300 Kerteminde
Tel *65 32 16 05*
ⓦ tornoeshotel.dk
Inexpensive, spacious rooms are available at this classic seaside hotel, which dates back to the 1600s and has offered lodging since 1865. Centrally located, most rooms feature fjord or harbour views.

The Danish flag flies above Pension Vestergade 44 in Ærøskøbing

For more information on types of hotels *see pages 244–5*

NYBORG: Hotel Villa Gule �
Value   **Road Map** D5
Østervoldgade 44, 5800 Nyborg
Tel 65 30 11 88
Ⓦ villa-gule.dk
This small hotel – dating from the
1800s and located in the centre
of medieval Nyborg – offers sea
views from many of the rooms,
good breakfasts and friendly
service. Two apartments are also
available in an adjacent building.

ODENSE: Hotel Domir ⓦ
Value   **Road Map** D5
Hans Tausens Gade 19,
5000 Odense C
Tel 66 12 14 27
Ⓦ domir.dk
A good budget option close to
the Kongens Have park and
central train station, this small,
privately owned hotel offers
comfortable, clean rooms,
friendly 24-hour reception and
a breakfast buffet.

RUDKØBING, LANGELAND:
Hotel Skandinavien ⓦ
Value   **Road Map** D6
Brogade 13, 5900 Rudkøbing
Tel 62 51 14 95
Ⓦ skanhotel.dk
This cosy little hotel from the
1600s is centrally located right on
the town's 'goose square'. In
addition to single, double and
triples, there is also a small
apartment with a kitchenette.

DK Choice

SVENDBORG: Stella
Maris ⓦⓦ
Luxury   **Road Map** D5
Kogtvedvænget 3, 5700 Svendborg
Tel 62 21 25 25
Ⓦ stellamaris.dk
Set in a converted building,
dating from 1904, Stella Maris
opened in 2014. It was originally
a stately home, and was
used as a Christian retreat for
a number of years. Now a
luxurious seafront boutique
hotel with a cocktail lounge,
smart bistro and bright, simply
decorated rooms. There is also
a farm shop in the grounds.

Southern and
Central Jutland

AARHUS: Simple Bed Hostel ⓦ
Value   **Road Map** D4
Åboulevarden 86, 8000 Aarhus C
Tel 53 23 21 89
Ⓦ simplebedhostel.com
Independent, self service hostel
with two dorms in a handy

riverside location. There's no
reception but the owners live in
the flat above. There's a shared
bathroom, kitchen and TV room.

DK Choice

AARHUS: Villa
Provence ⓦⓦⓦ
Boutique   **Road Map** D4
Fredens Torv 12,8000 Aarhus
Tel 86 18 24 00
Ⓦ villaprovence.dk
Many guests have fallen in love
with this small, intimate hotel
tucked away in a quiet corner
of central Aarhus. Despite its
nostalgic, guesthouse feel, Villa
Provence's modern facilities
include charging facilities for
electric cars. The Provence-
style rooms are spacious and
romantic; many have four-
posters and clawfoot tubs.

EBELTOFT: Hotel Ebeltoft
Strand ⓦⓦ
Family Friendly   **Road Map** D3
Ndr. Strandvej 3, 8400 Ebeltoft
Tel 86 34 33 00
Ⓦ ebeltoftstrand.dk
This modern seafront hotel
complex offers apartments
and double/family rooms, with
panoramic bay views and a smart
gourmet restaurant. Family-
friendly facilities include loan of
Nintendos and a kids' playroom.

ESBJERG: Hotel Ansgar ⓦⓦ
Character   **Road Map** B5
Skolegade 36, 6700 Esbjerg
Tel 75 12 82 44
Ⓦ hotelansgar.dk
A family-owned hotel for more
than a century, centrally-located
Ansgar prides itself on providing
personal service. Rooms are clean
and spacious, and both ferries and
trains are within walking distance.

Stylish guest room at the intimate
Villa Provence in Aarhus

FREDERICIA: Hotel
Postgaarden ⓦⓦ
Historic   **Road Map** C5
Oldenborggade 4, 7000 Fredericia
Tel 75 92 18 55
Ⓦ postgaarden.dk
This renovated hotel just outside
Fredericia's town ramparts offers
rooms in both a modern wing
and an older one, allowing guests
to choose between modern
comforts or old-world atmosphere.

HERNING: Best Western
Hotel Eyde ⓦⓦ
Historic   **Road Map** C4
Torvet 1, 7400 Herning
Tel 97 22 18 00
Ⓦ eyde.dk
On the town square in the centre
of Herning, this elegant hotel has
been thoroughly updated with
modern facilities including a gym
and a sauna. Breakfast is included.

HORSENS: Scandic Bygholm
Park ⓦⓦ
Family Friendly   **Road Map** C4
Schüttesvej 6, 8700 Horsens
Tel 75 62 23 33
Ⓦ scandichotels.com/Hotels/
Denmark/Horsens
This former stately home on the
outskirts of Horsens is now run
by the family-friendly Scandic
chain. In addition to enjoying the
modern facilities, guests are free
to wander around the vast park.

KOLDING:
Hotel Koldingfjord ⓦⓦ
Rural Retreat   **Road Map** C5
Fjordvej 154, 6000 Kolding
Tel 75 51 00 00
Ⓦ koldingfjord.dk
Built in 1911, this stately house,
ringed by forest and fjord, has
been transformed from a children's
sanatorium into an elegant hotel.
There is an impressive wine cellar,
marked walking trails plus a pool
and sun terrace.

RIBE: Weis Stue ⓦ
Historic   **Road Map** B5
Torvet 2, 6760 Ribe
Tel 75 42 07 00
Ⓦ weis-stue.dk
One of Denmark's oldest inns –
established in 1600 – this half-
timbered house on Ribe town
square has retained many early
18th-century features. Upstairs,
the quaint, antique rooms (shared
bathroom) breathe history.

RINGKØBING: Fjordgården ⓦⓦ
Family Friendly   **Road Map** B4
Vester Kær 28, 6950 Ringkøbing
Tel 97 32 14 00
Ⓦ hotelfjordgaarden.dk
Located amidst beautiful
countryside and a short walk

from the town, Fjordgården is a simple, family-friendly hotel. The rooms are clean and functional and the service is efficient.

SILKEBORG: Radisson Blu Papirfabrikken ⓀⓀ
Boutique **Road Map** C4
Papirfabrikken 12,
8600 Silkeborg
Tel *88 82 22 22*
W radissonblu.com/hotel-silkeborg
This former paper mill has been transformed into a modern design hotel with restaurant, riverside terrace and sleekly furnished rooms. Surrounded by woodland and water, but close to local attractions.

SØNDERBORG: Comwell Hotel Sønderborg ⓀⓀ
Luxury **Road Map** C6
Rosengade 2,
6400 Sønderborg
Tel *74 42 19 00*
W comwellsonderborg.dk
In a great location looking out over the Alssund, next door to Sønderborg Slot and within walking distance of Sønderborg centre, this hotel's four-star luxuries include a pool, gym and massage treatments.

VEJLE: Hotel Australia ⓀⓀ
Modern **Road Map** C4
Dæmningen 6, 7100 Vejle
Tel *76 40 60 00*
W hotelaustralia.dk
An inexpensive hotel in Vejle overlooking the fjord, with friendly reception and air conditioning in the rooms. It is well placed for the bus and train stations, as well as the town's pedestrian street.

Northern Jutland

DK Choice

AALBORG: Hotel Krogen ⓀⓀ
Character **Road Map** C2
Skibstedsvej 4, 9000 Aalborg
Tel *98 12 17 05*
W krogen.dk
Small, family-owned hotel-guesthouse in a palatial villa from 1872. Aalborg's bustling centre seems far away from its peaceful location in residential Hasseris, though the city's main sights are within walking distance. Aside from the romantically furnished rooms, the hotel's unique feature is its large miniature railway encircling the garden.

The impressive exterior of Hotel Krogen in Aalborg

FREDERIKSHAVN: Hotel Scandic The Reef ⓀⓀ
Family Friendly **Road Map** D1
Tordenskjoldsgade 14,
9900 Frederikshavn
Tel *98 43 32 33*
W scandichotels.com
Keep the kids happy with the tropical water park and family-friendly restaurant at this modern hotel with functional rooms.

HIRTSHALS: Hotel Montra Skaga Ⓚ
Value **Road Map** C1
Willemoesvej 1, 9850 Hirtshals
Tel *98 94 55 00*
W skagahotel.dk
Located just steps from Nordsøen Oceanarium, the exterior of this modern hotel block may not excite as much as the beauty of its windswept surroundings, between an orchard and the sea.

HJØRRING: Hjørring Kro Ⓚ
B&B **Road Map** D1
Birthesvej 2, 9800 Hjørring
Tel *98 92 53 29*
W hjoerringkro.dk
The rooms at this hotel are plain but clean and comfortable, and the restaurant serves traditional fare.

HOBRO: Hotel Amerika ⓀⓀ
Luxury **Road Map** C3
Amerikavej 48, 9500 Hobro
Tel *98 54 42 00*
W hotelamerika.dk
This country estate is surrounded by forest; a footpath from the 4-star hotel leads directly to Mariager Fjord. There is a spa, wellness centre and restaurant on site.

HOLSTEBRO: Centrum Bed & Breakfast Ⓚ
B&B **Road Map** B3
Sønderlandsgade 21, 7500 Holstebro
Tel *25 33 90 34*
W aas.dk
Close to the town centre, this well-equipped B&B offers breakfast from the adjoining Café Aas, as well as access to a communal kitchen. There are shared bathroom facilities and a pleasant outdoor terrace.

RANDERS: Best Western Hotel Kronjylland ⓀⓀ
Boutique **Road Map** D3
Vestergade 51–53,
8900 Randers
Tel *86 41 43 33*
W bestwestern.dk
Centrally located 300 m (328 yds) from the station, Kronjylland dates from the early 1900s, although its modern rooms have been decorated in clean Scandinavian style and reflects a boutique-like charm. Breakfast is included and there's Wi-Fi in the public areas.

SKAGEN: Bunken Strand Camping Ⓚ
Rural Retreat **Road Map** D1
Ålbækvej 288,
9980 Aalbæk
Tel *98 48 71 80*
W bunkenstrandcamping.dk
This well-equipped rural retreat which is located a few miles south of Skagen offers direct access to a sandy beach. In addition to several rental cabins and caravans, the campsite has two yurts imported from Mongolia.

SKAGEN: Hotel Plesner ⓀⓀ
Boutique **Road Map** D1
Holstvej 8, 9990 Skagen
Tel *98 44 68 44*
W hotelplesner.dk
This historic seaside hotel dates from 1907 and is close to Skagen's beautiful beaches and reknowned art galleries. Renovations have accentuated the boutique qualities at Hotel Plesner, with individually decorated rooms and a pristine, landscaped garden.

SKAGEN: Ruth's Hotel ⓚⓚⓚ
Luxury   **Road Map** D1
Hans Ruths Vej 1, 9990 Skagen
Tel *98 44 11 24*
Ⓦ ruths-hotel.dk
This legendary seaside hotel
opened as a small guesthouse in
1904. Several generations of the
Ruth family later, the place is
known for 5-star luxury, spa treatments and its gourmet restaurant.

THISTED: Hotel Thisted ⓚⓚ
Character   **Road Map** B2
Frederiksgade 16, 7700 Thisted
Tel *97 92 52 00*
Ⓦ hotelthisted.dk
In the centre of historic Thisted,
this small, family-owned hotel has
been well-maintained throughout its long tenure as a town inn.
Its French-Danish restaurant is
famed for homemade schnapps.

VIBORG: Oasen ⓚⓚ
B&B   **Road Map** C3
Nørregade 9, 8800 Viborg
Tel *86621425*
Ⓦ oasenviborg.dk
This inexpensive guesthouse in
central Viborg offers quaintly
decorated rooms and self-catering
apartments with breakfast. There
is a pleasant closed-in garden
patio and a coin-operated
laundry for guests.

Bornholm

ALLINGE: Hotel Friheden ⓚⓚ
Family Friendly
Tejnvej 80, 3770 Allinge
Tel *56 48 04 25*
Ⓦ hotelfriheden.dk
Modern, family-run resort hotel
with seaside location in Sandkås,
south of Allinge. The spacious,
well-equipped rooms have either
a balcony or terrace and a kitchenette; many also offer sea views.

ALLINGE: Pension Næsgaarden ⓚⓚ
B&B
Løsebækgade 20, 3770 Allinge
Tel *56 48 02 18*
Ⓦ naesgaarden.dk
An old-fashioned guesthouse
from the early 1800s, with a beach
on its doorstep, delightful cobbled
yard and fruit trees in the garden.
There's a small kitchen, and breakfasts are homemade and organic.

GUDHJEM: Hotel Klippen ⓚⓚ
Character
Grevens Dal 50, 3760 Gudhjem
Tel *51 83 60 22*
Ⓦ hotelklippen.com
A sprawling villa above Gudhjem
overlooking the sea, Klippen

offers a variety of rooms in
different annexes, with either a
terrace or a balcony. Nice café-
bar on the premises.

DK Choice

GUDHJEM: Stammershalle Badehotel ⓚⓚ
Historic
Sdr. Strandvej 128, 3760 Gudhjem
Tel *56 48 42 10*
Ⓦ stammershalle-badehotel.dk
Perched on the cliffs between
Allinge and Gudhjem, this
historic seaside hotel offers
dramatic Baltic views from
its bright, airy rooms. It features
an award-winning gourmet
restaurant, Lassens; full board
is available. Behind the hotel,
traces of the small zoo built
by the original owner can still
be seen.

HASLE: Hotel Herold ⓚ
Value
Vestergade 65, 3790 Hasle
Tel *56 96 40 24*
Ⓦ hotelherold.dk
A charming, friendly little hotel
on Hasle's renovated harbour
front. There are sea views from
many rooms, which offer the
opportunity to enjoy a perfect
Bornholm sunset. Good breakfasts are included in the room rate.

NEXØ: Hotel Balka Strand ⓚⓚ
Family Friendly
Boulevarden 9A, Balka, 3730 Nexø
Tel *56 49 49 49*
Ⓦ hotelbalkastrand.dk
Just 150 metres (164 yds) from
one of Bornholm's best sandy
beaches, this modern complex
comprises several buildings. All
rooms have furnished terraces.
The self-catering apartments can
sleep up to five guests.

RØNNE: Green Solution House ⓚⓚ
Boutique
Strandvejen 79, 3700 Rønne
Tel *56 95 19 13*
Ⓦ greensolutionhouse.dk
A modern, eco-friendly hotel
complex located just 200m
from the beach and about a mile
south of Rønne. The complex
has been custom designed for
a positive interactions with
its surroundings.

RØNNE: Griffen Spa Hotel ⓚⓚ
Luxury
Nordre Kystvej 34, 3700 Rønne
Tel *56 90 42 44*
Ⓦ bornholmhotels.dk
This resort is the largest hotel on
Bornholm. It's placed right on the

Historic seaside hotel Stammershalle
Badehotel at Gudhjem

seafront a short walk from the
ferry, with extensive spa, wellness
and bathing facilities.

SANDVIG: Hotel Hammersø ⓚⓚ
Luxury
*Hammershusvej 86, Sandvig,
3770 Allinge*
Tel *70 88 54 09*
Ⓦ hotel-hammersoe.dk
Located on the edge of
Bornholm's largest lake, this
adults-only, half-board hotel
offers old-fashioned resort
pastimes, a billiards room and
deckchairs to relax in around the
solar-heated swimming pool.

SVANEKE: Hotel Siemsens Gaard ⓚⓚ
Historic
*Havnebryggen 9,
3740 Svaneke*
Tel *56 49 61 49*
Ⓦ siemsens.dk
Situated behind the harbour in
a 17th-century merchant's
house, Siemsens Gaard was
rebuilt as a hotel in the 1930s.
Some rooms have a kitchenette
and a terrace opening onto the
peaceful rear courtyard.

Greenland

ILULISSAT: Hotel Avannaa ⓚⓚ
Character
*Nuussuattaap Aqq. 2,
3952 Ilulissat*
Tel *(+299) 94 40 02*
Ⓦ hotelavannaa.gl
Breathtaking views of Ilulissat
Ice Fiord are reason enough to
visit this small hotel/B&B.
All rooms have a balcony
and Internet access (fees may
be charged); some have a
kitchenette. Triples are available.

DK Choice

ILULISSAT: Hotel Arctic ⓚⓚⓚ
Luxury
Mittarfimmut Aqq. B-1128,
3952 Ilulissat
Tel *(+299) 94 41 53*
🅦 hotelarctic.com
As the world's most northerly luxury hotel situated right on the edge of the UNESCO-listed Ilulissat Ice Fiord, finding more stunning views from a hotel room would be a challenge. Ilulissat town is situated on the other side of the fiord to the south. The hotel offers both gourmet food and casual fare at its top-notch restaurant and café.

KANGERLUSSUAQ:
Polar Lodge ⓚⓚ
Value
Mitaarfiit Aqq, Postbox 1009
Tel *(+299) 84 16 48*
🅦 wogac.com/accommodation/
polar-lodge
This hostel is housed in a former US airbase, with Mount Hassel as its backdrop. Kitchen facilities, Wi-Fi and bike rental are available.

NUUK: Hotel Nordbo ⓚⓚ
Value
Vandsøvej 13, 3900 Nuuk
Tel *(+299) 32 66 44*
🅦 hotelnordbo.gl
Centrally-located, Nordbo offers a range of reasonably priced, simply furnished apartments with kitchen and laundry facilities, available for long- and short-term rentals.

NUUK: Hans Egede Hotel ⓚⓚⓚ
Luxury
Aqqusinersuaq, 3900 Nuuk
Tel *(+299) 32 42 22*
🅦 hhe.gl
The Greenland government uses this hotel for all of its conferences. Behind the unappealing façade is a well-equipped hotel housing one of Nuuk's best restaurants.

SISIMIUT: Hotel Sisimiut ⓚⓚ
Boutique
Aqqusinersuaq 86, 3911 Sisimiut
Tel *(+299) 86 48 40*
🅦 hotelsisimiut.com
Located just north of the Arctic Circle in the Sisimiut settlement, this hotel has friendly service and excellent rooms and suites.

TASIILAQ:
Hotel Angmagssalik ⓚⓚ
Value
PO Box 511, 3913 Tasiilaq
🅦 arcticwonder.com/hotels/hotel-angmagssalik
This pleasant hotel overlooks Tasiilaq settlement and is well

equipped will all the necesary amenities. Budget dorm lodgings are available in an annexe.

Faroe Islands

DK Choice

GJOGV, EYUSTUROY:
Gjaargardur Guesthouse
Gjogv ⓚⓚ
Rural Retreat
Dalavegur 20, 476 Gjogv
Tel *(+298) 42 31 71*
🅦 gjaargardur.fo/
An hours' drive from Tórshavn, amidst spectacular scenery, this eco-friendly guesthouse has a grass roof that blends into the surrounding hillside. It offers modern facilities, friendly service and will even make packed lunches on request. The attic rooms are cheaper with a shared bathroom, but offer spectacular views.

KLAKSVIK: Hotel Klaksvik ⓚⓚ
Value
Víkavegur 38, 700 Klaksvík
Tel *(+298) 45 53 33*
🅦 hotelklaksvik.fo
Great views from the rooms of Klaksvik's sole 3-star hotel, all but three of which are en suite. Note that although the hotel has two restaurants, both have a strictly no alcohol policy.

RUNAVIK, EYUSTUROY:
Hotel Runavik ⓚⓚ
Family Friendly
Heiðavegur 6, 620 Runavík
Tel *(+298) 66 33 33*
🅦 hotelrunavik.fo
The only hotel in this part of the Faroes is located in a former seaman's mission from the 1950s on Runavik's main street. Rooms are brightly furnished and well-equipped.

TÓRSHAVN: Bladypi
Guesthouse ⓚ
Value
Doktara Jakobsens gøta,
100 Tórshavn
Tel *(+298) 50 06 00*
🅦 hostel.fo/
One of the cheapest options in Tórshavn, this basic guesthouse is centrally located and offers both private rooms and hostel-style dorm accommodation. There are shared kitchen facilities as well.

TÓRSHAVN: Hotel Tórshavn ⓚⓚ
Boutique
Tórsgøta 4, 100 Tórshavn
Tel *(+298) 35 00 00*
🅦 hoteltorshavn.fo
A 3-star hotel with brightly decorated rooms and a brasserie restaurant. Centrally located near the harbour, some rooms at Tórshavn have sea views, though you'll pay a little extra for the privilege.

TÓRSHAVN:
Hotel Føroyar ⓚⓚⓚ
Luxury
Oyggjarvegur 45, 100 Tórshavn
Tel *(+298) 31 75 00*
🅦 hotelforoyar.com
This architecturally fascinating hotel is characterised by the way it blends into the surrounding landscape, with a grass roof, and light rooms. The hotel restaurant is equally innovative.

TVØROYRI, SUDUROY:
Guesthouse Undir Heygnum ⓚ
Rural Retreat
800 Tvøroyri
Tel *(+298) 37 20 46*
🅦 guest-house.dk
Remotely situated on Suduroy's northeastern shore, "Under the Hill" is a wood-framed 1920s villa. Guests can use the shared kitchen, enjoy the garden and, in summertime, go out on a boat.

Simple accommodation and spectacular scenery at Gjaargardur Guesthouse, Gjogv

For more information on types of hotels *see pages 244–5*

WHERE TO EAT AND DRINK

Denmark's restaurant scene is notoriously fashionable, and for good reason. The global trend for "New Nordic Cuisine" and the international fame of Copenhagen restaurant Noma, which bases its menu exclusively on locally produced, seasonal ingredients, has filtered down into all regions of Denmark. Even smaller, provincial eateries now offer a version of Nordic cuisine, with regional specialties such as horseradish and beetroot, and rye bread making a comeback. It's not only the big cities such as Copenhagen and Aarhus where diners can be assured a high culinary standard; the island of Bornholm, for example, has developed a reputation for its regional specialities and exceptional restaurants, while Greenland and the Faroes have their own gourmet restaurants that showcase local ingredients and take an innovative approach to traditional dishes. Travellers looking for more modest meals will find cafés in most small towns serving snacks, pastries and drinks, but traditional street stands offering the Danish hot dog *pølser* are becoming less visible.

Light-filled dining room at New Nordic restaurant, Orangeriet *(see p262)*

When to Eat and Opening Hours

Danish breakfast tends to be a fairly modest affair, though this is changing, especially in Copenhagen, where many cafés open from 7am. At weekends, hearty and wholesome brunches are popular, and cafés known for their brunches often fill up fast. As an alternative, many bakeries sell bread, pastries and coffee and occasionally provide a table at which to sit.

Frokost (lunch) is consumed between 11:30am and 2pm. It can take various forms, from a light meal to a large banquet of open sandwiches and salads. At lunchtime many restaurants also serve hot main courses such as meatballs, but the helpings are smaller and prices lower than the same meal at dinnertime. *Aftensmad* (dinner) is from 6pm onwards, with many restaurants closing their kitchens by 9pm. Evening dining can be expensive: it's not unusual for prices to rise

between lunch and dinner at the same establishment.

Bakeries open early, usually around 6am. Fast-food restaurants that serve breakfast open at around 8 or 9am. Restaurants that cater for the lunchtime trade generally open around 11am and often close around 3pm. Restaurants generally finish serving by 10pm, and restaurants that are not licensed to remain open all night close at 1am. Cafés tend to stay open all day and often late into the night.

What to Eat

New Nordic, pioneered by restaurants including Noma, is a seasonal cuisine trend that uses lesser-known regional ingredients, presented creatively. Traditional Danish cuisine remains popular and suits all budgets. The iconic *smørrebrod* remains popular, with *smørrebrod* restaurants ranging from old-fashioned to extremely innovative. For more information on types of food, see pp258–9.

Menu

Many restaurants have menus written in English. In addition to the full menu, some offer a specially priced *dagens ret*, or

Outdoor seating at a café along Nyhavn, Copenhagen

Sea views from the terrace at Kadeau Bornholm, Aakirkeby

"dish of the day", which is often written up on a board. Some restaurants serve good value fixed-price two-, three- or four-course lunches and evening meals. Seasonal changing set menus have become especially popular in "New Nordic" eateries, where a limited choice keeps prices down and the quality of ingredients high.

Children

Most restaurants in Denmark offer high chairs and special "child-friendly" menus and activity packs. The best time to take children to a restaurant is late afternoon. Eating at this time of day is quieter, less stressful and generally means that no one need wait long to be served.

Prices and Tips

Prices in restaurants vary enormously. Many cheaper Danish establishments offer set-price all-you-can-eat buffets at lunchtime, as do some of the Thai and Middle-Eastern restaurants. Some hostels also serve good value lunch and evening meals for about 100 Dkr. A three-course meal in a mid-priced restaurant will cost between 250–400 Dkr not including alcohol, while at an upmarket restaurant, diners should be prepared to pay in excess of 800 Dkr.

Soft drinks, beer and *akvavit* (a kind of schnapps) cost about the same in most places; however, prices for wines and liqueurs vary and tend to be steep in some of the upmarket restaurants.

In Denmark, a service charge and tax are automatically included in the price. Leaving no tip is not considered bad manners; however, it is customary to round up the bill. Most restaurants accept credit cards and display the appropriate signs at their entrance.

Reservations

Guests are generally required to book well in advance at the most popular restaurants. Even in quieter restaurants it is advisable to book at the weekend.

If it is too late to book, then the best option is to head to an area where there are clusters of restaurants.

Vegetarians

The diet in Denmark is heavily based on meat and fish. However, most restaurants should offer at least one vegetarian dish. Restaurants that serve only vegetarian food are a rarity.

Guests with Disabilities

Older establishments, particularly in bigger towns, are often located in basements, while more modern premises (such as restaurants attached to hotels and museums) are more likely to be accessible to all. It is best to check when booking. Local tourist offices should be able to help visitors locate accessible restaurants in the area. Another useful source for tourists is the Accessibility Label Scheme website (www.godadgang.dk), which lists establishments that have joined the scheme and are accessible to those with special needs.

Recommended Restaurants

The restaurants listed here have been carefully selected to offer a cross-section of options for every region. In addition to Copenhagen's best Michelin-starred restaurants, we have provided an alternative to suit all budgets and tastes, whether you are on a culinary tour or looking for a place to take the family for lunch. Danish cuisine is regarded among the world's best, and the "New Nordic" kitchen is heavily featured here, both in fine-dining and in more down-to-earth establishments.

The DK choice entries focus on those eateries that are exceptional and innovative in their use of raw ingredients, often produced locally at the restaurant's own farms. At many of them, advance booking is needed.

Selection of cakes on display at La Glace *(see p262)*

The Flavours of Denmark

Denmark's cuisine, like that of other Scandinavian countries, has always been rich in meat and fish dishes. Specialities from the sea include smoked salmon, pickled herring, eel and haddock. Cod is served baked, steamed, fried or dried *(klipfisk)*. The *kolde bord*, a lunchtime buffet, is a good way to try out various local dishes, with a selection of *smørrebrød*, cold cuts and hearty pork dishes. Most Danes have a sweet tooth and *wienerbrød* (Danish pastries) are eaten at any time of day. Berries appear in many desserts, and Danish ice cream is among the best in the world.

Danish pastries

Punnets of ripe strawberries, freshly harvested on Samsø Island

Smørrebrød

The classic *smørrebrød* (open sandwich) is as popular as ever with the Danes. Preparation is easy enough: buttered slices of *rugbrød* (unleavened rye bread) are topped with any number of sliced meats, fish or cheeses, such as prawns, smoked eel, ham, lamb and beef. They are then garnished with dill, cucumber, tomato or

lemon, a remoulade (mayonnaise-based sauce), caviar, or even a raw egg yolk served in its shell. Among national favourites are *Sol over Gudhjem* and *Bornholmer*, both variations on smoked herring fillets topped with an egg yolk, raw onion, chives and radishes. *Marineredesild* (vinegar-cured herring with onions and capers) and *Stjerneskud* ("shooting star",

fried fish fillet with prawns, lemon and dill) are also popular. Meat varieties include *dyrlægens natmad*, a towering creation laden with liver pâté, salt beef, flavoured lard, onion rings and watercress; *roastbeefmad*, rare roast beef with fried onions and grated horseradish; and *rullepølsemad*, slices of pork belly seasoned with raw onions, herbs, horseradish and watercress.

Roastbeefmad   Dyrlægens natmad   Prawns, caviar and lemon
            Bornholmer   Marineredesild
                                    Stjerneskud
Akvavit

Selection of typical Danish *smørrebrød*

Danish Dishes and Specialities

To this day, Danish cuisine retains a flavour of pre-industrial times, when the diet centred around rye bread, salted pork and herring – basically whatever could be grown and harvested in a short summer or pulled from the sea and preserved. This type of cuisine is enjoying quite a resurgence. Typical are dishes such as *øllebrød* (barley porridge), *æbleflæsk* (slices of pork with apples fried in the fat) and *grønlangkål* (thick kale stew with sausages and mustard). Many dishes are served with new potatoes and root vegetables. Cucumber salad, pickled beetroot, and peas and carrots in white sauce also appear. Desserts include Apple Charlotte with whipped cream, breadcrumbs and almonds, and *rødgrød med fløde*, a jellied fruit juice served with thick cream.

Dill

Frikadeller meatballs made of pork and veal are fried in Danish butter and served with boiled new potatoes.

Herrings hanging in a Bornholm smokery

Fish & Seafood

With its 406 islands, Denmark abounds with seafood. Herring is the most caught, cooked and consumed fish in the country. It is eaten fresh or preserved by salting, drying and smoking, and is served with sauces including curry, garlic, mustard and tomato. Salmon also features prominently, smoked, roasted, poached or cured in a salt-sugar-dill mixture, as do smoked eel, roe, mackerel and plaice. Fish fillets are often fried in butter and served with new potatoes and a buttery parsley sauce, washed down with lager or *akvavit* (Danish schnapps). Seafood is best enjoyed in the distinctive *røgeri* (smokehouses) found in harbours and pier restaurants all over the country.

Meat

Pork is the most common meat; there are four times as many pigs as people in Denmark, and Danish bacon is famous throughout the world. Traditional preparations include *stegt flæsk med*

Snegl (literally "snail") pastries in a baker's window

persillesovs, fried slices of pork with parsley sauce, served with potatoes; and *medisterpølse,* a thick and spicy pork sausage.

Sausages are popular, no more so than the ubiquitous *pølse,* a hotdog that is sold in kiosks everywhere and flavoured with any number of toppings. Though it is hardly haute cuisine, it is still a must for any visitor.

Beef, veal and lamb appear widely on menus, often in stews or minced to make rissoles and *frikadeller* (meatballs). In season, there are also game birds such as pheasant or duck, and venison and red deer.

DANISH PASTRIES

The "Danish" was introduced to Denmark in the 1870s, when striking breadmakers were replaced by Viennese immigrant bakers, with their repertoire of sweet breads, cakes and puff pastries. Pastries come in all shapes and sizes, and are filled with raisins, fruit compotes and custards, then topped with nuts and sweet icing. Some of the best examples are *spandauer,* a flat twist of dough filled with vanilla custard, and the almond-filled *hanekam.* Moist and light, all are perfect with a coffee. Note that the same cakes and buns will have different names in different regions.

Flæskesteg is a joint of roasted pork with crackling. It is usually served with cabbage and gravy.

Rødbeder is a side dish that consists of sliced pickled beetroot (beets). Horseradish sauce is also popular.

Risalamande is a Christmas rice pudding with almonds. It is served cold, topped with a rich, fruity cherry sauce.

What to Drink in Denmark

As far as drinks are concerned the Danes have two passions – coffee and beer. People over 60 are also very attached to their liqueurs, which come in a variety of flavours and appear under the common name of *akvavit*. The beer market is dominated by a handful of companies, of which Carlsberg is the best known, but there are also many micro-breweries, such as Mikkeler in Copenhagen. Danish beer comes in a variety of strengths and colours, from fairly tame draught Pilsner through to stout with an alcohol content of about 10 per cent. Wine was not always so popular but is readily available in supermarkets and restaurants. Non-alcoholic drinks include mineral water and numerous soft drinks.

Drinkers enjoying the sun outside one of Denmark's extremely popular bars

Lager

Lager is the most popular Danish beverage. Most Danish beers are of the Pilsner type with an alcohol content of about 4.5 per cent. They include brands such as Carlsberg, Grøn Tuborg, Faxe and Star. Before Christmas and Easter the shops sell Julebryg and Påskebryg in standard and strong varieties. These beers are slightly sweet and make perfect additions to *akvavit*. Bars and restaurants serve both draught beer *(fadøl)* and bottled beers. Sometimes draught beer is ordered in a jug. Beer is most often sold in bottles rather than cans.

Faxe Royal lager

Logo of the Carlsberg brewery

Beer is consumed throughout the day. It is not uncommon, and perfectly respectable, for Danes to drink beer in the park at lunchtime. It is rare to see drunkenness and drink-driving is not tolerated.

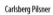

Carlsberg Pilsner   Tuborg lager   Faxe Classic

Carlsberg stout   Carlsberg Elephant

Brown Ale

There are over 400 varieties of beer produced in Denmark, including many fine brown ales. These generally have more flavour and are often stronger than Pilsner beers, with an alcoholic content of about 8 per cent or above. Some cafés and bars specialize in these beers, which tend to be slightly sweeter and less fizzy than lager. Among the popular brown ales are Carlsberg's Elephant and Sort Guld from the Tuborg brewery. The darkest beers are stouts and porters; these often have a higher percentage of alcohol. Organic microbrews, such as Thy Bryghus, also have a slice of the market.

Wine

The Danish climate does not allow for the cultivation of grapes, although a few enthusiasts are trying to introduce the hardier varieties to southern Scandinavia. So far their efforts have not yielded any commercially viable vintages, and Danes, who are increasingly swapping a tankard of beer for a glass of wine, have to settle for imported wines. White wine is referred to as *hvidvin*, red wine is *rødvin* and sparkling wine is *mousserende-vin*. Hot mulled wine, or *gløgg*, is served with almonds and raisins in the run–up to Christmas.

Gløgg – mulled wine

Hot Drinks

The Danes are coffee connoisseurs and coffee is the most popular drink in the country. Roasted beans are freshly ground on café premises and brewed in special jugs. Strong Italian espressos are also available, as are cappuccinos and increasingly popular lattes. Caffeine-free coffee is rarely found, but a delicious hot chocolate served with whipped cream is a fine alternative. Tea is not as popular in Denmark as coffee and consists of no more than a tea bag placed in a cup. Herbal teas are available in most cafés.

An aromatic herbal tea

A cup of black coffee

Liqueurs

The traditional Christmas feast is often accompanied in Denmark by chilled *akvavit*. This schnapps-like beverage comes in a variety of herbal flavours and often bears the name *akvavit* on the label. It is usually drunk in a single shot and is followed by a glass of beer. As well as schnapps, the Danes drink other strong alcoholic herb infusions. The most popular of these is Gammel Dansk, which is traditionally drunk early in the morning. Danes used to regard a small glass of this bitter herbal preparation as a preventative medicine. Another local drink is Peter Heering, a sweet liqueur made from cherries, which is sipped after meals.

Herb-flavoured Gammel Dansk

Akvavit –Danish schnapps

Soft Drinks

When ordering a meal it is customary to ask for a bottle or jug of water. Danish tap water *(postevand)* is perfectly safe. Still bottled water is *minaralvand;* the sparkling variety bears the proud name of *danskvand* (Danish carbonated water). All restaurants, bars and pubs also serve low-alcohol beer, known as *let øl*. Soft drinks such as Coca-Cola go by the name of *sodavand;* bottled fruit juices are known as *saft*. Drinking chocolate – both hot *(varm chokolade)* and cold *(chokolademælk)* – is popular.

Sparkling mineral water

Fizzy soft drink

Bottle of chocolate milk

Where to Eat and Drink

Copenhagen
North Copenhagen
Madklubben Bistro
De-Luxe ⓚ
Scandinavian **Map** 2 D5
Store Kongensgade 66,
1264 Cph
Tel *33 32 32 34* **Closed** *Sun*
The original restaurant in what is
now a string of Copenhagen
eateries, Madklubben is all about
serving simple, yet high-quality
traditional dishes such as soups,
fish and prime ribs cheaply and
informally. Vegetarian options too.

Mormors ⓚ
Café **Map** 2 E5
Bredgade 45, 1260 Cph
Tel *33 16 0 70*
A charming, nostalgic café with
friendly service and bar seating
next to the large street window.
Mormors serves tasty home-made
sandwiches and cakes – food like
"mormor" (grandma) would make.
Gluten- and lactose-free options
are available.

Café Petersborg ⓚⓚ
Danish **Map** 2 E4
Bredgade 76, 1260 Cph
Tel *33 12 50 16* **Closed** *Sat dinner,*
Sun
One of Copenhagen's oldest
restaurants, its name comes from
the visitors from the Russian
Consulate that was once above
it. The basement locale serves
traditional Danish fare in hearty
portions, for lunch and dinner.

Ida Davidsen ⓚⓚ
Smørrebrød **Map** 2 D5
Store Kongensgade 70, 1264 Cph
Tel *33 91 36 55* **Closed** *Sat, Sun;*
Jul
This famed, lunch-only *smørrebrød*
café has been run by the Davidsen
family for five generations, and in
its present location since 1974.
With more than 170 variations,
the *smørrebrød* list is record-
breaking; some are named after
royalty and celebrities.

The Red Box ⓚⓚ
Chinese Fusion **Map** 2 D5
Store Kongensgade 42,
1264 Cph
Tel *43 33 43 33* **Closed** *Sun*
A fresh, modern take on Chinese
food, fusing traditional Asian
dishes with the contemporary
European kitchen for meals that
are light and healthy. The decor is
similarly modern and minimalist,
the atmosphere relaxed.

Ché Fè ⓚⓚⓚ
Italian **Map** 2 D5
Borgergade 17A, 1300 Cph
Tel *33 11 17 21* **Closed** *Sun*
Organic trattoria Ché Fè
(meaning "What's up?" in Italian)
is run by the same team as
Christianshavn's Era Ora. The food
is not cheap, but the level of
quality and authenticity is high.

Koefoed ⓚⓚⓚ
New Nordic **Map** 2 D5
Landgreven 3, 1301 Cph
Tel *56 48 22 24* **Closed** *Sun, Mon*
In basement premises on a side
street near Store Kongensgade,
this simply decorated restaurant
in a former coal cellar specialises
in cuisine from the Danish island of
Bornholm. Free-range meat is
sourced from individual farms
to produce simple, seasonal
dishes. Large selection of
Bordeaux wines to chose from.

DK Choice

Lumskebugten ⓚⓚⓚ
Scandinavian **Map** 2 F4
Esplanaden 21,
1263 Cph
Tel *33 15 60 29* **Closed** *Sun*
(lunch & dinner); Mon & Tue
(dinners)
A former sailor's tavern situated
between the cruise ports and
Kastellet, *"Lumskebugten"* is
what Danes call a place to run
aground. The food is a modern
take on traditional Danish
dishes; open sandwiches and
fried fish are served simply with
delicious lightness. The setting
is cosy, with seating for around
30 diners, but as it's an old
building, the acoustics aren't
always perfect.

Serving counter at traditional Copenhagen
patisserie La Glace

Price Guide
Prices are based on a two-course meal
for one without alcohol or a tip, but
including tax.

ⓚ	up to 200 Dkr
ⓚⓚ	200–350 Dkr
ⓚⓚⓚ	over 350 Dkr

Orangeriet ⓚⓚⓚ
New Nordic **Map** 1 C5
Kronprinsessegade 13,
1306 Cph
Tel *33 11 13 07* **Closed** *Sun dinner*
Located in beautiful green
surroundings in a glass-fronted
conservatory in Kongens Have,
Orangeriet serves simple,
seasonal dinners and lunchtime
open sandwiches. There's also a
mouth-watering cake table on
Sunday afternoons.

Central Copenhagen
Atlas Bar ⓚ
International **Map** 3 B1
Larsbjørnsstræde 18, 1454 Cph
Tel *33 15 03 52* **Closed** *Sun*
A long-standing favourite with
the area's students, this casual,
inexpensive basement café
serves dishes from around the
globe with one of the best
vegetarian selections in the city.

Café Retro ⓚ
Café **Map** 3 B1
Knabrostræde 26, 1210 Cph
Tel *41 83 35 35* **Closed** *Mon*
A non-profit café with a pleasant
atmosphere run by a team of
international volunteers, with lots
of sofas and armchairs and an
upstairs room. There are no main
meals, but soups, cakes and
nachos are served.

La Glace ⓚ
Café **Map** 3 B1
Skoubogade 3, 1158 Cph
Tel *33 14 46 46* **Closed** *Sun (Easter–*
Sep)
An old-fashioned, rather genteel
patisserie dating from 1870.
Six generations later, La Glace
is much the same, with an
incredible selection of
elaborately decorated cakes.

Makke Kaffe ⓚ
Café **Map** 3 C2
Nybrogade 18–20, 1203 Cph
Tel *52 40 01 84* **Closed** *Sun*
Run by a smiling Italian
woman, this family-friendly
basement café on the canal side,
not far from the Nationalmuseet,
has sofas, books and toys.
It serves cakes, tapas and top-
quality sandwiches.

Rizraz Sticks 'n' Veggies ⓚ
Mediterranean   **Map** 3 B2
Kompagnistræde 20,
1208 Cph
Tel *33 15 05 75*
One of two Riraz eateries in
the city, the affordable and filling
all-you-can-eat Mediterranean
buffets served for both lunch and
dinner (lunch is cheaper) have
long been popular with
backpackers and students.

Slotskælderen hos Gitte Kik ⓚ
Smørrebrød   **Map** 3 C1
Fortunstræde 4, 1065 Cph
Tel *33 11 15 37*   **Closed** *Sun, Mon*
This classic *smørrebrød* lunch
restaurant dates from 1910 and
still looks much the same now as
it did then. Traditional open
sandwich toppings are served
with a lunchtime schnapps and
an old-fashioned atmosphere.

Aamanns Etablissement ⓚⓚ
New Nordic   **Map** 1 B3
Øster Farimagsgade 10–12,
2100 Cph Ø
Tel *35 55 33 44*   **Closed** *Mon, Tue*
dinner
Reinterpreting traditional *smørre-*
brød and Danish staples for a
contemporary audience, Aamanns
is both take-away deli and eat-
in restaurant (Etablissement),
serving open sandwiches, lunch
and dinner.

Bror ⓚⓚ
New Nordic   **Map** 3 A1
Sankt Peders Stræde 24A, 1453 Cph
Tel *32 17 59 99*   **Closed** *Mon, Tue*
The breakaway restaurant of a
couple of ex-Noma chefs, Bror is
similar in spirit, championing
seasonal, New Nordic dishes and
innovative taste pairings. It's far
easier to get a table here though.

Café Europa 1989 ⓚⓚ
Café   **Map** 3 C1
Amagertorv 1, 1160 Cph
Tel *33 14 28 89*
On one side of busy Amagertorv
Square, this café is a popular
meeting place and it can be hard
to get a seat. The cosmopolitan
decor and menu are both
influenced by the best of
European café traditions.

Café Norden ⓚⓚ
Café   **Map** 3 C1
Østergade 61, 1100 Cph
Tel *33 11 77 91*
A popular meeting spot overlooking Storkespringvandet in
the middle of Strøget. In summer,
tables tumble out onto the street
from the two-storey Art Deco
building. Enjoy coffee and cake,
brunch or various hot dishes.

Café Europa1989 on Amagertorv Square

Cap Horn ⓚⓚ
Organic   **Map** 4 E1
Nyhavn 21, 1051 Cph
Tel *33 12 85 04*
Dine outside on picturesque
Nyhavn's jetty or inside the
charming old building, which has
retained many original fixtures.
The seasonal, organic menu
offers a varied selection of fish,
meat and vegetarian dishes.

Geist ⓚⓚ
New Nordic   **Map** 4 D1
Kongens Nytorv 8, 1050 Cph
Tel *33 13 37 13*
Located amongst upmarket
restaurants on Kongens Nytorv,
Geist ("pleasure") is a stylishly
informal eatery where the menu
comprises many smaller dishes –
mix and match as you like.

Krebsegaarden ⓚⓚ
International   **Map** 3B1
Studiestræde 17, 1455 Cph
Tel *20 12 40 15*   **Closed** *Sun, Mon*
This small restaurant has built up
a following with a unique concept –
the menu is inspired by exhibitors
in the adjoining gallery (through
the courtyard), so may feature
specialities from their region.

> **DK Choice**
>
> **Marv & Ben** ⓚⓚ
> New Nordic   **Map** 3 C1
> *Snaregade 4, 1205 Cph*
> **Tel** *33 91 01 91*   **Closed** *Sun,*
> *Mon*
> This New Nordic gastro pub has
> a charming setting, in an old
> apartment building down a
> narrow cobbled street. It spans
> two floors (upstairs is more
> intimate, downstairs has the
> energy of the open kitchen)
> and offers four- to five-course
> set menus only; much of the
> produce is sourced from
> the restaurant's own gardens.

Royal Smushi Café ⓚⓚ
Café   **Map** 3 C1
Amagertorv 6, 1160 Cph
Tel *33 12 11 22*
The café of the Royal
Copenhagen store is a quirkily
decorated, pastel-toned place,
where *smørrebrød* is served in
dolls' sizes dubbed "smushi",
along with cakes and coffee –
all on blue fluted porcelain.

Uformel ⓚⓚ
New Nordic   **Map** 3 A2
Studiestræde 69, 1609 Cph
Tel *70 99 91 11*   **Closed** *Sat lunch*
& Sun
Located around the corner from
Palads cinema, this cool eatery,
furnished with dark wood decor,
is run by the team behind Formel
B. This is their cheaper, casual
option, serving a pick and
choose menu of starter-sized
gourmet dishes.

Krogs ⓚⓚⓚ
Seafood   **Map** 3 C1
Gammel Strand 38, 1202 Cph
Tel *33 15 89 15*
Krogs has been known as
Copenhagen's most exclusive fish
restaurant since 1910. In 2014 a
change of ownership led to a
more informal, bistro atmosphere
(and lower prices), but with the
same quality.

The Standard ⓚⓚⓚ
New Nordic   **Map** 4 E1
Havnegade 44, 1058 Cph
Tel *72 14 88 08* **Closed** *Mon (Studio)*
Actually two restaurants (plus
jazz club) combined in an Art
Deco, ex-customs building on
the harbour. Open for breakfast,
lunch and dinner, customers
can enjoy great food at either
Almanak, which serves
modern Danish fare; or the
Michelin-starred Studio, which
specializes in the innovative
New Nordic cuisine.

For more information on types of restaurants *see pages 256–7*

South Copenhagen

Rabes Have ⓦ
Smørrebrød **Map** 4 D3
Langebrogade 8, 1411 Cph
Tel *32 57 34 17* **Closed** *Mon, Tue*
Dating back to 1678, this traditional Danish lunch restaurant serves *smørrebrød* and schnapps in an authentic setting. Dine in the charming courtyard in summer. It can get very busy.

Nabo ⓦⓦ
New Nordic **Map** 4 D2
Wildersgade 10A
Tel *33 22 10 02*
🅦 nabonabo.dk
Named for its proximity to its older sibling, Michelin-starred restaurant Kadeau, "Nabo" means "neighbour". High-quality, good-value breakfast and dinner is made possible through classic and New Nordic options.

Restaurant Julian, Nationalmuseet ⓦⓦ
Scandinavian **Map** 3 B2
Ny Vestergade 10,1471 Cph
Tel *33 93 07 60* **Closed** *Mon*
The museum café focuses on Nordic cuisine and the Danish culinary heritage. It also produces "climate-friendly" menus where the carbon footprint is minimal. The weekend brunch buffets are very popular so arrive early.

Spiseloppen ⓦⓦ
International **Map** 4 F3
Bådmandsstræde 43, 1407 Cph
Tel *32 57 95 58* **Closed** *Mon*
A fixture in Christiania for decades, this restaurant offers fine dining and great cooking in premises that are never snobbish or exclusive. The international kitchen staff serve a global selection, and always offer vegetarian options.

Amass ⓦⓦⓦ
New Nordic
Refshalevej 153, 1432 Cph
Tel *43 58 43 30* **Closed** *Sun, Mon, Tue–Thu (lunch)*
In a former shipyard, quite a buzz surrounds Amass, an upscale but informal New Nordic eatery led by ex-Noma chefs. Communal dining is encouraged but not mandatory. Reservations are advised, with only five seats saved for walk-in diners.

Era Ora ⓦⓦⓦ
Italian **Map** 4 E2
Overgaden Neden Vandet 33B, 1414 Cph
Tel *32 54 06 93* **Closed** *Sun*
One of Copenhagen's best – and most expensive – Italian

restaurants, Michelin-starred Era Ora concentrates on the cuisine of Italy's northern regions, flying in fresh ingredients especially. Lunchtime dining is somewhat cheaper.

Kadeau København ⓦⓦⓦ
New Nordic **Map** 4 E3
Wildersgade 10A, 1408 Cph
Tel *33 25 22 23* **Closed** *Sun, Mon, Tue lunch, Wed lunch*
This Michelin-starred, rustic Christianshavn eatery was one of the forerunners of the New Nordic movement. Together with its namesake in Aakirkeby, Kadeau has elevated regional specialities from Bornholm to a higher gastronomic level, serving gourmet-quality set menus inspired and dominated by Bornholm produce.

DK Choice

Noma ⓦⓦⓦ
New Nordic **Map** 4 F1
Tel *32 96 32 97*
🅦 noma.dk
Pioneer of the New Nordic food movement, two Michelin-starred Noma was named the world's best restaurant from 2010–12 and again in 2014. It utilises only ingredients indigenous to Scandinavia – head chef Rene Redzepi having coined the culinary concept of "foraging". The famous restaurant closed in February 2017 and the staff opened a temporary pop-up in Mexico in the interim. The restaurant is due to reopen by 2018 – check the website for more information.

Restaurant Kanalen ⓦⓦⓦ
Danish-French **Map** 4 E2
Wilders Plads 2, 1403 Cph
Tel *32 95 13 30* **Closed** *Sun*
Upmarket Kanalen exploits its canalside location to the fullest, with al fresco dining in summer and cosy, candlelit dinners by the fire in winter. Its classic menus are Danish-French inspired and use fresh local ingredients.

Further Afield

Kates Joint ⓦ
International
Blågårdsgade 12, 2200 Cph N
Tel *35 37 44 96*
A small, cheap café that is one of the Nørrebro locals' best-kept secrets. Kate's menu travels the globe, changing continents daily, always with plenty of vegetarian options available. It is popular with the expat crowd.

The rustic yet chic dining room at Kadeau København

Namnam ⓦ
Singaporean
Vesterbrogade 39, 1620 Cph V
Tel *41 91 98 98* **Closed** *Sun*
This is a brightly furnished, casual Singapore street kitchen that hopes to introduce Danes and visitors to the vibrant tastes, smells and colours of the Paranakan kitchen – considered a melting pot of Asian cuisine – in a shared dining experience.

Bankeråt ⓦⓦ
Café **Map** 1 A5
Ahlefeldtsgade 27–29, 1359 Cph
Tel *33 93 69 88*
Though its name means "bankrupt", this is one of the area's most long-standing cafés. It is famed for its display of stuffed animals in home-made outfits and the local atmosphere. There's a good range of European newspapers to enjoy.

B'india ⓦⓦ
Indian **Map** 1 B1
Blegdamsvej 130, 2100 Cph Ø
Tel *35 43 88 38*
A smart and stylish Indian restaurant where the focus is on healthy, delicious dishes and subtlety of flavour. Vegetarian and children's menus are available, as well as changing weekly specials.

BioMio ⓦⓦ
Organic
Halmtorvet 19, 1700 Cph V
Tel *33 31 20 00*
The ultimate organic restaurant, a self-styled "people's kitchen" where guests dine communally at long tables in a renovated Bosch warehouse (the neon sign outside has been kept for posterity). There are plenty of vegetarian options.

Carte Blanche
French   Map 2 D3
Dag Hammarskjolds Alle 1B, 2100 Cph1 Ø
Tel *35 43 31 25*
This well-established, rather low-key French restaurant in the diplomatic district of Østerbro is ideal for a romantic dinner. The decor is charmingly old-fashioned and the menu majors on classic French dishes.

Cofoco
Danish-European
Abel Cathrines Gade 7, 1654 Cph V
Tel *33 13 60 60*   **Closed** *Sun*
The first restaurant of what is now a citywide chain, Cofoco radicalised Copenhagen's dining scene in 2004 by offering simple, quality dining at affordable prices. The menu consists of a variety of starter-sized dishes.

DK Choice

Enomania
Italian
Vesterbrogade 187,
1800 Frederiksberg C
Tel *33 23 60 80*   **Closed** *Sat–Mon; dinners Tue & Wed*
Located at the far end of Vesterbro, this cosy Italian restaurant and wine bar seats just 25, and is characterised by a passion for both food and wine. With its excellent reputation, reservations are advised.

Granola
Café
Værnedamsvej 5, 1819 Frederiksberg
Tel *33 25 00 80*
Entering this café is like walking through a time warp – the nostalgic diner has faithfully recreated a kitsch 1930s universe open for breakfast, lunch and dinner. Dishes on offer range from breakfast porridge to steak Parisienne.

Höst
New Nordic   Map 1 A5
Nørre Farimagsgade 41, 1364 Cph
Tel *89 93 84 09*
A New Nordic restaurant aimed at appealing to a broader audience with raw wooden furnishings and a seasonally changing set menu as well as à la carte. It is over two levels – street and basement.

Kaffesalonen
Café
Peblinge Dossering 6, 2200 Cph N
Tel *35 35 12 19*
A popular, long-established café with a fairly standard menu that is notable for its location on the lakes and terrace of outdoor tables, as well as its nostalgic, American diner vibe.

Kødbyens Fiskebar
Seafood
Flæsketorvet 100, 1711 Cph V
Tel *32 15 56 56*
This casual seafod joint in one of Kødbyen's typical white and blue buildings, serves freshly caught fish, shellfish (and meat/vegetarian options) of very high quality. It serves perhaps the best fish and chips in the city.

Mother
Italian
Høkerboderne 9–15, 1712 Cph V
Tel *22 27 58 98*
This trendy Kødbyen pizzeria serves top-quality, sourdough pizzas made with ingredients direct from Italy and cooked in a wood-fired oven. Delicious Italian antipasti, pastas and desserts are available too. The weekend brunches and weekday breakfasts are popular.

Pony
New Nordic
Vesterbrogade 135, 1620 Cph V
Tel *33 22 10 00*   **Closed** *Mon*
A more relaxed, bistro edition of Kadeau Copenhagen, which has moved out to Christianshavn. Pony offers simple dishes from the New Nordic kitchen with the focus – though not exclusively – on Bornholm produce.

Radio
New Nordic
Julius Thomsens Gade 12, 1632 Cph
Tel *25 10 27 33*   **Closed** *Sun, Mon, lunch) Tue–Thu*
An informal New Nordic restaurant that won't leave you out of pocket. Radio offers seasonal, locally grown produce in innovative but simple vegetable, fish and meat dishes. The wooden decor is minimalist but inviting.

Wokbaren Spicylicious
Thai/Vietnamese
Halmtorvet 10, 1700 Copenhagen V
Tel *33 31 13 11*
This brightly coloured, youthful Asian eatery has merged with Wokbaren in premises on Halmtorvet Square. The menu is a mixture of Thai and Vietnamese cuisine, prepared as vibrantly as the restaurant decor.

Frederiks Have
Scandinavian
Smallegade 41, 2000 Frederiksberg
Tel *38 88 33 35*   **Closed** *Sun*
A pleasant restaurant near Frederiksberg Runddel that's ideal for a romantic dinner, especially on a warm summer evening when the covered courtyard is open. It is pleasantly formal, with the focus on the Scandinavian kitchen.

Mêlée
French
Martensens Allé 16, 1828 Frederiksberg
Tel *35 13 11 34*   **Closed** *Sun, Mon*
A French bistro restaurant on a side street of Gammel Kongevej that honours the classic French kitchen with simple dishes, desserts and fine wines. It focuses on offering quality yet relaxed dining.

Nose2Tail
Organic
Flæsketorvet 13A, 1711 Cph V
Tel *33 93 50 45*   **Closed** *Sun*
Inspired by similar ventures in the UK, this white-tiled, basement restaurant in the meat-packing district is surprisingly warm and inviting. Every part of the free-range, locally sourced meat is used, "from nose to tail".

Romantic courtyard dining at Frederiks Have

Relæ ⓀⓀ
New Nordic
Jægersborggade 41, 2200 Cph N
Tel *36 96 66 09* **Closed** *Sun–Tue*
Ex-Noma chef Christian Pugsili's
Michelin-starred gourmet
restaurant attracts discerning
diners, despite its offbeat
location in Nørrebro. Organic
and seasonal set menus only are
served in the tiny basement
premises. There is always a
vegetarian and a meat option.

Northwestern Zealand

CHARLOTTENLUND: Café Jorden Rundt ⓀⓀ
Café **Road Map** F4
Standvejen 152, 2920 Charlottenlund
Tel *39 63 73 81*
In a carousel-shaped building
from the 1930s that was once
the public toilets, this eatery
serves typical, though mostly
organic, café fare, but its real
draw are the sea views from its
glass façade.

CHARLOTTENLUND: MASH Skovridderkroen ⓀⓀⓀ
Steakhouse **Road Map** F4
Strandvejen 235, 2920 Charlottenlund
Tel *33 13 93 00*
A countryside edition of the
popular Copenhagen steak-
house chain (MASH stands for
Modern American Steakhouse).
In an old inn between forest and
sea, the decor here is stylish
and modern, with lots of
red leather.

FREDENSBORG: Asminderød Kro ⓀⓀ
Danish **Road Map** F4
Asminderødgade 53, 3480 Fredensborg
Tel *48 48 00 02* **Closed** *lunch: Sun–Wed; dinner: Sun–Mon*
Traditional lunch and evening
restaurant in the historic setting
of a 17th-century coaching inn.
Renovated and modernised, the
inn offers classic Danish dishes
and friendly service.

FREDERIKSSUND: Restaurant Toldboden ⓀⓀ
European **Road Map** F4
Færgevej 1A, 3600 Frederikssund
Tel *28 80 36 00*
Ⓦ toldboden.nu
Found right on the harbour,
this restaurant offers ambitious
dishes inspired by both the
French and Danish kitchen.
A casual vibe inside, and guests
can dine outside outside in
the summer.

FREDERIKSVÆRK: Restaurant Tinggården ⓀⓀⓀ
French **Road Map** F4
Frederiksværkvej 182, 3300 Frederiksværk
Tel *48 71 22 35* **Closed** *Mon, Tue; Wed (Nov–Apr); open daily mid-Jul–mid-Aug (book ahead)*
Dine in an old (1702) farmhouse
between Helsinge and
Frederiksværk that divides its
tables between three small rooms
and, in summer, the cobbled
yard. Seasonal dishes are inspired
by the rustic French kitchen.

GILLELEJE: Casablanca ⓀⓀ
North African **Road Map** F4
Smidstrup Strandvej 14, 3250 Gilleleje
Tel *48 35 44 77* **Closed** *Oct–Apr; Sun evening*
Located on the coast road between
Gilleleje and Rågleje, Casablanca
is both restaurant, café and shop
selling Moroccan and Spanish
handicrafts. The speciality is the
Moroccan tagine, which can be
enjoyed in the garden in summer.

GILLELEJE: Brasseriet Gilleleje Havn ⓀⓀⓀ
Danish-French **Road Map** F4
Nordre Havnevej 3, 3250 Gilleleje
Tel *48 30 21 30*
Modern-looking eatery with
great views over the harbour
serving *smørrebrød* and other
Danish classics from its first floor
or outdoor terrace. There's no
shortage of fresh fish as the place
is owned by a fishmonger.

HELSINGØR: Spisehuset Kulturværftet Ⓚ
New Nordic Café **Road Map** F4
Allegade 2, 3000 Helsingør
Tel *49 28 37 51*
The café of the "Culture Yard", an
initiative in Helsingør's former
shipyard, boasts innovative
architecture and a seasonal,

Spartan interior at New Nordic
restaurant Relæ

New Nordic-inspired menu.
Organic and tasty burgers are on
offer, alongside sandwiches,
cakes and great fish and chips.

HELSINGØR: Amici Miei ⓀⓀ
Italian **Road Map** F4
Stengade 15, 3000 Helsingør
Tel *49 26 26 71*
A long-standing and popular
Italian restaurant in one of
Helsingør's oldest streets. The
café serves an excellent
lunchtime brunch menu, while
the evening menu focuses on
classic Italian pasta, pizza, meat
and fish dishes.

HELSINGØR: Madame Sprunck ⓀⓀ
European **Road Map** F4
Bramstræde 5, 3000 Helsingør
Tel *49 26 48 49*
There is both a café and a restaurant
in this centrally located, combined
hotel-eatery-cocktail lounge with
casual dining in the café and a more
formal setting in the restaurant of
this historic building.

HILLERØD: Spisestedet Leonora Ⓚ
Smørrebrød **Road Map** F4
Frederiksborg Slot, Møntportvej 2, 3400 Hillerød
Tel *48 26 75 16* **Open** *lunch only*
Frederiksborg Slot's restaurant is
located in what was once the
castle stables. The views over the
lake from the terrace in summer
are especially enjoyable over a
traditional *smørrebrød* lunch.

HILLERØD: Il Gallo Nero ⓀⓀⓀ
Italian **Road Map** F4
Torvet 1, 3400 Hillerød
Tel *48 24 35 33*
This upmarket, authentic Italian
is not far from the castle lake
and has quickly developed
a reputation with locals and
foodies alike. Four course set
menus available; booking advised.

HOLBÆK: SuRi ⓀⓀⓀ
Seafood **Road Map** E4
Havnevej 5, 4300 Holbæk
Tel *59 44 06 10* **Closed** *Sun*
Situated directly on the
rejuvenated Holbæk harbour
in an eye-catching wood and
glass building, SuRi is both a
fishmongers and a gourmet
seafood restaurant with high
ambitions on the culinary front.

HORNBÆK: Hornbæk Bodega ⓀⓀ
Smørrebrød **Road Map** F4
A.R. Friis Vej 10, 3100 Hornbæk
Tel *49 20 00 30* **Closed** *Mon*
A popular meeting place in the
1970s and 1980s, this eatery

reopened in 2016 with a nostalgic nod to Hornbæk's glamourous past. Serves the classic Danish *smørrebrød* or check out the *Dagens Ret* on the chalkboard.

HORNBÆK: Restaurant Olivia ⓚⓚⓚ
European **Road Map** F4
Havnevej 1, 3100 Hornbæk
Tel *49 76 11 77* **Closed** *Sun dinner, Mon*
Romantic, seaside eatery in the centre of resort town Hornbæk, inspired by Provençal cooking and decor. The patio garden is an especially pleasant spot for dining, while indoors, the decor is bright and airy.

DK Choice

HØRVE: Dragsholm Slot ⓚⓚⓚ
(ⓚⓚ in eatery)
Danish-European **Road Map** F4
Dragsholm Alle, 4534 Hørve
Tel *59 65 33 00* **Closed** *Sun, Mon, Tue (Sep–Jun), Wed (Sep–May), Thu (Nov–Mar)*
The gourmet Castle Kitchen at Dragsholm (also a hotel) attracts some of Denmark's best chefs and has lofty ambitions, not only culinary but also in highlighting its history and location, in a 17th-century castle, with atmospheric decor and locally-produced cuisine. Reservations are necessary.

HUMLEBÆK: Bolettes Gæstebud ⓚⓚ
Danish-French **Road Map** F4
Gl. Strandvej 7, 3050 Humlebæk
Tel *49 19 45 00* **Closed** *Sun, Mon*
Traditional *kro* restaurant serving classic Danish and French dishes with fresh fish and a daily menu. Enjoy a typical *smørrebrød* lunch on the pleasant terrace in summer, or a candlelit evening meal in cooler seasons.

HUMLEBÆK: Restaurant Sletten ⓚⓚⓚ
Danish-European **Road Map** F4
Gl. Strandvej 137, 3050 Humlebæk
Tel *49 19 13 21* **Closed** *Sun, Mon*
Sletten is run by the same team as gourmet restaurant Formel B in Copenhagen, but with an à la carte menu and cheaper prices. It has direct views of the Øresund and the dishes are exquisite.

JÆGERSPRIS: Gerlev Kro ⓚⓚ
Danish **Road Map** F4
Bygaden 4, 3630 Jægerspris
Tel *47 52 21 74*
This charming, thatched country inn close to Frederikssund golf

club might not actually have the historic heritage it suggests, but more than makes up for it in its warm welcome and traditional home-cooked meals.

KALUNDBORG: Hotel Ole Lunds Gaard ⓚⓚ
Danish **Road Map** E4
Kordilgade 1–3, 4000 Kalundborg
Tel *59 51 01 65* **Closed** *Sep–Mar: Sat*
A popular hotel restaurant close to Kalundborg's harbour that serves generous portions of classic Danish dishes and holds regular "family nights" on Fridays. The hotel courtyard is opened to diners in summer.

KLAMPENBORG: Den Gule Cottage ⓚⓚ
Danish-European **Road Map** F4
Strandvejen 506, 2930 Klampenborg
Tel *39 64 06 91* **Closed** *late Dec– late Feb.*
On the coastal road north of Copenhagen are two delightful country cottages, both restaurants. This – the yellow one – is the least formal of the two, offering upmarket yet relaxed dining in a romantic setting.

KONGENS LYNGBY: Brede Spisehus ⓚⓚⓚ
Danish-French **Road Map** F4
I.C. Modewegs Vej, 2800 Kgns. Lyngby
Tel *45 85 54 57* **Closed** *dinner Mon & Sun*
Lake views and a historic setting combine in a former canteen for local factory workers, which has been restored by the Nationalmuseet and is now part of Frilandsmuseet. The kitchen is surprisingly upmarket, and its dishes delicate and refined. The old-world charm of the interiors is complemented by the friendly and warm service.

Snekken restaurant in the harbour that overlooks Roskilde Fjord

KORSØR: Madam Bagger ⓚⓚ
Danish-French **Road Map** E5
Havnegade 17B, 4220 Korsør
Tel *58 37 01 49* **Closed** *Sun*
This traditional, historic restaurant is named after Korsør's beloved innkeeper, who fed its hungry residents during the 1700s and 1800s. Lunches are traditionally Danish, while in the evening, the focus is on the French-Danish kitchen.

ROSKILDE: Café Satchmo ⓚ
Café **Road Map** F4
Rosenhavestræde 2, 4000 Roskilde
Tel *46 35 03 15* **Closed** *Sun (except in Dec)*
Down a side street from Roskilde's main walking street, Café Satchmo is a pleasant café with a quiet back courtyard open in summer. It serves sandwiches, snacks and cakes, as well as a lunchtime brunch.

ROSKILDE: Snekken ⓚⓚ
New Nordic **Road Map** F4
Vindeboder 16, 4000 Roskilde
Tel *46 35 98 16*
Next to the Vikingeskibsmuseet, Snekken has teamed up with the museum on a menu of contemporary "Viking" cuisine, prepared only with those ingredients available to Vikings but using modern methods for a different yet delicious meal.

ROSKILDE: Mumm ⓚⓚⓚ
Scandinavian-French **Road Map** F4
Karen Olsdatters Stræde 9, 4000 Roskilde
Tel *46 37 22 01* **Closed** *Sun*
One of Roskilde's oldest restaurants, Mumm is tucked away on a small side street and seats just 40. The changing, seasonal menu comprises many smaller dishes, of which several can be combined for a blow-out dining experience.

For more information on types of restaurants *see pages 256–7*

SØLLERØD: Søllerød Kro ⓀⓀⓀ
French-European   **Road Map** F4
Søllerødvej 35, 2840 Holte
Tel *45 80 25 05*   **Closed** *Mon, Tue*
Michelin-starred Søllerød Kro offers
gourmet dining experiences in a
refurbished, 17th-century inn.
With views of the village pond,
a church and surrounded by
dense woods, it is not to be
missed. Set meals only;
reservation necessary.

**SORØ: Støvlet
Katrines Hus** ⓀⓀⓀ
Danish-European   **Road Map** E5
Slagelsevej 63, 4180 Sorø
Tel *57 83 50 80*   **Closed** *Sun, Mon;
middle 2 weeks in Jul*
Named after a distinguished
resident of the house, Støvlet
Katrine (1745–1805). The decor is
simple yet romantic and the gour-
met French-Danish kitchen offers
both set and à la carte menus.

**TISVILDELEJE: Den
Røde Tomat** Ⓚ
Pizza   **Road Map** F4
Hovedgaden 45, 3220 Tisvildeleje
Tel *48 70 45 46*
An informal pizzeria in what
has become a rather exclusive
seaside resort. Offers delicately
baked pizzas and sandwiches, as
well as selected wines and other
Italian imports from its deli counter.

Southern Zealand

KØGE: Café T Ⓚ
Café   **Road Map** F5
Nyportsstræde 17, 4600 Køge
Tel *60 17 27 65*   **Closed** *Sun*
Cosy, nostalgic coffee shop and
tea rooms serving home-made
cakes and waffles as well as
breakfasts. If you like the look of
the antique chair you're sitting
on, you can buy that too.

KØGE: Christians Minde ⓀⓀ
Chinese/Danish   **Road Map** F5
Brogade 7, 4600 Køge
Tel *56 63 68 56*
An interesting mix of traditional
Danish dishes and Chinese food
is served in this well-established
eatery in the centre of Køge.
At lunchtime enjoy open
sandwiches outside on the
cobbled square.

KØGE: Vallø Slotskro ⓀⓀⓀ
Scandinavian-French
     Road Map F5
Slotsgade 1, 4600 Køge
Tel *56 26 62 66*   **Closed** *Sun–Tue*
The gourmet kitchen of this
elegant castle restaurant serves
monthly changing menus based

on seasonal local produce. All
dishes are starter-sized; order
as many as you feel like.
Reservations are advised.

MARIBO: Restaurant B ⓀⓀ
European   **Road Map** E6
Vesterbrogade 23, 4930 Maribo
Tel *54 78 10 08*   **Closed** *Sun*
A popular restaurant with a
reliable menu, "B" offers good
quality steaks as well as more
adventurous seasonal
set menus in pleasant and
spacious surroundings.

NÆSTVED: Rådhuskroen ⓀⓀ
Danish   **Road Map** E5
Skomagerrækken 8, 4700 Næstved
Tel *55 72 01 56*   **Closed** *Sun*
One of Næstved's oldest
restaurants, this historic inn by
the town hall has retained its
atmosphere and tradition. It
offers an overwhelmingly Danish
menu, but with vegetarian
options available. There's pleasant
courtyard dining in summer.

**NÆSTVED: Restaurant
Ronni** ⓀⓀ
Thai   **Road Map** E5
Østergade 4, 4700 Næstved
Tel *55 73 45 64*
With vibrant red walls and plenty
of gold-coloured Buddhas, Ronni
offers inexpensive and authentic
Thai cuisine in the centre of town.
The service is efficient and friendly.

**NAKSKOV: Hotel
Skovriddergaarden** ⓀⓀ
Danish-European   **Road Map** E6
Svingelen 4, 4900 Nakskov
Tel *54 92 03 55*   **Closed** *Sun*
A hotel and restaurant surrounded
by woodland on the outskirts of
Nakskov, with an outdoor terrace
in summer. Despite the unassuming
facade, there is a surprisingly
varied menu card, including
vegetarian and organic options.

**NYKØBING F: Restaurant
Vinkælderen** ⓀⓀ
European   **Road Map** F6
Slotsgade 22, 4800 Nykøbing F.
Tel *54 85 09 10*   **Closed** *Sun, Mon*
In historic basement premises in
central Nykøbing, this stylishly
furnished, family-run restaurant
(previously La Comida) offers
seasonally changing a la carte
dishes from fresh locally sourced
produce.

NYSTED: The Cottage ⓀⓀ
Scandinavian   **Road Map** E6
Skansevej 19, 4880 Nysted
Tel *54 87 18 87*   **Closed** *Sun–Tue;
Dec–mid-Feb*
This charmingly romantic hotel
restaurant dating from 1908 is

Den Røde Tomat, in the seaside resort
of Tisvildeleje

located in an idyllic woodland
setting not far from the town
beach. The seasonal menus are
freshly prepared using locally
sourced produce.

**RINGSTED: Ferdinands
Bøfhus** ⓀⓀ
Steakhouse   **Road Map** E5
Nørregade 31–33, 4100 Ringsted
Tel *57 67 67 20*
This family-friendly steakhouse
is pleasantly decorated and
is a favourite with locals. The
extensive meny also offers pasta,
burgers and kids' meals, plus an
all-you-can eat brunch buffet
on Sundays.

RINGSTED: Raadhuskroen ⓀⓀ
Danish   **Road Map** E5
Sct. Bendtsgade 8, 4100 Ringsted
Tel *57 61 68 97*
This very traditional Danish
restaurant inn serves *smørrebrød*
lunches, juicy dinnertime fish
plates and a wide variety of
steaks (six different kinds). It's
a popular choice with locals.

**SAKSKØBING: Hotel
Saxkjøbing** ⓀⓀ
New Nordic   **Road Map** E6
Torvet 9, 4990 Sakskøbing
Tel *54 70 40 39*
Run by New Nordic food pioneer
Claus Meyer, the kitchen of this
hotel restaurant creates innovative
and exciting menus using produce
sourced from Lolland-Falster and
the surrounding islands.

STEGE: David's Ⓚ
Café   **Road Map** F6
Storegade 11, 4780 Stege
Tel *33 18 80 57*
In a striking glass house on
Stege's high street, this
lunchtime café serves quality
French-inspired dishes made
with fresh local produce, in a

pleasant setting with views of
the old church tower from its
cosy courtyard.

STEGE: Kaffehuset Møn Ⓚ
Café **Road Map** F6
Storegade 48, 4780 Stege
Tel *31 44 49 14* **Closed** *Nov–Mar*
Primarily a micro-roastery
that sells its own gourmet
coffee and tea blends, this
excellent coffee shop also
serves tasty breakfasts and
lunches in the pleasant setting
of the old apothecary.

DK Choice

VORDINGBORG:
Babettes ⓀⓀⓀ
Danish-French **Road Map** F6
Kildemarksvej 5,
4760 Vordingborg
Tel *55 34 30 30* **Closed** *Sun–Tue;*
last 2 weeks Jul; Dec–early Jan
This well-established, award-
winning gourmet restaurant
is known and respected as
one of the country's best
eateries. With the same kitchen
team since 1991, its solid
reputation is based on quality
seasonal and locally sourced
produce, predominantly
organic, deliciously refined
dishes and the simple yet
elegant surroundings.

Funen

ÆRØSKØBING: Restaurant
Mumm ⓀⓀ
Danish **Road Map** D6
Søndergade 12, 5970 Ærøskøbing
Tel *62 52 12 12* **Closed** *Sun, Mon*
A popular restaurant in an
atmospheric old building
next to Ærøskøbing's town
square, Restaurant Mumm
brings the best of modern
Danish cooking. The garden
courtyard is especially pleasant
in summer. House specialities
include freshly caught plaice
and teriyaki steak.

KERTEMINDE: Rudolf
Mathis ⓀⓀⓀ
Danish-French **Road Map** D5
Dosseringen 13, 5300 Kerteminde
Tel *65 32 32 33* **Closed** *Sep–Apr:*
Sun–Mon, Jan–Feb: Tue
The two white-painted
smokehouses of this gourmet
fish restaurant are a landmark in
the small town of Kerteminde.
A long-standing fixture on the
harbour, Rudolf Mathis offers the
best and the freshest seafood in
or around the area.

MILLINGE: Falsled Kro ⓀⓀⓀ
Danish-French **Road Map** D5
Assensvej 513, 5642 Millinge
Tel *62 68 11 11* **Closed** *Sun–Mon*
(Sep–Apr); Tue (Jan–Feb)
This romantic country idyll up the
coast north of Faaborg attracts
some of Denmark's top chefs.
Menus are planned around the
culinary calendar using local
produce; the brasserie lunch is
considerably cheaper.

MUNKEBO: Munkebo Kro ⓀⓀ
Danish **Road Map** D5
Fjordvej 56, 5330 Munkebo
Tel *65 97 40 30*
Set in a historic, half-timbered
inn overlooking the fjord, this
restaurant has a long-standing
gourmet reputation, though
the menu respects the traditional Danish kitchen over
innovative experimentation.

NYBORG: Lieffroy ⓀⓀⓀ
Danish-French **Road Map** D5
Skrædderggyden 34, 5800 Nyborg
Tel *65 31 24 48* **Closed** *Sun, Mon*
One of Funen's best restaurants
is situated right on the waterfront
in an idyllic rural setting.
Although the gourmet kitchen is
primarily French, ingredients are
locally sourced.

ODENSE: No. 61 ⓀⓀ
Danish-French **Road Map** D5
Kongensgade 61, 5000 Odense C
Tel *61 69 10 35* **Closed** *Sun, Mon*
Beautifully simple brasserie-style
restaurant in a lovely old building
with exposed beams and raw
wooden tables. Seasonal menus
take the best of Danish produce
and French culinary tradition
without charging the earth.

ODENSE: Restaurant
Nordatlanten ⓀⓀ
New Nordic **Road Map** D5
Nordatlantiske Promenade 1,
5000 Odense C
Tel *22 39 76 00* **Closed** *Sun dinner*

A contemporary Scandinavian
restaurant that takes its standards
from gourmet French cooking,
applying them to ingredients
sourced in the North Atlantic
region. Enjoy harbour views from
the panoramic windows.

ODENSE: Sieu ⓀⓀ
Asian fusion **Road Map** D5
Østre Stationsvej 40, 5000 Odense C
Tel *66 12 88 89* **Closed** *Sun, Mon*
Exciting contemporary Asian
restaurant with stylish decor,
where Thai, Japanese, Chinese
and Vietnamese cuisines form
the basis of elaborately arranged
dishes served on spotlessly white
oval dinnerware.

ODENSE: Den Gamle Kro ⓀⓀⓀ
Danish-French **Road Map** D5
Overgade 23, 5000 Odense C
Tel *66 12 14 33*
Situated in a 17th-century half-
timbered house in Odense's
historic centre, the premises are
an attraction in themselves
(check out the courtyard, with
its rolling glass roof). The food,
however, is top-notch.

ODENSE: Goma ⓀⓀⓀ
Japanese **Road Map** D5
Kongensgade 66–68,
5000 Odense C
Tel *66 14 45 00* **Closed** *Sun*
This stylish and sophisticated
restaurant inspired by the Kaiseki
style is considered to be the "haute
cuisine" of Japanese cooking. The
attached cocktail lounge is equally
adventurous in its drinks menu.

ODENSE: Sortebro Kro ⓀⓀⓀ
New Nordic **Road Map** D5
Sejerskovvej 20, 5260 Odense S
Tel *66 13 28 26* **Closed** *Sun evening*
At the entrance to Den Fynske
Landsby, this historic coaching
inn, with its half-timbered exterior
and thatched roof, offers gourmet
dishes made from locally sourced
ingredients. Booking essential.

Traditional setting at micro-roastery Kaffehuset Møn, Stege

DK Choice

ODENSE: Under Lindetræet ⓚⓚⓚ
New Nordic   **Road Map** D5
Ramsherred 2, 5000 Odense C
Tel 66 12 92 86 **Closed** *Sun, Mon*
Neighbour to H C Andersens
Hus, this gourmet restaurant
in Odense's oldest quarter is
located in an atmospheric
building from the 1700s.
Aside from the luxurious and
delicate five- and seven-course
evening menus, a four-course
weekend brunch is also served.
Reservations are advised.

SVENDBORG: Restaurant Svendborgsund ⓚⓚ
Danish   **Map** D5
Havnepladsen 5, 5700 Svendborg
Tel 62 21 07 19
Traditional Danish lunches and
evening meals are served in
historic surroundings, not far from
Svendborg harbour. This eatery
dates back more than 300 years
and remains popular with locals.

Southern and Central Jutland

AARHUS: Café Gaya ⓚ
Organic   **Road Map** D4
Vestergade 43, 8000 Aarhus C
Tel 86 18 14 15   **Closed** *Sun*
At this organic café the majority
of dishes are vegan/vegetarian
and the focus is on healthy
eating. Salads, soups, hot dishes
and burgers are served, plus
brunch on Saturday and live
music every Friday.

AARHUS: Forlæns og Baglæns ⓚⓚ
Tapas   **Road Map** D4
Jægersgårdsgade 23, 8000 Aarhus C
Tel 86 76 00 70   **Closed** *Sun–Tue;
Wed (Jan–Feb)*
Cosy tapas bar with lively atmosphere serving great-tasting dishes
to suit both large and small
appetites. Guests are packed
together and communal dining
is encouraged. Cocktails are
served at weekends.

AARHUS: Kähler Spisesalon ⓚⓚ
Scandinavian   **Road Map** D4
M.P. Bruuns Gade 33, 8000 Aarhus C
Tel 86 12 20 53
Stylish café-bistro that's designed
to perfection – Kähler is a world-
renowned ceramics manufacturer.
The *smørrebrød* is especially
rated, but the menu also offers
weekend brunch and hot meals.

AARHUS: Pinden ⓚⓚ
Scandinavian   **Road Map** D4
Skolegade 29, 8000 Aarhus C
Tel 86 12 11 02   **Closed** *Sun*
A good, old-fashioned Danish
lunch and dinner restaurant that
serves traditional and classic
dishes in generous servings. The
decor shows a similar respect for
long-standing Danish traditions.

AARHUS: Frederikshøj ⓚⓚⓚ
New Nordic   **Road Map** D4
Oddervej 19, 8000 Aarhus C
Tel 86 14 22 80   **Closed** *Sun–Tue*
Frederikshøj's head chef, Wassim
Hallal, is uncompromising in his
search for the ultimate gastronomic
experience. Beautifully located in
woodland in Aarhus' Mindeparken.

AARHUS: FRÜDno16 ⓚⓚⓚ
Scandinavian   **Road Map** D4
Europaplads 16, 8000 Aarhus C
Tel 86 20 88 00   **Closed** *Sun–Tue*
A trendy "concept" restaurant
where guests purchase dining
club tickets and arrive at the
same time to enjoy an identical
three-course gourmet menu. It
offers modern, minimalist decor,
and views out across the harbour.

AARHUS: Mefisto ⓚⓚⓚ
Seafood   **Road Map** D4
Volden 28, 8000 Aarhus C
Tel 86 13 18 13
In an old building in Aarhus' Latin
Quarter, this informal seafood
restaurant serves high quality sea-
food, always beautifully presented.
An outside courtyard opens in
summer. The brunch is also popular.

AARHUS: Nordisk Spisehus ⓚⓚⓚ
New Nordic   **Road Map** D4
M.P. Bruuns Gade 31, 8000 Aarhus C
Tel 86 17 70 99   **Closed** *Sun*
An innovative and adventurous
contemporary restaurant that

Decor reflecting a regularly-changing
theme at Nordisk Spisehus

takes up a new theme each month.
It is inspired by the world's best
gourmet restaurants, but uses
New Nordic ingredients and ideals.

AARHUS: Restaurant Miro ⓚⓚⓚ
New Nordic   **Road Map** D4
Marstrandgade 2, 8000 Aarhus C
Tel 86 13 87 00   **Closed** *Sun, Mon*
This is the oldest gourmet
restaurant in Aarhus, still with the
same owner. Creative seasonal
menus featuring the finest Danish
inputs paired with a sophisticated,
global wine list.

ÅBENRÅ: Knapp ⓚⓚⓚ
Scandinavian   **Road Map** C6
Stennevej 79, Stollig, 6200 Aabenraa
Tel 74 62 00 92   **Closed** *Mon*
In a 19th-century watermill that
was restored in the 1980s as a
restaurant and hotel, Knapp is
surrounded by parkland and
is a popular retreat for wedding
parties. It serves gourmet regional
three- to six-course dinners and
is filled with antique furnishings.

EBELTOFT: Molskroen ⓚⓚⓚ
French-Danish   **Road Map** D3
*Hovedgaden 16, Femmøller Strand,
8400 Ebeltoft*
Tel 86 36 22 00   **Closed** *Sun*
This gourmet restaurant with a
strong reputation for exquisite
French-Danish dishes attracts
some of the country's best chefs.
Reservations are essential. For
less formal dining, check out the
adjacent Strandhotel Brasserie.

ESBJERG: Café Le Chi ⓚ
Asian   **Road Map** B5
Englandsgade 23, 6700 Esbjerg
Tel 75 12 02 38
Casual and friendly Asian café/
takeaway that also serves breakfasts and sandwiches as well as a
variety of more exotic dishes,
mostly Vietnamese. All are fresh,
tasty and reasonably priced.
There's an Asian kids' menu too.

ESBJERG: Hav & Bøf ⓚⓚ
Seafood/Steak   **Road Map** B5
Britanniavej 3, 6700 Esbjerg
Tel 76 11 90 00   **Closed** *Sun*
Located in an historic port
building from 1900, this
beautifully renovated restaurant
overlooks Esbjerg. The menu
features the best regional
seafood and beef served every
way imaginable, from surf and
turf to shrimp cocktails.

FREDERICIA: Ti Trin Ned ⓚⓚⓚ
New Nordic   **Road Map** C5
Norgesgade 3, 7000 Fredericia
Tel 75 93 33 55   **Closed** *Sun, Mon*
In the basement of a former
distillery, gourmet restaurant

Ti Trin Ned (Ten Steps Down) is imbued with calm and simplicity. Innovative, beautifully plated dishes made with local produce.

GRAM: Gram Slotskro
Scandinavian   **Road Map** C5
Slotsvej 52, 6510 Gram
Tel *74 82 16 14*
Built in 1714 and adjacent to Gram Castle, the largest medieval castle in Denmark outside of Copenhagen, the location has an overload of charm. Chef Carsten Schrøder adheres to the hallmarks of classic Danish cooking and uses regional inputs. Open breakfast and dinner.

DK Choice

HENNE: Henne Kirkeby Kro
Danish   **Road Map** B4
Strandvejen 234, 6854 Henne
Tel *75 25 54 00*   **Closed** *Sun–Tue; Wed dinner*
Michelin-starred chef Paul Cunningham, formerly of The Paul in Tivoli, is head chef in this gourmet idyll in the heart of the Jutland countryside. Seasonally-changing set menus are stunning in their simplicity, locally sourced – often from the vast kitchen garden – and inspired by the global kitchen. Booking ahead is necessary.

HERNING: Restaurant Baghuset
Tapas   **Road Map** C4
Bredgade 12, 7400 Herning
Tel *97 21 71 74*   **Closed** *Sun dinner*
This family-friendly tapas bar is simply decorated with a stone tiled floor and rough brick walls. The menu features vegetarian, fish and meat dishes, and there is also a tapas buffet on weekends.

HERNING: Flammen
BBQ
Søndergade 15, Herning
Tel *44 22 33 54*   **Closed** *Mon*
A laid-back, family-friendly spot with superb grilled meat ranging from steaks to wild boar served fresh off the flames. A short list of starters includes potato soup and Danish smoked salmon.

HORSENS: Café Dolly
Danish   **Road Map** C4
Havnen 15, 8700 Horsens
Tel *75 62 34 81*   **Closed** *Sun*
Cosy and traditional Danish café-restaurant in a 100 year-old red brick building by Horsens

Pale wood decor at Jutland restaurant Henne Kirkeby Kro

harbour. It is known for its green-and-white checked tablecloths and house speciality, *stegt flæsk* (fried bacon with parsley sauce).

HORSENS: Mackie's
American   **Road Map** C4
Graven 2, 8700 Horsens
Tel *75 60 16 22*
American diner complete with red leather bar stools and Americana collectibles hanging from the walls. It is a popular meeting place for the town's younger residents, with live music several times a month.

KOLDING: Den Gyldne Hane
Danish-French   **Road Map** C5
Christian 4 Vej 23, 6000 Kolding
Tel *75 52 97 20*   **Closed** *Mon & Tue dinners*
This idyllic Danish *kro* in a thatched house is one of Kolding's oldest, surrounded by parkland yet minutes from the town centre. The old-fashioned kitchen respects both Danish and French culinary traditions.

KOLDING: Nicolai Biograf & Café
Italian Café   **Road Map** C5
Skolegade 2A, 6000 Kolding
Tel *75 50 03 02*
A combined café and cinema with a mostly Italian menu and wide selection of tasty pizzas to eat in or take away. There's a popular weekend brunch and an all-you-can-eat buffet on Sunday evenings. Very family friendly.

RIBE: Kolvig
Danish   **Road Map** B5
Mellemdammen 13, 6760 Ribe
Tel *75 41 04 88*   **Closed** *Sun*
Both lunchtime café and evening restaurant, this former chicory factory from the 1600s overlooks Ribe river; the outside tables have lovely riverside

views. The good-quality, seasonal menus are based on locally sourced produce.

RIBE: Sælhunden
Scandinavian   **Road Map** B5
Skibbroen 13, 6760 Ribe
Tel *75 42 09 46*
Historically placed in a half-timbered listed building that's over 400 years old, with lovely views of the river, especially from the small courtyard. The cuisine is Danish, generously served.

SILKEBORG: Gastronomisk Institut
European   **Road Map** C4
Søndergade 20, 8600 Silkeborg
Tel *86 82 40 97*   **Closed** *Sun, Mon; last 2 weeks in Jul*
A gourmet restaurant in Silkeborg's centre offering both a changing seasonal menu and a more fixed à la carte menu. Rooted in the classic French culinary tradition, both the cuisine and decor are European in outlook.

SILKEBORG: Piaf
Danish-French   **Road Map** C4
Nygade 31, 8600 Silkeborg
Tel *86 81 12 55*   **Closed** *Sun, Mon; Jul*
This small, rather understated gourmet restaurant in Silkeborg's Latin Quarter features simple, romantic decor. Rooted in the classic French kitchen, locally sourced dishes take inspiration from across southern Europe.

SILKEBORG: Traktørstedet Ludvigslyst
Organic   **Road Map** C4
Julsøvej 248, Svejbæk, 8600 Silkeborg
Tel *86 88 80 40*   **Closed** *Mon, Tue (except in summer), Sun dinner*
Located in a lovely rural setting close to Himmelbjerget peak, the rustic surroundings and decor of this out-of-town retreat complement the organic, locally sourced menu.

For more information on types of restaurants *see pages 256–7*

VEJLE: Tortilla Flats ⓌⓌ
Mexican **Road Map** C4
Dæmningen 44, 7100 Vejle
Tel *75 72 42 22*
This centrally located Mexican restaurant is especially popular for local family parties. The extensive menu offers a wide variety of Mexican dishes, including starters, desserts and vegetarian dishes.

Northern Jutland

AALBORG: Mumbai Ⓦ
Indian **Road Map** C2
Kjellerups Torv 1, 9000 Aalborg
Tel *98 16 41 22*
Aalborg's only Indian restaurant and café, Mumbai is located in the modern culture house, Nordkraft. It serves authentic and spicy Indian cuisine, including a very cheap lunch menu and many vegetarian options.

AALBORG: Penny Lane Ⓦ
Café **Road Map** C2
Boulevarden 1, 9000 Aalborg
Tel *98 12 58 00* **Closed** *Sun*
Cute, nostalgic café, bakery and shop with a reputation for baking some of the best bread in town. It is popular with locals, who enjoy the cosy atmosphere over coffee or breakfast. Lunch-time salads are also served.

AALBORG: Duus Vinkælder ⓌⓌ
Café **Road Map** C2
Østergade 9, 9000 Aalborg
Tel *98 12 50 56* **Closed** *Sun*
Situated under the arches of the historic Jens Bang Stenhus (built 1624), Duus is ideal for people watching in the city centre. In summer you can enjoy a traditional Danish lunch or afternoon tea outside. In winter, the medieval cellar is a cosy spot for wine and snacks.

AALBORG: Fusion ⓌⓌ
Japanese-Danish **Road Map** C2
Strandvejen 4, 9000 Aalborg
Tel *35 12 33 31* **Closed** *Sun*
Enjoy exceptional views across the Limfjord and the city's waterfront from this stylish modern restaurant that fuses European and Asian cuisine in a healthy and flavoursome combination. There is also a takeaway sushi bar.

AALBORG: Pingvin ⓌⓌ
Tapas **Road Map** C2
Adelgade 12, 9000 Aalborg
Tel *98 11 11 66* **Closed** *Sun*
Café Pingvin calls itself a tapas bar having redefined the term to mean tapas-sized dishes from anywhere in the world. This casual, lively eatery also boasts an incredible selection of wines.

AALBORG: Prinses Juliana ⓌⓌ
Seafood **Road Map** C2
Vestre Havnepromenade 2, 9000 Aalborg
Tel *98 11 55 66* **Closed** *Sun*
Dine in Aalborg's harbour – literally – on this floating gourmet seafood restaurant on a former Dutch training ship that has been serving dinner guests for over 30 years. Upmarket Danish-French kitchen.

AALBORG: Søgaards Bryhus ⓌⓌ
Danish **Road Map** C2
C.W. Obels Plads 1A, 9000 Aalborg
Tel *98 16 11 14*
This micro-brewery restaurant serves classic lunches and main meals from the modern Danish kitchen in light and informal surroundings. There's also a tasty daily brunch.

DK Choice

AALBORG: Mortens Kro ⓌⓌⓌ
European **Road Map** C2
Mølleå 4, 9000 Aalborg
Tel *98 12 48 60* **Closed** *Sun*
This stylish gourmet restaurant is one of the most exclusive in Aalborg, and hardly what you would call a *kro*: its luxurious designer decor is more metropolitan than historic, its clientele international and its flamboyant owner an award-winning chef. The innovative kitchen is Danish with a global outlook.

AALBORG: Sangiovanni La Cantina ⓌⓌⓌ
Italian **Road Map** C2
Vingårdsgade 25A, 9000 Aalborg
Tel *98 11 37 55* **Closed** *Sun, Mon*
A gourmet Italian restaurant located in a wine cellar that has been run by the Volpi family since opening in 1988. Champions of "slow food", dishes made from scratch with the very best ingredients.

FREDERIKSHAVN: Frida ⓌⓌ
Danish **Road Map** D1
Havnegade 5, 9900 Frederikshavn
Tel *70 70 74 88* **Closed** *Sun–Tue*
This stylish-looking restaurant opened in 2014. Visit in daytime for a light lunch, or after 5:30pm when a buffet served directly from the grill includes a large choice of different fish and meats.

Valuted-ceiling dining room at Sangiovanni La Cantina, Aalborg

FREDERIKSHAVN: Katfizk ⓌⓌ
Seafood **Road Map** D1
Søsportsvej 12, 9900 Frederikshavn
Tel *33 21 88 88* **Closed** *Mon, Tue*
This marina café-restaurant serves a huge seafood buffet for both lunch and dinner, much of it freshly caught. Dine directly on the terrace or indoors in bright, fresh surroundings.

HJØRRING: Bryghuset Vendia ⓌⓌ
Danish-French **Road Map** D1
Markedsgade 9, 9800 Hjørring
Tel *98 92 22 29* **Closed** *Sun*
This upmarket restaurant in a micro-brewery is positioned in the centre of Hjørring. The restaurant has two sections: gourmet and brasserie, offering formal evening dining and casual walk-in visits respectively.

HJØRRING: Restaurant Kamii ⓌⓌ
Japanese **Road Map** D1
Springvandspladsen 2, 9800 Hjørring
Tel *98 93 11 11*
Centrally placed Japanese restaurant and sushi bar that serves high quality, authentic dishes at very reasonable prices, especially Tuesday's 200 Dkr sushi menu, both to eat in and take away. Kids' sushi menu too.

HOBRO: Theater Restauranten ⓌⓌ
Steakhouse **Road Map** C3
Theatertorvet 1, 9500 Hobro
Tel *98 52 17 00*
Despite its Vietnamese head chef and owner, this traditional restaurant and steakhouse prepares classic old school Danish lunches and evening meals from the carvery at very reasonable prices.

**HOLSTEBRO: Borbjerg
Mølle Kro** ⓦⓦ
Danish **Road Map** B3
Borbjerg Møllevej 3, 7500 Holstebro
Tel *97 46 10 10*
This historic lakeside inn about
8 km (5 miles) northeast of
Holstebro sits next to a working
water mill. The restaurant offers
quality, locally sourced dishes,
from the Danish and global
kitchens. Very family friendly.

**HOLSTEBRO: Under
Klippen** ⓦⓦⓦ
New Nordic **Road Map** B3
Lille Østergade 3, 7500 Holstebro
Tel *97 40 66 55* **Closed** *Sun*
Shadowed by a huge artificial
rock – Holstebro's modern art
folly – between a glass-panelled
office block and car park is this
gourmet restaurant, where
seasonal Danish produce is
cooked to perfection.

LØNSTRUP: Villa Vest ⓦⓦⓦ
New Nordic **Road Map** C1
Strandvejen 138, 9800 Hjørring
Tel *98 96 05 66* **Closed** *Sun–Tue
(spring & autumn); lunch Wed & Thu
(except summer); Oct–Mar*
At this gourmet restaurant located
directly overlooking the North
Sea at Lønstrup Strand, exquisite
three- to five-course set menus
only are carefully prepared with
locally sourced produce. Advance
booking only; seasonal opening.

**MARIAGER: Hotel
Postgaarden** ⓦⓦ
Danish **Road Map** D3
Torvet 6, 9550 Mariager
Tel *98 54 10 12*
In a half-timbered, listed building
from 1710, this coaching inn
is found on a cobbled street in
the centre of Mariager village. The
restaurant is open for lunch
and dinner and serves classic,
traditional Danish dishes.

RANDERS: Fladbro Kro ⓦⓦⓦ
Danish **Road Map** D3
Randersvej 75, 8920 Randers NV
Tel *86 42 02 10* **Closed** *Mon, Tue,
Sun dinner*
This gourmet restaurant in a
historic inn situated near the
bridge over the river Nørreå
offers an innovative seasonal
menu that includes everything
from locally sourced vegetables
to kangaroo fillet. It is inspired by
the "slow food" movement.

RANDERS: Fru Larsen ⓦⓦⓦ
New Nordic **Road Map** D3
Østergade 1, 8870 Langå
Tel *86 46 83 88* **Closed** *Sun, Mon*
In a village 16 km (10 miles)
southwest of Randers, the

award-winning head chef of hotel
and restaurant Fru Larsen creates
gourmet dishes with Nordic
ingredients. Four- or five-course
gourmet menus or a simpler à la
carte option are available.

RANDERS: Østergade 1 ⓦⓦⓦ
French **Road Map** D3
Østergade 1, 8900 Randers
Tel *86 43 02 55* **Closed** *Sun, Mon*
Stylishly decorated, French-
inspired gourmet restaurant with
both à la carte and all-inclusive
menus. Dining is fancy yet casual.
Very centrally-located and with
high gastronomic ambitions.

**SKAGEN: Nordens
Folkekøkken** ⓦⓦ
New Nordic **Road Map** D1
Havnevej 11, 9990 Skagen
Tel *53 53 82 50* **Closed** *Sun–Tue;
Sep–early Apr*
Skagen's branch of the New
Nordic "people's kitchen" in
Aarhus is open in the summer
season only. Seasonally changing
menus are chalked across the
blackboard wall. Diners here
enjoy top quality Nordic produce
and relaxed gourmet dining.

SKAGEN: Skagen Bryghus ⓦⓦ
Danish **Road Map** D1
Kirkevej 10, 9990 Skagen
Tel *98 45 00 50*
This brewery-restaurant serves a
variety of classic fish and meat
dishes chosen to complement
the selection of beer. It also
serves a Sunday lunch buffet,
holds live concerts and offers
guided brewery tours.

SKAGEN: Kokkenes ⓦⓦⓦ
Danish **Road Map** D1
Havneplads 20, 9990 Skagen
Tel *98 44 48 48* **Closed** *Sun–Tue
(Sep–Apr); also Wed (Oct–Feb)*
A traditional and romantic
evening restaurant serving high
quality French-Danish dishes

with a prime location right on
the harbour. It has many loyal
return guests.

SKAGEN: Ruth's Hotel ⓦⓦⓦ
New Nordic **Road Map** D1
Hans Ruths Vej 1, 9990 Skagen
Tel *98 44 11 24* **Closed** *Sun, Mon;
Tue & Wed (May, Jun & Sep); Tue–Thu
(Oct–Apr)*
This legendary seaside hotel has
an equally renowned gourmet
restaurant that prides itself on
regional cuisine of the highest
quality. More casual is its classic
French brasserie, where you can
dine on the large terrace.

**VIBORG: For Enden
af Gaden** ⓦⓦ
International **Road Map** C3
Sct. Mathiasgade 9, 8800 Viborg
Tel *86 60 05 00*
"At the End of the Street" is a
lively café-restaurant in a lovely
old townhouse spanning three
storeys and serving everything
from snacks and cakes to top-
notch three-course dinners. Kids'
and vegetarian options too.

VIBORG: Latinerly ⓦⓦⓦ
Steakhouse **Road Map** C3
Sct. Mathiasgade 78, 8800 Viborg
Tel *86 62 08 81* **Closed** *Sun*
Despite its historic cellar locale,
Latinerly – one of Viborg's oldest
restaurants – is a modern steak-
house and café-bar-nightclub that
attracts the town's younger residents.
There's live music every Friday.

**VIBORG: Niels
Bugges Kro** ⓦⓦⓦ
New Nordic **Road Map** C3
Ravnsbjergvej 69, 8800 Viborg
Tel *86 63 80 11*
Historic inn overlooking Hald Sø
a few miles south of Viborg, where
walking and cycling routes abound.
Top quality Nordic dishes are made
with regional produce, in either
the inn or the adjacent restaurant.

Fru Larsen, an historic restaurant in Randers

For more information on types of restaurants *see pages 256–7*

274 | TRAVELLERS' NEEDS

Bornholm

AAKIRKEBY:
Christianshøjkroen ⓚⓚ
New Nordic
Segensvej 48, 3720 Aakirkeby
Tel *56 97 40 13*   **Closed** *Mon–Wed & Jan*
Partly a training project for mentally handicapped adults, this gourmet restaurant offers lunchtime *smørrebrød* and delicate set menus that change daily, made with organic and regional produce, in an idyllic woodland setting.

DK Choice

AAKIRKEBY: Kadeau Bornholm ⓚⓚⓚ
New Nordic
Baunevej 18, Vestre Sømark, Pedersker, 3720 Aakirkeby
Tel *56 97 82 50*   **Closed** *Mon–Wed (in low season); Oct–Apr*
Located in a renovated beach pavilion on the very south of the island, this Michelin-starred restaurant is surrounded by sea, beach and forest. Its white furnishings are as fresh as the food, which is exclusively regional, exciting and innovative. The restaurant is open from spring to autumn only; booking ahead is advised.

ALLINGE: Nordbornholms Røgeri ⓚ
Seafood
Kæmpestranden 2, 3770 Allinge
Tel *56 48 07 30*   **Closed** *Oct–Apr*
One of two smokehouses in Allinge, NRK is located south of the harbour on the cliffs. Various types of smoked fish are available, as well as an extensive buffet. There are open grounds and great sea views.

ALLINGE: Det Gamle Posthus ⓚⓚ
Regional Danish
Kirkegade 8, 3770 Allinge
Tel *56 48 10 42*
This historic building has been many things as well as a post office, including a sweet makers and a book store. The ambience and decor are welcoming, and the quality food is prepared with respect for Bornholm cuisine.

ALLINGE: Margeritten ⓚⓚ
Steakhouse
Kirkeplads 1B, 3770 Allinge
Tel *56 48 22 09*   **Closed** *Dec, Jan*
Family-owned steakhouse and restaurant that serves classic meat and seafood dishes at reasonable prices, in the centre of Allinge. There are lots of kid-friendly options, including pizza.

ALLINGE: No.9 ⓚⓚ
Danish-French
Havnegade 9, 3770 Allinge
Tel *31 32 74 85*   **Closed** *Sun–Thu; Oct–Mar*
A pleasant summertime gourmet restaurant on the seafront in Allinge with a limited but considered menu. Regional Bornholm produce, inspired by both French and Danish kitchens, is combined with great service.

CHRISTIANSØ: Christiansø Kro og Gæstgiveri ⓚⓚ
Danish-French
Christiansø 10, 3760 Gudhjem
Tel *56 46 20 15*   **Closed** *Nov–Mar*
The sole restaurant on tiny Christiansø (as well as its shop and inn) serves generous portions from a seasonally-changing, French-infused menu that always includes plenty of fish. If visiting during the off-season, it's wise to call ahead.

GUDHJEM: Café Provianten ⓚ
Café
Ejnar Mikkelsensvej 28, 3760 Gudhjem
Tel *21 68 00 19*   **Closed** *Sun–Tue*
Harbour-placed café serving hot and cold drinks, large sandwiches and tapas plates during summer, when it opens in the evenings, all of it organic. On Wednesdays, seating is arranged at long tables and everyone sits down to eat together at 5:30pm.

GUDHJEM: Pandekagehuset ⓚ
Café
Brøddegade 15, 3700 Gudhjem
Tel *56 48 55 17*
The pancake house sells exactly that, and has done for over 20 years. These are not just for the kids, either, as both savoury filled pancakes and dessert versions are available at all times of the day.

GUDHJEM: Lassen's Restaurant ⓚⓚⓚ
New Nordic
Sdr. Strandvej 128, 3760 Gudhjem
Tel *56 48 42 10*   **Closed** *Mon (Oct–Jun); Sun & Tue (Oct–Apr); Wed (Apr)*
Stammershalle Badehotel's restaurant, perched on the cliffs between Allinge and Gudhjem, attracts some of Denmark's top chefs. Simple, Nordic dishes are made to perfection from regional produce. Reservation advised.

HASLE: Hasle Røgeri ⓚ
Seafood
Søndre Bæk 20, 3790 Hasle
Tel *56 92 20 02*   **Closed** *Oct–Mar*
Smoking is still done here using traditional methods in open stacks. Come early and you can watch the herring being smoked before eating it. The fish buffet lets you try some of everything.

HASLE: Le Port ⓚⓚⓚ
Danish-French
Vang 81, 3790 Hasle
Tel *56 96 92 01*   **Closed** *Sun, Mon; Tue–Wed (in low season); Jan–Feb & Nov*
One of Bornholm's most established gourmet restaurants, Le Port specialises in Danish and French classics. The popular summer terrace enjoys lovely sea views and fantastic sunsets.

NEXØ: Restaurant Culinarium ⓚⓚ
European
Havnen 4A, 3730 Nexø
Tel *56 44 33 61*   **Closed** *Sat lunch*
This fairly traditional restaurant on Nexø's harbour is open for both lunch and dinner, serving an assortment of *schnitzels*, steaks and fish dishes alongside German wines and beers.

NEXØ: Restaurant Molen ⓚⓚ
Scandinavian
Havnen 6, 3730 Nexø
Tel *88 87 67 33*
Located right on the harbour, this ambitious, high-end restaurant offers mouth-watering, changing menus inspired by the sea and local ingredients.

ØSTERMARIE: Fru Petersens Café ⓚ
Danish
Almindingensvej 31, 3751 Østermarie
Tel *21 78 78 95*   **Closed** *Mon–Tue (Jun & Sep–Oct); Wed (Oct); Nov–May*
A charming café-restaurant in a fabulous half-timbered house

Lassen's Restaurant located in Stammershalle Badehotel, Gudjem

Key to Price Guide *see page 262*

serving classic Danish cuisine "like grandma used to make". Furnished like a private home from a century ago, both the menus and decor aim at historical accuracy.

ØSTERMARIE: Hallegård Gårdbutik Ⓚ
Café-deli
Aspevej 3, 3751 Østermarie
Tel *56 47 02 47* **Closed** *Sat, Sun; Oct–Mar*
Enjoy tapas and other handmade delicacies from this farm shop that makes its own organic hot dogs on the premises with locally sourced pork. Guaranteed fresh produce out in the countryside.

RØNNE: Restaurant Texas Ⓚ
American
Store Torvegade 14, 3700 Rønne
Tel *56 91 10 09*
At this American-inspired café-restaurant, centrally placed in Rønne's pedestrian street, steaks, pizzas, burgers and chicken wings are on the menu, all reasonably priced. It can get lively at weekends and in the evenings.

RØNNE: Selma's Home Cooking Ⓚ
International
Tornegade 6, 3700 Rønne
Tel *56 95 34 75* **Closed** *Sun–Wed*
This small, rather hard to find restaurant is a good budget option, with both buffet and hot dishes inspired by the global kitchen. It is family friendly, with a big focus on vegetarian dishes.

RØNNE: MådaGo Ⓚ Ⓚ
Café
Store Torvegade 29, 3700 Rønne
Tel *28 77 60 40* **Closed** *Sun*
A small, popular café-restaurant on the main square offering a simple, refined menu. Good quality lunches (in high season) and dinners in a light, airy setting and calm yet casual ambience.

RØNNE: Restaurant Di 5 Stauerna Ⓚ Ⓚ Ⓚ
Danish-French
Strandvejen 116, 3700 Rønne
Tel *56 90 44 44*
Fredensborg Hotel's gourmet restaurant comprises five inter-connected rooms (hence the name), and offers an intimate, romantic dining experience. The regionally-sourced dishes are inspired by French and Danish cuisine.

RØNNE: Restaurant Victoria Ⓚ Ⓚ Ⓚ
New Nordic
Nordre Kystvej 34, 3700 Rønne
Tel *56 90 42 44* **Closed** *in summer; selected days in winter, call first*
A window table is highly recommended at Hotel Griffen's smart restaurant, where the sea views are a big draw. The restaurant's signature "Sunset Menu" makes use of regional produce and Nordic inspiration.

SNOGEBÆK: Æblehaven Ⓚ Ⓚ Ⓚ
Danish
Hovedgade 15, Snogebæk, 3730 Nexø
Tel *56 48 88 85* **Closed** *Mon; Tue & Wed (Oct–May)*
A cosy, family-run evening restaurant with a small but select menu, on the harbour of the quaint fishing village Snogebæk. The Danish-French kitchen is given an Asian twist thanks to chef Sophia's Thai heritage.

SVANEKE: Aarsdale Silderøgeri Ⓚ
Seafood
Gaden 2, 3740 Svaneke
Tel *56 49 65 08* **Closed** *Mon (May); Sun–Wed (Oct); Nov–Apr*
Traditional smokehouse south of Svaneke near Paradisbakkerne that's been smoking locally caught herring for over a century. Individual portions are served with potato salad or you can order the large fish platter.

SVANEKE: Røgeriet Ⓚ
Seafood
Fiskergade 12, 3740 Svaneke
Tel *56 49 63 24* **Closed** *late Oct–early Apr*
The smokehouse in the centre of Svaneke sells smoked fish of all varieties as well as fish cakes to

Diners enjoying meals outside smokehouse Røgeriet, Svaneke

eat on the wooden tables outside, with views out to Christiansø, or to take away.

SVANEKE: Svaneke Ismejeri Ⓚ
Ice cream parlour
Svaneke Torv 3, 3740 Svaneke
Tel *40 74 65 35* **Closed** *Oct–Apr*
Svaneke's ice cream is considered one of Denmark's best, made from local and organic ingredients. Take a tour of the production area or sit in the café and choose from the range of daily flavours.

SVANEKE: Syd-Øst for Paradis Ⓚ
Beach Café
Skovgade 34, 3740 Svaneke
Tel *50 70 42 48* **Closed** *Sep–May or in bad weather*
This former ice cream stand, now a thriving summer café, calls itself "chirinquito", which is Spanish for "beach café with tapas". The café's speciality is a grill-it-yourself paella.

SVANEKE: Louisekroen Ⓚ Ⓚ
Danish
Bølshavn 22, 3740 Svaneke
Tel *56 49 62 03* **Closed** *Oct–Apr*
Traditional, half-timbered inn situated on the coast between Svaneke and Gudhjem. The decor is retro and many of the guests have been coming every year for decades. It is known for its good Danish steaks.

SVANEKE: Svaneke Bryghus Ⓚ Ⓚ
Scandinavian
Svaneke Torv 5, 3740 Svaneke
Tel *56 49 73 21*
In an 18th-century merchant's house on Svaneke's town square, this award-winning micro-brewery has an excellent restaurant with an extensive à la carte menu. Dining can be combined with a guided tour of the brewery.

Greenland

ILULISSAT: Restaurant
Icefiord Ⓚ Ⓚ
European/Thai
Jørgen Sverdrupip Aqq. 10, 3952 Ilulissat
Tel *(+299) 94 44 80*
The restaurant of Hotel Icefiord
serves both a seasonal menu
dominated by steak and fish
(although it includes regional
specialities like home-smoked musk
ox) and a cheaper Thai menu.

ILULISSAT: Marmartut Ⓚ Ⓚ Ⓚ
Scandinavian
Sermermiut Aqq. 4, 3952 Iulissat
Tel *(+299) 94 51 00* **Closed** *Sun*
This small, wood-framed
restaurant seats 40 and offers
views over Disko Bay. Add a head
chef with an impressive, lengthy
CV and lots of local specialities
like freshly caught ammassak fish,
a staple of the Greenlandic diet.

ILULISSAT:
Restaurant Ulo Ⓚ Ⓚ Ⓚ
Scandinavian
*Aaron Mathiesenip Aqquserna
B-1128, 3952 Ilulissat*
Tel *(+299) 94 41 53*
Hotel Arctic's gourmet restaurant
has great views and an ambitious
kitchen, headed by one of
Greenland's top chefs. Choose
three courses from the locally-
sourced, seasonal menu or go all
out with the chef's tasting menu.

KANGERLUUSUAQ: Restaurant
Roklubben Ⓚ Ⓚ Ⓚ
Greenlandic
P.O. Box 49, 3910 Kangerlussuaq
Tel *(+299) 52 45 26*
A few miles from its nearest
settlement Kangerluusuaq, this
established restaurant on the shore
of Lake Ferguson may look like a
hut from outside, but it serves
good, nourishing Greenlandic
specialities. Book ahead.

NARSAQ: Restaurant Klara Ⓚ Ⓚ
European
Sarquanguaqvej B-819, 3921 Narsaq
Tel *(+299) 66 12 90*
This is the restaurant of Hotel
Narsaq and pretty much the only
place to eat in town. The menu
can be rather limited depending
on what's available in the kitchen
that day, but staff are helpful and
eager to please.

NARSARSUAQ: Restaurant
Narsarsuaq Ⓚ Ⓚ
International/Greenlandic
Hotel Narsarsuaq, 3923 Narsarsuaq
Tel *(+299) 66 52 53* **Closed** *Oct–May*
The à la carte restaurant of
Hotel Narsarsuaq in southern

Greenland serves both
international standards
and regional specialities, along
with various imported wines
and Greenlandic coffee.

NUUK: Café Katuaq Ⓚ
Café
Imaneq 21, 3900 Nuuk
Tel *(+299) 36 37 79* **Closed** *Sun
dinner*
The pleasant in-house café of
Nuuk's cultural centre serves
quality dishes with regional
specialities such as snowcrab at
good rates, as well as good brunch.

NUUK: IGGU Ⓚ
Pizzeria
Sipisaq Avannarleq 10, 3900 Nuuk
Tel *(+299) 32 95 55*
This pleasant, brightly decorated
pizzeria in the centre of Nuuk
offers pizzas and a small range
of pasta dishes. Toppings include
halibut and musk ox.

NUUK: Café Esmeralda Ⓚ Ⓚ
Café
Aqqusinersuaq 6, 1st floor, 3900 Nuuk
Tel *(+299) 32 90 05*
This modern-looking, inviting
café is one of few places in
Nuuk where you can get a
fairly standard green and healthy
breakfast, brunch or lunch,
most of it homemade with
freshly flown-in vegetables. Cocktails are served later in the evening.

NUUK: Charoen Porn Ⓚ Ⓚ
Thai
Aqqusinersuaq 5, 3900 Nuuk
Tel *(+299) 32 20 20*
A Thai restaurant and takeaway
that is surprisingly authentic,
though not overly spicy,
considering its polar location.
It also offers some regional
specialities, including the
Greenlandic coffee ritual and a
popular local version of sashimi.

NUUK: Restaurant Bryggen Ⓚ Ⓚ
Danish
Godthåb Bryghus, Imaneq, 3900 Nuuk
Tel *(+299) 34 80 80*
A centrally located brewery
restaurant which prides itself on
being able to offer Greenland's
biggest all-you-can-eat buffet.
The emphasis is on meat, with
exotic types available at weekends.
Wash it all down with one of the
brewery's own ales.

NUUK:
Hereford Beefstouw Ⓚ Ⓚ Ⓚ
Steak
Aqqusinersuaq 1, 3900 Nuuk
Tel *(+299) 32 42 22*
Hotel Hans Egede's other restau-
rant is one of a Danish-wide chain

Patrons enjoying the surroundings of
Café Esmeralda, in Nuuk

of reliable steakhouses. This one
surely has the best views of all of
them, overlooking the fiord on
the hotel's fifth floor.

DK Choice

NUUK: Sarfalik Ⓚ Ⓚ Ⓚ
Nordic
*Hotel Hans Egede,
Aqqusinersuaq1, 3900 Nuuk*
Tel *(+299) 32 42 22* **Closed** *Sun
dinner*
The gourmet "gathering place"
in Hotel Hans Egede is a world-
class, innovative restaurant
that has put Greenlandic
cuisine on the culinary map.
More adventurous guests can
try the local menu, where
delicacies include indigenous
flora as well as reindeer and
musk ox, or the (slightly) safer
global menu. Book ahead.

QARQORTOQ: Inbox Café –
A Little Thai Corner Ⓚ Ⓚ
Thai
Torvet B 163, 3920 Qaqortoq
Tel *(+299) 64 22 39* **Closed** *Sun*
A genuine Thai café-restaurant in
this south Greenland settlement,
placed directly on the town
square. Do try the Greenland
style-sushi as well. Take away is
also available.

QAQORTOQ: Steakhouse
Nanoq Ⓚ Ⓚ Ⓚ
Steakhouse
*Anders Olsens Vej,
3920 Qaqortoq*
Tel *(+299) 64 22 82*
The steak restaurant in Hotel
Qaortoq serves a wide range
of meats as well as Greenlandic
beer made with water from
melted icebergs. Diners can
enjoy excellent views over the
town's harbour.

Faroe Islands

EYUSTUROY: Gjaargardur ⓚ ⓚ
Scandinavian
Dalavegur 20, 476 Gjogv
Tel *(+298) 42 31 71* **Closed** *Nov–Feb; open for light lunches only in Oct & Mar*
Situated in an isolated but beautiful landscape, it's advisable to call the house restaurant of this eco hotel ahead of arrival to avoid disappointment, particularly on Sundays, when a hearty three-course lunch is served.

KLAKSVIK: Roykstovan ⓚ
Pub
Klaksviksvegur 41, 700 Klaksvik
Tel *(+298) 45 61 25*
Together with the parish church, this red-and-blue painted pub overlooking the fjord is one of the town's landmarks and popular with locals. It serves bar snacks and pub food such as soups and burgers.

KLAKSVIK: Restaurant Hereford ⓚ ⓚ ⓚ
Steakhouse
Klaksviksvegur 45, 700 Klaksvik
Tel *(+298) 45 64 34* **Closed** *Sun, Mon*
On the town's main street looking directly out onto the fjord, this wood-panelled restaurant is furnished with cosy booths. The menu ranges from steaks and fresh lamb to puffin and chateaubriand.

TÓRSHAVN: Etika ⓚ
Sushi
Áarvegur 3, 100 Tórshavn
Tel *(+298) 31 93 19*
This trendy and stylish sushi bar with a cool, colourful interior, offers sushi boxes to eat in or take away. Fresh fish is a must for good sushi, and the salmon here comes fresh from Faroese waters.

TÓRSHAVN: Irish Pub ⓚ
Pub
Grims Kambansgøta 13, 110 Tórshavn
Tel *(+298) 31 90 91* **Closed** *Sun*
Generous portions of traditional but inexpensive pub dinners and lunches are served in this casual Irish pub, as well as a wide range of Faroese beer.

TÓRSHAVN: Barbara Fish House ⓚ ⓚ
Seafood
Gongin 4–6, 100 Tórshavn
Tel *(+298) 33 10 10* **Closed** *Sun*
A charming seafood restaurant in Tórshavn's old quarter with historic atmosphere and nostalgic decor. Fish dishes are served in tapas-sized portions to be shared by all at the table.

TÓRSHAVN: Hvonn Brasserie ⓚ ⓚ
International
Tórsgøta 4, 100 Tórshavn
Tel *(+298) 35 00 35*
The first floor restaurant of the Hotel Tórshavn has an international kitchen and a massive choice. It is open all day for steaks, burgers, sandwiches, pasta, pizza and curries.

TÓRSHAVN: Aarstova ⓚ ⓚ ⓚ
New Nordic
Gongin 1, 100 Tórshavn
Tel *(+298) 33 30 00*
This innovative gourmet restaurant in a charming, listed building in Tórshavn's old town specialises in local produce and regional specialities, with three and five-course menus. Book ahead.

DK Choice

TÓRSHAVN: Koks ⓚ ⓚ ⓚ
New Nordic
Í Geilini 13, Kirkjubøur, 175 Torshavn
Tel *(+298) 33 39 99* **Closed** *Sun, Mon, Nov–Mar*
It's been dubbed the Faroese Noma; an innovative gourmet restaurant that invites its diners to experience the changing seasons of the Faroes through its local produce. With its "Roots and Branches" menus, Koks even collaborates with local biologists in finding new Faroese fauna and flora to use. Book ahead.

TÓRSHAVN: Raest ⓚ ⓚ ⓚ
Scandinavian
Gongin 8, 100 Tórshavn
Tel *(+298) 41 14 30* **Closed** *Sun–Tue*
'Raest' means fermented in Faroese, and that is exactly what is on offer: a menu composed exclusively of traditional Faroese fermented dishes, served in the restaurant's creaky, 400-year old building on tables made from reclaimed ships.

TÓRSHAVN: Restaurant 11 ⓚ ⓚ ⓚ
Scandinavian
Tórsgøta 11, 100 Tórshavn
Tel *(+298) 31 16 11* **Closed** *Sat lunch, Sun*
A centrally located, quality restaurant serving both Faroese and European dishes, all well presented. The lamb is especially recommended. It doesn't tend to get crowded, so the service is very attentive and friendly. An excellent lunch buffet is also served.

TÓRSHAVN: Restaurant Hafnia ⓚ ⓚ ⓚ
Scandinavian
Áarvegur 4–10, 100 Tórshavn
Tel *(+298) 30 80 00* **Closed** *Sat lunch*
On the first floor of the Hotel Hafnia overlooking the main street, this quality restaurant makes good and original use of Faroese produce. A traditional roast dinner is served on Sunday afternoons and holidays.

VIDAREIDI: Matstivan hja Elisabeth (Elisabeth's Restaurant) ⓚ ⓚ
Scandinavian
Eggjarvegur 13, 750 Viðareiði
Tel *(+298) 45 12 75* **Open** *mid-May–mid-Aug only*
Seating just 30, Elisabeth serves local specialities such as fresh fish, guillemot and the national dessert, rhubarb trifle. The traditional Faroese knits on display are for sale in the shop next door. Reservations are required due to limited seating.

An atttractive display of Faroese dishes at Restaurant Hafnia, Tórshavn

For more information on types of restaurants *see pages 256–7*

SHOPPING IN DENMARK

Most major towns in Denmark have large, shopping centres and department stores such as the country-wide chain Magasin du Nord. Prices can be high, however, especially in the more exclusive shops such as those found along Strøget in Copenhagen (see pp102–105). Cut-price clothing can be found, especially during seasonal sales. Flea markets are widespread in Denmark – much of what is on sale is junk, but persistence and a keen eye can sometimes uncover real treasures. Countless independently run shops sell beautiful household goods, which satisfy the Danes' love of good design, while jewellery made from Danish amber is also popular and relatively cheap. Herb-flavoured *akvavit* (a kind of schnapps) comes in a variety of flavours and colours and makes a good present.

Shoppers at Illums Bolighus, a famous Danish home goods store

Opening Hours

In Denmark shopping days and opening hours are regulated due to union demands for reasonable working hours. The regulated hours are, for the most part, rigorously adhered to, although during the Christmas season and around busy tourist resorts longer openings are usual. Most shops open at 10am and remain open until 6pm Monday to Thursday. On Fridays many shops are open until 7 or 8pm. On Saturdays most shops close at about 2pm; some larger shops and department stores remain open until 4pm. Most shops now also open on Sundays, though opening times vary from store to store.

Some smaller, independent shops keep longer opening hours. Stores attached to petrol stations and kiosks found in town centres remain open 24 hours but offer a limited choice of goods.

In the run-up to Christmas and other festivals many shops and department stores in the capital and in larger towns extend their opening hours and often trade on Sundays.

Methods of Payment

The country's currency is the Danish krone (Dkr). Some shops also accept the Swedish krone and the euro, although the rate of exchange applied in such cases may not be advantageous. A few of the smaller shops may expect payment in cash, however the vast majority of outlets accept credit cards. This method of payment carries a small surcharge.

VAT

The rate of VAT (known as MOMS) is 25 per cent in Denmark; this is always already included in the selling price quoted. Some goods, such as alcohol, tobacco and petrochemical products, carry an additional excise. Visitors from outside the EU can claim a tax refund of between 13 and 19 per cent of the total price of an item on purchases over 300 Dkr. Shops operating this scheme carry a Tax Free logo. When making a purchase ask for a Global Refund certificate. The shopkeeper may ask to see a passport. On leaving the country the certificate must be stamped by a customs officer, who will need to see that the product is intact in its original packaging. The stamped certificate may be used when reclaiming VAT in allocated banks or border agencies. For more information, visit *www. taxfreeworldwide.com*.

Seasonal Reductions

Reductions on many items can be obtained by shopping during the sales, which are known locally as "Udsalg". In Denmark, the traditional months for sales are January and June/July, although many

12th-century cellars being used for wine storage

Bolia, one of the most popular design stores

stores shift their dates by one or two weeks either way. Sales are also held to mark the anniversary of a shop's opening or even the founding of a chain. As with most promotions, it pays to be cautious, however, as reductions can often be quite insignificant or apply only to a limited number of goods.

What to Buy

Denmark is the home of applied design, and those looking for homewares are spoilt for choice by the vast array of ingenious, smart, unusual and extravagant items on offer. The Danes like to dress smartly too, without spending a fortune, so it is worth checking out the sales for good quality clothes and footwear at bargain prices. The best times are in July and January.

While all the high-profile international designer labels are available, one of the pleasures of shopping in Copenhagen is discovering unusual and unique items unavailable back home.

Markets

Produce markets are very popular in Denmark, often held twice weekly in most towns; one of the best is the upscale Torvehallerne market in Copenhagen (see p104). The Danes also relish their flea markets, which are held periodically in many towns. Genuine antiques are mixed up with piles of bric-à-brac. Pre-Christmas fairs are also common. Seasonal fairs sell a variety of festive decorations including handmade wooden or knitted items, candles and colourful elves and gnomes fashioned from balls of wool.

Contemporary Design

Denmark is famous for its cutting edge design of ceramics, contemporary furniture and home accessories. Copenhagen has a wealth of independent outlets, but many brands are available throughout the country. The price of such merchandise can be high, especially for items by major designers, but smaller, more affordable items are available such as glasses by Bodum, silver Christmas tree decorations by Georg Jensen, cheese cutters or small porcelain items.

Food Products

Many types of cheese are produced in Denmark so there is no excuse for sticking to a simple Danish blue. Those who like sharp-tasting cheeses should go for "Gamle Ole". This strongly flavoured cheese goes particularly well with Danish rye bread, a dense and healthy loaf made with seeds and grains.

For those with a sweet tooth, chocolates and sweets are also well worth seeking out. Often these are handmade and far superior to the mass-produced variety. Hand-made boiled sweets are also good quality.

One of the Danes' favourite foodstuffs is pickled herring, which is served on its own and often on bread as *smørrebrød*. Many different recipes are used when marinating the fish to produce a wide range of tastes. Smoked fish, especially from Bornholm, is also popular.

The southern region of Jutland is famous for its meat products, which include salamis of various flavours and seasonings.

Assorted coffee-related gadgets such as grinders and percolators are often on sale in coffee shops, which sell a bewildering range of roasted beans from around the world.

Alcoholic Drinks

While in Denmark it is worth sampling *akvavit* (a form of schnapps). Many regions, and even individual restaurants, have their own special recipes for these flavoursome drinks, which are then sold as *husets snaps*. Visitors can, for instance, savour an Aalborg Porse flavoured with Jutland herbs. As well as *akvavit*, Denmark produces some excellent beers (see p260). Some of the lesser known brands and dark beers make a welcome alternative to the ubiquitous light Pilsners (see p104).

An antique shop in Copenhagen

ENTERTAINMENT IN DENMARK

The year round range of cultural events and entertainment in Denmark reflects the Danish national spirit, and the seasons have an important effect on what's on. In spring and summer, Danes celebrate light and life outdoors with every imaginable sort of festival and performance – from Viking markets to amusement parks and rock festivals, there's a full agenda of creative events for all ages. In autumn, theatres launch new programmes of plays, dance and opera, which continue through winter when coziness is most needed, and the Danish concept of *hygge* is at its best. Every town has at least one Christmas market, with the star among them being Tivoli, which has amazing decorations, seasonal indulgences and live entertainment. For information on entertainment in Copenhagen see pp106–109.

The performance hall at Odense Koncerthus

Theatre, Music and Dance

A visit to the theatre is one of the most popular pastimes in Denmark. Cultural life blossoms throughout the country, and university towns, such as Aarhus, Aalborg and Odense, have much to offer.

Aarhus is the biggest cultural centre after Copenhagen and has the **Musikhuset Aarhus**, a modern concert hall with four venues that stages musical and dance performances. It is home to Den Jyske Opera (The Jutland Opera) and the Jutland Symphony. Aalborg, in northern Jutland, has the cultural centre Nordkraft and a resident symphony orchestra, which often gives concerts in the **Aalborg Kongres og Kulturcenter**.

In Odense, the **Odense Koncerthus** has a regular programme of classical music, which includes performances of music by Carl Nielsen (1865–1931), a native of the city.

Most large towns have a large hall for concerts, theatre, ballet and modern dance performances. During the summer, Denmark hosts a number of open-air concerts, often in the grounds of manor houses. People bring along picnics for an evening of opera or classical music. There are also several rock, pop and folk music festivals. Visit *www.visitdenmark.com* for more details of live music in Denmark.

Amusement Parks

Denmark's amusement parks provide entertainment for children and adults alike. The parks are open mainly in summer, although some of them start their season earlier. One of the most famous is **LEGOLAND®** in central Jutland *(see pp196–7)*, which includes LEGO® sculptures along with high-octane rides. As with many of Denmark's amusement parks, the admission price to LEGOLAND® includes free use of all the attractions. Less high-profile amusement parks are dotted throughout the country and include fairgrounds, water parks and science centres. **BonBon-Land** in southern Zealand *(see p161)*, for instance, is packed with rides and amusements as is **Fårup Sommerland** in northern Jutland *(see p208)*.

In addition to its traditional zoos, Denmark has numerous safari parks and aquariums where visitors can see wild animals and aquatic creatures. Two of the best known are

Miniature buildings in LEGOLAND®

Det Kongelige Teater performance in Copenhagen *(see p73)*

Knuthenborg Safari Park

(see pp164–5) and Esbjerg's **Fiskeri-og Søfartsmuseet** aquarium *(see p198)*.

Nightlife

Apart from those in Copenhagen, the best clubs are in university towns, such as Aarhus, Aalborg and Odense, where they cater for the exacting demands of the student population. Among the most popular places in Aarhus are **Train**, **VoxHall** and **Musikcaféen**, which play a mixture of rock and techno depending on the night. In Aalborg **Skråen** and **The Irish House** have a lively feel. Two of the best clubs in Odense are **Posten** and **Jazzhus Dexter**. The latter has live jazz at the weekend. Performances in Danish music venues range from local bands to major acts from abroad. Many concerts are free although prices can be fairly steep for the biggest international names. Nightclubs are also popular and can be found even in some of the smaller towns. Clubwise, nothing really gets going until about 11pm in Denmark. Pubs and clubs usually stay open until 1am on weekdays. At weekends many of them don't close their doors until dawn.

Spectator Sports

Football (soccer) is a passion in Denmark and the Danish national side is one of the top teams in Europe. Watching football is a popular pastime and many games are attended by entire families. Three of the best-known clubs are **FC Midtjylland**, **FC København** and **Aalborg BK**. International matches are played at Parken, Denmark's national stadium and home ground of FC København.

Handball has quite a high profile following the gold-medal success of the women's team at the 2000 Olympics. Other common sports include ice hockey, badminton, dirt-bike racing and cycling. Gymnastics clubs are also popular, and shows and competitions are frequently advertised in smaller towns.

Players of FC Midtjylland, one of Denmark's premier football clubs

DIRECTORY

Theatre, Music and Dance

Aalborg Kongres og Kulturcenter
Europaplads 4, 9000 Aalborg. **Tel** 99 35 55 55.
Ⓦ **akkc.dk**

Aarhus Teater
Teatergaden, 8000 Aarhus C. **Tel** 70 21 30 21.
Ⓦ **aarhusteater.dk**

Granhøj Dans
Klosterport 6, 8000 Aarhus C. **Tel** 86 19 26 22.
Ⓦ **granhoj.dk**

Musikhuset Aarhus
Thomas Jensens Allé, 8000 Aarhus C.
Tel 89 40 40 40.
Ⓦ **musikhusetaarhus.dk**

Odeon Odense Koncerthus
Claus Bergs Gade 9, Odense C. **Tel** 66 14 78 00.
Ⓦ **odeonodense.dk**

Odense Teater
Jernbanegade 21, 5100 Odense C.
Tel 62 12 00 52.
Ⓦ **odenseteater.dk**

Nightlife

The Irish House
Østerågade 25, 9000 Aalborg. **Tel** 98 14 18 17.
Ⓦ **theirishhouse.dk**

Jazzhus Dexter
Vindegade 65, 5000 Odense C. **Tel** 63 11 27 28.
Ⓦ **dexter.dk**

Musikcaféen
Mejlgade 53, 8000 Aarhus C.

Posten
Ostre Stationsvej 35, 5000 Odense C. **Tel** 66 13 60 20.
Ⓦ **postenlive.dk**

Skråen
Nordkraft, Kjellerup Torv 5, 9000 Aalborg. **Tel** 98 12 21 89. Ⓦ **skraaen.dk**

Train
Toldbodgade 6, 8000 Aarhus C. **Tel** 86 13 47 22
Ⓦ **train.dk**

VoxHall
Vester Allé 15, 8000 Aarhus C. **Tel** 87 30 97 97
Ⓦ **fondenvoxhall.dk**

Spectator Sports

Aalborg BK
Hornevej 2, 9220 Aalborg Øst.
Tel 96 35 59 00.
Ⓦ **aabsport.dk**

FC København
Parken, Øster Allé 50, 2110 Copenhagen.
Tel 35 43 74 00.
Ⓦ **fck.dk**

FC Midtjylland
Kaj Zartowsvej 5, 7400 Herning.
Tel 96 27 10 40.
Ⓦ **fcm.dk**

OUTDOOR ACTIVITIES

The Danes are keen on sport and fitness, and many adults and most children participate in one sport or another. The country's gentle terrain and the many miles of well maintained cycle routes have helped to make cycling an integral part of Danish culture – it is not unusual for entire Danish families to embark on cycling holidays. Golfers are also well catered for and Denmark has over 100 courses, many of which can be found close to hotels and camp sites. With its many fjords, protected waters and tiny islands to explore, Denmark is a good place for sailors. The country is also ideal for water sports such as windsurfing and canoeing. The same sheltered fjords are perfect for novice windsurfers, and there are many companies near Danish holiday resorts that can arrange lessons. Horse riding and fishing are other popular activities.

Horse Riding

Equestrian pursuits are popular in Denmark and the country has a large number of riding stables. Some Danes have their own horses and keep them in community-style stables. Those who are unable to keep their own horses make use of the numerous riding clubs that offer riding lessons and provide horses for individual unsupervised rides. A small number of clubs will accept riders paying an hourly rate. Rides are also on offer in beach resorts such as Rømø, Thy and Løkken.

A good way for beginners to learn about riding and looking after horses is to sign up for a farm holiday *(see p247)*, some of which include riding lessons and accompanied treks through the countryside. Riding holidays on Icelandic horses (the traditional Viking horse) are available in Mols National Park.

Horse and driver on a carriage racetrack

For something a little different, it is possible to travel the country by wagon. Four to six people can usually be carried in the wagons, which are hired complete with horses from companies such as **Prærievognsferie Og Hesteudlejning** on Funen. Training is provided and the wagon is equipped with everything that travellers might need while on the road. A map is supplied marking the route to the camp site, where there is pasture for horses and often a welcoming bonfire. Prairie wagon holidays can be great fun, particularly for children. Contact **Dansk Ride Forbund** (The Danish Equestrian Federation) for details of activities in the area you are visiting.

For those who prefer to spectate, horse races are held in several towns, including Klampenborg, Aarhus, Fyn, Aalborg and Bornholm.

Horse riding – a popular pastime in Denmark

Water Sports

The many Danish lakes and some 7,300 km (4,536 miles) of coastline make Denmark a perfect location for water-sports enthusiasts. Equipment for windsurfing, water-skiing and sea kayaking can be hired in waterside resorts, as can jet skis and other gear. In Silkeborg it is possible to book canoeing holidays.

Visitors intending to take up some form of water sport should check in advance whether the region they plan to visit allows for such pursuits – for example, water-skiing is prohibited in some ecologically sensitive areas.

Fishing

Denmark is an ideal destination for anglers. Its many streams and lakes are well maintained and have healthy stocks of fish including plentiful supplies of pike and trout both for coarse

Windsurfers making the most of Denmark's coastal waters

and fly-fishing. The long coastline is also good for saltwater fishing and anglers can hope to catch sea trout, plaice, mackerel and cod. Anglers between the age of 18 and 67 must carry an appropriate licence. These are sold at post offices, tourist information offices and shops that sell angling equipment; they are also available at *www. fisketegn.dk*. Licences are issued for one day, one week or annually and cost 40, 130 and 185 Dkr respectively. Fishing in lakes and streams requires the permission of the owner, which often is the local angling club. Tourist offices will have details of angling holidays and some camp sites are especially geared for anglers with rooms set aside for gutting and cleaning fish.

Anyone fishing in Denmark will be expected to know the regulations concerning the size and types of species that may be caught. Some clubs may impose restrictions concerning the number or the total weight of the catch.

Those keen on deep-sea fishing can join the crew of a fishing vessel and head out to offshore fishing grounds, such as Gule Rev, in the North Sea off Hanstholm. The cutter **T-248 Skagerak** sails to this reef daily (weather permitting).

Anyone interested in a fishing holiday in Denmark should contact the local tourist office. The website *www.fiskekort.dk* provides maps of good fishing areas.

Motorcycle Tours

Touring around Denmark by motorcycle is a pleasant way to get to know the country. Traffic is reasonably light and many Danes are themselves keen motorcyclists.

Motorcycle rallies, known as *motorcykeltrief*, are organized countrywide. The size of events varies from small weekly meetings to large rallies that feature live music and competitions for the most impressive bikes. Major events can last days and attract locals as well as foreign enthusiasts.

Denmark has a network of scenic roads known as the Marguerite Route, which takes in some of the most beautiful parts of the country. The route consists mostly of secondary and minor roads and is marked on road signs by a white daisy on a brown background (see p301). Maps mark the route with green dots or a green line.

Anyone travelling in Denmark on a motorcycle should take into account the wind, which at times can be very strong and make riding difficult and sometimes even hazardous. When crossing bridges, particularly over some of the long straits, the wind can be especially strong and blow in sudden and unexpected gusts. When strong winds prevail, motorcyclists may be banned from using these bridges.

Motorcyclists in Denmark must adhere to the highway code. Riders and passengers are required by law to wear helmets and carry the necessary documentation at all times.

Cyclists on one of the country's many cycling routes

Cycling

Riding a bike is a hugely pop-ular activity in Denmark and the lowland areas especially are excellent regions for a cycling holiday, as is the island of Bornholm *(see p231)*. The whole country is criss-crossed with an extensive network of cycling routes. It is easy to plan a journey and routes take in most of the big towns and cities as well as more rural parts of the country.

Organized cycle races are common in Denmark. Many cover short distances and are open to amateurs. Races for elite riders include the Grand Prix Aalborg and the prestigious CSC Classic, where teams compete to earn points towards the world-ranking list. Races such as the CSC Classic are for serious competitors only.

Bikers and bikes at an annual motorcycle rally

Playing the green at a golf club near Gilleleje, northwestern Zealand

Cycling Tours

Cycling is an excellent way to tour Denmark, and enthusiasts are very well catered for. Specialist bicycle shops are found throughout the country. Alongside traditional touring bikes, they sell the very latest in cycling equipment. Dedicated maps for cycling make planning a tour fairly straight-forward. Maps are widely available and cover virtually every part of the country. The maps include not only cycle routes but all the major sights along the way such as museums and castles. In addition, they indicate which roads have cycle paths and on which roads it is forbidden or too dangerous to ride. Cycling maps are useful in a number of other ways. They often include details of camp sites and hostels, for instance, as well as grocery stores. Maps can be ordered from **Dansk Cyklist Forbund** (The Danish Cycling Federation) as well as from bookshops and tourist offices.

The Dansk Cyklist Forbund can also provide details of packaged cycling tours. Tours can be expensive but they have the advantage of providing suitable cycles and organizing the accommodation along the route. Tour operators often arrange for luggage to be carried, so that riders need not be weighed down by tents and other items.

Tandem bicycle, popular in Denmark

There are several places in Denmark where visitors can hire a bicycle; the local tourist office will be able to help. Larger towns usually have free city bikes available for short rides.

Finding someone to fix a bike is easy. Most cycling maps include details of cycle workshops where minor repairs such as mending a punctured tyre or fixing a spoke can be carried out quickly and cheaply.

Golf

Denmark has more than 100 golf courses. Most of them will honour the membership card of your own club, and most clubs admit novices as well as experienced players. Green fees vary but are fairly reasonable, averaging around 300 Dkr per day (370 Dkr at weekends). Buying a package golfing holiday that also includes accommodation can work out cheaper. Golf clubs generally hire and sell golfing equipment and also run improvement courses for all levels. The **Dansk Golf Union** can provide information about the country's golf courses.

Sailing

The waters around Denmark are dotted with islands, many of which have harbours in which to moor a boat. The coastline is highly diversified and there is plenty of scope for sailing at all levels of ability. Storms and gales are uncommon in bodies of water such as the sea between Zealand and Lolland as well as many of the fjords and these calm, forgiving conditions are perfect for novices and less experienced sailors.

If you wish to hire a sailing boat in Denmark, local tourist offices will be able to point you in the direction of a reputable company.

Sailing boats, a common sight on Danish waters

Coastal dunes, an ideal area for walks

All craft intended for charter must carry a seaworthiness certificate issued by the State Inspectorate of Shipping. When chartering a boat, it is important to ask to see this certificate before sailing.

Boat Cruises

Boat cruises are popular in Denmark and depart regularly from Nyhavn in Copenhagen, bound for the islands situated in the Øresund (Sound). It is even possible to book a cruise on a reconstructed Viking ship. Stationed in Roskilde harbour are several small ships that are faithful copies of 10th-century wooden Viking boats and these embark on regular cruises. Cruises of the lakes and rivers are another option. One popular jaunt is to jump aboard one of the small ships that depart from Ry harbour on a cruise along the Gudena river. Another alternative is to take a trip back in time on the *Hjejlen*, a paddle steamer that travels daily from Silkeborg to Himmelbjerget. A trip on one of the many ferries that link the various islands can be considered a pleasant cruise too.

Walking

Walking trails in Denmark are clearly signposted, with information boards giving the names of the destination points and the length of the route. In Denmark the public have conditional access to the coast even if the land is privately owned. Many signed walks follow the shoreline and are especially beautiful. The country's forests are also good for walking. Some marked trails lead across private land. When this is the case it is important to stick to the trail, otherwise walkers risk being arrested (although this is highly unlikely). Many routes are through nature reserves and may be marked with the sign of a daisy. Tourist offices and libraries often have brochures listing some of Denmark's best walks. The town of Viborg has a walking festival along old drove and army roads.

Denmark's hostels and inns are used to catering for the needs of walkers, as are the country's camp sites. **Dansk Vandrelaug** (The Danish Ramblers Association) provides maps (in Danish) for visitors.

Swimming

Denmark has many beautiful beaches. Most are ideal for swimming although the temperature can be on the chilly side. Even in summer, the water temperature rarely rises above 17° C (63° F). As an alternative, virtually all cities and major towns have swimming baths, which are well maintained.

Children may enjoy a visit to one of the many water parks, such as **Fårup Sommerland** *(see p208)* and **Brændesgårdshaven Bornholm** *(see p230)*, which have splash pools, waterslides and other entertaining facilities.

DIRECTORY

VisitDenmark
w visitdenmark.com

Sporting Organizations

Dansk Idræt Forbund
Idrættens Hus, Brøndby Stadion 20, 2605 Brøndby.
Tel 43 26 26 26.
w dif.dk

Horse Riding

Dansk Ride Forbund
Idrættens Hus, Brøndby Stadion 20, 2605 Brøndby.
Tel 43 26 28 28.
w rideforbund.dk

Prærievognsferie Og Hesteudlejning
Holmdrup Huse 3, 5881 Skårup, Funen.
Tel 62 23 18 25.

Fishing

Danmarks Sports- fiskerforbund
Skyltevej 4, Vingsted, 7182 Bredsten.
Tel 75 82 06 99.
w sportsfiskeren.dk

T-248 Skagerak
Vorupør Strand, 7700 Thisted.
Tel 97 92 07 41.
w skagerak-t248.dk

Cycling Tours

Bornholm Velcomstcenter (Visitors Centre)
Nordre Kystvej 3, 3700 Rønne. **Tel** 56 95 95 00.
w bornholminfo.dk

Dansk Cyklist Forbund
Rømersgade 5, 1362 Cph K.
Tel 33 32 31 21.
w dcf.dk

Golf

Dansk Golf Union
Idrættens Hus, Brøndby Stadion 20, 2605 Brøndby.
Tel 43 26 27 00.
w danskgolfunion.dk
w golf.dk

Walking

Dansk Vandrelaug
Kultorvet 7, DK-1175 Copenhagen K.
Tel 33 12 11 65.
w dvl.dk

SURVIVAL GUIDE

PRACTICAL INFORMATION

Large numbers of holiday-makers travel to Denmark each year, drawn by the wide range of attractions and accommodation on offer. The peak season is relatively short, however, since the winter months are cold and daylight hours few. The country has a good tourism infrastructure, with a network of efficient tourist offices. Information on destinations and attractions is easy to obtain, especially online, and planning a trip should be a straightforward undertaking, since most hotels and attractions have excellent English websites. Denmark's hotels and inns are welcoming and clean, as are the many good-value camp sites and hostels. The major museums and galleries display world-class collections, accompanied by English-language displays, guidebooks and even digital guides and apps to help visitors get the most from the exhibits.

When to Go

The best time to visit Denmark is during the milder months (mid-April–mid-October) or in December, when most of the country's towns and villages sparkle with festive Christmas decorations. The ideal time for cycling holidays is between mid-June and late August.

Most Danes go on holiday between late June and mid-August, to coincide with school vacations. During this time the camp sites, beaches and resorts tend to be full. A good time to visit, then, is in mid-August, after the schools have reopened – the beaches and attractions are less busy, but the days are still warm.

Visas and Passports

EU citizens do not need a visa to enter Denmark; visitors from other parts of the world should check if their country has reciprocal agreements on waiving visa requirements. Visitors not obliged to have a visa are allowed to stay in Denmark for up to 90 days.

Contact your embassy in an emergency, such as the loss of your passport. However, it is worth noting that embassies expect you to have your own travel insurance (see p291), and they are not likely to help if you have been jailed or fined for committing a crime. Most embassies are located in Copenhagen – visit the **Ministry of Foreign Affairs** website for a list.

Travel Safety Advice

Visitors can get up-to-date travel safety information from the **Foreign and Commonwealth**

Office in the UK, the **State Department** in the US and the **Department of Foreign Affairs and Trade** in Australia.

Customs Information

The customs allowance for EU visitors travelling to Denmark is 800 cigarettes and 10 litres of spirits; for people travelling from non-EU countries, it is 200 cigarettes and 1 litre of spirits. All food articles must be vacuum-packed by the manufacturer. Commercial quantities of a value exceeding 1,350 Dkr are subject to customs duty.

There is no limit – within reason – on how much alcohol or tobacco EU citizens can take out of the country. US citizens are allowed to take home $800 worth of goods before duty must be paid.

Tourist Information

Most Danish towns have tourist information centres with multilingual staff. They can supply maps and information on local sights and events; they will also hand out free pamphlets containing information on hotels, cycling routes, walking trails and disabled access to various attractions. In smaller towns with no tourist centres, visitors can usually get this type of information from their hotel. The official website of the Danish Tourist Board, **VisitDenmark**, is also very useful.

Aarhus, Denmark's second-largest city, relies heavily on QR tags and the Internet to deliver information to tourists.

Tourist information at the Shopping Street in Aarhus

Sign for a historical site

Admission Prices and Opening Hours

Some museums and historic attractions, especially those in Copenhagen, waive admission charges once a week (usually on Wednesday). In larger cities, visitors can purchase passes that combine reduced entry fees to museums and other attractions with unlimited use of public transport (see p302).

Many museums and galleries are closed on Monday, while some art museums, such as Louisiana and Aarhus' AroS, stay open late on selected days. Shops are usually open 10am–6pm; on Friday they close at 7 or 8pm, and on Saturday any time between noon and 4pm. Most shops are now open on Sundays too, though the opening hours can vary from store to store. In tourist resorts, shops are generally open seven days a week during July and August.

◄ Exploring Bredefjord and the Arctic Ocean, Greenland

Danish churches are open only on certain days and between certain hours, so it is wise to check in advance. Note that churches are closed to sightseers during services.

Tourist attractions often make seasonal changes to their opening hours. Some attractions and seaside restaurants close completely in January and February, while many restaurants and cafés in Copenhagen close in July.

Travellers with Disabilities

With a little forward planning, travellers with special needs should find a holiday in Denmark straightforward and enjoyable. Modern holiday centres, hotels, museums and other attractions generally provide wheelchair-accessible ramps and lifts, as well as facilities for the visually and hearing-impaired. However, hotels, museums and restaurants located in older buildings may not have such resources, and so you could find you have to negotiate stairs at street level and face space restrictions. It pays to check well in advance, either online or by phone.

Travelling with Children

Hotels, holiday centres and cottage-letting agencies in Denmark will often provide travel cots, high chairs, and garden toys such as swings. Taking children to a restaurant is perfectly acceptable, though it's best to go before 8pm.

Restaurants generally have children's menus, high chairs and changing facilities.

Most buses and stations on the public transport network are equipped with lifts that allow easy access for buggies.

Travelling on a Budget

Farm holidays and B&Bs offer fairly cheap accommodation, as do camp sites and hostels. YHA hostels have private rooms as well as dorms, and camp sites often offer accommodation in wooden chalets, a cheaper alternative to summer houses. Note that there is a charge at all Danish official camp sites; a free solution is to pitch a tent at a "nature camp" with only basic amenities (running water and a public toilet). See the VisitDenmark website for more information. **CouchSurfing** is free of charge, and is also a fun way to meet local people.

Savings can be made on train travel by booking tickets well in advance at "orange" saver rates (see p298). Alternatively, you can travel around the country by sharing a private car ride. Visit the **GoMore** website for a list of destinations and quotes.

Responsible Tourism

Denmark has always been progressive when it comes to environmental issues. Any bottles marked with the recycling logo can be placed in the machines (flaskeautomat) found in supermarket foyers. Press the green button for your receipt, which can then be

redeemed inside the shop for cash or goods. Other glass can be placed in the green recycling containers outside.

Many hotels and holiday centres are **Green Key**-certified, meaning they have adopted a number of eco-friendly initiatives. Organic, or økologisk, food is widely available, and there are also some organic restaurants. "Klima+" restaurants combine organic food with a policy of reducing carbon emissions.

DIRECTORY

Visas and Passports

Ministry of Foreign Affairs
w http://um.dk

Travel Safety Advice

Australia
w dfat.gov.au
smartraveller.gov.au

United Kingdom
w gov.uk/foreign-travel-advice

United States
w travel.state.gov

Tourist Information

Aalborg Tourist Office
Kjellerup Torv 5, Niveaub 13, 9000 Aalborg. **Tel** 99 31 75 00.
w visitaalborg.com

Bornholms Visitor Centre
Ndr Kystvej 3, 3770 Rønne. **Tel** 56 95 95 00. w bornholm.info

Copenhagen Visitor Centre
Vesterbrogade 4A, 1620 Copenhagen V. **Tel** 70 22 24 42.
w visitcopenhagen.com

Odense Tourist Office
Rådhuset, 5000 Odense C. **Tel** 63 75 75 39. w visitodense.com

VisitDenmark
Islands Brygge 43, 2300 Copenhagen S. **Tel** 32 88 99 00.
w visitdenmark.com

Travelling on a Budget

CouchSurfing
w couchsurfing.org

GoMore
w gomore.dk

Responsible Tourism

Green Key
w greenkey.global

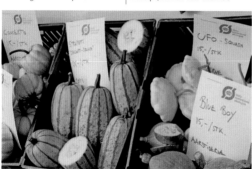
Certified organic vegetables for sale at a market stall

Personal Security and Health

Denmark is a safe country with low levels of crime. Even in the larger cities there is little likelihood of visitors encountering problems. The chances of falling victim to crime can be further minimized by not carrying excessive amounts of cash and by keeping credit cards, mobile phones and other valuables hidden away. In the event of a crime or accident, the Danish police and emergency services work very efficiently. Ask passers-by or witnesses to the event for their help. As a rule, Danes will not refuse such a request.

Ambulance with its lights on, attending to an emergency

White police patrol car parked in front of a shopping centre in Odense

Police

During the summer season the Danish **police** are dressed in blue shirts and black trousers; in winter they also wear black jackets. Road police generally wear all-in-one leather suits and ride large white motorcycles. Ordinary police patrol cars are white with the word "POLITI" in blue lettering, while the cars driven by the criminal division are dark blue. Criminal division police usually wear civilian clothes and will show their ID cards when required.

The majority of Danish policemen and policewomen will have at least a working knowledge of the English language. In most cases they will be able to provide some assistance, such as giving you directions or helping you contact a breakdown service.

Although they are not part of the police force, traffic wardens are entitled to check if someone has a valid parking ticket and can impose a fine for illegal parking (*see pp301 and 303*). Traffic wardens in Copenhagen wear dark green jackets.

What to be aware of

The summer months and the run-up to Christmas are the times when thieves are most likely to be operating, especially in busy places. Visitors are advised to be on their guard, particularly in the main train stations, such as Copenhagen's Central Station, as well as in the prime shopping areas. Valuables should be deposited at the hotel reception or kept in the safe in your room; money and documents should be carried under clothing rather than in handbags, backpacks or trouser pockets. Make sure all valuable items are out of sight if left in a car.

In an Emergency

In the event of a road accident, life-threatening situation, fire, attack or any other predicament that requires immediate intervention by the **emergency services**, visitors should call 112. This toll-free line is staffed by qualified operators who are able to speak several foreign languages, including English; they will determine which service should be sent to the scene of the incident.

Emergency telephones installed along the hard shoulders of motorways can be used to report a breakdown or accident. Special telephones found in S-tog railway stations and on metro lines enable passengers to contact railway duty officers when needed.

An accident or mugging should be reported to the police. The victim and any witnesses to the incident are entitled to give evidence in their native language.

Consulates and embassies can help to contact a visitor's family in the event of an incident, and they may also be able to provide financial help or advance the money for a ticket home.

Lost and Stolen Property

Any theft of money, travel documents, credit cards or other valuables, as well as any theft from a car or hotel room, should be reported immediately at the local police station, where an officer will issue a note confirming that the crime has been reported. This note may well be required when filling out an insurance claim or visiting an embassy or consulate to obtain a temporary passport.

If you have lost any personal belongings, enquire at the **lost property office** (*hittegods*) closest to the area where they went missing. There are *hittegods* at all local police stations. Any items left behind on a train, S-tog or metro should be reported to the duty personnel at the station; if lost on a bus, report it to the passenger service office of the appropriate bus company. Lost or stolen credit cards should be reported to the card issuer as soon as possible. Keep the relevant telephone numbers separately from your cards.

The entrance to a hospital in Copenhagen

Hospitals and Pharmacies

Addresses of doctors and hospitals can be obtained from hotel receptionists and camp site managers, or found in a telephone directory. Most Danish doctors speak English.

Note that not all hospitals in Denmark have an emergency department, and that the old word for emergency room, *skadestue*, is being replaced by *akutklinik*.

Pharmacies *(apotek)* are usually open from 9am to 5:30pm on weekdays and until 1pm on Saturdays. In larger towns there is always one pharmacy that is open 24 hours a day; the address will be displayed on the doors or windows of any pharmacy. You will usually have to call or buzz at a side entrance outside of normal opening hours (after 8pm Monday to Friday, after 4pm on Saturday and all day Sunday). A small surcharge is

generally added to the cost of non-prescription medicines purchased during these times.

If you require constant medication, be sure to take an adequate supply with you – medicines can be expensive in Denmark. Controlled drugs require a doctor's prescription.

Minor Hazards

Travellers to Denmark do not require any special vaccinations. Mosquitoes can be a problem near large lakes in the summer; spray-on repellents can be bought in any pharmacy. Those on hiking or camping holidays should check regularly for blood-sucking ticks, especially on children; ticks must be removed completely and any subsequent redness treated promptly with antibiotics. Note that antiseptic lotions, such as Savlon, are not available in Denmark, so it is advisable to bring some with you.

It is safe to drink tap water in Denmark, and stomach upsets are uncommon.

Travel and Health Insurance

Anyone with a medical emergency is entitled to free treatment in hospitals and doctor's surgeries in Denmark, provided that the person has not arrived in the country specifically for that treatment and is unfit to return home. EU visitors in possession of a European Health Insurance Card (EHIC) are covered by Danish national health insurance.

Greenland and the Faroe Islands are not part of the EHIC scheme. Non-EU citizens must have health insurance.

Travel insurance is advisable for all visitors, as it can make it easier to get treatment and should cover the cost of an ambulance (which the patient is responsible for) or an emergency flight home.

DIRECTORY

In an Emergency

Emergency Services
Tel 112 (toll free).

Police
Tel 114 (toll free).

Lost And Stolen Property

Lost Property Office, (Copenhagen)
Copenhagen police station,
Slotsherrensvej 113,
2720 Vanløse.
Tel 38 74 88 22.

Hospitals

Aarhus Universitets Hospital
Nørrebrogade 44, 8000 Aarhus C.
Tel 78 45 00 00.

Amager Hospital (Copenhagen)
Italiensvej 1, 2300 Copenhagen S.
Tel 32 34 32 34.

Odense Universitets Hospital
Sønder Blvd 29, 5000 Odense C.
Tel 65 41 22 71.

24-Hour Pharmacies

Aalborg Budolfi Apotek
Algade 60, 9000 Aalborg.
Tel 98 12 06 77.

Aarhus Løve Apotek
Store Torv 5, 8000 Aarhus C.
Tel 86 12 00 22.

Copenhagen Steno Apotek
Vesterbrogade 6C, 1620
Copenhagen V. **Tel** 33 14 82 66.

Copenhagen Sønderbro Apotek
Amagerbrogade 158, 2300
Copenhagen S. **Tel** 32 58 01 40.

Odense Apoteket Ørnen
Filosofhaven 38B, 5000 Odense C.
Tel 66 12 29 70.

A pharmacy in Copenhagen

Banks and Currency

Visitors arriving in Denmark from outside the EU are obliged to have adequate means to support themselves for the duration of their stay. Immigration authorities are usually satisfied with a verbal assurance regarding a visitor's credit card limit. While credit cards can be used almost anywhere, try to have Danish kroner to hand for buying small treats like ice creams, or to use on public transport and when travelling to the more remote islands.

A branch of Jyske Bank in Copenhagen

Banks and Bureaux de Change

Banks in Denmark are open from 10am until 4pm Monday to Friday, with extended opening hours on Thursday (until 6pm). Banks are closed on Saturday, Sunday and public holidays.

Be aware that banks in Denmark's smaller towns generally do not carry cash and will be able to provide money only from the ATM.

Foreign currency can be exchanged at many places throughout the country. Exchange booths at Copenhagen Airport are open most of the day. Hotels can also exchange money, though they offer the least favourable rates. Banks and special automatic money-exchange machines offer slightly better rates, but they also charge a commission. The best deals can generally be obtained at branches of **Forex**, since they do not charge a commission. In addition, their opening hours are usually more flexible than those of the banks. Exchange rates are usually displayed by the door. Anyone who wishes to bring more than 40,000 Dkr into the country or make a deposit of a similar sum must have a certificate confirming the legality of the money's source.

ATMs

All Danish banks have cash machines from which kroner can be withdrawn with a credit or debit card. ATMs are widespread in the towns and cities, and they all provide directions in English, as well as in a number of other European languages.

ATMs are not so readily available in more remote parts of Denmark, including some of its smaller islands, camp sites and summer house areas; anyone planning to visit these parts should have enough Danish kroner to last until they return to a larger town.

Credit and Debit Cards

Visitors to Denmark should have no problem using credit cards such as MasterCard, VISA or Eurocard, though some restaurants may charge a small fee for non-Danish cards. American Express and Diners Club are less readily accepted. Be aware that some shops may refuse to take credit cards as payment for low-cost items, while others accept only a Danish debit card called Dankort.

In many restaurants and shops, staff will use a reader to enter a card's data and ask the customer to sign a receipt or key in the card's PIN code.

In order to ensure your card works overseas, contact your bank or credit card provider before travelling.

If your credit or debit card is lost or stolen, report it to your card issuer immediately.

Currency

Denmark is one of the few EU countries to reject joining the European monetary union, keeping the krone (plural: kroner) instead. In large towns and tourist resorts, however, prices are often quoted in both kroner and euros. The Danish krone (or crown) is divided into 100 øre. Coins come in denominations of 50 øre, and 1, 2, 5, 10 and 20 kroner. Notes come in denominations of 50, 100, 200, 500 and 1,000 kroner. The Danish krone is written as DKK in most international money markets, but as Dkr in northern Europe and simply as kr in Denmark.

The Faroe Islands have their own version of the Danish krone, known as the Faroese krona, which has exactly the same value as its Danish counterpart. Danish currency is accepted on the Faroe Islands, but the Faroese krona is not accepted in Denmark, so exchange any Faroese krona notes at a bureau de change.

The Danish krone is the official currency in Greenland.

Be aware that while all Scandinavian currencies are called krone or krona, they are not interchangeable. Swedish kronar and Norwegian kroner, for example, are not valid currencies in Denmark.

Bank notes

Danish bank notes differ from each other in terms of size and colour. The lowest denomination bank note in circulation is the violet-blue 50-Dkr note. The largest denomination is the red-and-green 1,000-Dkr note.

50 kroner

100 kroner

200 kroner

500 kroner

Coins

The 10- and most of the 20-Dkr coins are golden in colour, with the queen's image on the reverse. The 1-, 2- and 5-Dkr coins are nickel with a hole in the centre. The 50-øre coin is copper-coloured.

50 øre

1 krone

20 kroner

10 kroner

5 kroner

2 kroner

Communications and Media

Danish postal services are very efficient. Letters and postcards take one to two days to reach their destinations within the country, and about two to four days within Europe. Telephoning abroad is straightforward, although public telephones are becoming increasingly rare. Nevertheless, visitors should be able to find a public telephone at a post office, railway station, camp site reception or hotel lobby. WiFi hotspots are generally easy to find throughout the country, particularly in cities, and data roaming is straightforward.

Dialling Codes

- To make an international call, dial 00, the country code, the area code and the number.
- Calling Denmark from abroad: 0045
- Country codes: UK 44; US/Canada 1.
- Directory enquiries: 118 (inland), 80 60 40 55 (overseas).

International and Local Telephone Calls

Denmark has no area codes, and all numbers consist of eight digits, generally written and read out by Danes in blocks of two. Numbers starting with 20 through to 31 are mobile numbers, while those starting with 32 through to 39 are Copenhagen landline numbers. Numbers starting with 80 are toll-free, while premium rate lines start with 90. Danes refer to land lines as *fastnet*.

Prepaid phone cards for calling overseas are available in many kiosks in the larger cities. Always state where you're calling for the best rates to that country. Prepaid phone cards can also be used with mobile phones.

Calling from a payphone is more expensive than using a private phone, but cheaper than phoning from a hotel room. The minimum charge for a call from a public phone is 5 Dkr, and denominations of 1, 2, 5, 10 and 20 Dkr are accepted; many payphones also take euros. All calls, including local calls, are charged by the minute. Clear instructions on how to make a call are displayed in English, and a list of dialling codes for other countries is usually available.

A public telephone that accepts both coins and phone cards

Skype is a free alternative to costly international phone calls. Anyone with a computer or phone with Internet access can use Skype, as long as they have registered for an account.

Mobile Phones

Most mobile phone networks provide the facilities for making international calls. Before departure, make sure that your phone will work in Denmark. The EU ended roaming charges in 2017, meaning European visitors travelling within the continent can use their mobile data abroad without incurring charges. Those travelling from outside the EU might find it cheaper to buy an local SIM card.

Making calls from Denmark is more expensive than calling from home;

incoming calls will also be charged at a higher rate. Receiving texts from abroad is free, but sending them is usually subject to a substantial fee.

For longer trips, your mobile phone needs often exceed roaming limits and it may be worth investing in a pre-paid Danish sim card.

Internet

Denmark moved swiftly into the broadband era, and free Wi-Fi connections are commonplace. Free WiFi is available in most tourist offices including the Copenhagen Visitor Centre, as well as in cafés and on some public transport, including the IC3, IC4 and IR4 trains throughout the country, the regional S-tog in Copenhagen and some buses. Wi-Fi is also available throughout Copenhagen Airport.

Most hotels in Danish holiday resorts can provide Internet access in hotel rooms and at reception. Many youth hostels and camp sites also have computers with Internet access.

The number of Internet cafés has declined, due to Wi-Fi becoming more widespread, but these can still be found in Danish towns and cities. Free Wi-Fi hotspots are available throughout Denmark. You can search for locations using **openwifi**. If you plan on using your own laptop, be sure to bring an adaptor suitable for Denmark's plug sockets and 230 voltage. If you anticipate needing

Free WiFi is available at many cafés in Denmark

constant internet access you can invest in mobile broadband access through a USB-modem.

Public Telephones

The increase of mobile phones in Denmark means that public telephone boxes are not as common as they used to be. Those that do remain are usually outside train stations. There are two types of phone booths: those that accept both coins and cards, and those that take cards only. Phone cards are available in post offices and many shops. Card phones also accept credit cards.

Danish postal services' logo

Bright-red Danish letterbox, showing collection times

Postal and Courier Services

Danish post offices are indicated by the word "POST" in white letters on a red background. Most post offices are open 10am–5pm Monday to Friday (until 6pm on Thursday) and 10am–noon on Saturday. You can post parcels, send registered letters and collect *poste restante* mail from all of Denmark's post offices.

Stamps can be purchased at post offices, in many souvenir shops and from vending machines. A letter sent to a European country requires a "Europa" tariff postage stamp.

Danish post boxes are painted red. They feature the crown and trumpet insignia of the national postal service and display the time of the next collection. International mail sent from Copenhagen should leave the country within 24 hours.

When posting something to a Danish address, you should include the name of the recipient, street, house number, town and a four-digit post code. It is important to include the post code, since many Danish towns, as well as many streets in Copenhagen, have the same name. For details of post codes, visit the website of **Post Danmark**, the national postal service provider. The address for an apartment may sometimes include the floor and staircase, as well as the number of the flat within a building. For example, the address may be written as "Bjergvej 20, 3.tv", where "3" stands for 3rd floor and "tv" stands for *til venstre*, meaning "to the left".

Express courier services such as **DHL** and **UPS** usually provide a telephone booking service in English.

Newspapers and Magazines

Most of the major foreign papers, including US and UK dailies such as *The Times*, *The Guardian* and the *Wall Street Journal*, can be found at train station kiosks and in some of the main newsagents in Copenhagen, and other large towns. Magazines such as *Time* and *The Economist* are also readily available. Libraries often provide free access to international newspapers.

Denmark's own press consists of about 50 regional and national daily newspapers. Of these, *Politiken* and *Jyllands-posten* have the largest circulation. The weekly *Copenhagen Post* has national news and a pull-out listings section in English; it can be found at kiosks and newsagents in Copenhagen, as well as in many cafés, public libraries and tourist offices.

DIRECTORY

International and Local Telephone Calls

Skype
W skype.com

Mobile Phones

Oister
Tel 70 31 30 70.
W oister.dk

TDC
Tel 70 11 03 30.

Telia
Tel 80 40 40 40.
http://telia.dk

Internet

openwifi
W openwifi.dk

Postal And Courier Services

DHL
Tel 70 34 53 45.
W dhl.dk

Post Danmark
Tel 70 70 70 30.
W postdanmark.dk

UPS
Tel 86 75 29 24 (Aarhus).
Tel 35 25 80 80 (Zealand).
W ups.com

Television and Radio

All television in Denmark is broadcast digitally. There are two public-service channels, DR1 and DR2, screening news and current affairs along with light entertainment. Other channels are more commercial in character, showing a large amount of soap operas and comedies. Many US and British programmes are shown with Danish subtitles. English-language news is often available on cable and satellite TV.

Many summer houses have satellite dishes that receive German, Norwegian and Swedish channels. German channels are largely available in Southern Jutland, while viewers in Northern Jutland should be able to pick up Swedish and Norwegian TV.

TRAVEL INFORMATION

Flights to Denmark from most parts of northern Europe are frequent. Planes from 60 airlines and over 100 cities worldwide land at Copenhagen, and the airport receives more than 27 million passengers a year. Frequent connections are available on internal flights. Fewer people arrive by train and ferry, although ferries are popular with visitors from elsewhere in Scandinavia. Ease of travel has increased with the construction of the Storebælt (Great Belt) Bridge, linking Zealand and Funen, and the fixed-link Øresund Bridge between Zealand and Sweden, but many of the smaller Danish islands can be reached only by ferry. Travelling on the mainland and around the major islands is easy, thanks to a network of well-maintained motorways and railways, and an efficient coach service.

Arriving by Air

Most visitors to Denmark arrive at Copenhagen Airport, located 12 km (7 miles) southeast of the city centre. **SAS** connects Copenhagen to most European capitals, and it also has non-stop flights from New York and Chicago. From Australasia the best connections to Denmark are via Bangkok. Other airlines serving Copenhagen include **British Airways**, **Norwegian**, **bmi** (from Edinburgh and Glasgow) and **easyJet** (from London Gatwick, London Stansted and Manchester, as well as other airports in Europe). **Ryanair** has daily flights from London Stansted to Aarhus and Billund, and also to Malmø, in Sweden, with a special connecting coach to Copenhagen.

Jutland can be reached via the international airports of Aarhus, Aalborg and Billund. **Aarhus Airport**, which is 40 km (25 miles) northeast of the city, receives flights from London Stansted and Barcelona among others. Buses link the airport to the city, dropping passengers off at Aarhus's railway station.

The journey time is about 45 minutes.

Billund Airport (for LEGOLAND®) is the largest international airport in West Denmark, and it receives flights from many European cities, including London (Stansted and City), Frankfurt and Amsterdam. Bus routes operate from here to Vejle, Horsens, Aarhus, Kolding and Esbjerg.

Aalborg Airport offers easy access to the very north of the country and receives flights from such places as London Gatwick, Berlin and Oslo. An express bus links the airport with the city centre.

Copenhagen Airport

The country's main airport is **Copenhagen Airport** (formerly known as Kastrup), situated on Amager Island, a short way from the city centre. It has four terminals: three for international flights and one for domestic flights. Terminal 4, which is known as CphGo, is used exclusively by easyJet and other low-cost airlines.

Bilingual information board at Copenhagen Airport

Copenhagen Airport has helpful staff and excellent information services. Facilities include shops and restaurants, cash machines and lockers. Cars can be hired at terminals 1 and 3.

The CPH Advantage programme is available to all passengers and allows free Wi-Fi access through all of Copenhagen Airport. Passengers flying business class can also enjoy the CPH Apartment, located within the transit hall, for free Wi-Fi, printing and recharging facilities, and light meals and drinks at a nominal fee.

Special assistance for passengers with disabilities is provided by **Falck**. However, note that this service should be booked in advance either via the airport website or by calling Falck directly.

A fast and economical train service runs every 10 minutes from the airport's Terminal 3 to Central Station in Copenhagen (a journey of about 12 minutes). Trains run throughout the day, as well as during the night, albeit less frequently. Many trains are listed as running to Helsingør because they continue up the

Sleek, streamlined interior of Copenhagen Airport

SAS aircraft on the tarmac at Aalborg Airport

coast after stopping at Copenhagen's Central Station. Passengers should be aware that trains from Copenhagen Airport also run in the other direction, to Sweden, so it's important to find the correct platform.

The metro also runs from the airport to the city centre, taking about 15 minutes and stopping at Kongens Nytorv and Nørreport stations. It's also possible to take the bus, which drops passengers off at Rådhuspladsen. The price of a bus ticket is the same as the train (38 Dkr), however, and the journey time is nearly three times as long.

Visitors with a lot of heavy luggage will find a taxi rank by the exit of Terminal 3. Rates to the city centre start around 250 Dkr and fares can be paid by credit card.

Tickets and Fares

Intense competition, rising airport taxes and CO_2 tariffs mean that airlines vary their prices continuously and it is difficult to be precise about fares. Booking in advance is recommended, as travellers who book at short notice invariably pay higher prices. It is always worth shopping around, and often the best deals can be found online.

It is possible to purchase a one-way, non-refundable ticket on a low-cost airline for as little as €35–45 (including taxes) from London, Berlin and other European capitals. Direct return flights with SAS from New York or Chicago to Copenhagen cost around

US$700, with no refunds or flexibility.

Most airlines connecting Denmark to other European destinations charge for light snacks. SAS still allows one piece of 23-kg (50-lb) luggage free of charge, as well as offering discounts to people over 65 and to children and students. Low-cost airlines offer good deals to people who bring only an item of hand luggage.

Internal Flights

Air travel within Denmark is fairly inexpensive, as long as you book your tickets a couple of weeks in advance of your departure date. The major domestic carrier is SAS.

A route that is particularly worth recommending is the one from Copenhagen to Aalborg (a 5-hour journey by car). Connections are frequent, especially on weekdays. Another important domestic hub is **Karup Airport**, which is located in the flatlands around Herning, in Jutland.

On Arrival

All visitors from EU countries must have their passport or ID card ready for exiting the arrivals area; this is usually a fairly quick process. Citizens of many non- EU countries, such as the USA and Australia, do not need a visa to enter Denmark, but they may need to show a return ticket and evidence of sufficient funds to cover the duration of their planned stay in the country.

Logo of SAS
(Scandinavian Airlines)

DIRECTORY

Arriving by Air

Aalborg Airport
Ny Lufthavnsvej 100, 9400
Nørresundby. **Tel** 98 17 11 44.
w aal.dk

Aarhus Airport
Ny Lufthavnsvej 24,
8560 Kolind.
Tel 87 75 70 00.
w aar.dk

Billund Airport
Passagerterminalen 10,
7190 Billund. **Tel** 76 50 50 50.
w bll.dk

bmi (British Midland)
Tel 0844 417 2600 (UK).
w flybmi.com

British Airways
Tel 0844 493 0787 (UK).
w britishairways.com

easyJet
Tel 0843 506 9856 (UK).
w easyjet.com

Norwegian
Tel 0843 378 0888 (UK).
w norwegian.com

Ryanair
Tel 0871 246 0000 (UK).
w ryanair.com

SAS
Denmark **Tel** 70 10 20 00.
Ireland **Tel** 01 844 5440.
UK **Tel** 0871 226 7760.
USA/Canada **Tel** 1800 221 2350
(toll free).
w flysas.com

Copenhagen Airport

Copenhagen Airport
Lufthavnsboulevarden 6,
2770 Kastrup.
Tel 32 31 32 31.
w cph.dk

Falck
Tel 70 33 33 11.
w falck.dk

Internal Flights

Karup Airport
N.O. Hansens Vej 4,
7470 Karup J.
Tel 97 10 06 10.
w krp.dk

Travelling Around by Train, Coach and Ferry

Danish trains are mostly run by the Danish State Railway (DSB) and Arriva; they are reliable and fast, making it possible to travel between Copenhagen and Aarhus in under 3 hours. Coaches run between the large cities and to other destinations in Europe; they take longer than the train, but they are cheaper. A network of ferries provides a convenient way to travel to some of Denmark's many islands, including the Faroe Islands, as well as between Denmark and countries such as England, Germany, Sweden, Norway and Iceland.

Arriving by Train

The most common railway routes into Denmark are from Germany to Jutland or via the Puttgarden-Rødby ferry from Hamburg to Lolland and up to Zealand. Many people also travel to Zealand by train from Sweden across the Øresund Bridge. Travel from the UK is generally via the Netherlands and through Germany.

Trans-European trains are fast and efficient, particularly the high-speed ICE services between Copenhagen and Gothenburg and Stockholm, in Sweden; and between Copenhagen and Hamburg and Berlin, in Germany.

Copenhagen's Central Station, in the heart of the city, is the main point of arrival for international rail services.

Main Stations

Danish railway stations are clean and well maintained. Facilities often include heated waiting rooms and snack bars. Copenhagen's Central Station has shops, ATMs, cafés, a currency exchange, a post office and a police station. Aarhus's Central Station is set in the middle of a shopping mall.

Domestic Trains

DSB's extensive network covers both local and long-distance lines. Long-distance trains, such as those that run between Copenhagen and Aarhus, are modern, safe and stylish. Seats are arranged in pairs facing each other. Above each seat is a reading light and, often, individual music jacks for headphones and power supply sockets for laptop computers. Many trains have Wi-Fi connections for an additional charge (29 Dkr); trains with Internet access are marked with a white logo on a dark background and the word "Internet". Intercity trains also offer payphones, baby-changing facilities and even children's play areas. Information displayed above each seat indicates whether a seat has been reserved and to which station. In some parts of the train, known as *stille zoner*, silence must be maintained, and the use of mobile phones is prohibited. On many routes, DSB also operates "business class" carriages, which supply passengers with Wi-Fi, free drinks, snacks and papers.

Local trains, many of which have double-decker carriages, tend to be slower and have fewer facilities.

On some routes, such as from Copenhagen to Aarhus, Bornholm and Odden, it's possible to buy a combined train-and-ferry ticket.

Details of the network and main schedules are available from all DSB stations.

Train Tickets and Fares

Tickets can be bought at train stations or by calling the DSB reservation line or logging on to their website. The **Rejseplanen** website offers useful information on train and coach travel.

Train passes such as InterRail (available to European travellers) and Eurail (for visitors from outside Europe) give the holders substantial discounts on travel in Europe and a flexible range of options. There are many other rail concessions within Denmark, so it pays to ask about discounts for off-peak travel, family tickets and return fares. Often the best prices can be obtained by booking early and online. Those travelling between Copenhagen and Jutland and Funen can get the best savings by booking an "orange" ticket well in advance via the DSB website.

Children aged between 10 and 15 travel for half price; adults with valid tickets can take up to two children under 12 for free. Further information can be obtained from DSB ticket offices.

A coach is often the cheapest way to travel around Denmark

Travelling by Coach

Abildskou travels to Aarhus from Berlin via Hamburg Airport. It also operates daily services from Copenhagen to Aarhus and Aalborg. Tickets can be bought on board, but it is wise to reserve a seat in advance. Between Monday and Thursday, discounts are available for students and the over-65s. The bus leaves from outside **Valby Station**, arriving in Jutland via Odden or the Mols-Linien ferry *(see opposite)*.

Eurolines operates coach journeys from the larger Danish cities to various European destinations. In Copenhagen, they depart from Ingerslevsgade, below the Central Station.

A domestic ferry sailing between Denmark's islands

Arriving by Ferry

The major international ferry companies are **DFDS Seaways**, **Stena Line**, **Color Line**, **Fjord Line** and **Scandlines**.

The opening of the bridges spanning the Øresund (Sound) and the Storebælt has greatly reduced the demand for ferries between Zealand and Sweden, and between Zealand and Funen. However, ferry travel remains a popular option with many visitors.

Main Terminals

Most ferry travellers from the UK will arrive at the port of Esbjerg. Other main terminals are located in Copenhagen, just north of the city centre, and Frederikshavn and Hirtshals, in northern Jutland.

There is usually a bus link between the port and the town's train station, as well as a taxi rank and long- and short-stay car parking.

Ferry passengers will often be asked to check in at least 1 hour before departure.

Domestic Ferries

Ferry services, such as those provided by **Færgen**, play a vital role in Denmark's transport infrastructure, linking a number of islands. Some routes are

very short, taking a matter of minutes, while the longest route (Køge–Bornholm) takes nearly 7 hours.

Ferries also link different parts of mainland Denmark. The **Mols-Linien**, from Odden in West Zealand to Ebeltoft or Aarhus in Jutland, is a popular alternative to the Storebælt Bridge, as it saves paying the bridge toll charge; the same is true of the **Kattegatruten** (Kalundborg–Aarhus). In the summer, **Smyril Line** runs two weekly ferries from Hirtshals to the Faroe Islands (journey time: a day and a half).

Most ferries take both foot passengers and cars, but there are some small islands where passenger-only ferries operate.

Ferry Tickets and Fares

Tickets for ferry services can usually be reserved online. Fares vary widely, depending on the season and the time of day. Substantial discounts are often available for students and young people with an international rail pass.

There is no need to book in advance on short routes, but it is compulsory to do so for longer journeys. Reservations should also be made when travelling at busy times (like Christmas) or with a vehicle.

International ferry connecting Denmark with Germany and Sweden

Travelling by Car

Although Denmark's public transport network is excellent, a car can still be a convenient way of travelling, especially when visiting out-of-the-way places. For groups of three or four people, a car can also reduce travel costs significantly. Danish motorways are toll-free, but the Storebælt and Øresund bridges are not. The major roads are well signposted and of a good standard, and travelling over one of the bridges, such as the Storebælt Bridge between Zealand and Funen, can be a truly breathtaking experience.

Arriving by Car

Most people driving to Denmark arrive from Germany, the country's only land border, or from Sweden via the Øresund Bridge. Immigration checkpoints between EU countries have been abolished; however, there are still customs checkpoints at sea and land borders with Germany.

The main routes into the country are the E45, running from the German border all the way through Jutland up to Frederikshavn; the E47, which connects Lübeck and Hamburg with Lolland via the car ferry from Puttgarden to Rødby; and the E20, which travels over the Øresund Bridge from Malmø in Sweden. From 2020, the Puttgarden–Rødby ferry will be replaced by the Fehmarn Belt Fixed Link, which will connect the German island of Fehmarn, north of Lübeck, with Lolland.

What You Need

Anyone driving in Denmark must have all the relevant documents, including insurance and an international driver's licence. Check that you have breakdown cover with a company that has reciprocal arrangements with Denmark. **FDM**, the Danish motoring organization, can provide further information.

While it is not compulsory to carry a first-aid kit, it is a good idea to have one in the car, in addition to a car fire extinguisher, a torch and a tow rope. A warning triangle must be kept in the car to be used to warn other motorists in the event of a breakdown.

Motorway road signs

Roads and Tolls

Motorway signs in Denmark are colour-coded and easy to understand. The blue signs indicate the exits, while the green ones indicate the cities that can be reached along the motorway.

Denmark has five trans-European motorways. The E20 runs west–east from Esbjerg through Kolding and Odense, across the Storebælt and on to Køge and Copenhagen; the E29 links Hirtshals to Nørresundby; the E45 crosses the German border and links Kolding, Aarhus, Aalborg and Frederikshavn; the E47 links Helsingør, Copenhagen, Køge, Maribo and Rødby harbour; and the E55 runs between Helsingør, Copenhagen, Køge, Nykøbing F and Gedser.

Part of the E20 consists of bridges over the Storebælt and Øresund (Sound). The toll charged to cross is collected at entry or exit points. The toll stations are equipped with card machines or manned by staff at busier times. The yellow

Danish motorway sign

Manuel lanes are for payment by credit card or cash.

The toll charge on the **Storebælt Bridge** is 235–370 Dkr, depending on the size and height of your vehicle. Similar toll charges apply for the **Øresund Bridge**. A BroBizz pass – a small transponder that you affix on the windscreen behind the rear-view mirror – can be used on both bridges and offers considerable discounts if you're making regular trips. Visit www.storebaelt.dk for more information.

Other major bridges in Denmark include the Farø Bridges that connect Zealand and Falster; the Lille Bælt Bridge, between Jutland and Funen; the Sallingsund Bridge, between Mors and Salling; and the bridge from Fyn to the island of Langeland. These bridges are toll-free.

A proposal that is likely to become reality within the next decade is the Kattegat Bridge, a bridge and tunnel connecting Kalundborg in Zealand with Aarhus via the island of Samsø.

Rules of the road

As in all continental European countries, the Danes drive on the right. Both cars and motorcycles must have dipped headlights during the day (cars from the UK will need to have their headlights adjusted). Seat belts must be worn at all times, and children under three must be in a child seat. When turning right, drivers must give way to cyclists on the inside.

The speed limit is usually 50 km/h (30 mph) in towns, 80 km/h (50 mph) on most roads and up to 130 km/h (80 mph) on motorways. A hefty on-the-spot fine may be charged for breaking the speed limit and for other motoring offences, such as not wearing a seat belt or talking on a mobile phone while driving. Being caught driving under the

A pretty country road next to a rapeseed field

influence of alcohol will incur even stiffer penalties and possibly imprisonment.

Parking

Tickets for parking are obtained from kerbside machines (billet-automat), which accept most coins and cards. In many smaller towns, parking is free and regulated by a parking disk that has an hour hand, which is available from all garages. Different zones are marked with a blue sign with the letter "P". Also on the sign is the time limit for parking; signs marked as 1 time mean you can stay for an hour; 2 timer is two hours and so on. When parking within these time zones, set the hour hand on your parking disk to indicate the time when you arrived and leave it on the dashboard, so that the wardens can check whether the limit has been exceeded. In larger towns, parking is often free 6pm–8am on weekdays, after 2pm on Saturday and all day Sunday. The Danish for "no parking" is parkering forbudt. For more information about parking in towns see p303.

Petrol

There is no shortage of petrol stations in Denmark, and most international brands are represented. Pumps are generally self-service, with daily opening hours from 6 or 7am to midnight. At 24-hour petrol stations, payment facilities are automated using Dkr notes, though you are unlikely to find instructions in English. Petrol is expensive, with prices slightly higher than in Britain or Germany. Autogas (LPG) is not widely used and is available only at a few selected petrol stations.

Breakdown Services

In the event of a breakdown, telephone the emergency number supplied by your car hire company or breakdown organization. Phones on motorways are placed at 2-km (1-mile) intervals. For other emergencies, dial 112 and ask for the relevant service. The main breakdown companies in Denmark are **Falck Autohjælp** and **Dansk Autohjælp**.

Car Hire

Representatives of most major car hire firms can be found at airports, upmarket hotels and in city centres. Car hire tends to be expensive in Denmark; booking beforehand through an international firm can work out much cheaper. Three of the major firms in Denmark are **Avis**, **Europcar** and **Hertz**.

DIRECTORY

What You Need

FDM
Firskovvej 32, 2800 Lyngby.
Tel 45 27 07 07.
Ⓦ fdm.dk

Roads and Tolls

Øresund Bridge
Tel 70 23 90 60.
Ⓦ oresundsbron.com

Store Bælt Bridge
Tel 70 15 10 15.
Ⓦ storebaelt.dk

Breakdown Services

Dansk Autohjælp
Tel 70 10 80 90.
Ⓦ dah.dk

Falck Autohjælp
Tel 70 10 20 30.
Ⓦ falck.dk

Car Hire

Avis
Tel 33 26 80 00.
Ⓦ avis.dk

Europcar
Tel 89 33 11 33.
Ⓦ europcar.dk

Hertz
Tel 33 17 90 00.
Ⓦ hertzdk.dk

Great Drives

The Marguerite or Daisy Route (Margueritruten in Danish) is a scenic motoring route indicated by a sign showing a daisy on a brown background. It was started in 1991 and named after Queen Margrethe II and Denmark's national flower. The route passes through more than 100 major attractions, including the castles of Egeskov and Kronborg, providing a pleasant alternative to travelling on the main highways.

One of the roads on the scenic Marguerite Route

Getting Around Danish Towns

Most Danish towns and cities can be easily explored on foot or by bicycle. Cycling is popular, and motorists treat cyclists as they would any other legitimate road user. Public transport in most cities is efficient, safe and reasonably priced. Taxis are another good way to get around, and they are especially convenient for anyone who is carrying heavy luggage or large amounts of shopping.

City bus – tickets can be bought on board or in advance

Green Travel

It is possible to travel around Denmark without leaving a massive carbon footprint thanks to the country's great train network and many ferry connections. Electric buses and cars are not as common as in neighbouring Sweden, but they are becoming more popular. The country's first electric taxis operate in Odense, and at least one taxi firm in Copenhagen is working towards making the move by 2020. In Copenhagen, some bus routes, including the sightseeing bus CityCirkel, use electric vehicles.

Cycling is widespread and it has been estimated that Danes cycle, on average, more than 600 km (373 miles) a year. Danish cities make many allowances for cyclists, including cycle paths and favourable laws regarding right of way.

Some small islands are virtually car-free, while some others offer the possibility of hiring a horse-drawn gypsy wagon for an especially green vacation.

Public Transport

Most cities in Denmark have well-run, modern public transport networks, so there is little need for a car. There are also well-maintained bus routes on all Danish islands, even the small ones. Here, bus timetables usually run in conjunction with ferry schedules, and a bus is likely to be waiting at the port as you disembark from the ferry.

Central bus stations in towns and cities are usually situated next to the main train station or by the ferry terminal. Maps and timetables that list the major bus and rail routes, as well as the most important sights, are available from tourist offices.

More information on public transport in Copenhagen can be found on pages 304–305.

Tickets

Multi-ticket clip cards (*klippekort*), valid on buses and local trains, are readily available in the major cities, such as Copenhagen, Aarhus and Odense. Travel passes bought in Copenhagen are also valid in other towns in the Greater Copenhagen (HT) region, including Roskilde, Helsingør and Hillerød. The Aarhus Pass and Odense City Pass allow unlimited travel on public transport and include discounted or free admission to some city attractions. Reduced-fare travel cards for children up to the age of 16 are also available.

In smaller towns, it is also possible to buy single tickets directly from the driver upon boarding. This is the best option if you are unlikely to be making multiple journeys. On the island of Mors, in the Limfjord, travelling on local buses is free of charge.

Walking

All of Denmark's towns and cities are compact, and most have pedestrianized areas. In addition, many sights tend to be closely grouped together, making getting around on foot a pleasant experience.

Nevertheless, pedestrians should observe the traffic regulations. Take care when crossing the road, although Danish drivers are very attentive towards pedestrians and would never enter a crossing when there are people on it. However, pedestrians who step on to the cycle lanes that run along beside the pavements are strongly frowned upon, especially during rush hour.

Walking tours provide a fun, alternative way to explore the major towns and cities in Denmark. Local tourist offices (*see pp288–9*) will be able to provide details of tours that are available in the area, as well as maps for those who wish to explore the city on foot without a guide.

Pedestrianized street in Aalborg

Visitors enjoying a walking tour

DIRECTORY

Taxis

Aarhus Taxa
Aarhus. **Tel** 89 48 48 48.

Dantaxi
Nationwide. **Tel** 70 25 25 25.

Taxa Fyn
Funen (incl. Odense).
Tel 66 15 44 15.

Cycling

Baisikeli Bike Rental
Copenhagen.
🌐 cph-bike-rental.dk

Bikes4rent.dk
Aarhus. **Tel** 20 26 10 20.
🌐 bikes4rent.dk

CSV Cykeludlejning
Odense.
Tel 29 29 25 89 (May–Sep);
66 12 12 58 (Oct–Apr).
🌐 odensecykler.dk
🌐 cityhotelodense.dk

Taxis

Taxis in Danish cities are plentiful, but they can be rather expensive. Taxi ranks can be found in front of all railway stations, airports and ferry terminals, as well as in town centres and major shopping centres. Cabs with a lit sign saying *fri* can be flagged down in the street. Taxis can also be booked on the phone. Fares start around 40–50 Dkr and then increase by the kilometre. A higher rate is levied at night and when booked by phone. Most taxis in Denmark accept credit cards, and there is no need to tip the driver.

TAXI
4 vogne
Sign for a taxi rank

Driving

Avoid driving in the larger towns if at all possible. As per its environmental policy, the Danish government does its best to discourage people from using their car. Most cities have designated car-free centres, and parking and fuel are very expensive, as is the cost of hiring a car. Cyclists and pedestrians take precedence on city roads, and when turning right, car drivers are obliged to give way to cyclists coming up on the inside and, even if there is a green light, to pedestrians crossing the road.

Parking

A fee is charged for on-street parking in Denmark's city centres between 8am and 6pm Monday to Friday and between 8am and 2pm on Saturday. It can be difficult to find a parking space at any time of day, especially in the centre of towns and cities. It can also be expensive to park a car. Some Danish cities have parking zones, with zones closest to the centre costing the most. High fines are charged for failing to pay parking fees or exceeding the time limit. See page 301 for more on parking in Denmark.

Cycling

Cycling is another popular and practical way to get around: bikes can be hired from hotels or special bike-hire places. In Aarhus, you can use free bikes supplied by the city and available at designated areas in the city centre (see p305). Bicycle lanes exist all over the country, in rural areas as well as in big towns, and you can obtain a map of scenic routes from tourist offices. Many Danes spend their holidays touring an island such as Samsø or Bornholm by bike.

Bikes and accessories such as helmets, child seats and even attachable trailers for transporting kids and heavy bags can be hired in many towns and cities from companies such as **Baisikeli**, **Bikes4rent.dk** and **CSV Cykeludlejning**.

Cycling is a fun way to get around, but a number of factors should be taken into account. Never leave a bike unlocked; expensive bikes, in particular, are highly desirable to thieves. In larger towns, attach the bicycle to a cycle rack. When using cycle lanes, cyclists must observe general traffic regulations, such as not jumping red lights. Buses often stop in areas allocated for cyclists, so beware of people getting off the bus. Bicycles must be equipped with lights after dark and have reflectors fitted at the back and front. Cyclists stopped under the influence of alcohol may not only incur a hefty fine but also lose their driver's licence. Everybody, especially children, should wear safety helmets.

Outside of peak hours, bicycles can be taken onto trains (excluding ICE trains) upon purchase of a special bicycle ticket. This is required on all trains, excluding Copenhagen's S-tog, but the cost is minimal.

Cycling is a popular form of transport in Danish towns

Getting Around Copenhagen

Copenhagen has an excellent round-the-clock public transport system, and you can use the same *klippekort* (clip cards) and travel passes on the buses, metro, S-tog and regional trains. Walking and cycling are also pleasant options. Copenhagen is one of the safest cities in Europe, and there should be no problem travelling alone, even at night, but visitors should remain vigilant.

The platform of a metro station in Copenhagen

Buses

Copenhagen's efficient bus network, run by **Movia**, shares its fare structure with the city's various train networks. Bus stops are marked by a yellow sign with the word "BUS" and display the relevant bus's timetable.

Insert your clip card into the yellow time clock next to the driver. If you don't have a clip card, you can pay the driver with cash; change is given, but be aware that large notes will not be appreciated. The next stop is displayed on a digital screen towards the front of the bus, and disembarking is via the central or back doors.

Buses, like trains, start running at about 5am (6am on Sunday). Less frequent night buses (marked by the prefix "N") operate on special routes.

Metro

Copenhagen's modern underground rail network, the **Metro**, has two lines, one of which links the airport to the city centre. The metro system, which complements the S-tog rail network, stops at Frederiksberg, Forum, Nørreport, Kongens Nytorv and Christianshavn in the city centre. A circle line (due by 2018) will stop at Nørrebro, Østerbro, Vesterbro and the Central Station. Metro stations are marked with the red letter "M" and can be spotted by the 5-m-(16-ft-) high illuminated information posts outside.

Metro trains are fully automated and consist of single driverless carriages that are sleek, bright and rarely feel crowded. The doors open automatically in line with the platform doors, making it impossible for anyone to fall on to the track. Call points by each of the carriage doors can be used in an emergency or by people with mobility issues. Travel cards must be punched into the yellow time clocks on the platform before boarding.

S-Tog

Copenhagen's rail system is known as **S-tog** and is run by the DSB state railway. This fast and convenient service consists of 10 lines that all pass through Central Station and run to the outskirts of the city. The DSB website *(see p299)* has a journey planner that allows you to find the best route around Copenhagen.

All S-tog trains have bright carriages with plenty of space for passengers with bicycles, prams and wheelchairs (outside of peak times). Screens in the carriages show traffic information and news in Danish, and there is also free broadband connectivity.

Tickets can be bought at the station. Travel cards must be punched into one of the yellow time clocks on the platform by inserting it with the magnetic strip facing downwards.

All trains are marked with a red hexagon bearing a white letter "S". Those marked with an "X" are express trains with limited stops. Most of the system has been adapted for disabled passengers, and there are lifts from street level to the platforms.

Trains operate from about 5am until around 1am during the week and on Sundays, and throughout the night on Fridays and Saturdays.

Cyclists boarding a train at Copenhagen's Central Station

Regional Trains

The Greater Copenhagen (HT) transport region stretches as far north as Helsingør and Hornbæk and as far east as Roskilde and Lejre. Many outlying attractions – including the Louisiana art galleries in Humlebæk – can be visited on a day trip using regional trains and a Copenhagen area *klippekort*.

Tickets

Public transport tickets in Copenhagen are valid on trains, buses and the metro, and it is possible to transfer from one mode of transport to another on the same ticket. Tickets are available from ticket offices, vending machines at stations and bus drivers.

The metropolitan area is split into seven zones. The cheapest ticket (billet) allows you to travel within two zones. Download the "Mobilbilletter Hovestaden" app from the App Store or Google Play and pay for your tickets on the go. You can also buy your bus, train and metro tickets online. Cards stamped for journeys within the same zone or between two or three zones are valid for 1 hour. Four-, five- and six-zone tickets are valid for 90 minutes, and tickets and stamped 10-trip cards for all zones are valid for 2 hours. Fares on night buses are the same. Travelling without a valid ticket carries a high penalty.

Special tickets that allow for unlimited travel over a 24-hour period are available. Tourist passes like the Copenhagen Card (for dealers, visit the Copenhagen Visitor Centre website, see p289) allow unrestricted travel on buses, trains, metro and harbour buses in all zones in the capital region. In addition, one gets free entrance to 72 major attractions and museums as well as discounts in several restaurants, sights, car rental and more.

Two children up to the age of 12 travel free when accompanied by an adult with the correct ticket. Children under 16 pay a child's fare when travelling alone.

Driving

Much of Copenhagen's city centre is car-free, and parking spaces are in high demand and expensive. Driving in central Copenhagen is therefore not recommended.

Taxis

Taxis operate all over the city at all times. To hail a cab in the street, simply wave to any that displays a lit fri sign. There are taxi ranks outside the Central Station, Nørreport Station and Kongens Nytorv.

Walking

Copenhagen is the perfect city for walking around. Green spaces and parks provide plenty of places to take a break. The tourist office (see p289) runs themed walking tours on subjects such as history, food and design. The more energetic visitor can join a **Running Copenhagen** tour.

Cycling

Copenhagen is one of the most cycle-friendly cities in the world, with cycle lanes over much of it, and cycle- and footbridges crossing the canals. Nørrebrogade is open to bicycles, pedestrians and buses only.

A hire scheme of intelligent City Bikes has been launched in Copenhagen and Frederiksberg. The bikes are available 24/7, 365 days a year. Each city bike has a handlebar-mounted touchscreen tablet used for navigation, payment and to guide users to points of interest. The first time you use the city bike, you enter your credit card information and unlock the bike on the touchscreen. The rental charge is 25 Dkr per hour. The bikes can be returned to any station in the system.

Cycling is a great way to see the city, and bikes can be taken free of charge on the S-tog. Guided tours, like **Bike Copenhagen With Mike**, are also available.

Take care when cycling in the city and obey the rules of the road at all times. Cycle lanes can be quite aggressive, especially at peak times.

DIRECTORY

Buses

Movia
Tel 36 13 14 00.
w moviatrafik.dk

Metro and S-Tog

Metro
Tel 70 15 16 15.
w m.dk

S-tog / Regional Trains
Tel 70 13 14 15.
w dsb.dk

Walking

Running Copenhagen
Tel 20 58 58 77.
w running-copenhagen.dk

Cycling

Bike Copenhagen With Mike
Tel 26 39 56 88.
w bikecopenhagenwithmike.dk

Waterbuses

Canal Tours Copenhagen
Gammel Strand 32. **Tel** 32 96 30 00.
w canaltours.dk

Waterbuses

A trip on a waterbus is a good way to see Copenhagen, as the city's canals lead past many of the major sights. The trips run by **Canal Tours Copenhagen** are accompanied by a guide and are particularly appealing to people with children. The yellow harbour buses 991, 992 and 993, operated by Movia and subject to the same fare system as buses and trains, are a cheaper alternative.

Departure point for a waterbus on a canal in Copenhagen

General Index

Acknowledgments

Hachette Livre Polska would like to thank the following people whose contribution and assistance have made the preparation of the book possible:

Additional Text Sue Dobson, Roger Norum, Marek Pernal, Jakub Sito, Barbara Sudnik-Wójcikowska, Jennifer Wattam Klit.

Additional Illustrations Dorota Jarymowicz, Paweł Pasternak.

Additional Photographs Oldrich Karasek, Ian O'Leary, Roger Norum, Laura Pilgaard Rasmussen, Jakub Sito, Jon Spaul, Barbara Sudnik-Wójcikowska, Monika Witkowska, Andrzej Zygmuntowicz and Ireneusz Winnicki, Juliusz Żebrowski.

Dorling Kindersley would like to thank the following people whose contribution and assistance have made the preparation of the book possible:

Publisher Douglas Amrine.

Publishing Managers Anna Streiffert, Vicki Ingle.

Managing Art Director Kate Poole.

Senior Editor Kathryn Lane.

Editorial Assistance Sam Fletcher, Anna Freiberger.

Additional Picture Research Rachel Barber, Ellen Root.

Cartography Vinod Harish, Vincent Kurien, Azeem Siddiqui, Casper Morris.

DTP Designers Uma Bhattacharya, Mohammad Hassan, Jasneet Kaur, Alistair Richardson.

Factcheckers Britt Lightbody, Katrine Anker Møller.

Proofreader Stewart J. Wild.

Indexer Helen Peters.

Jacket Design Tessa Bindloss.

Revisions Team
Marta Bescos, Lokesh Bisht, Subhadeep Biswas, Imogen Corke, Mariana Evmolpidou, Elisabeth Fogh, Jane Graham, Taraneh Jerven, Claire Jones, Laura Jones, Sumita Khatwani, Priya Kukadia, Jude Ledger, Delphine Lawrance, Carly Madden, Hayley Maher, Alison McGill, Vikki Nousiainen, Scarlett O'Hara, Catherine Palmi, Laura Pilgaard Rasmussen, Pollyanna Poulter, Akshay Rana, Lucy Richards, Ellen Root, Simon Ryder, Susie Peachey, Lokamata Sahoo, Sands Publishing Solutions, Susana Smith, Kathleen Sauret, Priyanka Thakur, Stuti Tiwari, Dora Whitaker, Conrad van Dyk.

Special Assistance and Permissions
The Publishers also wish to thank all persons and institutions for their permission to reproduce photographs of their property, for allowing us to photograph inside the buildings and to use photographs from their archives:
Amager Youth Hostel; Amalienborg, Copenhagen (S. Haslund-Christensen, Lord Chamberlain and Colonel Jens Greve, Palace Steward); Amber Museum, Copenhagen; Aquarium, Charlotten-lund; Arbejdermuseet, Copenhagen (Peter Ludvigsen); Bornholm Tourist Information Centre (Pernille Larsen); Carlsberg Brewery; Ceramics Museum, Rønne; Christiansborg, Copenhagen; Copenhagen Airports A/S (Bente Schmidt – Event- and visitor department); Copenhagen Town Hall (Allan Johansen); Corbis (Łukasz Wyrzykowski); Danish Tourist Board Photo Database (Christian Moritz – Area Sales Manager); Dansk Moebelkunst (Dorte Slot) (Bredgade 32, Copenhagen K) www.dmk.dk; Davids

Samling, Copenhagen; Danish Chamber of Tourism & SAS Group PR (Agnieszka Blandzi, Director); Egeskov Castle; Experimentarium, Copenhagen; H. Ch. Andersen Museum, Odense; Holmegaard Glass Factory; Jagna Noren – a guide to Bornholm; Jesper T. Møller and other employees of the National Museum in Copenhagen; Karen Blixen Museum; Knud Rasmussens Haus; Kronborg castle; Legoland, Billund; Lene Henrichsen – assistant to the director of the Louisiana museum; Louisiana – Museum for Modern Kunst (Susanne Hartz); The Museum of Holbæk and Environs, Holbæk; Det Nationalhistoriske Museum på Frederiksborg, Hillerød; Nationalmuseet, Copenhagen (Heidi Lykke Petersen); The Nobel Foundation (Annika Ekdahl); Ny Carlsberg Glyptotek in Copenhagen (Jan Stubbe Østergaard); Palaces and Properties Agency, Denmark (Peder Lind Pedersen); Pritzker Prize (Keith Walker) for making available the photographs of the interiors of Jørn Utzon's house; Ribe VikingeCenter (Bjarne Clement – manager); Rosenborg Castle – The Royal Danish Collection (Peter Kristiansen – curator); Roskilde Cathedral; The Royal Library, Copenhagen (Karsten Bundgaard – photographer); Royal Porcelain Factory, Copenhagen; Skagens Museum (Mette Bøgh Jensen – curator); Scandinavian Airlines SAS (Wanda Brociek i Małgorzata Grążka); Statens Historiska Museum, Stockholm; Statens Museum for Kunst: (Eva Maria Gertung & Marianne Saederup); Stine Møller Jensen (Press coordinator, Copenhagen Metro); Bo Streiffert; Tivoli, Copenhagen – Stine Lolk; Tobaksmuseet, Copenhagen (W.Ø. Larsens); Tycho Brahe Planet-arium, Copenhagen; Tønder Tourist Office (Lis Langelund-Larsen – tourist officer); Voergård Slot; Aalborg Symfoniorkester (Jan Bo Rasmussen); Østerlars Kirke, Bornholm (Ernst A Grunwald).

Picture Credits
Key: a = above; b = below/bottom; c = centre; f = far; l = left; r = right; t = top.

123RF.com: Vrezh Gyozalyan 4crb; Bernd Kroeger 171br; Mikhail Markovskiy 108tr. **4Corners:** Günter Gräfenhain 100b.

Aalborg Opera: 35cra. **Aarhus Kommune:** 298cr. **Agency for Palaces and Cultural Properties:** 131tl. **Alamy Images:** Arcaid Images 28–29c, 186; The Art Archive 168–9; Linn Arvidsson 120; blickwinkel 15bc; Bernie Epstein 80cb; imageBROKER 11br, 19, 94, 156; Ionotec/Thierry Lauzun 222bl; John Peter Photography 100tr; OJPHOTOS 161tl, 228–9 ; Robert Harding World Imagery 239br; Niels Poulsen DK 140–41; Niels Quist 14br, 33br; Pep Roig 258cl; Frantisek Staud 241tl; vario images GmbH & Co.KG/Stephan Gabriel 259tl; Vikslove 177b; Ken Welsh 258c; Westend61 GmbH 216–17. **Artothek:**209bl. **AWL Images:** Walter Bibikow 152–3; Hemis 54, 84, 176, 204.

The Bridgeman Art Library: Bonhams, London, UK/Private Collection *Street Scene* (oil on canvas), Danish School, (19th century) 8–9; Nordiska Museet, Stockholm *Bella and Hanna Nathansson* (1783–1853) Christoffer-Wilhelm Eckersberg 46tr; Skagens Museum, Denmark 13tc; Thorvaldsens Museum, Copenhagen *Shepherd Boy* (1817) Bertel Thorvaldsen 46bl.

Carl Hansen & Søn Møbelfabrik A/S: 29tl. **Cecilie Manz:** BRAHL FOTOGRAFI 29tr. **CinemaxX Danmark:** 107br. **Copenhagen Aiports:** Arne V. Petersen 296bl. **Corbis:** © Archivo Iconografico, S. A. 42–3c, 45br; © Bettmann 41bl, 42tr, 47bc, 48crb, 125crb; Francis Dean 291bl, 294tr; © Werner Forman 38cla, 38bl, 40bl; © Hulton–Deutsch Collection 49tl; Robbie Jack 130br; Wolfgang Kaehler 240tl, 240br; © Douglas Kirkland 125bl; © Bob Krist 12tr, 139br, 209cla, 209cr; © Stefan Lindblom 32cla, 49br; © Massimo Listri 31b, © Wally McNamee 49c; © Adam Woolfitt 58br. **CPH Living:** 249tr.